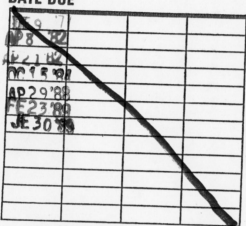

The American Party Systems

The

American

Party Systems

STAGES OF POLITICAL DEVELOPMENT

Edited by
WILLIAM NISBET CHAMBERS
and
WALTER DEAN BURNHAM

SECOND EDITION

Contributors
FRANK J. SORAUF
PAUL GOODMAN
RICHARD P. McCORMICK
ERIC L. McKITRICK
SAMUEL P. HAYS
DONALD E. STOKES
RICHARD E. DAWSON
THEODORE J. LOWI

New York 1975
OXFORD UNIVERSITY PRESS

To

S and T

From

B and D

FOREWORD

POLITICAL PARTIES have played, and play today, a variety of roles in the American political drama. Yet many aspects of their history and activity have remained obscure. Meanwhile an increasingly convergent interest in party development and behavior has emerged in the last dozen years among historians and political scientists, a convergence that may help to penetrate the obscurity. It is not too much to say that substantial numbers of political scientists have come to share the late V. O. Key's belief that parties and party systems can be fully understood only in their "dimension of time." Similarly, many historians have come to believe that party history can in turn be informed by the conceptual and theoretical tools that have been developed by the social sciences, including political science. A growing if often disparate body of research and analysis in both disciplines illustrates the point.

For the first time, the present volume joins the two disciplines in a systematic effort to illuminate problems of American political party development and action in a comprehensive way.

Of the ten chapters in this book, five are by historians and five by political scientists. One of the editors is an historian and the other a political scientist. Yet the contributions of the adherents of each discipline draw greater depth and breadth from the other, and all of the contributors are concerned with conceptualization and with analysis which involves the dimension of time. As a result of this virtually unique collaboration, the book is bound together by a shared interest in analysis of the development of the American party systems on the one hand, and the impact and behavior of parties in the contemporary American political scene on the other. The two disciplines are not only engaged in a dialogue, but their dialogue is given direction by common concerns.

The several essays in their present form are the product of a Conference on American Political Party Development held at Washington University, St. Louis, in April 1966. The Conference was jointly sponsored by the

Departments of History and of Political Science of Washington University; was financed by funds from the McDonnell Aircraft Foundation through the Department of Political Science, and from the Committee on Comparative Politics of the Social Science Research Council; and was made up almost equally of representatives of the two professions. The planning committee of the Conference, aided and supported throughout by Robert R. Palmer, then Dean of the Faculty of Arts and Sciences of Washington University, consisted of Carl A. McCandless and Robert H. Salisbury from political science, and Ralph E. Morrow, Rowland T. Berthoff and, later, Sam B. Warner, Jr., from history. The chairman of the planning committee was William N. Chambers, who had originally proposed the idea of an interdisciplinary inquiry into problems of party development and action.

Meetings continued for four days at the University's Bromwoods Conference Center. They were characterized throughout by a probing but amicable criticism of the original papers which have become the chapters of this book, and by a lively exchange of ideas and information. On the basis of the Conference discussion, recorded in a summary report prepared by John M. Murrin of Washington University, and of critiques by the editors, all papers were fully and carefully revised for publication. At the conclusion of the meetings, the committee asked Walter Dean Burnham, then of Haverford College, to serve as a co-editor of this book. The administrative assistant for the Conference was Harry Fritz, who has also assisted the editors in bringing the volume to press and in preparing the index.

In addition to the ten authors represented in this volume and the members of the planning committee, twelve other scholars participated in the Conference, making a total of twenty-seven. Participants included, among historians, Bernard Bailyn of Harvard University, Noble E. Cunningham, Jr., of the University of Missouri, Shaw Livermore, Jr., of the University of Michigan, Don E. Fehrenbacher of Stanford University, and Charles G. Sellers, Jr., of the University of California, Berkeley; and among political scientists, Charles D. Farris of the University of Florida, Richard Rose of the University of Strathclyde, Scotland, and John C. Wahlke of the University of Iowa. In addition four general discussants, Austin Ranney of the University of Wisconsin and Myron Weiner of the Massachusetts Institute of Technology, both political scientists, and David M. Potter of Stanford University and Marcus Cunliffe of the University of

Sussex, England, both historians, made particularly valuable contributions and provided the Conference with a most useful summary session on its last day.

This incisive criticism and exchange have had a profound effect on the chapters in this volume, and on their intellectual relationship with one another. That exchange among scholars and between disciplines has made *The American Party Systems* what it is—a systematic study of what American political parties are today and of how they got that way.

THOMAS H. ELIOT
CHANCELLOR

Washington University, St. Louis
June 1967

NOTE TO THE
SECOND EDITION

IN THE YEARS since the first edition of this book appeared, huge and very probably irreversible changes have occurred in the structure of American electoral politics. Cumulatively, these changes have been of overwhelming significance. If some of the questions raised by our 1967 essays have been answered by subsequent events, those events themselves raise a host of new and graver questions. As editors, we have assumed that the justification for a new edition of *The American Party Systems* lay in the intrinsic and enduring worth of the essays it contains. But we have also realized that, as wholly new chapters in the evolution—or degeneration?—of this political system are being written by the actors of politics themselves, so the book must end on a more up-to-date note.

W. N. C.
W. D. B.

Contents

The American Party Systems

I | WILLIAM N. CHAMBERS

WASHINGTON UNIVERSITY

Party Development
and the American Mainstream

FOR ALMOST as long as the national Constitution has been in effect the United States has only once been without a going, national, competitive two-party system. This enduring fact has had major significance for the course of American politics, just as the mainstream of American political development has had a major effect on the development of parties and party systems. The central problem of this volume is to provide some analysis and explanation of these aspects of American party development, and of the particular character of our political parties.

Individual parties have come and gone, and so have particular party systems. This birth and death enables us to count at least six major party formations in our history, from the Federalists, Jeffersonian Republicans, and short-lived National Republicans to the Democrats, Whigs, and modern Republicans. These parties in their contention for power, moreover, have provided the ingredients for five discernible national party systems, two before the Civil War and three during and after that great divide. Several third or fourth parties have also achieved at least passing significance, in that they have managed to win a crucial percentage of the popular vote for President larger than the over-all average for all third parties since 1828, when the selection of presidential electors by popular vote became the norm. These significant third parties include the Free-Soil party of 1848, the American or "Know-Nothing" party of the mid-1850's, the Constitutional Union party of 1860 and the Southern Democratic fragment of that year, the Populists of the late nineteenth century, the Socialist party briefly at its peak in 1912, and Progressive parties in 1912 and again in 1924. The Progressive and Dixiecrat efforts of 1948 did not win a high enough proportion of the popular vote to

3

qualify. Meanwhile innumerable lesser minor parties have come and gone or lived out a politically futile existence. Finally, party systems in the several states have varied immensely from place to place and from time to time, and state party systems have virtually led lives of their own.

In all of this historical flux and local variation, however, certain features have persisted. The first modern political parties arose in the United States, decades before they appeared in Great Britain and other nations; and this has meant that the first experiments in party politics were made in the American arena. Halting and uncertain in the first party system which emerged in the 1790's, these experiments advanced significantly in the second party system of the Jacksonian era. By sometime in the 1840's the general mold was set. Thus party development in the third, fourth, and fifth party systems has done little more than generate variations on the basic form and structure of the parties of the pre-Civil War era. The interplay of parties in the party system has also remained basically the same; despite significant third parties, the United States has always so far returned to a competitive two-party system. Finally, with limited but important exceptions, the American party systems have been moderate in character and less ideologically oriented than party systems in other nations.

All of this assumes something about the nature of political parties and party systems. An older historiography had it that political parties existed in the American colonies even before the Revolution; that the first national parties appeared with the emergence of Federalists and Anti-Federalists in the contest over the ratification of the Constitution in 1787-89; and that later national parties were simply an evolution of these earlier-day confrontations. In this view, conflicts of interest and voting blocs within the original states set the divisions which appeared in new form in the ratification controversy, in the rivalry of Federalists and Democratic-Republicans after 1789, in the party battles of Democrats and Whigs in the Jacksonian era, and in the competition of modern Democrats and Republicans. In short, parties were seen as a continuous flow from colonial times to the present, with little more than variations in dominant leaders and political labels.[1] Probably no reputable student believes this simplistic

---

1. For the older historiography of American political parties, not all of which subscribes precisely to the simplistic notion of continuity outlined here, see Charles A. Beard, *The American Party Battle* (New York, 1928); Wilfred E. Binkley, *American Political Parties: Their Natural History*, 4th Ed. (New York, 1962); Edgar E. Robinson, *The Evolution of American Political Parties: A Sketch of Party Development*

account of American political party development today, any more than any reputable student ought to believe that William Jennings Bryan lost the presidency in 1896 simply because industrial employers, under the prodding of Mark Hanna, threatened their workers with layoffs if Bryan were elected. Yet older conceptualizations die hard, particularly in the popular mind. This notion of continuous flow, moreover, is particularly dangerous in that it flattens out the variety of American party politics and makes it all but impossible to understand the actualities of our party history and party systems.

If the beginning of wisdom is to call things by their right names, some attention is due to what we mean by a political party and by a party system. Stated broadly, a political party in the modern sense may be thought of as a relatively durable social formation which seeks offices or power in government, exhibits a structure or organization which links leaders at the centers of government to a significant popular following in the political arena and its local enclaves, and generates in-group perspectives or at least symbols of identification or loyalty.[2] In this sense political parties were not discernible in the American colonies, which tended to get political business done through personal leadership, factions, cliques, courthouse juntos, or other means. From pre-Revolutionary times into the early nineteenth century, moreover, the conduct of politics often depended on habits of deference or subordination on the part of voters toward established notables in local communities, who were recognized as natural leaders. In the sense of continuing, identifiable formations, the so-called Federalists and Anti-Federalists in the years 1787-89 were also not parties, but rather congeries of local groups, factions, leaders and cliques, or other molecular elements of politics. Even after the

---

(New York, 1924); and, with a different and important approach, Herbert Agar, *The Price of Union* (Boston, 1950). The even earlier, magistral work by M. Ostrogorski, *Democracy and the Organization of Political Parties* (New York, 1902), is still important and suggestive.

2. The problem of conceptualization remains a difficult one, and it is probably easier to state a concept in the abstract than it is to apply it to the historical and contemporaneous study of party action. See, however, Frank J. Sorauf, *Political Parties in the American System* (Boston, 1964); William N. Chambers, "Party Development and Party Action: The American Origins," *History and Theory*, III (1963), 90-120; and Chambers, *Political Parties in a New Nation: The American Experience 1776-1809* (New York, 1963), for fuller, generally similar statements of the concept of political party. See also Neil A. McDonald, *The Study of Political Parties* (New York, 1955), for a discussion of concepts of political party from Max Weber and early American scholars to Maurice Duverger and other contemporaries.

establishment of the new national government, it was some time after Alexander Hamilton and Thomas Jefferson had come to face one another in the cabinet—"like two cocks," as Jefferson put it—before they became the rallying points for political parties. Yet it is in this sense of "party" that American politics can be said to have had political parties at all times from the mid-1790's to the present, except for one interregnum in the early nineteenth century.

American parties have also appeared as units within party systems, with a competitive two-party system as the norm. Indeed, it is one of the major themes of this volume that individual political parties cannot be fully understood except in terms of their place in a going party system. Most briefly, a competitive party system may be thought of as a pattern of interaction in which two or more political parties compete for office or power in government and for the support of the electorate, and must therefore take one another into account in their behavior in government and in election contests. This pattern of interaction, as compared with the fluidity of faction politics, is marked by durability and thus by relative predictability of consequences in both institutions and behavior. Such properties provide convenience for both political elites and the political public. A competitive two-party system may be defined as a system in which only two of the parties in the political arena generally have a significant chance of winning a preponderance of government offices and power.[3] It is in this sense that American politics on the national scene has, with rare exceptions, held to a two-party norm, although one-party or even multi-party systems have often characterized particular states. Variety of time or place remains, but viable concepts of party and party system may help us better to order and understand our politics.

In the 131 nations or states of the world today, party configurations range from the stable democratic two-party system of Great Britain to unstable multi-party systems in France or Italy, often characterized by intense ideological conflict; or from the single-party totalitarian system of the Soviet Union to the rise and collapse of mass nationalist parties in many new nations in Asia or Africa. Only 15 of the 131 nations or states of the world today have two-party systems.[4] For the American case, how-

3. See various standard works on contemporary parties and party systems, as well as citations to Sorauf and Chambers, above.
4. See e.g. Joseph LaPalombara and Myron Weiner (eds.), *Political Parties and Political Development* (Princeton, 1966); and summaries in Walter H. Mallory (ed.), *Political Handbook and Atlas of the World: Parliaments, Parties and Press 1966* (New York, 1966). Data compiled by Harry W. Fritz from the latter and other sources.

ever, a serious understanding of political parties can probably begin with the terms suggested here.

II

The course of American political party development can be broadly divided into three major stages. First came the stage of the virtual invention of parties, in the 1790's and again in the 1820's and 1830's, following the party interregnum during the presidencies of James Monroe and John Quincy Adams. In a second creative stage we find the development of American political party structure in its enduring form, in the Jacksonian era and its aftermath, a process which was virtually completed before the Civil War. The third phase of party development we may call a derivative stage, during which parties and party systems have responded, or sometimes failed to respond, to major currents in American social and political life.

In all three of these phases, parties and party systems have exhibited certain continuing or recurring patterns of activity. Insofar as they may play a significant part in the operation of the political system as a whole, these activities may be viewed as functions which parties or party systems have performed in the course of political development. This conceptualization is contested by Frank J. Sorauf and some other contributors to this volume, and the problem is indeed a thorny one; but it is difficult to analyze the relationship between parties and political development without drawing on some concept of function. First, parties and the party system appear to have served particularly significant integrative functions in the period of nation-building from the early 1790's to the end of the War of 1812, and have contributed in different ways and different degrees to integration and conflict resolution in later phases of development. Second, parties and party systems have at certain times also performed a significant function in shaping government policy and in mobilizing segments of the electorate behind such policy, as both the Federalists and Jeffersonian Republicans did in the 1790's, as modern Republicans did in the North during the Civil War, and as Democrats did to some degree in the era of the New Deal. Policy formation, however, has not been a prominent, regular undertaking of American political parties to the degree it has in many other party systems. More commonly, American parties and party systems have performed a third significant function in recruiting leaders in politics and providing personnel to fill the elective and appointive offices of government. Fourth, parties appear to have contributed also to the political socialization or acculturation of the American people, to have performed a roughly educational function. It is important to note, however, that the party system of our own time has not contributed as significantly to either of these last two functions as earlier party systems have.

In all three stages of development, American party systems, with few— though important—exceptions, have tended to contain or resolve political conflict more than they have tended to intensify or exacerbate it. This has been a result of their basic character and the way in which they have performed major functions.

1. *The stage of nation-building, 1789-1815.* The era of party origins in the American case provides a particularly useful laboratory for analysis. This is so not only for an historical explanation of party genesis, but also for a general understanding of the larger role party systems may play in a democratic polity. The American case involves not only the emergence of political parties at the national capital and in the national political arena, but also differential rates and patterns of party growth in each of the several states. Thus the first phase of American party development in the United States provides ample materials for a useful intra-national comparative analysis. The results of such analysis suggest that political parties are probably essential ingredients of any democratic or mass society of significant scale.

At bottom, four major conditions seem to account for the origin of parties and a party system in the American situation, and by hypothesis for the indigenous genesis of parties generally. These conditions are inter-related and appear to have acted on one another. Each of them appears to be a necessary condition for the emergence of parties, although no one of them alone is a sufficient condition; yet all taken together appear to constitute a set of conditions that is sufficient.[5] Each of the first three conditions also appears to have had an impact on the measure of party competition that developed at a given time or place, and on the shape of parties and the party system.

5. Cf. LaPalombara and Weiner, "The Origin and Development of Political Parties," and William N. Chambers, "Parties and Nation-Building in America," in LaPalombara and Weiner (eds.), *Political Parties and Political Development,* 3-42, 79-106; the second of these two chapters contains an earlier statement of the conditions for party genesis in the context of American political development. See also Seymour Martin Lipset, *The First New Nation: The United States in Historical and Comparative Perspective* (New York, 1963), 13-98, for the problems of political development in the era of nation-building.

The first two conditions have to do with matters of basic social structure and culture. The first condition may be described as the development of social or socio-economic structures that involve a substantial variety, differentiation, or complexity in society and economy, and consequently a variety of groupings or subgroupings in the population. Thus Pennsylvania, where a state party system probably had emerged in the 1780's and the national party system rapidly took root in the 1790's, was marked by economic variety and also by a variety of ethnic and religious groupings. The second condition is a situation in which popular, democratic, or mass styles of conducting politics obtain or are in the process of development, and in which emerging ideology or the political culture promises or emphasizes such popular or democratic modes of political life. The second condition can be stated conversely as the decline or collapse of the sway of deference politics, in which established notables could count on habits of political allegiance from men who held lesser status in the community. Thus the state of New York fulfilled the conditions of differentiation and complexity in social structure for party growth, but held on to the deference patterns by which family cliques could govern far more than Pennsylvania did; and the apparent result was that party development in New York was substantially slower than it was in its sister state. Meanwhile Virginia, for example, fell short of fulfilling either condition, with the result that party development and party competition in the Old Dominion was even more retarded.

A third condition for party genesis, obviously, is the existence of a common political arena, a condition that was provided on a national basis in the American case by the establishment of a national government through the new Constitution of 1789. Even more importantly, and less obviously, the precise character and structure of politics and government in a given political arena may have a profound effect on whether or not parties will arise, what their rate of growth will be, the form they will take, and how competitive they will be.[6] Thus, for example, variations in the structure of politics and government in the local arenas of Connecticut and South Carolina helped to account for variations in party development in the two states.

Variations in social structure, political culture, and political arena—basic contextual conditions for party development—may occur from time to time as well as from place to place. As both Goodman and McCormick

6. See Richard P. McCormick, *The Second American Party System: Party Formation in the Jacksonian Era* (Chapel Hill, 1966), as well as his essay in this volume.

show in their comparative studies of the first and second American party systems in this volume, such variations will in turn have an impact on the course of political party origins and development. The balance and inter-relations of these three conditions for party origins are immensely complex, but we can certainly suggest that they provide guidelines for research and analysis.

A final element in a historical explanation for party origins appears to have been some sense of felt need on the part of political elites for structures by means of which they could conduct political business in a reasonably predictable manner. Neither Hamilton, James Madison, nor Jefferson in the 1790's, nor many of the working politicians who gathered around Andrew Jackson in the late 1820's and early 1830's, were necessarily conscious that they were building political parties. Yet as they went about the business of trying to influence voters, win elections, satisfy diverse group interests, or conduct public affairs, this is in effect what they did. How difficult it is to manage political life without parties in a society in which the three contextual conditions for party development obtain is suggested by the fact that the disintegration of the first party system in the Monroe years was soon followed by the establishment of the second American party system. As we shall also see, moreover, political elites turned instinctively to partisan rather than factional ways of managing political business during the breakdown of the second party system in the 1850's. To working politicians, politics and the flux of interests and issues are uncertain enough as it is; and in order to act in any enduring context they tend to seek to maximize predictability in the complex political world. Thus their professional instinct is likely to incline them to establish relationships that are as stable and dependable as possible—relationships with each other and with the groups and voters who constitute their mass clienteles. This was one of the advantages Abraham Lincoln found in the Republican party during the strains of the Civil War years, as Eric L. McKitrick shows in his essay in this volume. Other politicians have learned the same lesson, and have thus tended to develop a penchant for the relatively ordered world of party procedures rather than the fluid uncertainties of non-party politics.

The contextual conditions associated with the emergence of parties support the hypothesis that parties and party systems of some sort are essential parts of a viable democratic polity in a complex society. Without the role party systems play in ordering political activity and facilitating the political process in such polities, these polities would scarcely endure as functioning entities. This appears to be the case despite variations in the character and functions of parties in the United States and other nations.

2. *The establishment of significant form, 1828-60.* The second stage of American political party development, the phase of the establishment of enduring significant form in party structure and action, was largely accomplished in the heyday of the second party system. Several important features of structure and activity appear and become fixed in this period, from the late 1820's to the early 1840's. Although a number of these features were foreshadowed by the first party system, they achieved their full flowering only in the second system. In considerable part these features developed because the Democrats and Whigs of the time were primarily concerned with winning a majority of the popular vote in contests for the presidency, contests which came to embrace virtually every state.

The salient characteristic of the second party system was the mobilization of mass participation in elections and in politics generally. In a time when Great Britain, even after the widely-touted Reform Bill of 1832, could boast an electorate of only about 650,000 out of a population of some 16 million, presidential elections in the United States were drawing turnouts of 1,153,350 in 1828, and 2,409,474 in 1840, even though total population amounted to only about 12 million in 1830 and 17 million in 1840. A venerable piece of doggerel expresses the American enthusiasm for politics in the nineteenth century—

> They marches in parades and they gets up hurrahs
> And they tramps through the mud for the good old cause.

This sense of popular engagement came to maturity in the second party system. In an era when men often lived far from one another and even town dwellers were often starved for entertainment and excitement, the party battle took on the form of a game and a major source of entertainment. It thus filled a need that has been served in our own times by the greater cultural advantages of an urban environment, and by theaters, moving pictures, sports contests, radio, and television. The heroes of popular culture a century and more ago were politicians like "Old Hickory," Henry Clay, "Old Tippecanoe" Harrison, Daniel Webster, "Old Bullion" Benton, or even Martin Van Buren—not cowboys in electronic transmission.[7] Thousands *did* march, flaunt transparencies of party heroes, cheer

7. This point was made particularly effectively by Marcus Cunliffe at the conference out of which this volume came; see also his *The Nation Takes Shape, 1789-1837* (Chicago, 1959) for a discussion of the relationship between the Jeffersonian and Jacksonian eras in politics.

at mass rallies in town squares or rural groves, and go to the polls to vote.

The outburst of popular participation was probably due in part to the ethos of Jacksonian, equalitarian democracy, but other factors were important too. Among these was the fact of nationwide party competition in an era of improved means of transportation and mass communication, including the emergence of a popular, partisan press. Voting turnout jumped from 26.9 per cent of white adult males in the multi-factional presidential election of 1824, in which six states still chose electors by legislature, to 57.6 and 57.8 per cent in 1828 and 1832, in the era of the restoration of parties. The election of 1840 brought voting participation to an unprecedented 80.2 per cent of white adult males,[8] and yet ironically it was an election in which issues were consciously de-emphasized by the victorious Whigs in favor of replicas of log cabins, chants of "Tippecanoe and Tyler Too," and red fire, an election in which keen rivalry between well-established Democratic and Whig party formations was the salient feature. Increased stresses toward participation by the populace imposed demands on party managers for new techniques to manage and mobilize masses of voters; and at the same time keen party competition spurred increased popular turnout. This relationship between a triumphant equalitarianism on the one hand, and the effect of close competition between far-flung popular parties in getting out the vote on the other, was the central political relationship of the age. The result was the democratization of parties and the party system, in popular participation and in the sources and kinds of leaders and cadres who came to the fore in both the Democratic and Whig parties. It was an age of the decline of the gentleman in politics as well as other aspects of life, and of the rise of professional politicians like Van Buren, the "Red Fox," or Francis P. "Bla'r," as Jackson called him, or the wily Thurlow Weed. Such managers quickly generated efficient means to manipulate the new mass ingredients of politics, but the sway of notables in a politics of deference was gone except for certain enclaves, mostly in the South. Political aspirants made a boast of coming from or pretending to come from *hoi polloi*, and "plain folks" was the theme in appeals to a mass electorate.

Meanwhile remarkable strides were taken in the development of party structures and mechanisms. Modern organization, in the sense of a continuing, rationalized division of labor and co-ordination of tasks to ac-

---

8. Here and elsewhere in this chapter I have used calculations of voting turnout made by Walter Dean Burnham, based as far as possible on primary sources.

complish the goals of party, had exhibited only a spotty development in the first party system, despite important initiatives among the Republicans in the 1790's and by younger Federalists in certain states in the early 1800's.[9] In the era of the second party system, however, party organization spread rapidly from state to state as a means of mobilizing the electorate and of winning elections, particularly crucial presidential elections. The final collapse in 1824 of the congressional caucus as a device for nominating presidential candidates opened the way for the establishment in the 1830's of the national convention system as a nominating agency. National conventions also took on the important function of mediating between state and regional elements or various factions within the national parties. In addition they assumed the task of providing a set of resolutions setting forth the party's policy position or ideology, and this practice was soon formalized into the party platform we know today. The system of organization was capped by the creation, by the Democratic National Convention of 1848, of the first national party committee, which served as an agency that could act for the party between conventions.

More-or-less popularly chosen delegate conventions in the states and counties also appeared as essential features of local party structure. Party affairs between conventions were managed by a variety of state and local committees, most of them at least ostensibly chosen by the popularly elected delegates to the appropriate local conventions. Party workers undertook systematic canvassing of voters in town and countryside; openly partisan newspapers at the national capital and across the country set forth partisan perspectives, kept leaders and followers informed, and bound the faithful to party standards; and partisan pamphlets flooded the land. A strong sense of identification with or loyalty to the party and its symbols, an attachment which had never developed in any significant measure in the first party system, became the order of the day. Men proudly carried party labels and loyalties to the edge of the grave. Party regularity was a virtue, straight ticket voting was the political duty of every good man, and switching from party to party was condemned as a vice.

Ultimately, under the impact of the sectional, ideological, and moral

9. See esp. Noble E. Cunningham, Jr., *The Jeffersonian Republicans: The Formation of Party Organization, 1789-1801* (Chapel Hill, 1957); Cunningham, *The Jeffersonian Republicans in Power: Party Operations, 1801-1809* (Chapel Hill, 1963); and David Hackett Fischer, *The Revolution of American Conservatism: The Federalist Party in the Era of Jeffersonian Democracy* (New York, 1966), for early party organization.

tensions of the slavery controversy, the second party system broke down. It is interesting, however, that the lineaments of a third party system were already apparent even before the schism of the Democrats at their national convention in Charleston in 1860 marked the disruption of the old national Democratic party.[10] Modes of party politics had become deeply ingrained in the outlooks and habits of men, and political elites turned quickly from the dying system of Democrats and Whigs to a new, emerging system of Democrats and Republicans. Even more important, the reestablishment of national competition between reunited Democrats and modern Republicans in a third party system after the Civil War built almost automatically on the foundations that had been laid down in the second system. Party competition in a new era rested on realignments in the electorate, but established ways of doing political business persisted.

3. *The derivative stage, 1865-1967.* It is the survival of early basic forms in the last hundred years that makes the third phase of American party development derivative, one of adjustment rather than creativity. Changes in ways of doing party business have occurred in the third party system, which lasted down to the early 1890's; in the fourth party system, down to 1932 or thereabouts; and in the fifth party system of the last three decades or more. These changes have been incremental, however, rather than basically creative.

A few leading instances will indicate the trend. The third party system saw the rise of the classical, corrupt, but assimilative urban boss and machine, and brought party loyalties to a pitch of almost military fervor and discipline. It also registered peaks of participation in presidential elections in 1876, 1888, and 1896 at or near 80 per cent of all adult males—including newly enfranchised Negroes. Yet the third system added little to the basic ingredients of party politics, and even the machine was but organization given a new bent and corrupted. The fourth party system of 1896 to 1932, under the impact of progressive reformers and critics in its early years, saw the establishment of the direct popular primary election for nominating candidates for local office. Hailed as a giant step in democratization, this reform also ultimately weakened party structure and the hold of parties on voters. In addition, voting turnout in presidential contests fell to 65.2 per cent of adult male citizens in 1904 and to 58.8 per cent in the three-party election of 1912, and turnout was to decline even further in the 1920's. The fifth party system struck a new balance between parties and local and national interest groups in a politics of welfare in the era

10. See Roy F. Nichols, *The Disruption of American Democracy* (New York, 1948).

of the New Deal, and brought participation back to 61 per cent and 62.4 per cent of adult citizens in the presidential races of 1936 and 1940. The fifth system also evolved new ways of campaigning in the era of television and pre-packaged candidate images; and if the 1870's and 1880's were decades of quasi-military drill in party politics, the 1950's and 1960's constitute an era overwhelmingly devoted to merchandizing or salesmanship styles in election campaigns. These developments, however, were more a matter of parties reacting to their environment than they were of parties acting on their own.

All told, the net result for our times has been a weakening rather than a strengthening of party bonds.[11] This remains the case despite a secular trend toward the nationalization of party politics as well as politics in general since the 1930's, and turnouts of 63.3 per cent and 64.1 per cent in the 1952 and 1960 votes for President. Parties have also lost the virtual monopoly over nominations, campaigning, and elections which they once enjoyed, as public relations firms and other agencies of political management have come to the fore, and the party system has come to play a less significant role than it once did. If party once was king in a democratic policy, it no longer reigns.

In all of these ways the long, derivative stage of American party development can best be seen as an exercise in adaptation and adjustment. The secular trend has been for party systems to adapt to forces generated outside of party politics itself—whether these forces involved a flood of new immigrants from Europe to American shores, the strains of economic depression, the impact on politics of an increasingly middle-class way of life, or new media of mass communication and political salesmanship—and to adjust political relations accordingly. To put the matter another way, the impact of social and political development in general on political parties in this era has been greater than the impact of parties on such larger lines of development.

Even so, the fact that American parties have by and large adjusted to the secular trend of change is in itself significant. In many other Western societies, among which France and Italy can be cited as examples, this kind of pragmatic adaptation or adjustment has not been the norm,[12] and such societies have paid high economic, social, and political costs as a re-

11. Cf. Walter Dean Burnham, "The Changing Shape of the American Political Universe," *American Political Science Review*, LIX (1965), 7-28.
12. See e.g. Giovanni Sartori, "European Political Parties: The Case of Polarized Pluralism," in LaPalombara and Weiner (eds.), *Political Parties and Political Development*, 137-76.

sult. Thus in the individual states, as Dawson points out in this volume, local party systems have not led the way in the transition to welfare policies, but they may well have facilitated that transition. While parties in recent years have seldom contributed significantly to policy initiatives, they have continued to provide an important addition to the constitutional framework in the political system as a whole, despite resistant tendencies toward localism and federalism in the face of great national problems. On balance, they have probably served to smooth the path to the solution of national problems and have thus helped to smooth the course of American development in general.

III

A deeper question than the development of parties as such is the relationship between parties and the broad mainstream of political development as a whole. Most Americans, and probably most American historians and political scientists too, have tended to take for granted the fact that the United States has elaborated a stable, functioning, and viable political system in the years since the establishment of the Constitution. Despite the strains imposed upon it by a vast, fast-changing, polyglot society, that system has broken down only once, in the schism of 1860-65. This is a record of continuity that no other major nation except Great Britain has matched in modern times.

Yet there is no reason to take the course of American political development for granted. To do so is to make a blind and arrogant assumption that Providence has granted to the American people some innate superiority in the management of public affairs. The span of world history, East and West, provides innumerable examples of the collapse or disintegration of nations or states, of turmoil and rebellion and revolution and civil war, of civil instability and political failure. The experience of would-be new nations in Asia and Africa today, moreover, is marked by repeated instances of frustration in nation-building or breakdown in political order. The comparative success of the American experience, of what the Founding Fathers thought of as their "republican experiment," calls for serious analysis and explanation. In that analysis, the relationship of parties and party systems to American development as a whole must certainly be examined as one element.

Any modern or modernizing nation, if it is to succeed in establishing a viable political system, must evolve some sort of solution for certain political problems. Solutions will vary from time to time and place to place, depending on history and circumstances; indeed, there is no guarantee that solutions will be found at all. At the outset a nation must establish some form of national authority, and win acceptance or legitimacy for that authority, if the writ of government is to run. If a nation embarks on a course which opens the way to substantial popular participation in politics, moreover, and particularly if it offers the democratic promise of government by consent, means must be found to absorb and manage the load of popular or mass participation. This is the problem of co-ordinating and rationalizing political activity in a situation which involves many rather than few, in which traditional patterns of deference, of government by local elites in a politics of factions or cliques, will not serve. In a politics of popular participation, again, authority and legitimacy will not be secure short of a significant degree of national integration, in the sense of an ongoing process in which various parts of the society are incorporated into a functioning whole. The problem of national integration in the United States has been a continuing one, as new groups, from propertyless males to fresh immigrants in the nineteenth century, and women and Negroes in the twentieth century, have demanded a place in society and a role in politics. In turn, the maintenance of authority, legitimacy, and integration depends on mechanisms in the political system which can at once express conflicting interests and resolve conflicts among them, short of immobilism or disruption of the society. In an open polity like that of the United States, this question has also involved the issue of open opposition to the men who happen to hold power in government at any given moment.

Even this does not complete the budget of problems which a viable political system must meet in some fashion. It is also necessary to recruit and train leaders for the political process at national and local levels. In addition, in democratic politics such political elites must be capable of mobilizing or responding to mass publics and electorates and of mediating between group and group. A political system, moreover, will stand or fall in part in terms of its payoff or policy output, particularly as this may involve meeting the problem of the distribution of the material and nonmaterial values that are the substance of the authoritative decisions of government. For a democratic polity to maintain stability, a substantial segment of the population must be convinced that the system is an instrument through which they have at least some chance to accomplish their objectives. In its relations with the rest of the world, finally, a nation—if it is to endure—must also evolve political means which will enable it to maintain its independence and autonomy.

These six basic, interrelated problems—establishing and maintaining authority and legitimacy, managing the demands and stresses of popular participation, achieving a workable measure of national integration, expressing and resolving conflicts of interests and meeting the issue of opposition, recruiting and training leaders for popular politics, policy-making and the distributing of values in the political process, and maintaining national independence and autonomy—have constituted the major problems of American political development. Many of them have been met more effectively in the American experience than they have at other times in history or in other places in the world, yet none of them have been solved automatically or even wholly resolved. The course of American development has often been halting or uncertain as elites groped for proximate solutions; the resort to arms in 1861-65 is only the most dramatic of instances of retrogression, of what may be called de-development, in our political history. In the process of development the American party systems have played various roles, ranging from proximate success to virtually total failure.

Against this background it is possible to define the concept of political development as it relates to the American experience as well as to other national experiences.[13] Political development is change through historical time, change which may in part be produced by and in part affect changes in other segments of the total society; but political development is not any political change. We would not call the dominance of one political party or another in any given era, for example, an instance of development. Political change may also constitute political development in one direction at the cost of de-development in another. Thus the establishment of the direct primary election in the early twentieth century was an instance of democratic development in that it did further democratize the political process. It was also an instance of de-development in the realm of parties, in that its ultimate effect was to help weaken party action.

Most broadly, political development can be characterized in terms of three crucial, interrelated processes, with a fourth variable related to them. First, political development implies the establishment and growth of a

13. For a fuller discussion of problems in political development, see Lucian W. Pye, *Aspects of Political Development* (Boston, 1966), *passim*.

capacity in the political system to maintain itself and its legitimacy; and this in turn implies a capacity to establish and maintain at least some workable measure of national integration. Second, this aspect of political development will depend in part on another, which may best be described as an increasing measure of differentiation and organization, and therefore of complexity in political structures and political activity, as differentiation and organization may promote efficiency in the political process. Such changes may at once reflect rising levels of differentiation and complexity in the society itself, and enable the political system to cope with such complexity. Third, and in part as the result of the first two elements, political development implies the evolution and maintenance of the capacity of the political system to meet or adjust to the problems and tensions of social change. Associated with these crucial processes of political development, we generally find a tendency away from localism and parochialism to some measure of centralization in political perspectives, decision-making, and activity as a concomitant aspect of development. Development in the political system as a whole also implies development in such sub-systems as the party system, although development in different areas of the total system are not necessarily precisely commensurate. Lag may occur at any point, and it often has in the American case.

Inevitably a difficult problem of analysis arises. It is the issue of whether political parties and party systems have had a major impact on American political development as a whole, or whether the general course of development has instead shaped parties and the party systems. Insofar as party systems have met the first criterion and provided significant innovations in the political process, they may be thought of at least in part as independent variables. If, on the other hand, parties and party systems have been shaped by the general course of development far more than they have shaped that course, they appear as dependent variables, as Sorauf argues. Analysis of American politics and party action in a dimension of time suggests that cases may be made for both points of view, but at different junctures in the American experience. The problem is treated in various ways in several chapters of this volume, generally with a contemporary emphasis. It may be well to approach it in terms of a longer span of historical time.

Certainly in the first two stages of their development, American political parties and the party systems had a significant impact on the course of political development as a whole. This is not to say that parties and the

party systems were not also shaped by society and culture, by the course of political development in general, and by the nature of the governmental and political framework as well. The process, not surprisingly, involved interaction.

The first party system was in itself a significant innovation.[14] Its evolution constituted nothing less than the creation of the machinery to handle the new national politics in a period of still modest but expanding political participation. As both Federalists and Republicans accepted and subscribed to the new constitutional system, and as both parties provided channels for the expression of interests and opinion, the party system also helped to give legitimacy to the new national authority. As the party system linked men and groups from region to region and state to state, providing a national framework for political expression within which both Massachusetts men and South Carolinians could be Federalists, and both New Yorkers and Virginians could be Republicans, it served to advance the process of national integration. This is so on balance despite the divisive conflict and competition between parties which often erupted out of immediate issues and in election contests.

In itself the first party system also entailed a significant differentiation of political structures and activity. As parties moved to establish increasingly durable relationships between leaders and followers, and increasingly regularized ways of conducting political business, they advanced the course of differentiation in the political system as a whole. In addition, the first party system served to stir increased outpourings of popular participation in politics and to provide vehicles for such participation, as increasing levels of voter turnout in the 1790's and early 1800's show. Parties in the first party system also recruited and trained leaders for the new popular politics, played an unusually significant role in proposing and shaping public policy, and contributed to solving the problem of national independence and autonomy. Finally, while neither the Federalist nor Republican parties were fully centralized formations, their national character and interstate linkages represented a movement away from the ex-

14. For the first party system, see Joseph Charles, *The Origins of the American Party System* (Williamsburg, Va., 1956); Manning J. Dauer, *The Adams Federalists* (Baltimore, 1953); and Paul Goodman, *The Democratic-Republicans of Massachusetts: Politics in a Young Republic* (Cambridge, Mass., 1964), and his essay in this volume. See also Chambers, *Political Parties in a New Nation, passim;* and Fischer, *The Revolution of American Conservatism, passim.* For the net balance of integrative effects in the first party system, cf. Chambers, "Parties and Nation-Building in America," loc. cit. 98-106.

treme localism and parochialism of previous political action. In all of these ways the first party system appears to have provided essential ingredients for the capacity of the political system to maintain itself. Yet the first party system failed in the end, in a process of de-development in which national parties disintegrated.

In the second phase of party development, the stage of the development of significant, recognizably modern form, parties and the party system also generated important innovations.[15] Probably the most significant contribution of the second party system to American political development was the activity the Democrats and Whigs of the 1830's and 1840's undertook at once to mobilize mass, *hoi polloi* participation in politics and to provide mechanisms for channeling such participation. Problems of authority and legitimacy were no longer so serious as they had been in the era of nation-building, but in its national and nationalizing characteristics the second party system apparently played a significant role in national integration, and thereby in the maintenance of national authority. Representation of interests and opinion continued, although the second party system probably contributed less significantly to the evolution and shaping of public policy than the first party system did, despite high measures of party cohesion in congressional roll-calls in the 1840's and early 1850's.[16] Recruitment and leadership training continued, but in new dimensions that were made necessary by the increasingly mass character of politics and party action. Elaborate organization involved still further differentiation of political structures and activities, although the national focus of a federally structured party system remained far from centralized, and somewhat tenuous.

Parties in the second system appear once again to have contributed to the capacity of the political system to carry on its various functions. Although the second party system also ended in failure, its contribution to basic patterns of party organization and action remained.

The impact of party systems on political development diminishes in

15. For the second party system, see McCormick, *The Second American Party System,* and his essay in this volume; also Richard P. McCormick, "New Perspectives on Jacksonian Politics," *American Historical Review,* LXV (1960), 288-301; Robert V. Remini, *Martin Van Buren and the Making of the Democratic Party* (New York, 1959); and Lee Benson, *The Concept of Jacksonian Democracy: New York as a Test Case* (Princeton, 1961). See also Arthur M. Schlesinger, Jr., *The Age of Jackson* (Boston, 1945), and other general histories.

16. Joel H. Silbey, *The Shrine of Party: Congressional Voting Behavior, 1841-1852* (Pittsburgh, 1967).

the later phases of party history. The Republican party and the party system in the Union during the Civil War made a vital contribution to popular mobilization for the war and to the evolution, coherence, and co-ordination of policy, as McKitrick shows in his chapter in this volume; and political efficiency in the Confederacy suffered from the collapse of party politics. The classical bosses and machines of the last decades of the nineteenth century, in part for their own purposes and certainly for a price, nonetheless provided important functions of political socialization and integration among the masses of newly arrived immigrants. Yet the orientation of party structures to parochial, community cultures rather than to more cosmopolitan, society-wide concerns, as Hays points out, resulted in resistance to movements toward centralized political decision-making to match centralized direction in the economy and in corporate structures. In the twentieth century, particularly in the era of the Great Depression and Franklin D. Roosevelt, parties did revamp their outlooks and to some extent their activities to cope with demands for welfare, the need to meet the effect of massive economic collapse, and problems of economic management in a mixed economy. Once again, however, the effect of a federally structured party system was often to fragment or federalize national policies or programs, as Lowi observes.

In our own times parties have become more issue-oriented and national in character. A general nationalizing of political attitudes, not only in the more cohesive party system of Great Britain but in the American instance too, as Stokes shows, has resulted in elections turning more on national vis-à-vis local constituency factors than they once did. Yet today parties must also share more and more of their role in elections and in political management with agencies outside of the party system. By taking up the demands of Negroes for recognition and equality in our own time, both of the major national parties today have probably helped to deal with this most recent great problem of national integration. Yet here again, the parties have responded to forces coming from outside the party system rather than undertaking innovation on their own. On many counts, indeed, critics find our party system today a laggard in political development on both the national and state levels.

On the basis of this analysis, it is possible to offer a general hypothesis. Probably the most nearly precise way to summarize the relationship between political parties and the course of political development in general during the last hundred years and more is to say that the role of parties and party systems has changed to one of adaptation and adjustment rather than of innovation. It follows that parties appear in the second long stage of their development as dependent variables far more than they do as independent variables. The party system probably still contributes to the maintenance of legitimacy and to national integration, and thereby plays a part in giving the political system as a whole the capacity to maintain itself. Parties do not stand out in the era of Lyndon Johnson, however, as the initiating, guiding forces they once were when a Jefferson or a Jackson held sway.

In summary, American political development as a whole, like the development of other stable polities, can conveniently be divided into two broad eras. The first is the phase of establishing the nation as a going entity, with all of the peculiar problems this process involves. In the American instance this phase can be said to have extended from the Revolutionary era down to sometime around 1815, when the American triumph at the Battle of New Orleans symbolized the coming of age of the United States as an established nation with its place in the world reasonably assured. The second era of political development can be described as a continuing phase of reaction to social change and the problems it brings with it. In this context the role of party systems has on the whole been one of adjustment. Their chief function during the last century has probably been the function which Lowi in this volume calls "constituent," in the sense of mediating relations between government on the one hand and voters on the other, and of providing a sense of involvement and consent. In their constituent function, furthermore, party systems have helped to give shape to the course of politics and to the agenda of policy issues.

In this constituent function, parties may greatly facilitate the workings of the political process. Our party systems have still served the nation in the third phase of party development by providing an adaptive, generally pragmatic mechanism within the political process; indeed, pragmatic adjustment has become virtually a way of life in and between American political parties. This way of party life has, with a few rare exceptions, helped to keep the temperature of American politics low and thus to minimize or resolve conflict. If we compare these aspects of American party politics with the exacerbation of social cleavages, ideological tensions, and conflict by parties in many other nations, the value of the moderating effect of the party system in American politics becomes readily apparent.

This adaptive, pragmatic character of political parties in the American system calls in turn for analysis and explanation; and once again the explanation cannot be grounded in the realm of party action alone.

IV

Certain major features of American life appear to have shaped the particular course of American political development. Together, they may provide the ingredients for a set of general hypotheses for an historical explanation of that course and its relationship to political party development. Set down in brief outline, these features appear to have been—

A *liberal tradition*. Since the time of the Revolution, the liberal philosophy of John Locke and the Enlightenment has more and more been incorporated into American thought and into American political culture until it became virtually "the common sense of the subject," as Jefferson put it. It became an unconscious mood in the American presence and the basis for an emerging political consensus.

Relative economic abundance. The existence of immense resources in a rich continent and the emergence of vigorous human resources, including skills in technology and economic organization, have made the United States an affluent, middle-class nation in comparison with other countries of the world, have provided a generally high standard of living, and have thus helped to provide a favorable economic and social environment for American political development.

A *pragmatic strain*. An ingrained pragmatic tendency, presumably stimulated by the experiences of facing a new continent, characterized the attitudes of most Americans as well as the famous Yankee tinkerer long before philosophers coined the term "pragmatism." This tendency has become a common heritage among Americans, and has been incorporated into the conduct of political as well as other kinds of business.

All of these features have been mixed in the interplay of American life. They may thus be taken as interrelated factors or variables in the historical explanatory scheme which is suggested here to account for the particular course of American development. Probably the liberal tradition would not have flowered so readily on American soil were it not for the fact that it could grow in an environment of comparative economic abundance, and could gain sustenance from the pragmatic tendency among Americans to find workable solutions to political as well as other problems, solutions which often meant the way of compromise and adjustment. Political prag-matism, moreover, can probably grow most readily in an environment in which a common political mood and a generally accepted, if often half-conscious, notion of political fundamentals exists. A pragmatic politics is also favored by an environment in which relative economic abundance tends to keep clashes between social classes or groups at a comparative minimum and provides a considerable margin for the pragmatic process of trial and error without the risk of economic catastrophe. The problem of explanation is to set forth the interrelationships between these variables more precisely, and to show how they have affected the course of political development.

At the center, the liberal tradition which Americans borrowed from Europe and shaped into the core of an indigenous political culture became the basis for consensus on political fundamentals. The liberal tradition emphasized the value of the individual man and his freedom and rights, the belief that the legitimacy of government and its actions could rest only on the rational consent of the governed, and a civic sense of community. Political thought in the liberal mood began not with the idea of historically established orders, estates, or classes ranged in a hierarchy of privilege and status, but with the notion that individual human atoms were the units of politics and the only proper foundations of legitimate government. Such ideas were subversive of the whole notion of feudal hierarchy or corporate gradations in society and politics. Indeed, as Louis Hartz has pointed out, the absence of a feudal past and feudal traditions in America was probably a major explanation for the ready rise to ascendancy of liberal ideas in our political culture.[17] Americans living in an already largely open society found it easier to adopt such ideas than their Euro-pean cousins did. The fact that the American Revolution was not a social revolution of class against class or system against system, as the French Revolution and other European social upheavals have been, probably also facilitated the acceptance of the liberal strain in American life. The pe-culiar character of the American national revolution, again, stands in con-trast to the deeper tensions of movements for independence in many new nations in our own times.

Finally the liberal tradition carried with it the notion of the basic moral

17. The most powerful statement of the whole contention is Louis Hartz, *The Lib-eral Tradition in America* (New York, 1955), although he sometimes overstates the case.

equality of men, an idea that was to prove as powerful in American development as it was ambiguous. This idea of equality was proclaimed in the Declaration of Independence and the Gettysburg Address, was at the heart of the thrust of Jacksonian democracy, and was heavily involved in the promises of the New Deal. Today, it has been part of the motive force of the civil rights and Negro movements of our time. The stress toward equality has been by far the most controversial aspect of the liberal tradition in application, while at the same time it has been one of the strongest driving forces in the course of American development.

At the outset of American national political history, the liberal tradition had yet to achieve the status of a general commitment. In its larger promises at least, it commanded far more support from Jeffersonian Republicans than it did from many or most Federalists, and for a time it stood almost as the ideology of one party against the other. It worked its way more and more into the minds of men, however, and after the War of 1812 it was clearly a central strain in our political culture. The notion that the units of politics were free, equal, independent men who must consent to government was obviously at loggerheads with older patterns of deference politics based on habits of social subordination to local elites. The liberal equalitarian outlook was a major factor in producing both new forms of party competition and in the collapse of deference politics in the early nineteenth century. By the age of equality, of which Andrew Jackson became the symbol, even this most controversial aspect of the liberal perspective had triumphed as an idea if not in actuality. The Whigs of the 1830's contrasted sharply with the Federalists of the 1790's in their readiness to accept the rhetoric and at least some of the substance of the equalitarian thrust. At least since the election of 1840, moreover, no major party has failed to pay its respects to liberal, equalitarian symbolism and ideas.

Yet the question of why the liberal tradition should have experienced such a comparatively easy growth on American soil requires further analysis. The absence of a feudal past and the peculiar nature of the American Revolution do not constitute a sufficient explanation. Certain more specific factors associated with social and economic structure are also crucial. American society even in the colonial years of the eighteenth century was not so sharply or so rigidly graded into ranks or classes, much less orders or estates, as European society was during the same span of historical time. Another crucial aspect was the movement even of eighteenth-century Americans toward comparative abundance. As Douglass North and others have pointed out, most plain Americans were probably better off by the end of the century than their European counterparts, despite the comparative lag of industrial development in this country.[18] Later dramatic thrusts in economic development in the nineteenth and twentieth centuries have made the Americans a "people of plenty," in David Potter's telling phrase.[19] Americans have moved more and more toward middle-class ways and standards of life, despite the continuing economic and cultural poverty of significant components of the society. These aspects of the society and economy have had profound effects on the course of American political life.

A society which has lacked rigid class structures is less likely to generate a politics of sharp social or class conflict than societies—like those of most of Europe—that have been dominated by such class structures. Where developing abundance rather than scarcity is a fact of economic life, moreover, conflict over the distribution of values through the authority of government is likely to be less deep, less intense, and less disruptive than it is in societies that do not enjoy such comparative affluence. Thus the attitude of most Americans toward the problem of distribution, as Potter has commented, has been "deal me in," rather than "soak the rich"—and, he might have added, rather than "expropriate the expropriators," or "smash the capitalist class." In comparison with Europe, the interplay of politics and the contention of political parties have not centered on basic, deeply divisive issues of social class and social or economic structure. Rather, they have revolved around questions of a better balance in distribution or of incremental change. In such a society it is far easier for the liberal outlook to become the accepted norm than it is in societies that are deeply divided on economic and class lines, and hence along ideological party lines.

All of these elements provide foundations for an historical explanation of the moderate, pragmatic, adjustive character of American politics and political party action. The hypothesis is that these factors of economic plenty, a social structure that minimized class divisions, and the liberal ethos or tradition have, as fundamental forces, helped to move American development toward a politics of limited conflict and moderation; and they have thereby provided a favorable context for a politics of mediation, of group brokerage looking toward formulas of agreement in broad partisan

18. Cf. Douglass C. North, *Growth and Welfare in the American Past* (Englewood Cliffs, 1966), chaps. 2, 3, *passim*.

19. David M. Potter, *People of Plenty: Economic Abundance and the American Character* (Chicago, 1954), *passim*.

combinations, of conflict resolution and adjustment, of compromise—in short, a politics of pragmatic adaptation. Where men are broadly agreed —if half-consciously—on the fundamentals of society, the Constitution, political structure, and political ways and means, it is comparatively easy to maintain such political practices. Despite occasional lapses and the great breakdown of the Civil War, and despite the dramatic rhetoric and recurring logomachy that has characterized our political history, this has been the broad course of American development.

To be sure, pragmatism in politics and in the larger society has often entailed significant costs, as such critics as Richard Hofstadter among others have pointed out;[20] but it has become a standard way of life in the political realm and particularly in the conduct of party politics.

V

The basic factors in American development stressed here have also probably tended to make American politics less oriented to ideology than the politics of many other nations, and American parties less significant in performing continuing policy-making functions than parties elsewhere. These factors may, in addition, help to explain the persistence of the two-party norm in our politics.

Ideological tensions have run higher at certain junctures of American development than at most other times. Important instances are the controversies over Jay's Treaty and world politics in the 1790's, the moral and ideological strife over slavery and the place of the Negro in American life in the middle decades of the nineteenth century, and the tensions of the New Deal years in the 1930's. The content of ideology has also run unusually high in certain election campaigns, most notably those involving William Jennings Bryan's agrarian-Democratic following in 1896 and Barry Goldwater's conservative-Republican stalwarts in 1964. But it is also worth noting that both Bryan and Goldwater suffered disastrous defeats, defeats which followed in large measure from the campaign strategies to which their ideological commitments bound them. Other cases might be noted, from John Randolph's purist quid pronouncements of 1805 to the thrust of Jacksonian equalitarianism.

20. Cf. in particular Richard Hofstadter, *Anti-Intellectualism in American Life* (New York, 1963), and his discussion of the decline of the gentleman and the general impact of pragmatism and equalitarianism on American culture, within and outside of the political realm.

Finally, it may be that the mid-1960's will mark another period of comparative ideological stress. Frustrations and tensions have brought not only liberal-conservative contention but the rise of a militant Negro movement, the combat of New Left and Radical Right, and new political associations of various hues. Ours are troubled times for Americans, at home and as they face—or fail to face—the revolutionary tensions of world politics and the strains and costs of an undeclared war in Vietnam. Perhaps 1964, the ambiguous unsettlements and Republican gains of the 1966 elections, and talk of significant Left and Right presidential candidacies in 1968, foreshadow the emergence of a new party alignment. If so, it will have been heralded, as often in the past, by ideological rumblings.

Ideology, however, has not been of the American mainstream. It was Jefferson who, after he and his party had won power, remarked that "what is practicable must often controul what is pure theory." In his turn, Lincoln took a pragmatic approach to the problems of slavery and emancipation, as he did toward Reconstruction in the South; and the Compromise of 1877 which finally closed out the Reconstruction controversy was a thoroughly pragmatic bargain.[21] Despite the tensions of the problems of recovery and reform in the 1930's, Roosevelt himself was virtually the epitome of pragmatism and experimentalism. Even at its peak, ideological contention in the United States has never reached the extremes that have often characterized the politics of other nations in Europe, Africa, or Asia. Moreover, ideological thrusts have usually been followed in American development by a new political balance within standard pragmatic bounds. Indeed, pragmatism and ideology stand as virtually opposite approaches to political affairs, if not as antonyms; where pragmatism has become the norm, the politics of ideology is unlikely to find widespread favor. This equation in American politics and party action has tended to facilitate the resolution of political conflict, and to keep the intensity of politics comparatively low.

In the end result, American political development in general and political party development in particular have tended to follow a roughly cyclic pattern. Times of stress or tension produce new demands, relative ideological ferment, and new issues; and thus they provide a kind of motive force in the course of politics. As political elites and political parties re-

21. See the probing analysis in C. Vann Woodward, *Reunion and Reaction: The Compromise of 1877 and the End of Reconstruction* (Boston, 1951), and also the discussion of the effects of the bargain on parties and party action.

spond to such pressures or undertake initiative on their own, these materials break into the political arena and come to a head in periodic crucial elections—elections like those of 1800 and 1828, the contests of 1856 and 1860, the congressional and presidential races of 1894 and 1896, and (after some foreshadowing in 1928) the elections of 1932 and 1936. In all of these instances but one, these elections have brought about realignments of party forces and popular followings which have resulted in the establishment of new party systems. Such realigning periods, however, have generally been followed by pragmatic adaptation to the new direction of politics by major elements in the leadership of the defeated party or its successor; and politics is reoriented around new rather than old issues. Thus, for example, the Republican regime of Dwight D. Eisenhower in the 1950's scarcely even contemplated rolling back the measures of its predecessors, of the New Deal and the Fair Deal. This historical phenomenon, which V. O. Key, Jr., has aptly referred to as dualism in a moving political consensus,[22] is in itself a kind of pragmatic historical adaptation. Starved for office, if nothing else, the "out" party wants once again to be "in," and particularly to win the presidency. Its major national leaders generally modify their policy views accordingly, although frustration with change may leave some measure of intransigence. By and large, however, the enthusiasms of old causes or ideology are drained away, and politics proceeds on its normal course of business as usual.

This cyclic ebb and flow, together with the pragmatic bent of American party politics in general, helps to explain why American parties have not regularly undertaken policy-shaping functions to the degree that European and other parties have. In general, the American party systems have tended to assume a major role in policy formation, and in mobilization of public support for particular policy directions, primarily in times of relative social tension and ideological concern, although the impact of parties on policy-making has probably also varied with the degree of cohesion and organization within parties at any given time. Federalists and Jeffersonian Republicans, in the era of nation-building and concern for the direction the American republican experiment would take; the Republicans of Lincoln and the Radicals, in the turbulent years of the Civil War and Reconstruction; and the new national Democratic party, in the era of the New Deal—these significant instances of party systems playing ma-

22. V. O. Key, Jr., *Politics, Parties, and Pressure Groups,* 5th Ed. (New York, 1964), 222-7.

jor roles in the formation of public policy are also precisely instances of relatively high social strain and ideological attachment. Thus they support the argument that the role of party systems in policy-making will vary with these kinds of conditions.

These inferences from an intra-national time comparison are buttressed by the results of an international comparison. Observers appear to be agreed that party systems outside of the United States have, by and large, performed policy-making functions more steadily, more significantly, and more effectively than American parties have. It seems probable that this fact is in turn the consequence of associated conditions that have obtained more fully in Europe and in other societies than they have in the United States—conditions of continuing and often deep social tensions, which produce a corresponding, enduring emphasis on political ideology. If this is the case we would expect party systems in such societies to participate more significantly in policy-making than party systems in the United States, just as we would expect American parties to undertake policy functions in larger measure in times when these characteristics have reached comparatively high levels in our own society. At bottom, again, the impact of the three major factors in American development that have been stressed here probably explains why such undertakings have not been the norm.

Finally, these factors may help provide an explanation for the persistence of the two-party system in American political life. A variety of approaches to this problem have been advanced in the literature on political parties, but none of them appear to be wholly satisfactory.[23] It may be, again, that historical analysis through a substantial dimension of time will carry us further toward a solution. Minor parties we have always had with us—at least since 1840—but the average vote for all minor party candidates taken together in presidential elections from 1828 through 1964 has been only 5.2 per cent of the total popular vote. The number of third or fourth parties that can qualify as "significant," on a criterion of having won a popular vote for their presidential candidates at least equal to this standard of 5.2 per cent, is limited to only seven in the 120 years since 1848, with none qualifying since 1924. The relevant instances occurred in 1848, in 1856 and 1860, in the early 1890's, with both the "Bull Moose" Progressives and the Socialists in 1912, and in 1924. At all other times party

23. Cf. Sorauf, *Political Parties in the American System;* Key, *Politics, Parties, and Pressure Groups;* and other standard sources.

politics has proceeded as usual, and has returned to and sustained the two-party norm.[24] Undoubtedly factors of constitutional and institutional structure, particularly the presidency and electoral institutions, are relevant to the problem. Yet for a variety of reasons they do not seem to constitute a sufficient explanation.

Perhaps a new approach will prove fruitful. It seems probable, as a hypothesis, that such factors as consensus, the absence of continuing, deep economic or class cleavages, and the persistence of pragmatic adjustment of political tensions, have all had something to do with the maintenance of the two-party system as a norm. In terms of an intra-national historical comparison, it appears that third-party thrusts of significant dimensions in the American experience have developed in periods, first, when tensions and frustrations have been unusually high, and second, when pragmatic adjustment through the major parties has broken down. When these disturbing variables have been relatively low, two-party politics as usual has persisted. An apparent exception, the failure of a significant third-party movement to emerge after the Great Depression, is probably not an exception but a confirmation. In this instance the Democratic party under new leadership undertook precisely the kind of pragmatic adjustment that has characterized the American mainstream, and with reasonable success, whereas in other instances of crisis, as they have been marked here, pragmatic adjustment between and within major parties failed. The whole problem calls for much more research and analysis. The notions of a liberal tradition, relative affluence, and a pragmatic bent in politics, however, should provide fruitful ingredients for such work.

In any case the interplay of these crucial elements appears to constitute the most likely basis for an understanding of the emergence of the peculiarly American way of party life.

24. These and other data on third-party votes as they relate to the two-party norm have been calculated for me by Harry Fritz from a variety of statistical sources, including *Historical Statistics of the United States: Colonial Times to 1957* (Washington, 1960), and others.

II | FRANK J. SORAUF

UNIVERSITY OF MINNESOTA

Political Parties

and Political Analysis

To RAISE THE QUESTIONS of developmental analysis and theory as they relate to political parties is to raise a host of theoretical issues. Developmental analysis most certainly brings up the broadest issues of social change, and questions of social change can scarcely be separated from any questions of generalization and theory. Generically the developmental questions do not differ from those that explain political phenomena at any one particular moment. We are concerned with explaining variation and uniformity, and it makes no fundamental difference whether that variation or uniformity occurs over time or space. In fact, the search for separate theories of change in the social sciences in the past may have been so relatively fruitless simply because that search was organized on the premise of the distinctiveness of such theories. And by the same token, the search for general theories has undoubtedly been hampered by the relative inattention paid to change and development over time.

While the question of change and development cannot be separated from the more general questions of any theory, it is true that one may develop implicit understandings of reality that are more applicable to the explanation of static relationships than they are to the more elusive matters of change. And therein may lie one of the explanations for the paucity of developmental theory in the social sciences. In the past large numbers of social scientists have adopted theoretical models and systems which focused on the fixed rather than the changing. Within many equilibrium models, for example, the movement of all factors is toward balance and rest and away from motion, disturbance, or change; at best they detail the compensating reaction of the system to change. Within the disciplines of history and political science the working out of developmental theory has also been beset by a dispiriting tradition of developmental theorizing that can perhaps best be called "evolutionary." Among the ancient Greeks it was typified by the cyclical theories, heavy with historical teleology, in which political forms matured until, overripe, they decayed into some new and emergent form. With the Hegelians disembodied historical forces chased each other across the panoramas of history in a series of combining and refining encounters. Evolution informed those who found their theories of social change in analogies to the biological laws of Darwin. These approaches and their contemporary variants have lost a great deal of favor. They smack too much of descriptive explanation in that they mistake the fact of the cycle for an explanation of change. Their analysis also too often disappears in the mists of metaphysics or teleology.

The working out of a more empirical and analytical set of developmental theories is well under way. Some important intellectual issues remain, however, and this paper will in part focus on two of them. The first is the problem of choosing among possible models of the political system and of the relationship between its totality and its parts. At the present that problem centers on the usefulness of the assumptions of functionalism. The second is the question of the proper and most fruitful level of analysis for the development of theories about the political system. In terms of the present task it is the question of how one integrates the study of the development of political parties themselves into the study of the development of entire political systems. Is it merely a matter of shifting from the party as a dependent variable to party as one of a set of independent variables affecting the development of the system? Can one indeed think of party development as a process independent and separable from that of the development of the total system? These particular issues, along with the more general problem of a theory of political parties, furnish the major concerns of this essay.

II

It is necessary, first of all, to be clear as to what we are talking about. While on some levels the American political party—or any other political party, for that matter—is easily identifiable, on others it is amazingly elusive. The elusiveness is both definitional and empirical. In a stipulated definition the political party is not easily separated from hundreds of interest groups or from non-party political organizations such as the Americans for Democratic Action or Barry Goldwater's Free Society Association. At least in the American context some of these non-party organizations do not differ vastly in organization from the political party, and increasingly some of them are sharing the traditional party activities of contesting elections and mobilizing the men and machinery of government. All political organizations, whether political parties or not, serve as political intermediaries between the micro-politics of the individual and the macropolitics of political institutions and political systems. They all mobilize and organize the fragmented, minuscule political power of individuals into more effective political aggregates or conglomerates.

The only major characteristic which consistently separates the political party from other political organizations is its conventional inclination to offer its name and collectivity to candidates for their public identification. Especially where political parties have lost control of nominations they are marked chiefly by their specific electoral role. In an important, if secondary, way, it is also true that political parties have, historically, been more stable, more ongoing, and longer-lived than other political organizations. They have also been more inclusive, more willing to embrace large and heterogeneous groups of citizens, and more apt to assume an independent, symbolic presence to which the individual can attach his loyalty and to which he might look for guidance and cues.[1] There does remain the question whether the impact or consequences of the activities differ so greatly in quality or quantity from the consequences of the actions of other political organizations as to set them apart. In short, by exaggerating the differences between political parties and other political organizations we may have closed off the fruitful possibility of a level of analysis between party and total political system: that of the full range of political organizations.

More serious has been the empirical elusiveness of parties. It is clear from the literature on political parties that in the name of "political parties" scholars have been studying a considerable range of phenomena. Even the most cursory examination of the histories of American parties suggests that much of our work has centered on the quadrennial nominating conventions, the campaigns, and the presidential election itself. Candidates af-

1. For an extended, perceptive definition, see William N. Chambers, "Party Development and Party Action: The American Origins," *History and Theory*, III (1963), 108ff. I have also dealt with the problem in the first chapter of my *Political Parties in the American System* (Boston, 1964).

flicted with the presidential "bug," dramatic convention scenes, rousing oratory, and the vying for great regional blocs of votes make for compelling narratives, but through it all we see the political party *qua* party only dimly—unless one conceives of political parties only as a complex of candidates, campaigns, issues, and voters in presidential campaigns. Furthermore, most studies of voting behavior treat the voting decision apart from the impact and effect of the political parties in the campaign. The political party in these studies is little more than an aggregate of voter perceptions and loyalties; it has little substance as a palpable organization operating in a real political world. Or to take an additional example, studies of party cohesion (i.e. of party discipline) in legislative voting in the United States talk of "party," but it is only "party" in the sense of aggregates of party affiliations. Nowhere does the party as an organization, with leaders, whips, and caucuses, make a substantial appearance.

Apparently limited data, and perhaps limited interest, encourage us to say little of the political parties as organizations, of their strategies and leadership, their activities as organizations, their long-term activists and loyalists.[2] It is true that the American political parties are marked by an organizational looseness and evanescence—who indeed *are* the Democrats and the Republicans?—but they do nonetheless have palpable organizational characteristics. The great theoretical tradition in the study of political parties was established by men with a distinctly organizational approach to the study of political parties—one need mention only the names of Moisei Ostrogorski, Roberto Michels, and Maurice Duverger.[3] More recently one of the major American theoretical advances in the study of political parties, that of Samuel Eldersveld, has also reflected an organizational approach to political parties.[4] There is a strong case, in other words, that the major theoretical contributions to the study of political parties have come from that sector of the literature in which the party as an empirically observable organization dominates the work. If that is so, the moral, and the lesson, are clear.

2. A word ought also to be said in candor about the disproportionate attention we have given to the minor parties in American history. The very size of this literature suggests the power of colorful leaders and burning issues to distract scholarly attention from party organizations and activities.

3. See esp. M. Ostrogorski, *Democracy and the Organization of Political Parties* (New York, 1902), and *Democracy and the Party System in the United States* (New York, 1910); Michels, *Political Parties* (Glencoe, 1949); and Duverger, *Political Parties* (New York, 1954).

4. Samuel J. Eldersveld, *Political Parties: A Behavioral Analysis* (Chicago, 1964).

For the sake of simplicity and clarity the political party can be thought of as a tripartite organization or structure. It is composed of three elements.

1. *The organization proper.* The political party *is* an organization which men and women join for concerted action to achieve goals. And this party organization has an internal life of its own, as does any organization or institution. It recruits members, elevates men to positions of leadership, and works out a division of labor. It develops norms and loyalties of its own; for its activists the party *itself* may even become a goal. It pursues goals and makes decisions important both for its internal goals and for the performance of its activities in the external political system. Within it power and influence and authority are distributed, and consent and resources must be mobilized. It must find essential resources and decide how to expend them. This, quite simply, is the political party of the party officials, the activists, and the members; it is the purposeful, organized, initiating vanguard of the party.

2. *The party in office.* Partisans are organized as partisans in virtually all legislatures of the democracies. In the legislatures of the United States the legislative party organizations are those of caucuses, floor leaders, and whips. The party organization in the executive in parliamentary systems is merely an extension of party organization in the legislature; in non-parliamentary systems it is more casual and difficult to identify. Within the American practice it appears most prominent in those states in which governors are armed with a substantial appointive power, both in regard to top-level policy-making positions and to the lower-level positions so appropriate for patronage use. But the important point is that, while the parties in office represent an organized, goal-seeking wing of the party, their goals, incentives, and rewards are different from those of the organization proper. An American legislative party, for example, controls a separate system of rewards and punishments for its members; it awards status and power, and it may approve or defeat the legislative projects of individual members. It generates its own goals and responds to its own perception of its special constitutional responsibility. Those goals and those perceptions may or may not be the same as those of the organization proper. They can and do conflict, for instance, in such matters as the legislative party's responsibility to the party's platform or manifesto.

3. *The party-in-the-electorate.* The least stable, least active, least involved, and least well organized of these three sectors of the party is the

THE AMERICAN PARTY SYSTEMS

party-in-the-electorate.[5] It is composed of those partisans who attach themselves to the party either by regular support at the polls or through self-identification with it—"I am a Republican," "I am a Democrat." They may perceive the party symbolically rather than organizationally; they may see it as an extension of a personality or as a traditional duty to the loyalties of their fathers. But they are "of" the party by reason of a somewhat stable, persistent attachment to the party on which the party organization can "count," and on the basis of which the individual orders a sizable portion of his political perceptions and actions. The party is for him a symbol that provides cues and order to the political cosmos; to the party, the individual constitutes part of a loyal clientele, but not so loyal that it does not have to be propitiated. In activity and involvement the dividing line between the partisans of the organization and those of the party's electorate is, of course, imprecise; individuals cross freely from one to the other and back again.

To put the matter briefly, a meaningful approach to political parties must be concerned with parties as organizations or structures performing activities, processes, roles, or functions.[6] At the risk of appearing to be an unreconstructed formalist, I would say that the logical intellectual and analytical point of reference is the party as a structure. Activity (or function) is certainly important, but one must begin by knowing who or what is acting. Much of the complexity of "party" behavior can indeed be explained in terms of the relationships among the three sectors of the party and the need to co-ordinate their differing goals and incentives. One party differs significantly from another, both organizationally and in its capacity for action as the pattern of relationships among the three sectors differ. And if by "party" we mean, for example, a party candidate and his personal views, or, on the other hand, the total group of voters who happen to vote for him, I doubt very much that it *is* a party to which we refer.

The organizational approach to political parties runs counter to many of our intellectual predispositions, for American parties have been and are classically underorganized by the standards of the ideological parties of Europe. We have often in the past deduced statements about a party from our assessments of the activity of some part of the party or the perceptions of an electorate. It is easy and tempting, for example, to begin with gross

5. The term has been made popular by V. O. Key, Jr., in *Politics, Parties, and Pressure Groups* (New York, 1964); he in turn attributed its origin to Ralph Goldman.
6. Here and elsewhere I am employing a broad concept of organization; I am, in fact, using the term synonymously with structure.

election totals, analyze their patterns and determination, and from them deduce the presence and activity of party organizations. The party's candidate lost a ward, a county, or a state by a particularly overwhelming margin; hence the "party" is especially weak there. Or we speak blithely of the President as a leader of his "party," even though he may have an absolute distaste for partisan politics and will have no truck with the affairs of his party. In these and so many other ways we reconstruct an image of something we imprecisely call a political party. But surely a theory of the political party, developmental or other, must begin with more than a "party" that is only an inference or a deduction.

III

A developmental analysis of political parties looks in two directions. On the one hand it considers the development of the parties themselves: how and why changes occurred in the organization and/or activities of the parties and how changes will occur if we alter some critical part of their political environment—say, for example, if we replace their convention nominations with a direct primary. But, on the other hand, developmental analysis considers the political party not as the dependent variable but as an independent variable—the political party as a contributor to or a cause of the political development of the entire political system. Here one is, for example, concerned with the role of the party in building those processes, perceptions, and behavior we associate with changes in the system as a whole. Such a distinction may very well be an artificial one in reality, but it is a helpful one for analysis. First of all, then, there is the problem of a developmental theory of political parties.

The achievement of any theory is more than a matter of finding the appropriate theoretical touchstone. It is as well a matter of resolving less glamorous and more practical problems of method and technique and of setting appropriate research priorities. For the study of political parties the problem of priorities is an especially acute one. It has succumbed in some degree to what Abraham Kaplan has called the Law of the Instrument, best expressed in the analogy of its formulator: "Give a small boy a hammer, and he will find that everything he encounters needs pounding."[7] The availability of methods rather than theoretical needs and guidelines determines the expenditure of scholarly effort and, thus, determines re-

7. Abraham Kaplan, *The Conduct of Inquiry* (San Francisco, 1964), 28.

search priorities. That law can probably be broadened to include a Law of Available Data: the easy availability of data, either because they come "naturally" or because we have the means to gather them conveniently, similarly determines research priorities and the contours of knowledge in a discipline. Thus, the availability of aggregate vote totals and then of survey data about American voting behavior has encouraged us to permit the study of elections and electoral behavior to dominate the study of political parties. The writing of party history has emphasized ideological issues and presidential elections at least in part because data was easily available.

It is unlikely that the laws of the instrument and available data will soon be "repealed." Several scholarly evasions of them may, however, be attempted. In the first place, scholars may use the old, conventional data more imaginatively. As an example one thinks of Walter Dean Burnham's use of aggregate data on the American electorate.[8] Secondly, we may exploit new sources of data—especially the data of extensive field work, as, in the terms of the anthropologists, either participant or observer or both. We can observe party activity in nominations (do the parties endorse candidates?), in elections (do they control electoral finance?), and in governmental power (what sanctions do they exercise over the party mavericks?). Even in the more difficult past eras, personal memoirs, contemporary accounts, party records, newspapers and periodicals, and government records must certainly yield more than the stuff of presidential campaigns and elections.[9]

At the moment the study of political parties is suffering from an acute shortage of data. We have in the last generation added only one new body of data to our limited resources: sample survey data, most of it on the voting behavior of the American electorate.[10] But survey methods, like all other methods, have their limitations, and they are not ideally suited to the analysis of organizations and structures—in either their internal life or their external activities.[11] As a mark of the paucity of data on American

8. Walter Dean Burnham, "The Changing Shape of the American Political Universe," *American Political Science Review*, LIX (1965), 7-28.

9. Note the success of William N. Chambers in *Political Parties in a New Nation: The American Experience 1776-1809* (New York, 1963).

10. The most important source, of course, is the Survey Research Center of the University of Michigan; see Angus Campbell, Philip E. Converse, Warren E. Miller, and Donald E. Stokes, *The American Voter* (New York, 1960).

11. With all deference to Samuel Eldersveld's excellent and perceptive work, *Political Parties*, I would suggest that sections of it illustrate the difficulties of analyzing a party organization with survey data.

parties, which are the best described and most thoroughly analyzed of them all, one need only note the almost total absence in the literature of any work on party organization and activities in rural and suburban settings. Finally, it is necessary only to note the scarcity of longitudinal studies of the kind that might contribute to a theory of party change or development. The analysis and correlation of time series is an old and honorable scholarly enterprise. We already have at hand the kinds of data that would, for example, permit a study of primary competitiveness, legislative party cohesion, or electoral turnout over a period of time. If we are to pursue a theory of change and development, should it be necessary to suggest that we must first describe the relevant change?[12]

In such a condition of data poverty we have two quite human inclinations. The first is to subject our limited data to an ever more refined analysis, with the consequent danger of passing a point of diminishing return. We may fail to recognize that at some point so many units of scholarly effort and resources would be better invested in the acquisition of new data than in the further analysis of the old. The second is to tend to look to some theoretical system or model as a way of transcending the restrictive limits of our data and knowledge. We may see "theory" as a sure way of getting more mileage out of less data, and the law of parsimony becomes more a desperate hope than a statement of theoretical efficiency.

New data will certainly move us closer to a theory of party development, but there remain deeper, troubling problems of conceptualizing about social change. To a considerable extent any theory is a theory of change. Generalizations or theories about the relationship between statutory regulation and the forms of party organization in the fifty American states should, for example, illuminate the expected changes in any one state if the legislature should alter its regulations concerning parties within the state. Two extended illustrations may make the point clear, and they can serve as a beginning for the exploration of the issue of change in American parties.

1. *The decline of the urban machine.* The classic "machine" form of party organization is yielding in considerable measure to a more relaxed, middle-class form of party organization. Only in a few urban centers does the machine, with its omnipotent "boss" and its army of local precinct workers, continue to have any vitality. It has been replaced by any num-

12. For examples of the relatively scarce longitudinal studies, see Burnham, "The Changing Shape of the American Political Universe"; and V. O. Key, Jr., *American State Politics* (New York, 1956).

ber of less aggressive and less articulated party structures, ranging from minimal, "shadow" organizations led by a handful of activists to the new "club-style" membership parties of the urban reformers. Their leaders range from public officeholders to the upper-middle-class, avocational leaders of the suburbs.[13]

In more analytical terms, party inputs have changed. The new party activists and leaders are generally better educated and carry higher socio-economic status than their predecessors. They come to party work not so much in search of a patronage job or some other form of political prefer-ence, but out of a combination of ideological and social purposes. The party itself as a decision-making system has been changed. The new activists, unlike the old, make heavier demands as participants: they especially de-mand a fuller measure of intra-party participation and democracy. Party goals change also: ideology and interest now may seem more important than, or as important as, the winning of elections. And since changed in-puts have altered the kinds of political skills on which the party can draw, so too the performance of party activities has changed. No longer does the party send out an army of precinct workers in door-to-door canvassing. It relies instead on local radio or television appearances, on hand-shaking at the local supermarket, and on coffee hours in comfortable living rooms.

Changes in formal party organization, in the nature of party activists, and in the manner and style of party activities over the past seventy or eighty years are marked.[14] Observers of American parties have noted these historical transformations. Among students of parties there is a high degree of consensus on the changes or conditions outside of the parties which are associated with these transformations within the parties.

—the replacement of patronage systems by various kinds of merit ap-
    pointment programs.
—the rising educational level, increased literacy, and greater political
    sophistication of the American electorate.
—the replacement of old-style campaign techniques by those centering
    on the mass media and its associated arts, such as public relations ex-
    pertise, opinion polling, and advertising skills.

13. See James Q. Wilson, *The Amateur Democrat* (Chicago, 1962), for a study of one form of replacement.
14. On the decline of the machine, see Edward Banfield and James Q. Wilson, *City Politics* (Cambridge, 1963), chap. 9; and Seymour Martin Lipset's introduction to his recent abridgement of M. Ostrogorski's *Democracy and the Organization of Political Parties* (New York, 1964).

—the assumption by government of the social welfare programs once carried out by the urban political machines, such as finding jobs for the unemployed or delivering food and fuel to the needy.

—the development of a more issue-oriented politics and a consequent general national party alignment along lines of socio-economic status.

—the growth of alternative and competitive political organizations, such as interest groups.

—the increasing centralization and nationalization of government and politics—and political issues and personalities—in the United States.

—the rise in skill levels, standards of living, and employment stability in the American economy.

Yet the major analytical issue still puzzles one. Do changes in the parties originate because of changes internal to the parties (new activists with new goals and skills) or because of changes external to them (new demands from the electorate, new political techniques available, new competitive challenges)? Do the changes originate, in other words, with changes in party structure or in party activities? Or both simultaneously? Somewhere in that confused complex of conditions or causes lie the clues to an understanding of change in the political parties. But the truth is that we cannot yet answer the artless question of our students: what caused the decline of the urban machine?

2. *Variation in legislative party cohesion.* A cursory look at American state legislatures will indicate that the legislative parties in the fifty states differ widely at this particular point in time. They generate different degrees of cohesion in roll call votes, and they show varying measures of party control over the organization and business of the legislature. They mobilize legislators representing different kinds of constituencies and constituency parties; their members may, too, be men of different experience, skills, and expectations. As organizations they may also differ; the disciplined state party may meet more frequently in caucus, may invoke harsher sanctions, and may exercise greater control over positions of leadership in the legislature than less disciplined parties. Obviously, their comparative impacts on legislation differ.

Because our data are so recent, we are forced to frame these observations about legislative parties at one point in time. But assuming that fundamental and important environmental factors remain constant, there is no reason why they cannot be projected over time. Various scholars have related the variations in legislative parties and their activities to the centralization of the state parties, to the degree of two-party competitiveness, and to the ideological polarization of the electorate and the legislative constituencies.[15] But one ought to be able to say on the basis of these findings that as industrialism and changes in the economy of the state produce a polarization of politics along socio-economic status lines, we might expect the development of more cohesive legislative parties.

As in the case of the decline of the urban machine, we face enormous problems here in unraveling the explanations behind the relationships. Do differences in legislative parties result from changes in organizational capacities, or in the expectations or competitions which affect activities and goals? Or, indeed, does the political environment work at all points simultaneously? Do we labor a false distinction, in other words? Or is it possible that strong and willful party leadership in the legislature may muster the internal resources to alter the structure and thus alter the activities of the party? Is it possible that powerful leaders may develop a legislative party marked by more discipline in roll call voting, without antecedent changes in the environment or in the other two sectors of the party?

These two cases—and everything else we know about change and variation in American parties—suggest the outlines of the major variables and the chief relationships underlying the theoretical problem. But before we venture into an ordering of them, one point—the competitiveness of the parties—must be emphasized. It is conventional in our categorization of party systems to indicate the number of competitive parties in the political system; hence the one-party, two-party, and three-party systems. But that terminology conveys an understanding of competitiveness badly deficient in at least two ways. It is first of all based on an assumption that electoral competition is the main, if not the sole, form of competition involved. But major, electorally competitive parties "compete" with minor ("third") parties in non-electoral ways; they compete for political resources and activists, and in their activities they compete in their attempts at political education and socialization. And, second, the conventional criterion of competitiveness is expressed within the limits of a "party system," and hence fails to consider the party's competitions with non-party political organizations. They compete for activists and for skills and resources with interest groups, *ad hoc* voluntary organizations, candidate followings and campaign organizations, ideological clubs, and local cliques and elites.

15. For example, see Malcolm Jewell, *The State Legislature* (New York, 1962), chap. 3.

The party organization itself, as Figure 1 indicates, may be thought of as a self-contained structure. It must recruit, as inputs, the skills, manpower, money, involvement, and other resources it expends in its political

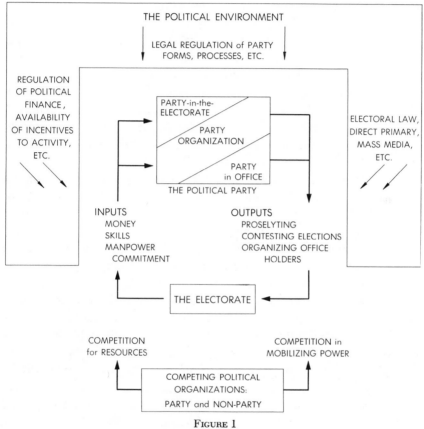

FIGURE 1
The political party: Processes and relationships

outputs or activities. It maintains its own system of incentives by which to attract and hold these resources; the maintenance of the incentives, in turn, is clearly related to the operation of the party organization itself and its political activities. The goals and demands of activists may be directed both to the internal operation of the parties, such as participation in its internal decision-making or in its social good fellowship, and/or to its external political activities, such as the quest for public office, for patronage appointments, for ideological converts. The kinds of political activities the party engages in, its priorities and strategies in engaging in them, its style and manner of operation, all depend on the nature of the resources it attracts and the capacity for action it thus builds.

But the political party is self-contained only in an artificial sense—only if "all other things are equal." It operates within the context of an external environment which limits its organizational structure (statutes which control its raising of money, set its organizational pattern, regulate its conventions), and also conditions its activities in mobilizing citizen power (the primary which limits its selection of candidates, media skills which alter its campaigning techniques, and electoral systems which affect its electoral outcomes). But more than this, political parties compete with other parties and other political organizations for the support of the citizenry. Like the other political organizations, parties mobilize political power in the broader political system. They are great aggregating intermediaries which seek their own political goals by winning support for their candidates, their ideas and programs, or the programs of their elected office-holders. But they compete for more than the support of electorates; they also compete in their attempts to mobilize money, skills, concern, and manpower. For parties and other political organizations compete for scarce resources that can be used to mobilize scarce political power behind controversial goals in the political system.

The crucial relationship for the political party is the one between its committed activists, loyalists, and officeholders on the one hand and the general electorate on the other. The general electorate holds the fate of the political party through three key relationships.

—It is the reservoir of the resources, skills, and personnel on which the party draws.

—It controls the party's environment; it may spur legal restrictions, and its norms and values set real, if informal, limits to party organization and activity.

—It is the consumer of party activity, the instrumental object of party strivings and wooings.

Changes in the electorate may be felt by the parties in any one or all of these directions. Increasing prosperity and literacy in the electorate affects the skills recruited into the party; changes in the electorate's political norms may be translated into new legal restrictions; and the electorate's shifting political concerns, goals, and information—its increasing ideological information and involvement, for instance—alter the goals, the styles, and the strategies of party activity. These changes in turn come generally from a number of more basic sources. They may reflect more general changes in social attitudes or culture, for example, changing feelings about the social role of women which lead to the expansion of the suffrage and then to greater recruitment of women into party activity. Changes may also occur in educational patterns, in communication systems, in agencies and processes of socialization, and in a wide range of social and economic institutions and processes, from growing urbanization to changes in income levels and income distribution. Finally, changes may reflect the numbing political effects of crises such as wars and depressions.

The political party, therefore, competes to mobilize the political power and political demands of individuals and groups in the public. Changes in its organizational form and its activities reflect changes in the resources it recruits, in the competitive pressures it feels from other political organizations, in the environmental limits on its organization and activities, and in the goals, demands, and perceptions of the electorate. The transition from old-style party campaigning to contemporary personality-centered and media-centered campaigning, for example, reflects all of these factors: changes in party personnel, the decline of machine organizations, the encroachments of non-party organizations specializing in new skills, the sheer availability of new political technology and the money to pay for it, and changing expectations of clienteles about what a campaign ought to be. Even the decline of residential and social patterns that made old-style canvassing possible is relevant.

Apparently the direction of change moves chiefly from outside into the political party. To be sure, some short-run change may be initiated within the party itself. Party leadership may make more efficient use of existing inputs to increase party activity levels, or a powerful majority party may alter election laws in its favor. There is, in other words, a degree of "play" or looseness within the party that permits some degree of internally generated change or innovation. In the long run, however, the gross and important changes will come from outside the party. But it is more difficult to judge whether the external impact impinges primarily on the party organization or on party activity. Are party structures, in other words, shaped directly by external influences on the recruitment of resources or indirectly through the shaping of party activities and thus the shaping of the needed organization? Very probably the political forces outside the party work simultaneously on both organization and activity. To state the point in illustrative form: the decline of the urban machine reflected both changes in the party's inputs and in the organizational imperatives of its changing activities.

Thus, American parties have changed and developed with broader changes in American society and in the population. Their organizational forms in this century mirror contemporary American society as those of the nineteenth century mirrored the society of that time. So, too, do their activities: if torchlight rallies in the streets typified the politics of earlier times, media-based campaigns and political coffee hours typify ours. As America has become middle class, so have the styles and forms of its partisan politics. A contemporary swing toward ideology in American parties —note the rise of reform and club parties, the multiplication of non-party ideological groups, the Goldwater candidacy of 1964—just as surely reflects rising levels of literacy, education, and political knowledge in the electorate.

IV

The relationship of the political party to development or change in the total political system is, it seems to me, a far more puzzling problem.[16] Here we confront the issue of the parties' role in or contribution to processes of change or patterns of development in the system—or how, in fact, they relate to the system as a whole, developing or not. The parties cease to be dependent variables; we stop looking for a theory of the political party and turn instead to a theory of the complete system and changes in it over time. And that shift in focus involves the fundamental issue of how we conceptualize the whole political system and the relationship to it (the role, the functions, the contributions, the activities, or whatever one will) of any particular part, any particular structure or process.

American students of political parties have long celebrated the parties' contributions to the stability and democratic health of the American political system. They have not blushed, in fact, to equate party with democracy, to call parties the agents of democracy, and to refer to partisan politics (when carried on through the two-party system) as the method of democracy. Their texts and treatises are full of references to the func-

16. I am leaving aside the question of whether by "political development" we mean ordinary change in the system or some special, generically distinct, type or pattern of change associated with political modernization. I think my comments here apply in either case.

tions of the parties—major, competitive parties, that is. The parties are said to mobilize majorities, organize dissent and opposition, recruit political leadership, socialize voters into the norms of the system, legitimize the decisions of government, and so on.[17] With these ascriptions or imputations of role or function I have two main arguments. One is with the assumption of the primacy of the political party, the other, with the use of functional categories and assumptions.

1. *The assumption of party primacy.* Writers on American parties have tended to consider them as independent agencies in the political system— as some *élan vital*, some autonomous, ordering force set loose in the system. It has been customary, for example, to speak of the parties as "democratizing" American politics as if they were reforming missionaries from some far-off places. The implication is often clear that the parties are structures independent of the forces which shape and limit other political structures; that they are more a product of political will and ingenuity than of the social and political environment.

Perhaps such claims for the power and effect of the political parties in the political system are a result of the identification of scholars with the organizations they study. Perhaps such claims also flow from the belief that the parties are more flexible, adaptable, and malleable than are the constitutionally mandated political institutions. In any event, the myth of party primacy is not limited to a central, governing role for the parties in political development. Much of the reformist literature on the desirability of more "responsible" American parties suffers from the same assumption.[18] There, too, the political party is to be the initiator and instrument of change, the first political structure to cast off the chains of the social and political environment.

In the context of political development the assumption of party primacy suggests that the party guides, or even shapes, the developmental processes. For example, one distinguished scholar writes:

> The parties, in fact, have played a major role as *makers* of governments, more especially they have been the makers of democratic government.

17. Perhaps it will be sufficient here merely to refer to my own acceptance of that tradition in my *Political Parties in the American System* (Boston, 1964). As the next few pages indicate, I now have some qualms about what I wrote there about party functions.

18. The literature on party responsibility is diverse; for a good bibliography, see Austin Ranney, *The Doctrine of Responsibile Party Government* (Urbana, 1954); for a recent example, see James M. Burns, *The Deadlock of Democracy: Four-Party Politics in America* (Englewood Cliffs, 1963).

It should be stated flatly at the outset that this volume is devoted to the thesis that the political parties created democracy and that modern democracy is unthinkable save in terms of the parties.[19]

And another writes of single-party systems in West Africa:

Mass parties strengthened democratic forces, in the third place, to the extent that they encouraged social equality. . . . The fourth contribution of mass parties to the prospects of democracy is setting conditions in which opposition is possible.[20]

The argument is more than that the party performs a function. It is that the party initiates or "engineers" a change—that it, rather than the needs and conditions of the system, determines its own role or function. But the political party is itself a product of the forces of the political system. It is as much a product and a result of change or development as it is its shaper. The same changes and conditions which produce political development produce change or modification in the parties. They cannot step outside of the political system in order to get greater leverage on it.

Part of the tendency to the myth of party primacy may spring, as I have suggested, from scholarly identification with the objects of scholarship. It may also flow from reformist zeal for change, especially in the direction of stable, healthy, Western-style democracies, with which we associate the presence of healthy party systems. Or it may result from a misunderstanding of the implications of "function."

2. *The use of functional categories.* Functional terminology has been an accepted part of the analysis of American parties for almost the full span of that analysis. Those parties have been variously said to
—simplify political issues and alternatives;
—produce automatic majorities;
—recruit political leadership and personnel;
—organize minorities and opposition;
—moderate and compromise political conflict;
—organize the machinery of government;
—promote political consensus and legitimacy; and
—bridge the separation of powers.

19. E. E. Schattschneider, quoted in Theodore Lowi, "Toward Functionalism in Political Science: The Case of Innovation in Party Systems," *American Political Science Review*, LVII (1963), 570-83.
20. Ruth Schachter, "Single-Party Systems in West Africa," *American Political Science Review*, LV (1961), 304-5.

The list could be expanded, but with no real point. Since most of the contemporary literature on political development and developing areas contains some variety of functional analysis, the mating of the older and newer scholarship was perhaps inevitable.[21]

The issue of functionalism immediately raises the counter-question: whose functionalism? For most students of political parties it is clearly not the total-system functionalism of Talcott Parsons or Marion Levy. It is far more likely to be a more modest subsystem functionalism that two critics have called "empirical functionalism."[22] It involves making functional statements about party activity without necessarily relating them to functional requisites or needs of the system. It is indeed a form of "function" which the systems theorists might hesitate to recognize. More frequently it comes very close to the functional types of Robert Merton: the manifest functions (the obvious tasks the parties perform intentionally) and the latent functions (those unintended, felicitous by-products of the manifest ones).[23] It is especially the latter, latent functions, that much of the literature on political parties refers to simply as "functions."

Although this is hardly the occasion for a full-dress review or critique of functionalism, let me briefly suggest some of the reasons for my reservations about functional terminology and categories.

The lack of clarity about function. Even if we concede, for the sake of argument, the possibility of a meaningful functional statement that is not system-related, it is not clear how a function differs from an activity, a task, or a role. Is the function the actual behavior, the observable activity, or is it a consequence or result we infer or deduce from the observable activity? If the concept of function is to have any meaning apart from activity, it must refer to the result or consequence of activity and relate to the ongoing operation or needs of some other or larger social system or entity. "Functions" such as political socialization or the recruitment of political leadership seem to be little more than the activity of the party,

21. Lowi, "Toward Functionalism in Political Science," provides an excellent summary of the traditional reliance of party scholars on functional categories; an influential example of functionalism in scholarship concerning developing areas is provided by Gabriel A. Almond and James S. Coleman, *The Politics of the Developing Areas* (Princeton, 1960).

22. William Flanigan and Edwin Fogelman, "Functionalism in Political Science," in Don Martindale (ed.), *Functionalism in the Social Sciences*, Monograph 5 in a series of the American Academy of Political and Social Science (Philadelphia, 1965).

23. See Robert Merton, *Social Theory and Social Structure* (Glencoe, 1957); it is interesting to note that Merton's distinction was developed in the analysis of the American urban political machine.

distinguished perhaps by the fact that it is not always the party's main, goal-oriented activity.

The absence of consensus on functional categories. Quite simply, students of parties, and particularly American parties, seem unable to agree on a common set of party functions in the political system. It may be that the number of functional categories is really limited only by the deductive ingenuity of man, especially when one may logically infer a function or set of functions at every point at which party activity touches the system or some other part or process within it. We come very close, in other words, to a set of categories which can explain everything and, thus, nothing. On another level, the party itself may even be thought of as the system, the totality; and structures and processes within it can thus be said to perform functions related to the party as a whole. For example, it has been argued that the presidential nominating conventions, in addition to their obvious tasks of nominating candidates and writing platforms, also perform a valuable integrative function for the heterogeneous and often divided parties. But whatever the cause, the sheer proliferation and variety of functional categories—and above all, the fact that one scholar's list rarely coincides with that of another—unquestionably stand in the way of additive, replicative scholarship.

The problem of measurement. The problem of measuring any relationship is considerable, but that of measuring functional relationships is especially vexing. To use the terms of Almond and Coleman, how is one to compare two political parties in the same system—or one party at two different points in historical time—in their performance of the functions of "interest aggregation" and "interest articulation"—or in the building of consensus? How is one to develop empirical measures or indices which will permit us to test propositions cast in functional terms and categories? It is one thing to say as a matter of logic or insight that a party *does* perform those functions. It is quite another to measure performance with the kinds of magnitude and precision necessary for the statements required in the building of theoretical propositions.

V

Without belaboring the complexities of functional analysis further, I should perhaps state my personal preference for a developmental analysis of party activity in the political system. In a discipline that has traditionally been short of data, it is probably a strategic mistake to adopt a set of functional categories that create further problems in obtaining it. The case is strong, it seems to me, for making a conscious decision to keep concepts and categories close to the operational terms of the actual activity. Functional categories undoubtedly offer heuristic and analytic insight, but the developing and testing of theoretical propositions require the vast and varied quantity of "hard" data that can best be expressed in categories of behavior or activity. An emphasis on activity also avoids the plethora of functional categories and the debilitating confusion among system function, subsystem function, function as role, and function as activity or process.

Political parties—and all other political organizations—are political structures mobilizing or aggregating political influence. Or if one prefers, they are agents of representation, bridging the political distance between individual citizens and small groups on the one hand and the institutions of government on the other. They organize and mobilize political resources and support for the achievement of political goals, and this they do through three main groups of activities.

— They select candidates and contest elections (or they offer themselves and their symbols in election contests).

— They organize (or attempt to organize) the elected decision-makers of government.

— They attempt to win converts to their ideologies or issue positions.

Political parties carry out these three chief activities in competition both with other parties and with other political organizations.

The contribution of the parties and political organizations to the political system is perhaps best expressed simply in the terms of these activities through which it mobilizes political resources behind aggregate political goals. The relationship of the political party to the political system, therefore, is observable and measurable, first of all in its activities and their styles and strategies, and second in the relative position of the scope and success of those activities *vis à vis* other political organizations.[24] Changes in pattern or style of activity may then be related to characteristics of, or changes in, the political system as a whole or to some other structure or process within it. At this point then, if we choose to make functional statements, their empirical base will at least be firmer and clearer.

24. Note, therefore, that we need more study of non-party organizations, such as interest groups, for an understanding of parties in the political system.

Even in so literally empirical an approach as this to the relationship between party and political system, the distinction between the party as a dependent variable (theory of party) and the party as an independent variable (in a theory of the political system) cannot be maintained for anything more than scholarly convention and convenience. We need an understanding of the political party *per se* and its activities even for a theory of the system, such as one of political development. Thus, I would personally be more at ease with an approach to a theory of the political system that begins with the parties as structures, moves to their activities, and only then to the relationships between those activities and other political activities and processes, and between those activities and characteristics of the system. One of the dangers of some functionalism is that it begins with assumptions that, given the nature of the system, functions a, b, c, and so on, must be performed; it then, so to speak, goes in search of them and the structures performing them. One then arrives at the actors in the political system—in this case the political parties—in part by indirection and deduction. The result is often an imperfect knowledge of the parties themselves.

In looking at American parties over the last fifty or sixty years, two facts in their development stand out. The two-party system has produced a heightened two-party competition everywhere; today, for example, there remain virtually no substantial pockets of one-partyism in the United States. But while the parties are locked in a new competitiveness, there are signs that they also have been losing their monopoly over the political activities (or functions) they have traditionally performed. The parties lost control of much of the nominating process to the direct primary, and now their control of election campaigning is slipping away. Increasingly, candidates rely on public relations and ad men, media specialists, interest groups, *ad hoc* volunteer campaign organizations, and personal followings for support in elections. The political party no longer monopolizes the important political skills or manpower. By nineteenth-century standards the parties "remain at best only indifferently successful at mobilizing a stable, predictable mass base of support."[25] Indeed, it is now possible to "rent" a private enterprise "political party"—such as Spencer Roberts in California —which will do everything that any party organization can do, and a great deal more than most are capable of.

In the broadest outlines, then, we can see American parties reacting to

25. See Burnham, "The Changing Shape of the American Political Universe," 23.

the loss of their political monopoly. This loss has resulted from the increasing diffusion of political skills, the specialization of political organization, and differentiation in individual political roles. Individuals and political organizations are increasingly selective, both in the choice of political goals and in the use of political skills and strategies. Behind these differentiations and specializations lies the refinement of individual political interests, attention, and loyalty. In this context of increasing political sophistication and proliferating political organization, it is inevitable that the major parties should lose their omnibus control of political mobilization.[26] The two major American parties, awkwardly large and undifferentiated, make blunt instruments for a specialized and precise politics of interest and political pluralism. Or to put the point more broadly, political development —with its broad social, economic, and political changes, especially in the period of mature industrialism—has been accompanied by parallel changes not only in the parties *qua* parties, but in their competitive positions as political organizers. All this may even suggest that politically sophisticated electorates in heterogeneous and pluralistic political systems have come to depend less and less on the organizing medium of the political party.

26. Douglas Chalmers, *The Social Democratic Party of Germany* (New Haven, 1964), makes the same point about the relationship of the SPD to proliferating interest groups.

III | PAUL GOODMAN

UNIVERSITY OF CALIFORNIA, DAVIS

The First American

Party System

THE FEARS that haunted Americans in the decades preceding the Revolution continued to trouble the Revolutionary generation as it reconstructed political authority on "pure" republican foundations. No longer feeling themselves subjects of a corrupt kingdom, Americans were free at last to devise political arrangements that would reconcile the competing claims of liberty and authority, protecting them from the aggressive and tyrannical propensities of power, and yet restraining those forces which threatened to disrupt communal order.

The solution was expected to come from a diligent study of politics, "the divine science." For two decades Americans wrote and rewrote constitutions, confident that appropriate constitutional mechanisms would tame faction, enable diverse and conflicting interests to secure justice, and lay the foundations of a great republic which was strong yet free. These high hopes, elaborately expounded during the formation of the federal Constitution, generated expectations that the young nation would avoid the rivalry and corruption, the tumult and violence that had infected and doomed earlier experiments in free government. The new frame of government was supposed to deliver Americans from the squabbling petty interests whose representatives schemed for the immediate, selfish advantage of their parochial constituencies.

The first decade's experience under the new regime was profoundly disillusioning. In the eyes of many the republic seemed to split into warring factions as dangerous as citizens had feared; as they saw it, forces lurked everywhere bent on subverting the carefully wrought structure of 1787 and overturning the social order. Networks of aristocrats, monarchists, and

Jacobins, financial manipulators, "wild Irishmen," clerical bigots and blaspheming *Illuminati*, paid foreign agents and sowers of sedition and treason, they thought, roamed the republic plotting its destruction. In the decade preceding the Revolution, and recurrently throughout their history, Americans believed that sinister elements threatened their existence.

These perceptions of experience and the actual realities of public affairs were disturbingly incongruent. Those who built the first political party system in the 1790's mistook parties for factions, assuming that those with whom they differed were disloyal to the nation and its ideals. Though vastly different in structure and function from earlier forms of political organization, the first parties were confused with factions because the modern political party was outside the range of this generation's experience as well as its historical consciousness.[1] Federalists and Republicans alike regarded themselves not as parties but as embodiments of the nation's will. When out of office, their duty was to recapture power from those temporarily and illegitimately exercising it; when in office, their task was to keep it from those ready to usurp and misuse it. Unconscious builders of political parties, Federalists and Republicans were prisoners of inherited political assumptions which distorted their understanding of the innovations stemming from the creation of a strong central government in a federal system. Viewing the political parties of the 1790's as alliances of factious elements, many Americans believed that factions had achieved cohesiveness, organization, and unity which made them more dangerous than ever, capable of overwhelming the constitutional mechanisms designed to restrain them.

Yet Americans were slowly learning from experience to accept the legitimacy of organized political activity in support of or in opposition to those who exercised the powers of government. In time political parties came to be recognized as institutions essential to the survival of free government, providing an orderly means of articulating the majority's wishes and settling differences among contending groups. The acceptance of parties, and their incorporation into the structure of American politics, constituted a recognition that the forces which generated them were inherent in an open society.

1. For the innovative character of the early parties see William N. Chambers, *Political Parties in a New Nation* (New York, 1963); and William N. Chambers, "Parties and Nation-Building in America," in Joseph LaPalombara and Myron Weiner (eds.), *Political Parties and Political Development* (Princeton, 1966), chap. 3.

II

Unlike later nation-builders, the Americans had no contemporary models for guidance; nor were the lessons of history useful except as they helped them avoid the errors of others. Though unaware that they were experiencing political modernization, the necessities of circumstance forced them to change their ways of managing public business.

If crises in participation promote the growth of political parties, the contours of such crises in America differed noticeably from similar phenomena in other times and places. No fundamental social or economic transformation preceded the emergence of the early party system, nor was "the extension of the suffrage," as LaPalombara and Weiner, and others, have suggested, "the real impetus for the creation of some form of party organization at the local level."[2] The Revolution did not radically alter the productive system or the social structure, and suffrage had not been monopolized by a few even before independence. The absence of a native hereditary aristocracy, the superficiality of royal control, the great instability in the fortunes of leading men, and the constant need to recruit additional leadership to govern a new and rapidly expanding society, made it difficult to exclude the most talented and persistent elements which sought to participate in public affairs. The colonists did not experience full-scale democracy, but those who exercised power had never been as secure as their counterparts in the Old World were.

The movement for independence which expressed the Americans' determination to preserve self-government had failed to generate parties such as those which appeared in the 1790's. The Revolutionary leaders did not, as later ones did, need to create a party to mobilize support outside the government, because they already dominated much of the existing political structure. They were not conspirators forced to operate outside the framework of established authority, but parliamentary leaders, accustomed to exercise power and able to work through established institutions. The members of the Stamp Act Congress were selected by provincial legislatures, as were the delegates to the Continental Congress. To the very end the Revolutionaries remained loyal to the British constitution, as they understood it, seeking to preserve, not destroy it. Thus independence hardly

2. LaPalombara and Weiner (eds.), *Political Parties and Political Development,* 14-19.

disrupted the continuity of constituted authority within the states. Connecticut and Rhode Island continued under their old colonial charters; Massachusetts waited five years before adopting a constitution; and elsewhere royal authority dissolved almost imperceptibly into the new republican sovereignties. The Revolutionary forces thus always enjoyed the legitimacy of being part of constituted authority. Accustomed to authority, the revolutionary leaders did not depend prim~~ ~~ ~~n~~ mass movements to organize resistance.

When political parties did emerge in the 1790's, t   effect radical change in the *formal* terms of participation in go.   Rather they mobilized previously inactive elements, bringing into the political arena citizens and groups that had had the right but not the desire or incentive to participate. Far more important in broadening the base of popular government than liberalization of the suffrage was erosion of the habits of deference which had enabled those claiming social superiority to command the respect and support of their inferiors. The decline of deference had its roots in the social disorganization accompanying the transplantation of traditional English institutions and attitudes to America. Because the American social order lacked either a nobility or other familiar ruling elements, its leadership strata was self-made and recruited from the middle and lower strata; and because abundant resource opportunities enabled the shrewd and enterprising to rise, the composition of the leading strata lacked permanence, as newcomers edged their way to prominence. The Revolution intensified the degree of social disorganization, as established elements were swept away by war, and further undermined the capacity of leaders to lead, making it harder than ever for citizens to know to whom they should defer when so many, often new faces, competed for their fa   olitical parties hastened the decline of deference by legitimizin   utionalizing competition for the electorate's favor and by enhai   elihood that challengers might succeed in ousting established   . Thus instead of being the product of an enlarged franchise, the first American party system generally sharply increased the level of voter participation.

3. For democratization in the recruitment of political leadership see Jackson T. Main, "Government by the People; the American Revolution and the Democratization of the Legislatures," *William and Mary Quarterly*, XXIII (July 1966), 391-407; see also David Hackett Fischer, *The Revolution of American Conservatism: the Federalist Party in the Era of Jeffersonian Democracy* (New York, 1965), where the decline of deference is a major theme.

In addition to resolving crises of participation, political parties, as La-
Palombara and Weiner suggest, emerge during crises of legitimacy. By
proclaiming themselves instruments of the majority, parties authenticate
a regime's claim to represent the popular will. The new Revolutionary
regimes in America, following the Declaration of Independence, enjoyed
legitimacy from the outset without the aid of modern parties to express
majority will. The Revolutionary cause never became a party cause because it was seen as a defense of established units of local government
against the usurpations of king and parliament. The colonists believed they
were upholding the British constitution against those who sought to sub-
vert it, and with relatively little difficulty the new regimes quickly assumed
the right to exercise all the functions of government. These regimes suffered few doubts about their legitimacy, for the logic of the Revolutionary
argument left no other conceivable claimant to sovereign power. Those
Americans who opposed the Revolutionary movement either went into
exile or quietly submitted, so the new republic was spared the challenges
of potentially disloyal elements receptive to opportunities for restoring the
old regime. In two states there was resistance to Revolutionary authority,
but by supporters of the patriot effort: in Massachusetts and Pennsylvania
some citizens refused to accept the constitutional settlements which they
believed did not adequately protect their interests. But in both cases the
disaffected recognized existing authority while attempting, successfully,
to modify it. The only case of violent resistance to the new state regimes,
Shays's Rebellion, was generally condemned and enjoyed scant support
even among farmers and artisans.

The most troublesome problem of authority arose over the establishment
of the national government. Those who favored strengthening the Confederation at the expense of the states, and who later wanted to scrap the
Articles entirely, attacked the adequacy rather than the legitimacy of existing arrangements. And those who unsuccessfully but vigorously fought
adoption of the new federal Constitution quietly and rapidly submitted to
the new regime, without entirely abandoning their doubts. In the 1790's
also, Americans often divided over the course the new government was
steering, but few wished to undo the settlement of 1787. From time to time
the disaffected lost hope that their interests could be advanced within the
established political framework. Some of these elements joined the Whisky
Rebellion in 1793 or Fries's Rebellion in 1799, or toyed with separating
from the Union, as did some Republicans in the Old Southwest in the

1790's and some Federalists in New England after 1800. On the whole, however, while political activists professed to believe that their opponents plotted their downfall and endangered the social order, they argued that the evil stemmed from a perversion of legitimate authority which could be cured not by rejecting authority as such but by changing the men who held the reins of power. No *Putsch* could hope to succeed as long as most citizens had faith in peaceful change, and hence no group, however alienated, could reasonably expect to get its way through violence. Even hopelessly discouraged minorities, such as the later Federalists, became resigned to their fate.

The establishment of a national center of decision-making generated greater tensions than the framers had foreseen. Many feared for the stability of the social order or doubted that the new framework of government would enable Americans to master the forces that threatened survival. By 1815, however, these fears and doubts had subsided. The nation experienced a series of internal and external challenges but emerged with its constitutional fabric intact and its citizens more nearly united than ever. By providing orderly means of determining the majority's will and enabling conflicting forces to settle their differences peacefully, the first political parties authenticated government's claim to represent the people. Yet in the early years of party development their functions were obscured because no one had anticipated how difficult it would be to articulate the national will in a republic that was larger in territory, and more diverse in its social components, than any in the past. The new government immediately faced a series of decisions on problems whose specific outlines and complex dimensions could not be foreseen in 1787, and whose solutions were likely to lead to disagreements. Though nearly all agreed that public policy must be based on the majority's wishes, no one could authoritatively know or interpret the majority's wishes because the people themselves often had no opinion, and when they did, it was hopelessly divided or fragmented. The task of the early political parties was to attempt to clarify, to articulate and channel, the majority's preferences. Though the clash of parties helped to give legitimacy to the policies adopted by government, citizens often found it difficult to accept this mode of decision-making because the deferential style of politics lingering from the past assumed that a disinterested, virtuous, and wise few were to be entrusted with power. But party politics assumed that no group had either a prescriptive right to govern or an inherent monopoly of wisdom or competence.

Like the crisis in participation and legitimacy, the American version of the crisis of national integration also diverged from the experience of many other new nations. In certain critical respects, a large measure of integration had been achieved before the 1790's. From the beginning the republic enjoyed territorial integration, with territorial limits defined by the boundaries of the colonies which the new nation automatically incorporated. Predominantly English in nationality and Protestant in religion, the colonists had also long shared a common culture inherited from Britain. Even more important were experiences which shaped a new sense of identity, transforming Britons into Americans. "What is an American?," Crèvecœur asked, and announced that "a new race of men" had appeared whose ideas and institutions distinguished them from those they had left behind in Europe. Long before Americanness was embodied in a sovereign state, the colonists had sensed that they shared a common nationality born of their unique experiences—the product not simply of a common language, culture, religion, or long identification with place, but of being uprooted and replanted in the wilderness. The Americans assumed that they were unique and superior because they assumed that their society was enlightened beyond any other.

From another perspective, they had achieved a degree of modernization far in advance of other societies. Never burdened by a feudal past, they never had to liquidate the remnants of the medieval social order which were obstacles to modernization elsewhere. Established churches either never took root or repeatedly succumbed to the forces undermining their position; enclosures and the whole process associated with the transformation of manorialism and the modernization of European agriculture were unnecessary in America, where individual holdings on large and small scales of enterprise prevailed; and the American economy had achieved capacities for sustained expansion long before Hamiltonian mercantilism attempted to speed up the rate of economic development. Similarly, political modernization had been under way long before the Revolution. A liberal suffrage and the sensitivity of colonial governments to recurrent pressures from personal factions and socio-economic interests suggest that the terms of political participation were being enlarged. Finally, the social structure was one in which birth counted for less and individual achievement more in determining one's position than anywhere else. It was because of these and related changes that Americans could no longer be thought of as Europeans. When the Revolution came, Americans and their admirers abroad universalized this example as a model for mankind, defining more clearly than ever before the nature of American nationality. Thus shared ideals and experiences helped to unify a heterogeneous people, even before they embarked on national independence.[4]

Yet integration was incomplete; like the crises of participation and legitimacy, the crisis of integration was subdued and prolonged. At first Americans misjudged the extent to which independence required the centralization of authority. They believed that by locating sovereignty in the states, power would be less dangerous to liberty; diversity, they thought, was not inconsistent with national prosperity and survival. The experiment in decentralization foundered when citizens discovered that their well-being required a redistribution of power. The new federal Constitution attempted to achieve a greater degree of national integration, sufficient to promote "the general welfare" without eliminating local authority but limiting its scope. The Constitution created a new locus of power which promoted greater integration by requiring the articulation of a national will to decide those policy questions which had become the responsibility of all the people, the voters in the Union. But it provided no mechanism for focusing national attention on the pressing issues of the day or for collecting popular sentiment. The first political parties, offsprings of a national center of decision-making, performed that task.

As long as the states had been sovereign during the Confederation, conflicts of interest were played out within the arenas of state politics. The members of Congress in the Confederation were ambassadors from their states, and in most matters local perspectives were decisive. The new Constitution shifted the locus of decision-making, and for the first time citizens elected a Congress and President to grapple with problems on a scale and in a context that were new. Whether the nation survived and prospered now depended on what happened at the national capital. Federal power was not distant and abstract but could reach into a citizen's pocketbook, hale him before the courts, and determine whether he lived at peace or war with other nations. Centralization also vastly multiplied the numbers and complexity of the groups competing for advantage. By throwing representatives of diverse elements together under one jurisdiction, the Constitution heightened the sense of group differences and local senses of identity. Frustrated Virginians became exploited planters and Southerners;

4. For a quantitative analysis of the growth of American nationality, see Richard L. Merritt, *Symbols of American Community, 1735-1775* (New Haven, 1966).

disappointed Massachusetts men became aggrieved merchants and East-
erners. The multiplication of heterogeneous elements, each prone to identify its own interests with what it regarded as the national welfare, certain
that anything threatening its special interests jeopardized the common
good, increased the intensity of political life. Groups used to getting their
way at home were unused to being thwarted in the new arena. But
there they repeatedly encountered frustration and discouragement, which
aroused suspicions that "the general welfare" was being sacrificed to
faction.

The only way to resist was to find new methods of arousing the electorate to the presumed dangers and to forge a national coalition to install in
the legislative and executive branches men devoted to "the common good."
To do this, electoral alliances among elements in the various states were
indispensable, especially in the organization of Congress and the choice
of a President. Paradoxically, though centralization promoted national
integration, it also led to the polarization of the nation into parties by
generating conflicts which required new institutions for their management
and resolution. The parties divided people as they united them. Each party
brought together diverse elements previously little known to one another,
elements whose common fears and interests dictated their union and required the formulation of an ideology which defined their purpose and
could claim to represent the national ideals. To form an effective party
coalition, the diverse social materials were forced to accommodate to one
another and to formulate a program and ideology vague and broad enough
to carry a wide appeal. Once in power, parties learned that the compromises that had brought them into office could help keep them there by
accommodating the opposition when feasible. Thus parties organized conflict and in doing so intensified it, but they also instituted an orderly means
of settling differences without resorting to violence. Parties offered hope to
the threatened or discouraged that the next election would bring a change
in fortune and the restoration of virtue to the seats of power. And when
that happened, the Union once more would be whole: "We are all republicans, we are all federalists," as Jefferson put it.[5]

The first American party system made leadership and policy formulation
sensitive to the conflicting demands of diverse elements scattered across an
extensive republic and thereby helped to reconcile these heterogeneous
elements to the Union. It did not, however, resolve the crisis in integration

5. See Chambers, "Parties and Nation-Building in America," 98-104.

for the long run; by the middle of the nineteenth century, altered circumstances intensified the long smoldering crisis of national integration beyond the capacity of the party system of that time to resolve.

III

The course of party development in the 1790's was slow, uneven, and incomplete. Parties appeared earlier in some communities than elsewhere, and though they eventually spread into most states, they barely took root in some. In some states a strong two-party system developed and persisted; in others it did not survive much beyond the election of 1800, and one party dominated thereafter. In some of the two-party states the contending forces were evenly balanced, but elsewhere they were unevenly matched. Some second parties became, after a struggle, the major party; others never achieved power. The peculiar circumstances of each state shaped the timing, direction, and precise course of party development.

Party evolution in the states was determined by conditions that preceded the appearance of stimuli to party growth and influenced the extent to which competitive politics flourished. The most important were the political infra-structure—the constitutional mechanisms and procedures, formal and informal, which defined the rules of the game—and the social structure, which influenced the range and intensity of group conflict. Both determined the strength with which habits of deference endured.

Some social structures nourished competitive politics while others discouraged it. States with a high degree of social differentiation and social change experienced tensions that weakened habits of deference and generated rivalry which promoted party development. Demographic patterns and shifts were one persistent important source of conflict. The influx of new population into an area was an index of the opportunities that attracted settlers to a region. The older and more densely settled areas, often the smaller states, exerted less pull on prospective emigrants because there was little good land left, and the few that might venture into such communities found it much harder to penetrate the established order. Unsettled areas not only offered land to newcomers but, since there was no pre-existing social structure, permitted settlers to fashion one themselves. All positions of influence were up for grabs where no established groups controlled them. Yet the unsettled areas were not the only ones experiencing high rates of population growth. Rapidly developing urban areas with expanding commercial economies, such as Baltimore, offered considerable opportunity to newcomers. Whatever reasons pulled men, the rapid influx of population into western Pennsylvania, up-country South Carolina and Georgia, Maine, and central and western New York introduced disruptive elements that required assimilation into the social structure; in turn, this usually meant a redistribution of power. Differential rates of growth within a state gave a sectional or regional pattern to politics as new groups concentrated in certain areas and challenged the authority of those situated in older, more stable communities.

Population growth often brought increased demographic heterogeneity. Some states already had highly differentiated populations before the Revolution. Pennsylvania had large numbers of Germans, fragmented into a variety of Protestant denominations, with the Lutherans the largest and most active; Scots-Irish who were also Presbyterians; and English and Welsh who were generally Quakers or Episcopalians. These ethnic and religious groups were concentrated in certain parts of the state which gave them a greater degree of self-consciousness, cohesiveness, and political force than they would have had were they distributed more evenly throughout the colonies or within the state. Similarly, in the 1790's a highly visible and often vocal influx of English and French émigrés from the tyranny and turmoil of Europe added troublesome new elements.

Memberships in ethnic and religious groups mediated an individual's relationships with authority. Americans, then as later, perceived political events as they believed they affected the well-being of the primary groups with which they identified. Was war with England in the mid-1790's good for the peace-loving Quakers? Was the defeat of the French armies which had brought liberation to their brethren abroad good for the Jews? Were the Alien and Sedition Acts, which invaded the rights of conscience, good for the Baptists? The fragmentation of religious affiliation into numerous, competing denominations was a potent source of differentiation and group tensions.[6]

Demographic change and heterogeneity were sources of differentiation that promoted political competition. As people moved in groups from the older to the newer areas, they brought with them their culture, churches, traditions, and leaders. Thus the influx of New Englanders into western New York significantly altered the ethnic-religious balance in that state. Settlers from North Carolina and Virginia flocked into the Georgia up-

6. See e.g. Niels H. Sonne, *Liberal Kentucky, 1780-1828* (New York, 1939).

country, settling among their own kind in a way that gave a special identity to their new community. Into Ohio poured three streams of migration, from Virginia and North Carolina via Kentucky, from western Pennsylvania, and from New England via New York. Though membership in a given group influenced the way individuals responded to the political stimuli of the 1790's, the partisan preferences of groups were not simply a function of their being Quakers, Germans, Methodists or Scots-Irish. A group's relationship to other groups in the local community also influenced partisan choice. If it was estranged from rival groups, its preference might be dictated according to which party its antagonists favored. Thus local conditions in Delaware led Quakers to become Republicans, while in Pennsylvania most of the sect preferred Federalism; but in both cases the decision was influenced by the way people thought politics affected them as members of a particular community. Sometimes objective interests appear to explain partisan choice, as when religious dissenters supported the Republicans because they were opposed to religious bigotry and establishments. In other instances a group's party preference seemed to depend on its leaders' personal ambitions and antagonisms. These could, however, be reconciled with the group's interests, since support of its leaders was a way of asserting the group's dignity and expressing its desire for proper recognition in the community. Ethnic and religious influences on party preference were also complicated by the looseness of party identifications, which could easily be altered. Thus Pennsylvania Germans generally voted Federalist until the late 1790's, when the direct tax, reminding them of the hated hearth tax in Europe which went to fill the coffers of Rome, turned them toward Jeffersonian Republicanism in 1800. A further complication was that individuals were subjected to multiple pressures, such as occupational and regional ones, which might reinforce or conflict with ethnic and religious ones.

Conflict rooted in competitive economic interests has traditionally become a primary focus of political history. The difficulty with the conventional economic interpretation is that economic or occupational groups in America did not form homogeneous classes and were usually deeply divided. Men differed on the best ways to advance their material well-being; but more importantly, their political preference was colored by the totality of their social situation, which included other roles besides occupational ones. Thus a Quaker merchant might have thought Federalist foreign policy was good for business, but his view might also have been shaped by his desire to harmonize his role as a merchant with his cultural ties with England, or with his fear of those who challenged his position through the Republican party. Though the conventional picture that the early parties stemmed from conflicts between agrarian, commercial, financial, and manufacturing interests is no longer persuasive, economic development was an important source of social differentiation. Some states and certain regions within a state experienced much less economic growth than other areas. Where rapid growth did occur, it generated rivalries that contributed to party development. Thus the emergence of Baltimore as a leading commercial center produced a powerful, ambitious group of Republican merchants, revolving around Robert and Samuel Smith and their connections, who successfully challenged the power of an old-line Federalist leadership entrenched in the rural counties. Similarly, in such bustling ports as New York, Salem, or Charleston, Republicans exploited the grievances of the new merchants and tradespeople excluded from the banks, insurance companies, and social circles of the established elite.

Sectional and provincial loyalties further complicated the political picture. Whether one left one's native region or stayed behind, place of birth was a source of pride. People thought of themselves as Virginians or Massachusetts men, Northerners or Southerners, as well as Americans. Presidential ticket makers knew this when they balanced George Washington with John Adams, Adams with Charles C. Pinckney of South Carolina, Thomas Jefferson with Aaron Burr, James Madison with Elbridge Gerry of Massachusetts. "How shall we conjure down this damnable rivalry between Virginia and Massachusetts?" John Adams asked Jefferson some years after they had done battle as representatives of their beloved rival commonwealths and regions.[7]

Whatever its sources, diversity produced tensions in the social structure that undermined habits of deference, fostered competition, and promoted party growth. The variety of groups produced many different perceptions of self-interest and attitudes toward public policy, gave individuals an incentive to participate in public affairs to further their own group interests, and threw up leaders who expressed different perspectives. Wherever social diversity was greatest, it was most difficult for leadership to exercise power unchecked or to continue to receive uncritical deference from the citizenry. Where many competed for advantage in an open society, few

7. Lester J. Cappon (ed.), *The Adams-Jefferson Letters* (Chapel Hill, 1959), II, 348.

could long resist pressures from the excluded. Hence states with highly differentiated social structures were likely to exhibit a more competitive politics than states with a low degree of differentiation. Since aristocracy also ran afoul of republican ideology, thwarted or endangered interests conventionally sought to discredit opponents by denouncing them as "aristocrats." Resistance to change was taken as proof that some Americans presumed illegitimately to possess a superior right to govern and sought to perpetuate temporary advantage, recently acquired, by transforming it into permanent privilege. The result, presumably, would be an hereditary aristocracy, without the birth, blood, or antiquity with which such groups traditionally justified their position. The father of Jeffersonian Republicanism proclaimed the party faith by demanding "equal rights for all, special privileges for none," a theme that reappeared in Republican rhetoric in endlessly different forms like a Wagnerian leitmotif. Here was a doctrine that, theoretically at least, tolled the death knell for the politics of deference.

Diversity of political interests and perspectives not only increased the desire of people to participate politically; it also created obstacles to national integration. The great range of varying interests competing for influence made the achievement of a national consensus no easy task. The first American party system played a critical role, not only in providing a means for various groups to influence decision-making through alliances with others which gave them effective political striking power, but also in promoting trust and a willingness to compromise among disparate forces separated by parochial perspectives and preferences. As the first parties integrated diverse social materials into effective institutions, they provided an instrument by which the nation could accommodate rivalries. For these reasons, not only was a heterogeneous social structure a precondition for the development of political parties in general, but the special form party development took in a particular community reflected in addition its own unique configuration of social forces.

Fragmentation in the contest for power persisted despite the centralization accomplished by the establishment of the federal system. After 1789 parochial forces had to compete for power within a national political arena, but they also had to secure and maintain an effective power base in their local communities which chose congressmen, senators, and presidential electors. In states where politics was highly competitive before 1793 and deference patterns weakened in the 1790's, a vigorous two-party system was likely to develop. In other states, where citizens were more inclined to defer to traditional ruling groups, politics was relatively uncompetitive and after 1790 one party usually prevailed. These differences, reflecting in large measure the nature of the social structure, influenced the way political authority was reconstructed in the states.

For almost a generation Americans engaged in a great deal of constitution-making. The particular arrangement agreed upon was the product of colonial experiences and existing power relationships, as well as historical investigation and philosophical reflection. Each state's constitution influenced the extent to which its politics was competitive, for the rules of the game usually shaped patterns of political expression.[8] Thus, in states where informal procedures had traditionally played an important role, inferiors customarily deferred to their superiors; politics was likely to be less competitive than it was in states where leadership recruitment and decision-making were formalized as the result of open rivalry. Formalization promoted political polarization on a statewide basis, sharpened divisions between contending forces, and stimulated coalitions among those with common interests. Where local offices were largely appointive rather than elective, informal arrangements were likely to prevail. Self-perpetuating town and country cliques took turns in office with each member getting an opportunity to enjoy the perquisites and profits of office, as long as he demonstrated appropriate loyalty and patience. Ambitious newcomers were neutralized by admitting them to the favored circle, placing them at the bottom of the ladder but assuring them of eventual ascent. Since disaffected members of the group or excluded elements had no recourse to the electorate to gain access to office, it was nearly hopeless to fight the system, especially since the dominant loyal group easily controlled the county's only elected official, the representative in the legislature. Where local office was elective, on the other hand, political procedures were usually more formalized and open and the opportunities of electoral choice encouraged competition for office. The excluded and disaffected had a more reasonable chance to unseat an entrenched group, which found it much harder to monopolize patronage and office.

A deferential style of politics was strongest where informal procedures and appointive office went together with a constitution which dispersed

8. For a systematic historical study of the relationship between constitutional structures and early American politics see Richard P. McCormick, *The Second American Party System: Party Formation in the Jacksonian Era* (Chapel Hill, 1966).

decision-making in the towns and counties. The more the political structure was decentralized, the more difficult it was to organize on a colony-wide or statewide basis. A strong executive with patronage and the veto, independent of the legislature because he owed his election not to its favor but to a popular vote in a statewide constituency, and who could succeed himself repeatedly, was a centralizing force which promoted political competition. Independence and resources gave a governor autonomy from the legislature and local cliques within it; though he usually had connections among both, he need not be simply the creature of others. By linking up with dissident elements challenging the dominant county leadership, he could use patronage and his personal popularity to undermine them and at the same time build a power base in areas of weakness. "Wherever you find a strong executive," Nathaniel Macon instructed a leader of the Ohio statehood movement, "in a country which has any liberty, you will also find violent parties. Examine the state constitutions, and by the power of the Governor you may very nearly ascertain the general state of party as it relates to state affairs." Fear of executive influence stemming from experience with royal governors and a belief that the monarchy had corrupted English political life led Revolutionary constitution-makers to strip the governor of power: they had him chosen by the legislature, limited his length of service, and denied him the veto and patronage. Thus, Macon argued: "The executive should not appoint a single office except as the North Carolina constitution directs; the appointment by the legislature is much better than by the Executive; because it destroys patronage, and prevents sycophants from obtaining office by dint of courtship. . . . When the governor has no appointments to bestow, the elections will be made without riot or tumult. . . ."[9] This was the constitutional practice of many Southern states, which also usually showed a limited range of political competition.

The size and structure of electoral units which chose officials also had important bearing on the extent of competitiveness. The larger and more diverse an electoral unit was in population and social structure, and the greater the number of different social groups it contained, the harder it was for a few to control things through informal arrangements. Thus, there was more likely to be competition for the governorship, where the entire state in all its diversity was the electoral unit, than competition for mem-

9. Macon to Thomas Worthington, Buck Spring, September 1, 1802, quoted in William T. Utter, *The Frontier State, 1803-1825* (Columbus, Ohio, 1952), 17-18.

bership in the legislature, where towns or counties were the electoral units. Similarly, it would be difficult to arrange the election of the President informally, where an entire nation was the electoral constituency. Likewise, the election of congressmen was a disruptive innovation because congressional districts cut across town and county lines, combining several of them into one district. Early congressional elections often generated such a proliferation of candidates that none had a majority and repeated runoffs were required. The plethora of office seekers revealed that traditional methods of recruitment, even where politics had customarily been uncompetitive and deferential, broke down under altered conditions. When several county cliques were thrown together in one congressional district, they could not rely on the usual methods of buying off competition and informal rotation. The alternative was for several groups to muster their maximum support in their bailiwicks behind favorite-son candidates, sometimes making deals with other groups against the rest of the competition.

The political infra-structure of each state was the product of its own peculiar historical development. Whether a state relied on formal or informal procedures, recruited its leaders through election or appointment, centralized or decentralized power, or had a strong or a weak executive, was not entirely fortuitous but reflected the distribution of forces and power in the community and the way citizens thought it best to manage their public affairs. The shaping force in making constitutions was not logic but experience and expectations.

IV

A competitive social and political structure was a necessary precondition for party growth, but not a precipitant. Before 1789 rivalries generally involved provincial interests within the states. The federal Constitution, however, pushed citizens into a national political arena since the locus of decision-making was now divided between central and local governments. This change rendered inadequate the older methods by which public affairs were managed and stimulated the invention of new ones.

The parties which emerged in the 1790's were distinguished from the factions and *ad hoc* interest groups that had competed for advantage in the colonial and Revolutionary years by their elaboration of structures and functions.[10] Parties systematically organized electoral processes by devel-

10. See Chambers, *Political Parties in a New Nation*, esp. Prologue, chaps. 1 and 5.

oping techniques for nominating candidates and persuading the citizens to vote for them on election day. The elaboration of ideologies and party structure, the recruitment of party leadership at different levels, the enlistment of a faithful cadre of party workers, and the development of party loyalty within the electorate gave the first American party system an institutional complexity and stability that earlier political forms lacked. As alliances of heterogeneous elements within a state and among groups in different states, parties also developed a territorial range and social density that made them national in scope and function.

The struggle over centralization during the 1780's, culminating in the federal Constitution, polarized the nation, as widely dispersed and diverse citizens collectively decided how best to manage the affairs of the republic. The newly established national government was also a potential source of continued polarization. The problems confronting the country and the policy choices adopted would affect citizens wherever they lived, and recognition of this fact worked against traditional parochial outlooks. The developing national perspectives of farmers, merchants, manufacturers, mechanics and artisans, holders of public securities, and others were now sharpened and deepened as they sought to shape public policy at the national capital after 1789. As the new government chose between competing courses, it won increased favor among some but disappointed others. Groups learned that they could effectively promote their interests only through national authority, but that rival groups could also thwart their desires through that same authority. Conflicts, compromises, bargains, and deals with distant and often unfamiliar elements were necessary before decisions could be reached. The first American party system became the principal means by which the complex array of interests and local perspectives sorted themselves out and joined together in electoral alliances to promote their welfare.

In the early 1790's Congress became a dramatic arena within which rival groups quarreled over policy questions. Should the state debts be assumed by the federal government, how should the federal debt be funded, how should the tax burden be distributed, should a national bank be established, how should the public domain be managed—these were some of the many vexing questions facing the new government. As a consequence of repeated clashes in the legislative chambers there was an increasing polarization within Congress around particular leaders and issues. As members of Congress articulated differences inherent in the electorate and fought to gain their way, newspapers and other communications media made citizens more aware than ever of the differences that divided them. As divisions emerged in Congress, legislative leaders became keenly interested in the outcome of congressional elections which would determine the strength of their troops at the next session. In this way, national leaders came to take a growing interest in the politics of the various states, while at the same time voters now were making choices that would influence, and were influenced by, national perspectives.

Presidential elections had a similar effect. The obvious preference for George Washington in the first two presidential elections delayed the nationalizing and polarizing impact of a contest for the presidency, and hence its contribution to political party development. The absence of consensus over the succession in 1796, however, encouraged leaders in the capital to form alliances and make arrangements with the various elements that influenced the choice of presidential electors in the states in order to mobilize support behind particular candidates. The previous divisions in the Congress, in the executive branch, and in the states simplified the task of presidential ticket-makers, since lines of opposition had been drawn more and more clearly in many communities before the intrusion of the presidential question.

Thus differences over policy produced national perspectives among interests and voters, splits in the Congress, and rivalry over the presidency, and in turn promoted party development. So too did personal rivalries and conflicts of interest within the states, many of which preceded party development but nonetheless fed the flames of party battle in the 1790's. In many states persisting antagonisms influenced the way people chose sides in the controversies which began to erupt in the capital. The Washington administration could not appoint all those who desired recognition, and those who were disappointed added to the numbers of the disgruntled. Traditional enmities, such as those between the Livingston and Schuyler families in New York, Governor Hancock and his critics in Boston, eastern and western Pennsylvania politicians, and the Marshall and Blount factions in Tennessee, continued into the 1790's. Such rivals often ended up in different political parties.

Yet none of these divisions aroused an often lethargic electorate in the way the ideological and diplomatic crisis generated by the French Revolution did. The outbreak of war in Europe in 1793 between Revolutionary France and the coalition of old regimes which were determined to crush republicanism agitated Americans profoundly. The Revolution in France forced them to choose between peace and war, between a French or a British alliance, between lining up with "the party of humanity" or backing "the forces of reaction." Determined to remain neutral in deed, if not in thought, Americans could not escape a choice. Their prosperity was closely bound to ties of trade with the belligerents, and their security and sense of destiny deeply involved in the fate of French republicanism.

At the center of party conflict in the mid-1790's, moreover, was a widespread belief that the future of the republic was threatened. Those who considered themselves Republicans had believed even earlier that the decisions made by the early, Federalist-dominated Congresses had departed from republican principles by benefiting the few at the expense of the many. But Federalists were equally convinced that those measures, denounced as anti-republican by their critics, actually promoted the stability and prosperity of the nation and thereby helped to assure the success of the republican experiment. When Federalists moved to prevent British interference with American trade with France from precipitating war, they confirmed Republican suspicions that they were aristocrats with British sympathies. When Republicans in turn sought to block ratification of Jay's Treaty in 1795 and thereby risk war with Britain, Federalists were confirmed in their suspicions that the Republicans were Jacobins with French sympathies. The crisis of the mid-1790's affected people wherever they lived and whatever their local circumstances, and had a saliency that earlier issues had lacked. By arousing widespread, deep, and fierce partisan sentiments, it simplified and dramatized electoral choice.

The Republican party continued to attract many of those who had already been alienated by the policies of the federal government. Now it also came to encompass others who had once supported Federalist domestic policy but would not support Federalist foreign policy, and still others who had previously taken little interest in public affairs but were aroused by what they saw as new dangers. Although most Republicans prudently wished to avoid involvement in foreign wars, they could not hide their sympathies, and now perceived their own Revolution as the first act in the drama of mankind's regeneration through the American example. Should the votaries of superstition and oppression crush republicanism in Europe, they thought, it could not long survive in America. Moreover, French defeat would bring into question the universality of America's own Revolutionary example and strike a mortal blow at the party of humanity. The Jeffersonians, along with many European *philosophes*, saw the American

Revolution as the most important event in human affairs since the coming of Christ. As Jesus had delivered mankind from the tyranny of sin and death, so republicanism, inspired by the American model, promised to free mankind from civic inequality and slavery.

Other Americans, of course, disagreed. Most had welcomed the French Revolution in its early years, but as it became violent and expansionist, and threatened to disrupt peaceful and profitable ties with the rest of the world, the consensus dissolved. Federalism expressed the fears and disillusionment of those who believed that France discredited republicanism by its inability to reconstruct a stable fabric of government at home and by its insatiable lust for conquest abroad. The future of republicanism rested not on the outcome of events abroad but on the establishment of a strong and stable republic at home, they thought, and the export of Jacobinism to the United States was now the most serious threat to the survival of the republic since the crisis of the 1780's. Thus the Federalist and Republican parties, both devoted to republicanism, each believed that the other threatened its survival at home. For the Republicans, those who favored a protective alliance with Britain and were willing to join the war against France betrayed the country's ideals and its mission. In turn, Federalists believed that men who were incapable of distinguishing between genuine republicanism and Gallic tyranny were at bottom American Jacobins who endangered the social order.

Whether citizens chose Federalism or Republicanism depended on their attitudes toward national authority and the way in which they thought it affected their vital interests. Federalist leadership was mainly drawn from elites who had achieved positions of prominence before or during the Revolution, but who were insecure because of challenges from below. These challenges they perceived as attacks on constituted authority, and thus they looked to the national government to protect them from disorder and the spread of "French principles." Republican leaders were more often ambitious newcomers, outsiders who had been excluded by dominant groups from positions of prestige and power. Denied equal access to government, they believed that they were the victims of an erstwhile aristocracy; and thus they regarded national authority as a potential instrument of local aristocracy and identified emotionally with French Revolutionary attacks on entrenched privilege. These alienated elements were galvanized, organized, made self-conscious through the leadership of elites in other states which did not feel threatened within and hence felt no fear of Jacobinism at home, but were disaffected from national authority because they believed they were denied their rightful place in the national councils. For them, the necessities of the national political arena required that they enlist support from among discontented elements in other states even though such allies might be their social inferiors.

V

The history of party growth in four states—South Carolina, Delaware, Connecticut, and Virginia—illustrates some of the varieties of party development. Although nationwide forces or pressures promoted parties, the precise course party development took in a given state depended on its particular social structure and constitutional arrangements.

In South Carolina the Federalists emerged as dominant in the late 1790's only to be challenged by the Republicans, who gained the upper hand in 1800 and thereafter remained supreme.[11] Until the late 1790's, the groups that had led South Carolina through the Revolution maintained a firm grip on the state. Centered in the low country where family fortunes had been built on rice and indigo plantations, this elite lived in and around Charleston, the capital until 1790. Such families as the Smiths, Izards, Pinckneys, and Rutledges, together with their relatives, business and professional associates, and friends, formed extensive and powerful connections, and relied on informal procedures to control politics after independence. Although the Smith-Izard group became early supporters of the national administration under Washington, the Rutledges and Pinckneys were critical of Jay's Treaty, and the state backed Jefferson in 1796. Subsequently, however, the Charleston elite was driven by anti-French sentiment into the Federalist camp and worked hard for President Adams's re-election in 1800.

As the leading families joined under the Federalist banner, a coalition of elements drew together to challenge their authority. The Republican

11. The most helpful studies of South Carolina politics are William A. Shaper, *Sectionalism and Representation in South Carolina*, Report of the American Historical Association, 1900 (Washington, 1900); J. H. Wolfe, *Jeffersonian Democracy in South Carolina* (Chapel Hill, 1940); David Ramsay, *The History of South Carolina* (Charleston, 1809); Charles C. Rogers, Jr., *Evolution of a Federalist: William Loughton Smith of Charleston, 1758-1812* (Columbia, S.C., 1962); and the extremely good contemporary travel account, J. F. Jameson (ed.), *Diary of Edward Hooker, 1805-1808*, Report of the American Historical Association, 1896 (Washington, 1897), vol. I.

party was an alliance of leading citizens in the middle and up-country who had long been excluded from what they regarded as an equitable share in decision-making, and of discontented elements in the low country who were detached from the established leadership. The architect of this alliance was Charles Pinckney, a turncoat low-country planter of prominent family ("Blackguard Charlie," he was called) whose ambitions brought him into conflict with his own group. He discovered that rapid social change and extensive diversity made South Carolina a fertile field for party building, and brought together an extensive connection in the low country among young men, Presbyterians, Charleston mechanics, tradesmen, striving merchants, French *émigrés,* and Jews. The key to Republican success, however, was the vote-rich up-country. Barely settled before 1760, this virgin territory underwent a massive influx of farmers just before and especially after the Revolution; and these newcomers turned it into a land of small farms with relatively few slaves. Coming from the upper South rather than from the eastern coastal region, many of its citizens were Scots-Irish Presbyterians, like the Calhouns of Abbeville, who lived in crude and primitive surroundings in contrast to the polished society of the downstate planter elite. The rapid introduction of cotton culture in the 1790's speeded development and advanced the prosperity of the newer regions. Until the Revolution the back country had played little part in South Carolina politics, but during the war it fought a long guerrilla campaign against the British after the low country fell to the enemy. The prominent role the up-country men played in the resistance must have whetted their appetite for greater recognition once peace returned.

After the war, however, the back country was denied equal representation in the legislature, as the low-country elite successfully prolonged its control. Because malapportionment prevented the up-country from amending the constitution, it needed support from allies downstate if it was to end low-country domination. Such an alliance was the foundation of the Republican victory in South Carolina in 1800. Thereafter the party of Jefferson chose the governor; controlled the legislature and with it the patronage; amended the constitution to reapportion the legislature, extend the suffrage, and make certain local offices elective; chartered new banks to cater to investors excluded from the older ones; and repealed the low-country ban on the importation of slaves, which were badly needed by inland cotton growers. The Republican social base became so broad that the Federalists disappeared as an effective political force. After 1800 South

Carolina became virtually a one-party state. In time even the up-country and low-country elites were reconciled, as the maturing of the newer areas narrowed differences that had once divided them.

Rapid social change brought diversity and political conflict to South Carolina, and fed the growth of two-party politics in the 1790's. The low-country elite had traditionally commanded deference as natural leaders, but patterns of subordination dissolved as new groups emerged; and as the back country developed its own political leadership and self-confidence, it refused to bow to the downstate rice planters. The idea was catching and spread to Charleston, where divisions within the ruling gentry encouraged the lower orders to assert their independence. It was no longer clear who, if anyone, was entitled to deference. But as the social order matured and stabilized, tensions declined, and South Carolina's vigorous but short-lived two-party system declined also.

Like South Carolina, Delaware too came under Federalist control in the 1790's, but unlike their South Carolina brethren the Federalists of Delaware successfully resisted the Republican challenge.[12] Delaware was largely rural and experienced little social change in the Revolutionary era, and the colonial gentry had supported independence and remained in firm control. Indeed, the habit of deference ran so strong among Delaware's farmers that Jefferson described the state as virtually "a county of England" in its political patterns. Many of the state's most prominent families lived on large estates in the lower two counties. Anglicans before the Revolution, many subsequently became Methodists, a shift which strengthened their authority by tying them to a popular denomination. When party rivalry began to emerge, the center of the Republican challenge was in the northern county. Socially much more mixed than the southern counties, northern Delaware was the home of the state's commercial and manufacturing interests, especially the merchants, millers, artisans and mechanics of Wilmington, the leading city. It was also the home of Scots-Irish Presbyterians, Swedes, and a recently arrived French family, the du Ponts. The Republicans' most prominent and respectable leader was Caesar A. Rodney, who, like Charles Pinckney in South Carolina, came from a good, old family but deserted the state's elite to champion the interests of his social inferiors. By making inroads into the two Federalist southern counties from

12. For Delaware see John A. Munroe, *Federalist Delaware, 1775-1815* (New Brunswick, 1954); and Morton Borden, *The Federalism of James A. Bayard* (New York, 1955).

their northern Delaware power base, the Republicans hoped to forge state-wide majorities that would bring them statewide control. But the habit of deference persisted in the lower counties; their social structure remained homogeneous and stable in the absence of an urban area such as Wilmington, where diverse groups rubbed shoulders and competed for advantage. Since the majority of the state's voters still reside in the lower counties and were content to follow the established gentry, Delaware remained a Federalist bastion.

Party development in Connecticut paralleled Delaware's experience in several ways.[13] During the heyday of the first American party system, when many states had arrived at vigorous two-party competition which resulted in a transfer of power, the Federalists in Connecticut turned back persistent Republican challenges. As in Delaware, a Republican minority formed in the late 1790's, fusing various discontented elements. It was unable to broaden its electoral base sufficiently to win a majority until the second decade of the nineteenth century, however, when almost everywhere else the first American party system was disintegrating.

The Revolution did not greatly alter Connecticut's social structure or political life. Governed under the same charter which had prevailed during the colonial period, the state retained the methods by which an elite of prominent families and Congregationalist ministers alternated in office, recruited new blood, and kept control. Compared to neighboring New York and Massachusetts, where party rivalry was in the process of development, Connecticut's social order was relatively static. Ethnically homogeneous, its dissenters weak and divided, its economy stagnant, without large and rapidly growing urban centers or newly settled regions, Connecticut experienced fewer of the tensions that diversity and change generated elsewhere. The ambitious and discontented often left for better opportunities in other communities. Men who chafed under the Congregationalist establishment, and others who were excluded from power by the secular and ecclesiastical elite, were too weak to challenge effectively a group that enjoyed all the advantages of the state's constitutional arrangements. Elections for Congress and the Council which controlled much patronage were conducted on a statewide basis, thereby making it difficult for a minority to secure an effective power base even where it was numer-

13. For Connecticut see Richard J. Purcell, *Connecticut in Transition, 1775-1818* (Middletown, Conn., 1963); for a comparison with neighboring Massachusetts, see Paul Goodman, *The Democratic-Republicans of Massachusetts: Politics in a Young Republic* (Cambridge, Mass., 1964).

ous. Moreover, a rigged system for nominating candidates, which was unique to Connecticut, gave those in office an effective device for determining the outcome of elections. Connecticut entered the 1790's inexperienced in open, competitive politics and with its citizens habituated to bestow their suffrage on their social superiors. Yet even in the Land of Steady Habits some men dissented from the prevailing Congregationalist-Federalist orthodoxy. Though it remained in control long after entrenched groups elsewhere were ousted, Connecticut's elite was defensively sensitive to dissent and easily alarmed by the threat of Jacobinism in the 1790's —a threat they saw as embodied in a Republican minority in the legislature. The religious establishment was an anachronism, and the alliance between the clergy and secular leadership was increasingly strained because of growing impatience with excessive ministerial influence.

Eventually even the unity of the Federalist elite of Connecticut disintegrated. By 1810 more and more Connecticut citizens found it hard to take seriously the danger of Jacobinical *Illuminati* in America, a danger which a decade earlier had seemed real and frightening. Time not only eroded the cohesiveness of the state's leadership as the more secular-minded broke with their orthodox brethren among the clergy and laity, but also increased the degree of diversity in social structure. Religious dissenters became more numerous, the influence of the Congregationalist clergy waned even among members of the established faith, and a modest urban and commercial boom in the eastern towns produced new fortunes and new claimants for recognition. Led by socially respectable, anticlerical ex-Federalists, dissenters and other excluded elements formed the Tolerationist party, which won control in the state, wrote a new constitution, separated church and state, and redistributed public offices. As the ruling group split apart and the number of restless outsiders increased, it was no longer clear who was entitled to lead, and habits of deference broke down. All of these changes promoted party development after 1810 as a means for managing public affairs in a community where open, formalized clashes of interests and personalities now determined how power would be exercised.

Paradoxically, a homogeneous and stable social structure and persistent deference patterns also enabled a dominant Republican elite in Virginia to maintain supremacy.[14] Though much larger in size and population,

14. Studies of Virginia politics in this period are inadequate, but the most useful are Charles H. Ambler, *Sectionalism in Virginia from 1776 to 1861* (Chicago, 1910);

Virginia, like Connecticut, did not experience significant change during the Revolutionary decade. The Tidewater and Piedmont elites led the Revolutionary cause, Tories were few, and many of the same people governed after the Revolution as before, using similar methods. The new state constitution of 1776 reduced the influence of the executive and intensified and legitimized the power of the county courthouses, where self-perpetuating cliques of planters and lawyers prevailed. Most offices were appointive, and local elites nominated candidates to fill vacancies. As justices of the peace and militia leaders, the gentry often held office during most of their active years unchallenged, while the ambitious and talented usually accepted the promises and security of a seniority system that offered eventual reward for faithful service. There was a narrower suffrage base in Virginia than anywhere else, and the level of popular participation was also lower. "In no state," one scholar concludes, "were democratic procedures and beliefs more firmly resisted or with greater success."[15]

Social structure did not sustain competitive political development in Virginia because, despite its size, the Commonwealth was remarkably homogeneous. Largely rural, the state had a stunted urban development. Its religious dissenters were pacified by disestablishment, and its ethnic and sectarian groups were concentrated west of the Appalachians, where they posed no serious threat to the eastern elite who dominated the region containing the majority of the state's population. Malapportionment, moreover, kept the western counties under-represented even as they filled up with people. In the older eastern regions striking inequalities of wealth made the social and economic distance between the gentry and the common folk greater than in neighboring Pennsylvania and North Carolina. The restless and ambitious could leave for Kentucky, Tennessee, and the lower South where opportunities were presumed to be greater, and thousands did. Pockets of Federalist strength developed among elements imperfectly integrated into this static social order, such as mercantile interests in Richmond and Norfolk who were scorned by the planter elite, the independent Lee and Marshall families in the northern counties,

Harry Ammon, "The Formation of the Republican Party in Virginia, 1789-1796," *Journal of Southern History*, XIX (1953), 283-310; Harry Ammon, "The Jeffersonian Republicans in Virginia: An Intepretation," *Virginia Magazine of History and Biography*, LXXI (1963), 153-67; and Anthony F. Upton, "The Road to Power in Early Nineteenth Century Virginia," *Virginia Magazine of History and Biography*, LXII (1954), 259-80.
    15. McCormick, *The Second American Party System*, 179.

and the isolated northern neck gentry. A number of Federalists also appeared in the Great Valley, inhabited by Germans and Scots-Irish from Maryland and Pennsylvania, a region of small farmers and few slaves which was chronically discriminated against by the eastern planters. But these enclaves of dissent were not large enough to alter the political balance. Secure from challenge within, Virginia's leadership welcomed the French Revolution and became its foremost champions in America as well as leading critics of national authority.

In the late eighteenth century, as its economy stagnated, Virginia lost population to other regions that offered greater opportunity, and its leaders' commitment to the ideology of the Declaration of Independence was compromised by their inability to make their institutions conform to their ideals. For a while in the 1780's some were inspired by a national vision and the vague conviction that Virginia's problems might be solved in a strong Union, and as a result they championed centralization. But the policies pursued by the national government after 1789 seemed to threaten the interests of many Virginians and only intensified their chronic frustration. As charter members of the party of humanity in America, the Jeffersonians who had sought to transform Virginia along pure republican lines had repeatedly met defeat. Primogeniture and entail were abolished and the Anglican church disestablished, but neither had been essential to the elite's control.

On other occasions Jeffersonians were denied even symbolic victories. They favored democratizing the state constitution, enlarging the franchise and strengthening the executive, and reapportioning representation, but the planters would suffer no dilution of their influence. Though widely regarded as a moral blot inconsistent with republicanism, slavery was more and more fixed on the Commonwealth as the number of Negroes surpassed the white population east of the Blue Ridge in the 1790's. Universal education was deemed an indispensable pre-condition of self-government, but Virginia's privileged orders would not consent to the creation of common schools. The Jeffersonians hoped to diversify the state's economy, force urbanization, and encourage more efficient methods of agriculture, but in every case the conservatism of Virginia's gentry resisted change. Trapped at home, the Jeffersonians blamed their declining fortunes on others, notably the national government which, they insisted, had been captured by a paper aristocracy whose tariffs and navigation acts, taxes and funding schemes exploited agricultural interests, especially in the South. Picturing themselves as the nation's true Republicans, they grossly exaggerated the extent to which they had democratized Virginia, claiming that a natural aristocracy governed their society in contrast to the coalition of hereditary aristocrats and clerical bigots alleged to dominate New England. Meanwhile they hoped to regain their weight in the Union by assuming leadership of Americans elsewhere who were still battling against privilege in the national arena. Thereby they would vindicate their devotion to Revolutionary ideals and demonstrate their unique capacity to lead.

Unlike Republicanism generally, which tended to draw its greatest support from the excluded, the newcomers, and restless and ambitious members of the gentry, Virginia Republicanism was the party of an established elite that continued to enjoy the deference of its social inferiors, much as Federalist elites did elsewhere. And as in other states where one-party dominance managed to resist challenges to its rule, Virginia's social structure lacked the degree of vitality and diversity that would generate rival interests sufficiently numerous and powerful to upset traditional patterns of governance and establish competitive party politics.

Social orders whose roots went back to the seventeenth century were still prominent in South Carolina, Delaware, Connecticut, and Virginia. In the late eighteenth century, however, new societies were just beginning to take form in Georgia, Kentucky, Tennessee, and Ohio as these areas were settled and underwent social development. Though various groups in these states called themselves Federalists or Republicans, political parties had at best a shadowy existence. Most voters considered themselves Republicans and candidates usually ran under that label, but contests occurred primarily among numerous loosely organized factions which were usually powerful in a particular region and influential in a particular bloc in the legislature. In each state the leading factions were for one reason or another alienated from national authority during the years of Federalist rule in the 1790's. Thus Kentuckians and Tennesseans formed a French Revolutionary Legion and entered into fantastic schemes to secure the right to navigate the Mississippi; Georgians denounced the federal government's alleged sloth in removing Indians from the paths of speculators and settlers and also blamed the Federalists for the Yazoo land frauds; and Ohioans had to overcome obstacles a Federalist territorial governor and his clique placed in the way of immediate statehood.

Yet the rivalry of factions and sections in these newer communities did not generate political parties. Their social orders were too loose and unstructured, and there were few well-entrenched elites to challenge or to feel threatened by alleged Jacobinical assaults. As settlers poured into these virgin territories, it was possible to accommodate the ambitious because land, offices, and rank were easy to acquire. Where no established elite had existed, and the ruling groups were newly arrived and self-made, habits of deference were likely to be weak. As a result, a bewildering variety of personalities and factions made and broke alliances to achieve limited and immediate goals. In short, politics exhibited neither the organizational structure nor the complexity of function that distinguished party politics elsewhere.

Not until the social structure of the new communities achieved a degree of differentiation and stability that generated clear-cut, continuous lines of conflict among persisting rival interests would the pre-conditions for party development exist.

VI

Even where conditions were most favorable to party growth, the first American party system failed to survive. In some states where the Republicans won majorities in 1800, Federalists perceived only the dimmest hopes of making a comeback, and many simply gave up the fight. Others invested new energies in party activity, though often with disappointing results. The crisis in foreign affairs after 1805, culminating in the unpopular Embargo of 1807 and the divisive decision to go to war in 1812, caused dissension among Republicans and led to a brief revival of Federalist strength, which, however, fell far short of enabling the party to recapture national power or even to regain it for long in many states. By 1815 Federalism and Republicanism no longer divided the nation into rival political formations. Party organizations decayed, ideological and programmatic differences were blurred, and many Federalists in search of office joined their erstwhile enemies. With each passing year, Jefferson's vision was increasingly coming to pass—"We are all republicans, we are all federalists"—although the emphasis fell on the former term.

Most explanations of the first party system's arrested development have focused on the Federalist decline. Some have argued that the party was deeply divided in the late 1790's between Hamiltonian war Federalists and Adams peace Federalists,[16] and that this division cost the party dearly in the election of 1800 and unity was never restored. But why not? Why didn't the necessities of defeat, the experience of being a minority, force discordant elements to bury their differences sufficiently to form an effective opposition and regain power? Another analysis suggests that the Federalists were doomed by their conservative, aristocratic ideology, which was increasingly incongruous in a society of ongoing democratization.[17] But why didn't the Federalists make a greater effort to adjust their ideology to political realities, as politicians usually do if they desire to regain power? And why were Republican elites so successful in building a party whose *raison d'être* was the destruction of aristocracy? Some have argued that Federalist principles made them loath to resort to the political methods and machinery which the Jeffersonians used so successfully to win office. But why should Federalist gentlemen have been less willing to innovate than Republican gentlemen? Moreover, recent studies suggest that younger Federalists did build elaborate party organizations in many states after 1800 without abandoning their basic ideology. Yet despite such efforts, the party failed to arrest decay.[18]

Another course of explanation seems to be in order. It might begin with the fact that the first political parties were new and fragile institutions, lacking deep roots in political experience, and that party identification and loyalty was recent and weak. It is often difficult to fix clearly a politician's partisan identity in the 1790's and early 1800's, and shifts from one party to another occurred frequently. Party organization was also new and often rudimentary, falling short of stable institutional foundations; thus the early parties were not autonomous institutions, but hastily formed, loose alliances of individuals and groups. Should disaffection or apathy overtake these groups the party would wither away, because the party structure, as such, had only a weak claim to citizen support. Before the 1790's no one had been born a Federalist or Republican, and thus most ordinary citizens and voters did not inherit an ancestral party loyalty. The superficiality of party development helps explain why so many

16. See Stephen G. Kurtz, *The Presidency of John Adams: the Collapse of Federalism 1795-1800* (Philadelphia, 1957); and Manning J. Dauer, *The Adams Federalists* (Baltimore, 1953). See also Chambers, *Political Parties in a New Nation,* chaps. 7 and 8.

17. Shaw Livermore, *The Twilight of Federalism: the Disintegration of the Federalist Party, 1815-1830* (Princeton, 1962), chap. I.

18. Fischer, *The Revolution of American Conservatism, passim.*

party leaders, especially Federalists, retired from battle, and why still others defected to the Republicans.

Party growth had thrived on the tensions of the 1790's, but those tensions ebbed in the years that followed Jefferson's election. As the Republicans took power, most Federalists learned that, after all, their old fears of Jacobinism were unfounded. In office the Republicans left many important Federalist policies undisturbed, carefully cultivated support from moderate Federalists they hoped to convert, retained many Federalist job-holders and made removals covertly and piecemeal, so as not to alarm the opposition. Victory was also sobering for the Republicans. Their assumption of power reduced their fears of monarchy and restored their faith in peaceful means of effecting change. Controlling the presidency and Congress, Republicans were no longer hostile to national authority; and power gave them confidence, especially as their continued rule became assured. The more secure and dominant they became, the more they were prone to split into warring factions, especially in states where Federalists no longer effectively challenged them. On this count too, men of virtually all persuasions came to think less and less in party terms.

In this situation, the first party system withered away because most of its builders did not regard themselves as professional party politicians. Such leaders as Washington, Jefferson, and Hamilton had seen themselves as disinterested statesmen, not as political brokers among competing interests or as election managers, even when necessity forced them to behave as though they were. Confidence in their rectitude and the wisdom of their policies made Federalists insensitive and indifferent to the political dangers their rhetoric and programs entailed. In a social order where habits of deference still persisted, a statesman was accustomed to doing what he thought right regardless of personal risk, whereas a professional politician typically calculates risks and maneuvers accordingly within the mainstream of popular currents. The Federalists claimed to be statesmen, not professionals. To most early Republican as well as Federalist leaders too, politics was not a profession. It was rather a duty, a responsibility of gentlemen whose primary commitment was to planting, or trade, or law, or medicine, and the good life. Most hated to stand for or serve in public office. Party leaders often had to plead with popular vote-getters to run for office and with men of special talent to accept major appointments. Despite grave fears for the future of the republic, Thomas Jefferson fled public life in 1793 for Monticello, and not to build an opposition party, as mythology tells it. While President, John Adams spent so much time at home amid comfortable surroundings, neglecting affairs of state, that he temporarily lost control of his own administration. Men unaccustomed to the stinging shafts of political attack, thin-skinned, unused to the rough and tumble of political warfare, preferred to retreat to their firesides rather than remain as targets for mudslingers. If a man was disappointed or defeated, he gracefully retired; one's career did not revolve around winning and holding office. Once again, this was particularly the case among Federalist leaders.[19] For the professional whose occupation is politics, there is nothing else to do but plan, work, wait, and hope for the next election. He knows that there is rhythm in political life and that eventually his fortunes will improve; tomorrow's possible victory makes it easier to accept today's defeat and inspires new energies to hasten the time of his return to office. But for defeated Federalists there could be no such expectation, if only because they had no experience with the cyclical alternation of parties in and out of power. Defeat, when it came, was total.

The Revolutionary generation did produce some prototypes of the political professional, men like Aaron Burr and DeWitt Clinton of New York, whose careers revolved around the pursuit of office. But such individuals inspired distrust and contempt even among those temporarily allied with them, those who needed and used their skills and strength. One could never quite trust men who were governed exclusively by selfish desires, devoid of principle, willing to resort to almost any means to gain their ends. During the deadlocked presidential election of 1800 that ended in the House of Representatives, Alexander Hamilton urged Federalists to support Jefferson over Burr because he thought that the Virginia gentleman, for all his faults, was far less dangerous than the unscrupulous Manhattan politician. In the eyes of the patrician leaders of the first party system, men like Burr lacked the essential moral qualities political leadership demanded. Only those recruited from among the "real" interests of the republic—merchants, farmers, and planters—could understand and would serve the people's needs. Lawyers, the occupation from whom professional politicians were to be recruited, were suspect since they were

---

19. See Morton Borden, *The Federalism of James A. Bayard*, 159: "To Bayard the Senate was a job and not a career, a position of dignity and respectability rather than a battleground under observation by the nation." For John Adams's difficulty in recruiting a cabinet see Kurtz, *Adams*, chap. 12. Typical was Benjamin Stoddert's reluctant acceptance of an appointment as Secretary of Navy though he much preferred "to spend my life in retirement, and ease, without bustle of any kind."

widely viewed as social parasites, producing no wealth but prospering off the miseries of those who did. To keep public life pure, officials should receive small salaries that would discourage service by any except virtuous men motivated by civic responsibility. A hireling political leadership was as unacceptable in a republic, they thought, as a hireling clergy in a reformed church, and equally dangerous.

One day the republic would need the services and skills of professional politicians. The Revolutionary generation had already discovered that the tasks of governance were far more difficult and complex than they had at first realized. As nation-builders the Americans were amateurs who sailed into rough and uncharted waters, only vaguely aware of the difficult storms ahead. At each step of the journey, none could quite see where it all would lead; but each decision confronted citizens with pressing new problems and choices. Winning independence did not so much create a nation as give men a chance to discover arrangements by which power could be harnessed in the service of liberty and the common good, so that a republic justified by the principles of the Declaration would be more than a short-lived utopian dream. The first efforts to reconstruct political authority in the Confederation by centering power in the states proved incomplete, but the new federal system invented by the Constitution-makers of 1787 was likewise no magic solution. Neither was the first American party system, although it did offer new hope and provide experience on which the organizers of later party systems could draw.

IV | RICHARD P. McCORMICK

RUTGERS UNIVERSITY

Political Development

and the Second Party System

HISTORIANS engaged in the study of political parties in the United States have commonly focused their attention on individual parties as distinctive entities or on the contests between parties. Studies of particular parties abound, both at the state level and in larger contexts, and much of our political history is written in terms of the clashing rivalry of Jeffersonian Republicans and Federalists, Whigs and Democrats, or Democrats and Republicans. This approach has tended to emphasize the differences between parties, especially in terms of their ideologies and their constituencies. Worthy, rewarding, and time-honored as this usual type of inquiry may be, there is an alternative—or complementary—approach that can be expected to yield important insights into American political development. We can view the parties in existence at any given time as comprising a party system; and with the party system, rather than individual parties, as the phenomenon under scrutiny, we can proceed to new categories of questions and hypotheses.

In studying individual political parties, for example, we may properly direct our attention to certain activities in which parties engage, such as nominating candidates, conducting campaigns, aggregating interests, formulating ideological positions, and managing governmental power. We may also be concerned with the structure, or pattern of organized relationships between leaders and identifiers, of a particular party. If on the other hand the party system is the object of our concern, we may endeavor to formulate understandings of how and under what circumstances party systems emerge, define the character of the party system in terms of various proposed typologies, and evaluate the contribution of the party system —as an element in the larger political system—to the handling of certain "problems" or the meeting of specified "crises." To the degree that we are able to develop suitable and meaningful concepts of broad applicability, we can engage in the comparative analysis of successive party systems within our own nation over a period of time as well as of party systems in different nations. By engaging in such comparative studies, we may hope to formulate and test hypotheses regarding the role of party systems in our culture.[1]

Proceeding within this frame of reference, we can say that in the period between the establishment of a new government under the federal Constitution in 1789 and the disruption of the Union in 1860, two party systems rose and declined and a third was in the process of being formed as the nation confronted the crisis of disunion. The first party system, properly recognized as the first modern party system in any nation, was formed in the 1790's, deteriorated after 1815, and in a loose sense came to an end in 1824. The second party system had its origins in the presidential contest of 1824, acquired its full dimensions by 1840, and began to disintegrate in the early 1850's. By 1856, with the sudden rise of the Republican party to national prominence, there were signs that a third party system was emerging, although the disunited condition of the opposition parties down through 1860 and the cataclysmic effects of the Civil War and the subsequent era of Reconstruction left the eventual outlines of this party system in doubt until the 1870's.[2]

These three party systems shared many attributes. They were all, for example, two-party systems. But they differed in the circumstances surrounding their origins—and in the cases of the first and second party systems in the circumstances associated with their disintegration—as well as in such important respects as the character of their sectional alignments,

1. My own intrest in the comparative study of party systems has been influenced in various ways by Gabriel A. Almond and James S. Coleman (eds.), *The Politics of the Developing Areas* (Princeton, 1960); Maurice Duverger, *Political Parties: Their Organization and Activity in the Modern State* (New York, 1954); Seymour Martin Lipset, *The First New Nation* (New York, 1963); Sigmund Neumann (ed.), *Modern Political Parties* (Chicago, 1956); and Joseph LaPalombara and Myron Weiner (eds.), *Political Parties and Political Development* (Princeton, 1966). For an admirable and full bibliography, see the last work, pp. 439-64. William N. Chambers has broken new ground with his brilliant conceptualizations of American party systems in *Political Parties in a New Nation: The American Experience, 1776-1809* (New York, 1963); and in "Party Development and Party Action: The American Origins," *History and Theory*, III (1963), 111-17. I have found many of his formulations suggestive.

2. Two useful but outdated standard histories of American parties are Wilfred E. Binkley, *American Political Parties: Their Natural History* (New York, 1962); and Edgar E. Robinson, *The Evolution of American Political Parties* (New York, 1924).

the comprehensiveness of their appeal to potential participants, and their apparent capacity for resolving conflicts. They are, however, comparable, and when sufficient descriptive studies become available, it should be fruitful to engage in a comparative analysis of all three. Then it may be possible to identify similarities and differences and advance hypotheses to explain them.

II

This brief introduction will suffice to establish the general conceptual framework within which my particular subject—the second American party system—is presented. My main concern will be to offer a descriptive account of the formation of this party system and its growth to maturity in the 1840's.[3] In order to place the subject in proper perspective, I shall deal briefly with some aspects of party development before 1824 and after 1840 and suggest some comparisons among the party systems under consideration.

By way of background, it is relevant to offer some very general observations on the conduct of politics before the emergence of the first party system. Unlike most nations of the world, the United States had considerable experience in operating representative institutions long before the advent of parties. Passing over the colonial period, which, as current research has demonstrated, was marked by a lively brand of politics inspired by an ideology that came to assume an increasingly democratic thrust, it should be recognized that even after 1776 republican governments functioned without political parties. In all of the states leaders were recruited, substantial proportions of the adult males were involved in the electoral process, stability was maintained, the legitimacy of governmental authority was recognized, and important conflicts were resolved. In this era of popular or semipopular non-party politics, independence was secured, grievous postwar problems were met, a new Constitution was adopted, and the federal government was established. Many of the obvious pre-conditions for the rise of parties existed in many of the states—elected legislatures, broad suffrage provisions, open competition for offices, a society of differentiated interests sharing common goals—but there was no semblance of a national party system, and, with two or three

3. Much of the material in this essay is drawn from my study, *The Second American Party System: Party Formation in the Jacksonian Era* (Chapel Hill, 1966).

interesting but questionable exceptions, no party formation at the state level. Politics remained essentially local in scope and factional in character, and was therefore readily managed through informal structures.

Any general approach to the comparative study of American party systems must surely include some analysis of this pre-party era, for only through such an analysis can we test adequately any hypotheses that may be advanced to explain the emergence of parties shortly after 1789. Similarly, by comparing how certain functions conventionally ascribed to parties were actually performed in the pre-party period and after the advent of parties, we may be able to obtain valid understanding of what parties have contributed to our political system. Or, to put the matter differently, what obvious deficiencies existed in the political system before the 1790's that were rectified by the formation of parties? These questions can only be raised at this point; not until we have available well-conceived studies of colonial and state politics before 1789 can they be answered with any assurance.

National parties did not form during the Confederation period, but within a few years after the establishment of the new federal government, and surely by 1795, there were clear signs that party formation was well under way at all levels of government.[4] The origins of these parties can be detected first in cleavages that developed within the highest level of the national administration. Next, comparable factions formed within Congress. The emergence of these congressional factions encouraged the formation of parties at the state level. Finally, successive contests for the presidency in 1796 and 1800 provided an additional stimulant and served to focus and reinforce party feelings.

In endeavoring to account for the creation of parties at this particular time, we are obliged to ask what new conditions arose in the 1790's that seemingly created an environment more favorable to the formation of national parties than had maintained a decade earlier. It is my view that

4. In addition to Chambers's *Political Parties in a New Nation*, which provides the best summary account of early party formation, two outstanding works are Joseph Charles, *The Origins of the American Party System* (Williamsburg, Va., 1956); and Noble E. Cunningham, Jr., *The Jeffersonian Republicans: The Formation of Party Organizations, 1789-1801* (Chapel Hill, 1957); see also Manning J. Dauer, *The Adams Federalists* (Baltimore, 1953). I share many of the understandings that Paul Goodman has set forth in his essay on "The First American Party System," in this volume. In particular, I agree with his insistence that the creation of a national political arena and its particular character was the crucial factor in the array of preconditions for the formation of national parties.

the critical new factor was the creation of a national political arena as the result of the adoption of the federal Constitution. Politics assumed an entirely new dimension—a national dimension—and the informal techniques of political management that had sufficed previously were replaced by party techniques. In particular, the constitutional arrangements for electing a President encouraged co-operation among political leaders throughout the nation in behalf of particular candidates. In quite a different way, the election of members of the House of Representatives by popular vote served to relate state and national politics. As parties were delineated on this national basis, the same alignments became operative in contests for state and even local offices.

Overly simple as this formulation may appear, it is not without its complications. It would seem that down to 1796, at least, we are confronted with a fairly clear case of parties whose origins were of the "interior" type, or "internally created" parties, to employ Maurice Duverger's typology.[5] That is, parties were formed first within the Congress and then were extended to the electorate. The complication arises because almost at once —in 1796—quite a different influence entered the scene; namely, the contest for the presidency. The rivalry between John Adams and Thomas Jefferson in 1796 and again in 1800 served not only to dramatize and polarize the emerging partisan cleavage: it also enlarged party strife beyond the bounds of congressional districts, bringing it to embrace entire states and, by extension, the whole nation. Without pausing to develop this admittedly crucial point, I would contend that it was the contest for the presidency that was to exert the determining influence on the structure of the American party system.

The first party system, launched with such enterprise and vigor in the 1790's, soon entered upon what might be termed a stage of arrested development. It did not become established in the newer states that entered the Union after 1796; it soon languished in the Southern states; and in some other areas it succumbed to factional discord. By 1824 the remnants of the first party system possessed some vitality in only five states—Maine, Massachusetts, New Jersey, Delaware, and Maryland—although there were numerous isolated instances elsewhere of Federalists still offering challenges to their Republican adversaries.[6] Vestiges of old party organ-

5. Duverger, *Political Parties*, xxiii-xxxvii.
6. Contrary to some understandings, the Federalist party did not experience an abrupt demise in 1815. Indeed, it was still amazingly vigorous as late as 1826 in

izations survived in some cases and party identities lingered on, but elections were rarely contested within the framework of the party system.

The first party system, then, can be seen in terms of failure as well as success. It failed to achieve truly national dimensions and, quite obviously, it failed to survive; and it also came perilously close to recording an even more serious failing. As the party system matured it became increasingly unbalanced. That is, the Republicans achieved such a lopsided superiority on a national basis that their Federalist opponents could scarcely hope to compete. What rendered this situation especially ominous was that the Federalist strength was sectionally concentrated, chiefly in New England, and that strength could now scarcely be effective in national politics. In consequence, the Federalists experienced a keen sense of political frustration, amounting to a sense of loss of their political efficacy. Much of New England's disaffection during the War of 1812 can be related to this factor, and the Hartford Convention, with its demands for revision of the constitutional "rules of the game," and even its implied threat of a division of the Union, brought the tensions to a crisis. What the ultimate result might have been had Andrew Jackson's victory at New Orleans in 1815 not transformed popular reactions to the war and to the record of the national administration must remain problematical. It can at least be suggested that the first party system as of 1814 was failing lamentably in achieving national integration and was even bringing the very legitimacy of the government into question. In other terms, the first party system was a failure because the parties became excessively unbalanced and took on a sectional alignment to the point where one sectionally oriented party, feeling that it could not compete, would no longer play the game according to the recognized rules.

In sequel, the first party system in its latter years—after 1815—can be held responsible for a peculiar example of a "crisis of participation." Having failed to secure a revision of the rules, and having lost any prospect of electoral success, the Federalists in many states simply withdrew entirely from the arena of politics. In New Hampshire, for example, where the Federalists ceased to contest for state offices after 1817, voter participation declined from a high of slightly more than 80 per cent of those

Delaware—see John A. Munroe, *Federalist Delaware, 1775-1815* (New Brunswick, N.J., 1954). Two of the best studies on the Federalists are David Hackett Fischer, *The Revolution of American Conservatism: The Federalist Party in the Era of Jeffersonian Democracy* (New York, 1965); and Shaw Livermore, *The Twilight of Federalism* (Princeton, 1962).

eligible in the gubernatorial election of 1814 to a low of 44 per cent by 1822. In Connecticut, for similar reasons, voter participation dropped from 45 per cent in 1819 to 22 per cent by 1822; in Vermont there was a comparable decline from 66 per cent in 1818 to 25 per cent by 1821; and in Rhode Island there was an abrupt falloff from nearly 50 per cent in 1818 to 15 per cent in 1819.[7] In other states, as party competition languished, voter participation generally sank to a low level.

Why did the first party system disintegrate? If we could answer this question with complete authority we should no doubt possess an important key to understanding the nature of the system. Without attempting to offer a comprehensive explanation for the breakdown of the parties, we could propose the simple proposition that the failure of the Federalists to extend, or even maintain, the bases of support they held in 1800 brought about a condition of extreme party imbalance. At this point the Federalists confronted the alternatives of rebelling against the system or withdrawing from it. After experiencing failure with the first alternative, they adopted the second in most states. No longer confronted by a formidable opposition, the Republicans in most areas succumbed to internal factionalism.

Approaching the problem from even a narrower perspective, we could advance the hypothesis that the first party system disintegrated because the chief purpose for which it had been formed had lost its urgency. That is, the fact that the contest for the presidency subsided after 1800 deprived the party system of the main source of its vitality and even the reason for its existence. The fortuitous availability of the members of the "Virginia Dynasty," the succession of Jefferson, Madison, and Monroe, and the failure of the Federalists as politicians to grasp the full significance of the importance of the presidential contest, together with certain impediments that inhered in the existing constitutional and social environment, all combined to reduce and ultimately eliminate the contest for the presidency as the stimulus to party action. This hypothesis—that the contest for the presidency provided the first party system with its crucial function—would obviously require extensive testing. Here it can only be noted that in the absence of a contest for the presidency there was little tendency for parties to form within individual states for the purpose of competing for state and local offices. Moreover, there is no evidence to suggest that cleavages within the Congress, even after 1815, could provide the basis

7. For the sources of these, and other voting data cited, see my *Second American Party System*, 373-9.

for the rehabilitation or reconstruction of the party system. Finally, the revival of the contest for the presidency after 1824 had the immediate effect of stimulating the formation of a new party system.

As the national party system disintegrated, especially after 1815, it is noteworthy that there was not much of a tendency toward the formation of state-oriented parties, that is, parties organized solely for the purpose of contesting offices at the state level. The obvious exceptions to this generalization were New York, with its Bucktail and Clintonian parties; Georgia, with its peculiar Troup-Clark alignments; and Kentucky, where Old Court and New Court parties carried on a brief struggle.[8] It is also significant, I believe, that divisions did not form within Congress to provide the basis for a new party alignment even when such crises as those attendant upon the economic depression of 1819 or the furore over the admission of Missouri to statehood agitated public feelings.

III

It would seem to be quite clear that the stimulus for the formation of the second party system was supplied by the revival of the contest for the presidency in 1824. With the expiration of Monroe's second term there was no notable Virginian to take his place; the weak and discredited Republican congressional caucus was unable to produce a disciplined solution to the problem of succession; and soon there were four candidates— all self-styled Republicans—contending for the presidency. Except in New England, where John Quincy Adams had virtually no opposition, the contest was extremely confused and did not at once produce new party alignments. Because it was so chaotic, and also because in many states one or another of the candidates enjoyed overwhelming support from local political leaders, voter participation was remarkably low.

The most important consequence of 1824, in terms of party formation, was that it projected Andrew Jackson to the fore as the rival to Adams. Looking ahead to 1828, rival political leaders from state to state began to calculate their courses of action with respect to what was termed the "presidential question." Obviously, many considerations entered into their

8. Although I recognize that some may contend that the formations in New York, Georgia, and Kentucky were not parties, I believe that they are entitled to this designation. The point to be emphasized, however, is that these formations were exceptional and that in the absence of the stimulus of the contest for the presidency, parties did not form around state issues or group cleavages within states.

appraisals, but the fact that loomed largest, no doubt, was the highly sectional nature of the appeal of the two candidates.

This sectional bias was clearly revealed in the election of 1828. Adams swept New England, securing majorities of three-to-one or better in four of the six states. Jackson was equally impressive in the South, and won commanding majorities in most of the newer states of the West. Having no sectional candidate of their own in the race, the Middle States provided the major battleground of the election, and—except in Pennsylvania —the vote was extremely close. The party alignments that formed in the Middle States by 1828 tended to be durable, as Table 1 shows,[9] although in both New York and Pennsylvania the anti-Jackson forces lacked co-

TABLE 1

Differential between Percentages of Total Vote Obtained by Major Presidential Candidates, 1828-44

STATE	1828	1832	1836	1840	1844
Maine	20	10	20	1	13
New Hampshire	7	13	50	11	19
Vermont	50	10	20	29	18
Massachusetts	66	30	9	16	12
Rhode Island	50	14	6	23	20
Connecticut	50	20	1	11	5
New York	2	4	9	4	1
New Jersey	4	1	1	4	1
Pennsylvania	33	16	4	1	2
Delaware	—	2	6	10	3
Maryland	2	1	7	8	5
Virginia	38	50	13	1	6
North Carolina	47	70	6	15	5
Georgia	94	100	4	12	4
Kentucky	1	9	6	29	8
Tennessee	90	90	16	11	1
Louisiana	6	38	3	19	3
Alabama	80	100	11	9	18
Mississippi	60	77	2	7	13
Ohio	3	3	4	9	2
Indiana	13	34	12	12	2
Illinois	34	37	10	2	12
Missouri	41	32	21	14	17
Arkansas	—	—	28	13	26
Michigan	—	—	9	4	6
Average Differential	36	36	11	11	9

9. See Table 1 for an index of the balance—or imbalance—of parties in each state for the presidential elections from 1828 through 1844. It will be observed that the average differential between the total vote obtained by the presidential candidates in 1828 was 36 points, which would mean an average percentage of 68 for the victor and 32 for the defeated candidate.

hesion and were distracted by Antimasonry. With these important exceptions, we could say that a new two-party system had emerged in the Middle States by 1828 and that it had been given definition by the presidential contest. In New England, because of the overwhelming loyalty to the sectional favorite, the opposition Jacksonian parties were able to make little headway until after Adams had been defeated. But by 1829 the political balance had altered considerably, and the Jacksonians rapidly moved into a competitive position in most states. In the South and West —except for the very special case of Kentucky—the election of 1828 stimulated the temporary formation of parties. Once the election was over, however, the alignments did not persist and politics continued to be conducted in what was essentially an unstructured fashion.

Despite the large issues that presumably were involved, the election of 1832 had remarkably little effect on party formation. In the South and West there were feeble efforts to organize support for Henry Clay, but in most states he fared even less well than had Adams in 1828. In the Middle States, the close balance that had become evident in 1828 persisted. The most striking shift occurred in New England, where in every state the Jacksonians made tremendous gains and captured Maine and New Hampshire. Perhaps this remarkable upheaval can be attributed to the popularity of Jackson's policies regarding the bank, tariff, and internal improvements. Yet I am inclined to believe that the explanation is to be found quite simply in the fact that Clay lacked the strong sectional appeal that Adams had possessed.

How well developed, then, was the new party system by the end of 1832? In broad terms, it was well established in New England and the Middle States, despite the complications of Antimasonry. In every state the Jacksonians had acquired recognized leaders, constructed an elaborate party apparatus, and enlisted in their ranks multitudes of voters who identified with the Jackson party. The opposition, plagued by the lack of a persistent standard bearer, nevertheless managed to maintain a competitive position, whether under the Adams, National Republican, or Antimasonic label. The South, except for Kentucky, could best be described as politically monolithic. Where nearly all political leaders and candidates were nominally, at least, of the Jacksonian persuasion, there could scarcely be a functioning two-party system. In certain of the newer states of the West what can only be described as a dual party system existed. There were temporary party formations in 1828 and 1832 for the purpose of contesting the presidential election, but in state and congressional elections the contests were either conducted on a non-party basis or, in some instances, on the basis of alignments quite different from those that obtained in the presidential elections. It is common, in describing American politics in this era, to assert that by 1828 or by 1832 a functioning party system existed; but it would be my contention that in many states the crucial stage of party formation had not yet been reached.

Slight as was the effect of the election of 1832 on party formation, it did reveal an undercurrent that was soon to assume the proportions of a tidal wave. Although Jackson retained, and even increased, his huge majorities throughout the South, there were strong manifestations of dissatisfaction with his running mate and heir-apparent, Martin Van Buren of New York. In Virginia, North Carolina, Georgia, and Alabama, factions that professed loyalty to Jackson also launched organized efforts to oppose Van Buren's candidacy for the vice-presidency, and there were similar signs of restiveness in other Southern states as well. Some of these early anti-Van Burenites were admirers of John C. Calhoun, and others were appalled at the prospect of having to support a Northerner for the presidency. Still others, no doubt, were calculating how they might exploit anti-Van Buren sentiment to advance their political fortunes within their particular states.

What can best be characterized as a political explosion rocked the South from Virginia to Mississippi in 1834 and 1835. With Jackson nearing the end of his tenure, the political consensus that seemingly had prevailed was abruptly replaced by a sharp cleavage in almost every state. Those who remained loyal to the Jackson party found themselves confronted with a virulent opposition that shared a common antagonism to Martin Van Buren. While some of those "antis" continued to profess their undying loyalty to Old Hickory and his policies, others declaimed against executive usurpation, the removal of bank deposits, and the tariff, or sounded the changes on states' rights. The new sides were drawn in the state and congressional elections of 1834 and 1835, and by 1836 the Southern opposition parties—often bearing the name Whig—had found their standard bearer in Hugh Lawson White of Tennessee.

In the Western states, too, the approach of the election of 1836 spurred the slow process of party formation. More-or-less well-organized Van Buren-Democratic parties faced bitter struggles with opposition parties pledged variously to a local hero—William Henry Harrison of Indiana—

or to mixed White-Harrison tickets. In part because of the unprecedented personal campaign waged by Harrison, the election aroused considerable interest. The alignments that emerged in this election persisted, even though state elections in Illinois, Indiana, and Missouri continued for a few years to bear only a vague resemblance to party contests.

The least studied of all our presidential elections, the election of 1836, was of crucial importance in determining the ultimate outlines of the second party system. In marked contrast to the situation that had existed in 1832, there were now two parties contesting elections in every state, and—no less significantly—in the large majority of the states the parties were competitive. Although Van Buren eked out a victory in the 1836 election, the party that he headed had very different dimensions from the one that had twice swept Jackson into office. In the South, where Jackson had encountered little more than token opposition, Van Buren polled slightly less than 50 per cent of the popular vote. Jackson had won 100 per cent of the votes in Georgia and 95 per cent of the votes in Tennessee in 1832; Van Buren lost both of these states in 1836. In the West, too, Van Buren's strength was far less than that of Jackson. Only in New England did Van Buren enhance the strength of the Democratic party. In the evenly balanced Middle States there was no large shift.

In brief, the effect of Van Buren's candidacy was to end the monolithic character of Southern politics and delineate and strengthen alignments in the West, thereby giving a truly national dimension to the second party system. While in 1832 the victorious candidate had secured a two-to-one margin in eleven states, only one state remained in that category in 1836: New Hampshire, which Van Buren carried by a three-to-one margin. Fittingly enough, the state in which Van Buren found his weakest support was Vermont. Here, indeed, is a conundrum for political analysts.

The anti-Van Buren or Whig parties that had formed in the several states between 1834 and 1836, together with those in New England and the Middle States that had originated earlier, had yet to develop national cohesion and leadership. Such an achievement would be essential if they were to contest successfully for the presidency. Meeting at Harrisburg in December 1839, in one of the most astutely contrived conventions ever held, they performed the difficult feat by agreeing to unite on the best available hero, Old Tippecanoe Harrison, and by sedulously avoiding any semblance of a party platform. Thus effectively mobilized, the Whigs proceeded to put on a spectacular campaign that was to fix a new style in

American political drama.[10] The exciting contest, waged furiously now in every state, stimulated an unprecedented outpouring of voters and sent Van Buren down to a crushing defeat in the electoral college, although the popular vote was far less lopsided.

The campaign of 1840 brought the second American party system at last to fruition. In every region of the country, and indeed in every state, politics was conducted within the framework of a two-party system, and in all but a handful of states the parties were so closely balanced as to be competitive.[11] In broad terms, it was the contest for the presidency that shaped this party system and defined its essential purpose. The same party system, however, was to be utilized as the framework within which competition for office at all other levels of government would be conducted. The two parties were similar in structure, employed similar campaign techniques, and performed similar functions. Although in specific features the parties remained somewhat differentiated from state to state, there had in fact occurred a nationalization of institutional forms and political styles. There was also a nationalization of political identities. Voters everywhere would respond to candidates and issues as Whigs or Democrats.

IV

With this brief and even partial synopsis of party development in mind, it becomes possible to attempt some analyses of what it all signifies. We can approach this question by attempting some broad comparisons between the first and second party systems. But before engaging in this exercise, we might well pause to consider how politics was conducted in the absence of parties, for only with some understanding of this phase of our political history can we measure and evaluate the effects of parties.

Even after the appearance of the first party system, many states continued to conduct politics on a non-party basis. An example is Tennessee, which did so for roughly forty years.[12] With no vestige of political parties,

10. The story of this memorable campaign is ably detailed in Robert G. Gunderson, *The Log Cabin Campaign* (Lexington, Ky., 1957).

11. See Table 1. In twenty of the states in 1840 the margin between the two parties was 15 points or less and the average differential was only 11 points. Note the contrast between 1832 and 1840.

12. Tennessee might be called a "one-party" state in the sense that nearly all public figures, as well as voters, identified thmselves as Jeffersonian Republicans, or— after 1824—as Jacksonians. But there was no formal party structure, and vigorously contested elections were conducted without relevance to parties.

the Tennessee brand of politics featured hard-fought contests for seats in the legislature and in Congress that not uncommonly brought over 70 per cent of the electorate to the polls. In the process, the state produced a host of outstanding political figures, including not only Andrew Jackson but James K. Polk, Hugh Lawson White, John Bell, and Felix Grundy as well. Reference could readily be made to a dozen other states where as late as the 1820's, or even 1830's, political parties were nonexistent. Leaving aside the intriguing question of why parties were not formed, at least for the purpose of conducting state politics, it would no doubt be illuminating if we could answer the question of what functions usually ascribed to political parties were not being performed in some manner in Tennessee and other non-party states. Probably none of us would insist that representative government was inconceivable without political parties, but we may readily err in attributing to parties a larger and more comprehensive role in the American political process than they in fact deserve. Unfortunately, we know even less about pre-party politics in the United States than we do about party politics, with the result that as yet we are not well prepared to make reliable comparisons between the two systems.

We are on slightly firmer ground when we endeavor to compare the first and the second party systems, although admittedly our knowledge of both is inadequate and the conceptual framework within which we structure our comparisons is incomplete. For the purposes of this essay, the comparative analysis must necessarily be kept within brief limits and deal only with large and readily visible attributes.

The first and second American party systems did not have precisely the same origins. It would seem that cleavages within Congress preceded and even forecast the formation of parties in the 1790's. In theoretical terms, it would be extremely important to be able to affirm that the first party system represented an "internally created" or "interior" type of party formation. Unfortunately, we cannot be sure how far this interior process of party formation might have proceeded, for superimposed on the impulse supplied by the congressional parties was the mobilization for the presidential contests in 1796 and 1800. It is my view that these contests for the presidency supplied a greater stimulus to party formation than did the congressional groupings. Nevertheless, the early existence of congressional alignments in the 1790's has no counterpart in the 1820's. Moreover, the parties of the 1790's possessed at the outset an issue-orientation that can hardly be discerned in 1824 or 1828. Finally, the first party system had a relatively rapid emergence, whereas the second was formed in stages over a period of roughly sixteen years.

Both party systems, the second more clearly than the first, were oriented toward contesting presidential elections. This orientation presents a striking contrast to the situation in other Western political systems, where parties have been oriented toward securing as large a representation as possible in the national legislature (although it must be noted that in most cases it has been the legislature that names the functioning executive in such systems). It is this peculiarity, among others, that makes it so difficult to conceptualize American party systems in terms that would be relevant to other nations. In organizational terms, the congressional district has presented awkward problems for our parties, quite unlike the parliamentary constituencies in Europe. Why should the executive rather than the legislative branch have been the focal point for the party system, especially in the first half of the nineteenth century? No doubt an extended answer to this question could tell us much about the special character of American parties.

There were pronounced differences in the organizational structures of parties in the first and second party systems. The caucus reflected in part the prominent role taken by legislators—national and state—in guiding early party development, and it was extensively employed as a management device under the first party system.[13] In most states, as well as at the national level, party members within the legislature, often joined by non-legislators, performed extensive nominating functions and—usually through such agencies as central committees—directed party affairs generally. In many states, conspicuously in New England and Virginia, the caucus and its agencies operated a highly centralized party apparatus, although in time local party units increasingly employed delegate conventions to nominate candidates for lesser offices. Two states, New Jersey and Deleware, were exceptional in that they instituted the state convention. Because of the great variations in constitutional structures from state to state, the precise forms of party organization and even the functions performed by the caucus differed widely; but in its most highly developed form—notably in Massachusetts—the caucus structure was highly inte-

13. For interesting material on the caucus-style party organization under the first party system, see Cunningham, *Jeffersonian Republicans,* 162-6; Cunningham, *The Jeffersonian Republicans in Power: Party Operations 1801-1809* (Chapel Hill, 1963), 111-12, 127, 133, 137, 142, 145-6; and Fischer, *Revolution of American Conservatism,* 60-90 *passim.*

grated and extremely efficient. At the national level, party management was relatively weak. The Republican congressional caucus was a promising institution, which under slightly altered circumstances might have exerted a lasting influence on the structure of American parties, but for reasons that must be passed over it failed to develop and maintain its authority and grew increasingly ineffective, especially after 1816. The Federalists, with their small and geographically unrepresentative delegation in Congress, could scarcely use the caucus as an authoritative national agency, and they had little success in developing the convention as an alternative.

Under the second party system, the caucus was almost completely replaced by the convention as the characteristic device for party management. The changeover, which has not yet been studied thoroughly, had great theoretical significance. In addition to reflecting demands for popular participation in party affairs the convention also represented a highly practical solution to problems facing party leaders at a time when party identities in legislative bodies were extremely confused, or when incipient parties had too few legislative representatives to organize a respectable caucus. Much might be made of the fact that the Antimasonic party, the first clear example of what Maurice Duverger calls an "externally created" or "exterior" type of party in the United States, was especially zealous in developing the convention technique and, as we know, held the first national party convention. Whether the extralegislative origins of the Jackson and Adams parties in most—but not all—states would justify our describing them as "exterior" parties could lead to considerable debate. What would seem to be indisputable is that the shift from caucus to convention implied a loss in the political authority of legislative bodies. While they were suffering this loss, they were also experiencing general curtailment of their elective functions, as evidenced by the trend toward the popular choice of electors, governors, and other state officials. Again, one would like to be able to understand fully why this downgrading of the legislative branch occurred and what implications it had for our system of politics.

The widespread adoption of the convention system in the 1830's, with its hierarchy of delegate conventions and party committees extending from the smallest electoral unit up to the national conventions, made for an exceedingly elaborate and complex organizational structure. Because candidates had to be nominated at so very many different levels of government, elections were held so frequently, and the party system embraced the entire range of offices, the organizations that had evolved in most states by the 1840's were marvels of ingenuity and intricacy and required enormous manpower to staff them. In contrast to the diversity of organizational forms under the first party system, there was now a high degree of uniformity throughout the nation and in both major parties.

It is possible that the shift from the caucus to the convention may have tended greatly to emphasize the purely electoral functions of the party apparatus. The members of a caucus, in their dual capacity as legislators and party managers, may have been more concerned with matters of program and policy than were the members of conventions. It would also appear that in its most centralized form, the caucus structure imposed a much higher degree of discipline than was to prevail under the convention system. Despite their elaborate organization, the new parties of the second party system were actually decentralized structures. The party apparatus at each level of government, or within each type of constituency, possessed considerable autonomy. Party mechanisms were better designed for achieving agreement on nominations than for formulating policies. Perhaps the very complexity and magnitude of the formal organizational structure contributed to the rise of the professional party manager and the informal leader, or boss.

In discussing any formal party structures, whether of the caucus or convention type, the problem inevitably arises as to whether the formal structure reflected the actual locus of power or influence. Superficially, the delegate convention system of the 1830's and 1840's resulted in the "democratization" of parties, but we have yet to determine the degree to which conventions were genuine decision-making bodies. Perhaps they were, but they must also be viewed as having what might be termed a cosmetic function; that is, they gave a democratic appearance to what might in fact have been decisions determined by a party oligarchy. Indeed, Ostrogorski used the term "democratic formalism" to describe the convention structure.

The two party systems could also be compared with respect to participation. The installation of the convention party structure unquestionably multiplied opportunities for party followers to assume roles as activists. This development was especially prominent in those states where previously there had been little or no formal party organization, but its effects could be noted everywhere. Moreover, intense inter-party competition stimulated unprecedented levels of voter participation, not uncommonly rising to 80 per cent of the electorate, whereas prior to 1824 in a very large number of states it was exceptional for half of the eligible voters to participate regularly in elections.[14] Both in the comprehensiveness of their structures and in the universality of their appeal, then, the new parties could truly be characterized as mass parties.

One may properly speculate as to whether the measurable increase in voter participation had a direct influence on party programs and governmental actions. To put the question differently, when vast numbers of men who had formerly lacked the franchise or who had been apathetic entered the electoral arena, were there discernable shifts in party attitudes or public policy? Did the parties and the governments become more "democratic"? This would be an extremely difficult question to answer, but I have the impression that the "new" voters tended to divide between the two parties in much the same proportion as the "old" voters.[15] We might conclude that both parties accommodated the new voters by modifying their appeals and their programs. An alternative conclusion could be that because the new voters did not enter predominantly into one party and make it the instrument for achieving their political goals, they had no great effect on the parties. Any sure evaluation of the effects of enlarged participation must depend on further studies, but at least we might agree that the mass participation that we associate with the second party system did affect the style of politics.

The extended form of participation in politics in the era of the second party system can scarcely be comprehended in purely political terms— that is, only in terms of rivalry between opposing power elites or interest groups for dominance in the state and for control over public policy. It would be difficult to account for all the phenomena of the system within

14. See my "New Perspectives on Jacksonian Politics," *American Historical Review,* LXV (1960), 288-301, for illustrative data on the increase in voter participation. In those states where the parties were competitive after 1800, it was not uncommon for 70 per cent or more of the adult white males to vote, and on occasion higher levels were reached. But in states where the parties were unbalanced, or where elections were not contested on a party basis, participation would usually be under 50 per cent. There are, however, curious exceptions to these generalizations. Alabama recorded the suspiciously high figure of 97 per cent in a gubernatorial election in 1819, and Tennessee reached 80 per cent in the gubernatorial election of 1817. These, and other data that could be cited, suggest that high participation could be achieved in the absence of parties, and even in the absence of the stimulus of a presidential contest.

15. See my "Suffrage Classes and Party Alignments: A Study in Voter Behavior," *Mississippi Valley Historical Review,* XLVI (1959), 397-410.

these limited concepts, and the varieties of experiences that parties in this era afforded to the electorate went beyond the political sphere.[16] Those tens of thousands of men and women who attended the mammoth Whig festival at Nashville in 1840; those untold millions who carried torches, donned uniforms, chanted slogans, or cheered themselves hoarse at innumerable parades and rallies; those puffed-up canvassers of wards, servers of rum, and distributors of largesse; and all those simple folk who whipped themselves into a fury of excitement and anxiety as each election day approached, were thrilling to a grand dramatic experience, even a cathartic experience. There was no spectacle, no contest, in America that could match an election campaign, and all could identify with and participate in it.

Innumerable foreign observers saw clearly this amazing dimension of American politics. As Michael Chevalier perceived it, the political campaign and all its attendant pageantry and exaltation meant to Americans what religious festivals had meant to the peoples of Catholic Europe. Witnessing a post-election celebration of New York City Democrats, he was struck by the resemblance.

> The procession was nearly a mile long; the democrats marched in good order to the glare of torches; the banners were more numerous than I had ever seen them in any religious festival; all were in transparency, on account of the darkness. On some were inscribed the names of the democratic societies or sections, . . . others bore imprecations against the Bank of the United States; *Nick Biddle* and *Old Nick* here figured largely and formed the pendant of our *libera nos a malo.* Then came portraits of General Jackson afoot and on horseback . . . Those of Washington and Jefferson, surrounded with democratic mottoes, were mingled in all tastes and of all colors. Among these figured an eagle, not a painting, but a real live eagle, tied by the legs, surrounded by a wreath of leaves, and hoisted upon a pole, after the manner of the Roman standards. The imperial bird was carried by a stout sailor, more pleased than ever was a sergeant permitted to hold one of the strings of the canopy, in a Catholic ceremony. From further than the eye could reach, came marching on the democrats. I was struck with the resemblance of their air to the train that escorts the *viaticum* in Mexico or Puebla. . . . The democratic procession, also, like the Catholic procession, had its halting places; it stopped before the house of the Jackson

---

16. M. Ostrogorski, among other foreign observers, has some extremely perceptive comments on the "ritual character" of American parties in *Democracy and the Party System in the United States* (New York, 1910), 408-12.

men to fill the air with cheers, and halted at the doors of the leaders of the Opposition, to give three, six, or nine groans.

. . . If these scenes were to find a painter, they would be admired at a distance, not less than the triumphs and sacrificial pomps, which the ancients have left us delineated in marble and brass; for they are not mere grotesques after the manner of Rembrandt, they belong to history, they partake of the grand; the are the episodes of a wondrous epic which will bequeath a lasting memory to posterity, that of the coming of democracy.[17]

Finally, the first and second party systems exhibited pronounced differences in their extent and their alignment. The parties of the 1790's had never really been extended to more than fifteen states, and in several of those they scarcely became rooted. The second party system comprehended every state, although there might well be some reservations about South Carolina. The first party system was, from one point of view, very badly aligned. Early in its history the New England states were heavily inclined toward the Federalist party, while in the South the Republicans possessed a lopsided supremacy. Although New England in time achieved a brief balance of parties, the South became virtually a one-party region. The second party system was extraordinary in that the two parties were fairly evenly balanced in every region.[18] Between 1836 and 1852, as in no other period in our history, each of the parties was truly national in its extent.

V

It would be possible and even profitable to explain why the two party systems differed in so many attributes, but such a disquisition would probably have to be very lengthy if it were to be at all persuasive. Within the limited compass of this essay it is appropriate to attempt no more than a brief reference to the most salient factors.

Of foremost importance in affecting the structures of parties as well as the specific tasks that elements within the party organization had to perform were certain fundamental changes in the constitutional and legal environment.[19] To put the matter simply, the rules under which the po-

17. Michael Chevalier, *Society, Manners and Politics in the United States* (Boston, 1839), 318-19.
18. See Table 1.
19. Constitutions and electoral laws, as demonstrated by the studies of Duverger and others, strongly conditioned the nature of party systems. This is not to maintain

litical game was to be played changed greatly between 1800 and 1840. The most obvious development was a trend from diversity to uniformity in governmental structures and electoral procedures from state to state. The magnitude and significance of this quiet revolution in the electoral environment has generally been ignored, except for a curious preoccupation with modifications in suffrage qualifications.[20] We have yet to assess adequately the relevance to our party system of the movements toward the popular, at-large election of presidential electors, the choice of congressmen by districts, the popular election of governors, and the multiplication in numbers of locally elected officials. In a related realm, the adoption of printed ballots, the creation of small voting districts, and the consolidation of elections on a single day had enormous consequences for political parties.

One general effect of this quiet revolution was to complicate the tasks of the parties. In a situation where, for example, members of a legislature were elected from the county as a unit and where the legislature in turn appointed the governor, presidential electors, and county officials, parties would have very limited tasks, as contrasted with a situation where members of each house of the legislature were chosen from different constituencies, and presidential electors, the governor, and county officials were popularly elected. Compelled to elaborate an intricate organization capable of making nominations and conducting campaigns within a bewildering variety of constituencies, and obliged at the same time to appeal for the broadest possible base of support, the new parties confronted a staggering challenge, especially when they might be called upon to engage in electoral combat two or three times within a single year. It is no wonder that they were reduced to little more than electoral machines.

If one change in the electoral environment loomed larger than all the rest it was the shift to the popular, at-large election of presidential electors. This development gave a popular dimension to the contest for the presidency, reduced the political authority of the state legislatures, called

---

that all attributes of parties are explainable in these terms, and in seeking to account for cleavages between parties, political styles, or the characteristics of political elites, for example, relevant social factors must be considered. But I would agree with Lipset that "electoral laws determine the nature of the party system as much as any other structural variable." See Lipset, *The First New Nation*, 293.

20. There have been scarcely any comparative studies of constitutional change at the state level, although this field offers rich opportunities for scholars. For a pioneering study, which still stands alone, see Fletcher M. Green, *Constitutional Development in the South Atlantic Sates, 1776-1860* (Chapel Hill, 1930).

forth elaborate and intensive campaign efforts, facilitated the building of national parties, reduced the effectiveness of third parties, and made the presidential election the focal point of the party system—to suggest but a few consequences. How and through what influences this transformation of the process of choosing electors was brought about has yet to be studied, but a complete understanding of its implications might well be crucial to any conceptualization of the American party system.

The political environment was profoundly influenced not only by these constitutional and legal developments, but also by fairly obvious technological, economic, and social changes. Revolutionary improvements in means of transportation and communication made it feasible, for example, for parties to hold state and even national conventions and conduct nationwide campaigns. Rising economic expectations associated with the transformation and expansion of the economy gave new energy to democratic dogmas and spurred mass participation in politics. The entrance of new states into the union broadened the spatial dimensions of the party system, and the growth of urban areas and the sharp rise in immigration created new challenges. Above all, the increasingly egalitarian flavor of American society, now given voice in an incontestable rhetoric, compelled both parties to project the same democratic image.

These briefly enumerated changes in the constitutional and cultural environment may account for certain fairly obvious differences in organization and style between the first and second party systems. But they do not fully explain what was most distinctive about the latter, namely, its lack of sectional bias. As the second party system reached maturity in the 1840's, it scarcely reflected the fact that the basic cleavage within the nation, transcending all others, was that which may be vaguely defined as North-South sectionalism. The first party system had mirrored this tension to the degree that after 1800 the Federalists were very largely a Northern party. The third party system as it finally became aligned in the 1870's also contained a decided sectional bias, with its solidly Democratic South and its Northern-oriented Republican party. In attempting to explain how the second party system produced not sectional parties but parties that were remarkably well balanced throughout the nation, we are confronted with a paradox. In the successive contests for the presidency between 1824 and 1836 strong sectional loyalties shaped the responses of political leaders and voters in each region to the opposing candidates. But by 1836 the end result of the series of realignments was a sectionally balanced party system. In brief, the explanation for the paradoxical character of the second party system is to be found in the peculiar circumstances associated with the contests for the presidency.

To recapitulate, the second party system did not emerge suddenly; it developed in a series of stages, and at each stage it was shaped by the sectional identifications of the candidates. With Andrew Jackson and John Quincy Adams as the candidates in 1828, a highly sectionalized vote resulted; New England went almost as overwhelmingly for Adams as the South did for Jackson; only the Middle States were evenly divided. When Henry Clay was substituted for Adams, New England was no longer held together by its loyalty to a sectional favorite, and parties throughout the North came into balance. When Martin Van Buren was substituted for Jackson—and opposed by White and Harrison—the South and much of the new West ceased to be politically monolithic, as anti-Van Buren parties quickly mobilized. These sectional responses to the presidential candidates were crucial at the time of party formation. Once the parties had been formed and identities had been acquired by the voters, alignments tended to remain relatively firm. Thus highly sectional responses in a series of presidential elections resulted in the formation of non-sectional parties.

Merely to emphasize their distinctiveness, I have chosen to call these national parties "artificial" because their ultimate alignments bore no direct relationship to the realities of sectional antagonism. At maturity, each party sought to aggregate interests that were national in scope; and within each party almost equally powerful Northern and Southern wings contested for supremacy. Intra-party tensions were greater than the tensions between the two parties. The federalized character of our constitutional structure and the inability of any national party agency to exercise firm discipline made it all but impossible to restrain the intra-party tensions. Responsible leaders of both parties understood that such parties could be destroyed by issues that were sectional in character. The parties could indulge themselves in furious controversies over the "Monster Bank," but they might be rent asunder by such issues as expansionism or the status of slavery in the territories.

The second American party system was truly a wondrous creation. Emerging over a period of sixteen years from the circumstances associated with the successive contests for the presidency, it elaborated a complex organizational structure within which there could be orderly competition for offices at all levels of government. It also provided maximal opportunities for mass participation and produced a political style that took on the aspects of a democratic religion. It could perform a wide range of electoral functions, and it could resolve conflicts that were not highly charged with sectional antagonisms. But, like the first party system, it, too, met with failure.

Apparently it was still in a healthy condition down to about 1850. Then, under the strain of the sectional issues confronting the nation, it began to crumble. The first sign was the collapse of the Whig party in the lower South, and by 1856 the already altered Democratic party was confronted by the newly marshalled Republican party and, in some areas, by the short-lived American, or "Know-Nothing," party as well. At last, in 1860, the Democrats succumbed to a fateful division and the Civil War followed. Although in the North a viable new party system operated, it was not until the 1870's, with the nation reunited and the South released from the abnormal years of Reconstruction, that the third party system assumed national dimensions.

Why did the second party system fail? One answer could be that it was inadequate to cope with conflicts that arrayed section against section. The first party system had come perilously close to foundering on this rock in 1814; but the second party system, for the reason that its parties were truly national in scope and lacked a pronounced sectional bias, was presumably better designed to manage divisive pluralism. Here we face a dilemma. If in a democratic two-party system the parties became so aligned as to reflect crucial ideological, class, social, or sectional cleavages, and they therefore present the electorate with drastic alternatives, the strain on the political system as a whole, and particularly at the level of government, may be disruptive. If, on the other hand, each party is expected to mediate conflicting interests by aggregating the broad spectrum of those interests, the strain on the political system at the level of the parties may be disruptive. I have no solution to propose to this dilemma, other than to suggest that a party system that is *too* comprehensive—as was the second party system—may be potentially as explosive as a party system that is polarized around drastic alternatives—as was the third party system in its formative years.[21] Perhaps this is to say that threatening

21. For an interesting discussion of the conditions under which a two-party system may be less able to resolve conflict than a multi-party system, see Lipset, *The First New Nation*, 308-12.

problems or the strains of crises must be shared between the party system and the government.

VI

In conclusion, some crude assessments of the contributions of the party systems to American political development down to 1860 might be attempted. Such an appraisal must be extremely tentative because the concept of political development, as formulated by LaPalombara and Weiner or others, is awkwardly elusive.[22] And even if one accepts the notion that such problems as national integration, political participation, distribution, legitimacy, and management of conflict are relevant to political development, it is all but impossible to measure the specific contributions of party systems to the solution of those problems. Consequently, what follows must be regarded as impressionistic and even subjective.

We must begin with the understanding that the United States in the 1790's did not confront crises of the same kind and magnitude as those facing the newly emergent nations of today. An extensive experience with the operation of representative institutions that dated back to early in the seventeenth century gave the new nation a politically skilled leadership corps, a broad and alert electorate, and an informed respect for constitutional order. In addition to possessing a common language, a cultural heritage that stemmed largely from British origins, and a relatively homogeneous Protestant religious background, the former colonies had strengthened their sense of national identity through their struggle for independence and had reaffirmed their unity by adopting the federal Constitution. The legitimacy of the new government was not challenged by a party of disaffection, nor was it threatened with subversion by a hereditary elite, an entrenched bureaucracy, or a powerful military establishment. The economy seemed to be capable of gratifying the expectations of the citizens. In relative terms, a high degree of literacy existed;

22. The discussion that follows draws upon some of the concepts advanced by La-Palombara and Weiner in *Political Parties and Political Development*, 399-435. Similar concepts have been perceptively applied to an analysis of American party development by William N. Chambers in an extremely important essay in the same volume, "Parties and Nation Building in America," 79-106. For a contrasting view, which minimizes the effects of parties as independent variables, see Morton Grodzins's essay, "Political Parties and the Crisis of Succession in the United States: The Case of 1800," in the same volume, 303-27. I would suggest that the election of 1824 is an even better illustration of Grodzins's point.

and a flourishing, free press sustained political communication. Not least of all, if we accept the persuasive formulation of Louis Hartz concerning the flowering of a liberal tradition in America, there was consensual agreement on basic national values.[23]

The new American republic was designed as a federal republic, however, in recognition of the sovereign authority held by the several states, and the powers assigned to the national government were explicitly limited. This intricate, carefully adjusted political system was decidedly experimental, and by its very nature it placed restraints on national integration and even permitted the possibility of contests over legitimacy between state and national authorities. Given the complex of factors that conditioned the formation of the national union, we can appreciate the virtues of these arrangements, but they were to occasion very special problems for American party systems. These problems were to become especially formidable as the nation expanded in size and—most ominously —as sectional interests diverged and took precedence over other cleavages.

In gross terms I would take the view that the first and second American party systems were not confronted with serious crises of participation, nor with major crises of distribution. Neither were they required to meet challenges to the legitimacy of the constitutional regime, unless we choose to regard the menace of secession as a threat to legitimacy rather than to national integration. The two areas in which the party systems might be expected to contribute to political development were in advancing national integration and in managing conflicts.

We know, of course, that internal conflicts were not successfully managed in the 1850's and that the nation disintegrated in 1860-61, after having somewhat fortuitously averted a similar crisis in 1814. Now two possible courses of argument are open to us. We might adduce evidence to sustain the position that the first two party systems, despite their defects, held the nation together and resolved a number of conflicts over a period of sixty years, only to fail when confronted by irreconcilable cleavages. Or we might defend the position that the party systems, perhaps because of the difficulties inherent in the federal system, were ill-adapted to resolving conflicts that were sectional in character and that in 1814 and again in 1860 they were malintegrative in their effects.

Whichever position seems to us most plausible, one conclusion is inescapable: the early American party systems are no less notable for their

23. Louis Hartz, *The Liberal Tradition in America* (New York, 1955).

failures than for their successes. We may properly hail the ingenuity of the political architects who constructed the first modern party system in history, but we must record that that party system fell victim to a kind of entropy after 1815. We can marvel at the comprehensiveness and popularity of the second party system, and at the incredible technical proficiency of its professional corps of managers, but that system collapsed within a generation. And as the third party system began to form, the nation divided. Whatever the contributions of the party systems to American political development, they were not after all adequate to avert the disaster of civil war.

V | Eric L. McKitrick

COLUMBIA UNIVERSITY

Party Politics and

the Union and Confederate War Efforts

The Civil War has always lent itself naturally and logically to the comparative method. Comparing the resources of the Union and the Confederacy in everything conceivable—manpower, brainpower, firepower—has been highly productive in helping us to understand the process whereby the North ultimately overwhelmed the South. But it is in the realm of government, where the process of historical comparison normally begins, that the results are on the whole least conclusive and least satisfying. The two sets of institutions exhibit a series of uncanny similarities. We may think we can detect in the Southern body politic a certain pallor, a lack of muscle tone that is in some contrast to the apparent resiliency of the North. But this is only a suspicion. We have not been very certain about how to get at such a subjective matter as the health of a metaphorical organism.

The Union and Confederate governments, as set down on paper, were almost identical. The Confederacy deliberately adopted the federal Constitution with very few changes, some of which might have been improvements had they been carried fully into effect. Cabinet members might sit in Congress, though few did; the executive had an itemized veto on appropriation bills, though it was a power he did not use; and bills for departmental appropriations had to be initiated with an estimate from the department concerned. The general welfare clause was dropped, but the "necessary and proper" clause—so useful for expanding national power—was kept. The states were "sovereign" but had no power to make treaties, which meant that they were in fact not sovereign. Nothing was said about the right of secession, and it was not as though no one had thought of it. The relations of the states to the central government would, in the course

117

of things, reveal some crucial differences, but it is hard to find much evidence for this in the organic law of the two governments. A trend toward centralized power was perfectly possible within either of the two constitutions, and it could proceed just as far under the one as under the other.[1] The co-ordinate branches of government were constitutionally the same, though in the election and term of office of the executive there were certain differences. As for the judiciary, the Confederacy too was to have had a Supreme Court, though it never actually got around to establishing one. In the Confederacy judicial review (with generous citations from *The Federalist,* as well as from the opinions of Marshall and Story) occurred in the states. How much difference this made may be debated, though historians have not in general made an issue of it. In any case, of the three branches of government on either side, the judiciary seems to have made the least impact on the waging of war. With regard to the two Congresses, the practices and procedures were strikingly similar. It might be said that even their membership overlapped, since a number of men had served in both.[2]

The same executive departments were established in both governments, and with one exception the positions in each president's cabinet were the same. There has been some debate on the competence of the men who filled those positions. It is generally supposed that Lincoln's cabinet was the "better" one, though there is little clear agreement as to the reasons. One authority emphasizes the over-all deficiencies of the Confederate cabinet; another calls attention to its many merits. It is at least clear that both cabinets contained a mixed lot. Each had its good administrators, and on both sides there was incompetence. Leroy Pope Walker may have made a very poor Secretary of War, but the Union had to fight the first nine months of the war with Simon Cameron. Comparisons on this level,

1. The Confererate constitution may be found in James D. Richardson (ed.), *A Compilation of the Messages and Papers of the Confederacy, Including the Diplomatic Correspondence, 1861-1865* (Nashville, 1906), I, 37-54; or in *War of the Rebellion: A Compilation of the Official Records of the Union and Confederate Armies* (Washington, 1880-1901), G.P.O. 4 Ser., I, 136-47. See also Albert N. Fitts, "The Confederate Convention: The Constitutional Debate," *Alabama Review,* II (1949), 189-210.

2. Sidney D. Brummer, "The Judicial Interpretation of the Confederate Constitution," in James W. Garner (ed.), *Studies in Southern History and Politics Inscribed to William Archibald Dunning* (New York, 1914), 105-33; J. G. deR. Hamilton, "The State Courts and the Confederate Constitution," *Journal of Southern History,* IV (1938), 425-8; William M. Robinson., Jr., *Justice in Grey: A History of the Judicial System of the Confederate States of America* (Cambridge, Mass., 1941), xix-xxi, 39-69; Wilfred Buck Yearns, *The Confederate Congress* (Athens, 1960), esp. 236-44.

in short, are certainly enlightening, but they take one just so far.[3] So much has been said about executive leadership that this almost constitutes a separate literature. It seems apparent that the leadership of Abraham Lincoln was superior to that of Jefferson Davis, though the fact of Northern victory is naturally quite helpful in making the case. Lincoln was "flexible," Davis "rigid." And yet conditions may have been such, above and beyond the two men's personal characteristics, as to make Lincoln's flexibility and Davis's rigidity unavoidable political responses to the requirements of war as experienced in their respective sections.[4]

But what were those conditions? What was the nature of the political setting, beyond the actual structure of government, within which the two leaders had to operate? Was it—a subject that has never been systematically investigated—affected by the presence or absence of political parties?

II

All such comparisons as those just surveyed, enlightening as they are, must be made within certain limits. Attention is always in some way directed to the formal structure of government and to the individuals occupying the formal positions established by that structure. But comparing these formal arrangements, even in the broadest and most extended way, still does not bring us a very clear idea of why the North won and where it drew the necessary energy for sustaining a long drawn out war effort. At this point one normally retreats to the "concrete realities" of military power and material resources, the logic of which has a reassuring finality. Military and economic organization—"in the last analysis," as we say—is what tells.

Still there may be, as I think, much more to be said for the way in which political organization, in and of itself, affected the respective war efforts. And if so, it is most likely to be found by moving to another level altogether: by turning from the formal to the informal functions of pol-

3. There was no Interior Department in the Confederate government. For differing appraisals of the Confederate cabinet, cf. Burton J. Hendrick, *Statesmen of the Lost Cause: Jefferson Davis and his Cabinet* (Boston, 1939); and Rembert W. Patrick, *Jefferson Davis and his Cabinet* (Baton Rouge, La., 1944). See also Hendrick, *Lincoln's War Cabinet* (Boston, 1946); and Clarence E. Macartney, *Lincoln and his Cabinet* (New York, 1931).

4. See e.g. Allan Nevins, *The Statesmanship of the Civil War* (New York, 1953); and David M. Potter, "Jefferson Davis and the Political Factors in Confederate Defeat," in David Donald (ed.), *Why the North Won the Civil War* (Baton Rouge, La., 1960), 91-114.

itics, from its official to its unofficial apparatus, from the explicit formulations to the implicit understandings. For at least a generation prior to the Civil War, the most salient unofficial structure in American public life was its system of political parties. No formal provision was ever made for such a system. Yet in this system of parties may be found historically the chief agency for mobilizing and sustaining energy in American government. It thus seems reasonable to consider how, as a matter of actual practice, the energies of government may have been affected by the workings of this unofficial system in waging the American Civil War.

In an essay published in 1960, David Potter suggested "the possibility that the Confederacy may have suffered real and direct damage from the fact that its political organization lacked a two-party system."[5] This, with its implications, constitutes in my opinion the most original single idea to emerge from the mass of writing that has been done on the Civil War in many years. It implicitly challenges two of our most formidable and consistently held assumptions regarding political life of the time, assumptions which until recently have gone unquestioned. One is that Lincoln's leadership of the Union war effort was severely and dangerously hampered by political partisanship——that is, by obstructions put in his path by Democrats on the one hand and, on the other, by extremists within his own Republican party. The other assumption is that Davis and the Confederate government, by deliberately setting aside partisanship, avoided this difficulty. There were no parties in the Confederacy, and thus the South, in this respect at least, had the advantage.

In order to show these notions as fallacies, following Potter's cue, it should not be necessary to claim that the South "ought" to have encouraged the establishment of a party system. Even had such a system been seen as a positive value—which it was not, either North or South—there was probably a variety of reasons why an effort of that sort on the eve of war would have been out of the question. Such things must in any case grow naturally or they do not grow at all. Indeed it might better be wondered why the South did not put itself in an avowedly revolutionary posture and run its government as a kind of Committee of Public Safety, a procedure which could have given it maximum maneuverability for achieving what was in fact a set of revolutionary objectives. And yet this course was in reality even less thinkable; the mentality needed for it simply did not exist. The Confederates again and again insisted that they

5. Ibid. 113.

were not in rebellion, that it was not a civil war, that they were not truly engaged in a revolution. The South's ideological strategy was to declare, in effect, to the people of the United States: our constitutional title to exist is legally purer than yours. We are in fact the "true" United States; we are more faithful than you to the spirit of the Founders; it is you, not we, who have departed from it; it is you who are the rebels.[6] The Confederates, in short, put an unusual amount of effort simply into behaving as a fully constituted nation, and they seemed to feel an almost obsessive need to clothe their government with as many of the symbols and minutiae of legitimacy as they could. They imagined themselves engaged not nearly so much in a revolutionary struggle for liberation as in a fully mounted war between two sovereign powers.

It is only necessary, then, to take the Confederates for the time being on their own terms: as a government possessing all the formal incidents of constitutional legitimacy, but lacking at least one of the informal ones —a system of political parties—possessed by their opponents. This discrepancy, it is here suggested, has much to tell us about the vigor of the respective war efforts. It is further suggested that the persistence of party contention in the North all through the war was on the whole salutary for Lincoln's government and the Union cause. The war was, of course, in addition to all else, one long political headache, tying up much of the executive's valuable time and attention. Obstacles of opposition were bound up again and again with the most annoying kind of partisan politics. Nobody at the time, so far as is known, ever explicitly thanked the Almighty for parties. But by the same token, it was partisan politics that provided the very framework within which these same obstacles could be contained and overcome. To Jefferson Davis's government such a framework was not available. Everything, to be sure, has its price; there were functions and dysfunctions. But it may well be that on balance the functions outweighed the dysfunctions, and that the price was worth paying.

III

The functions of party in the formation of a government seem to involve, on the face of it, something fairly direct and straightforward. But the process has its subtleties, which become apparent where there are

6. Thomas J. Pressly, *Americans Interpret their Civil War* (New York, 1965), 87-98.

two governments being formed at the same time, under comparable circumstances and by men sharing many of the same political traditions, but where, in one of the cases, the principle of party is not a factor.

The rapid growth of the Republican party in the brief span of five or six years prior to 1860 had generated certain by-products. It had certainly dissipated the malaise of the early 1850's in which the expanding anti-slavery and free-soil sentiment of the North had been, for a time, without any clear vehicle for political organization. There were, moreover, established public men who had come to be identified with this sentiment, and whose careers could no longer be promoted without stultification amid the dissolution of the Whig party and the conservatism of the regular Democrats. Such men, of whom William H. Seward and Salmon P. Chase were conspicuous examples, now found in the Republican party a welcome field for their talents and leadership. In addition, the very effort required in organizing the new party in state after state brought to the fore hundreds of new men within the same short space of time. The very marching clubs which sprang up everywhere—the so-called "Wide Awakes"—amounted to much more than a freakish social phenomenon. They represented the "progressive" element of the community. That the Republicans by 1860 had elected governors in every Northern state, to say nothing of capturing the national government, is evidence of a vitality going far beyond the ordinary. The period was one of mounting public crisis; what has been less noticed is that precisely at this time public life began to present an expanding field for younger men of talent, ambition, and energy.[7]

By the time the Confederacy was being established, politics was not attracting the South's best men to anywhere near this degree. An obvious immediate reason, of course, was that the war crisis naturally brought many of the Southern elite into the army, and many writers have commented on this. But antecedent factors were more pervasive. The chief mechanism for managing political talent and bringing it forward—party organizations—had in effect disintegrated in the South by the time the war began. The organizational stability of both the Whig and Democratic

7. There is a hint of this, though little more, in Andrew W. Crandall, *The Early History of the Republican Party* (Boston, 1930), 285-6. Much more work needs to be done on the manner in which changes in the organization of parties affected careers in the 1850's. For a work of great insight and distinction, dealing with a single individual in these terms, see Don E. Fehrenbacher, *Prelude to Greatness: Lincoln in the 1850's* (New York, 1962).

parties at local and state levels all over the country, ever since the emergence of such organizations in the 1830's, had depended on their maintaining some sort of national orientation and national interests. In the South, the growth of a sectional, state-centered ideology in defense of slavery had steadily undermined such interests, and with them, whatever stability such organizations had once had. Thus the collapse in the South of the existing parties—the Whigs in the early 1850's and the Democrats in 1860—had created a setting in which the only real political issue came down to that of whether a man did or did not support secession. "Opposition" implied disloyalty, unless it could be based on state particularism —which was exactly the form opposition would in fact take. There was thus no national (that is, all-Confederate) basis on which a system of parties might be re-fashioned. Meanwhile those organizations which do so much to define political skill and political success, and to measure the satisfactions of politics for all from the humble to the high, had in most respects simply vanished.[8]

How, then, would this affect the standards—of duty and commitment, as well as ability—to be used in the forming of a government?

The vice-presidency might be taken as a minor, though interesting example. The significance of Hannibal Hamlin has never inspired the historian; as with many a Vice-President of the nineteenth century, Hamlin does not even have a modern biographer. Yet in 1860 the man played a role whose specifications were clearly understood by all, especially by those most responsible for placing him in it. He represented an interest within the Republican party which might "balance" a national ticket, broaden its support, and thus help it to win an election. He had already served in Congress as a Democratic representative and senator, and he had been one of the chief organizers of the Republican party in the state of Maine. He could speak for the antislavery element of New England, having strong sympathies with abolition. As Vice-President, Hamlin

8. For comments on the quality of political leadership in the Confederacy, see Hendrick, *Statesmen of the Lost Cause*, 9-11; E. Merton Coulter, *The Confederate States of America, 1861-1865* (Baton Rouge, La., 1950), 134-48; Clement Eaton, *A History of the Southern Confederacy* (New York, 1954), 54-60; and Nevins, *Statesmanship of the Civil War*, 24-56. For the process whereby the coercions of party allegiance upon Southern leaders broke down in the 1850's, see Roy F. Nichols, *The Disruption of American Democracy* (New York, 1948). The indispensability of national connections in maintaining the stability and continuity of local party organizations over time has been very convincingly shown in Richard P. McCormick, *The Second American Party System: Party Formation in the Jacksonian Era* (Chapel Hill, 1966).

hardly made a ripple on the surface of events, which is to say he played with unassuming perfection the role marked out for him. His one chance for fame—the presidency itself, which would have fallen to him upon Lincoln's death—was snatched away in 1864 when it was decided that the ticket of that year might be better balanced, in yet a different manner, by someone else, Andrew Johnson, a former Democrat from Tennessee. But in certain small ways Hamlin made himself useful from the first—for example, in the diplomacy of cabinet-making, in the choosing of officers for Negro regiments, and in testing the weather on emancipation. Despite his disappointment, he made no complaint at being superseded in 1864, supported the new ticket, and was eventually compensated in good party fashion with the Collectorship of Boston.[9]

Had any such standards of choice governed the Confederate delegates at Montgomery, the last man they would have picked as Vice-President would have been the distinguished Alexander Stephens. The principal criterion in this case seems to have been the delegates' feeling that something was needed to placate the state of Georgia for having failed to elect a Georgian as President. Yet Stephens had strongly opposed secession, did not really believe in the Confederacy and hardly even pretended to, and had no inclination whatever to stay in Richmond and preside over the Confederate Senate. He spent most of his time at home in Georgia grumbling against his own government and actually attacking it in venomous letters and speeches for usurping the rights of citizens. Few men did more to undermine Davis's administration than his own Vice-President. Perhaps Stephens's one positive act, if such it may be called, was going to meet Lincoln on an unsuccessful peace mission. Davis himself once offered to resign, his one condition being the resignation of Alexander Stephens.[10]

The choice in the one case had been a party matter; in the other, it had been made on a regional, "popular-front" basis. Hamlin's career was tied to the Republican party, and therefore to the success of the Lincoln administration; Stephens had been placed in the Confederate government mainly as a gesture toward the state of Georgia and to the former members of a political party (the Whigs) that no longer existed. He and his friends thus had no direct vested interest in the day-to-day success of the Davis administration.

9. Charles Eugene Hamlin, *The Life and Times of Hannibal Hamlin* (Boston, 1899), 301ff., 331-51, 368-75, 424-35, 490, 500-503.
10. James Z. Rabun, "Alexander H. Stephens and Jefferson Davis," *American Historical Review*, LVIII (1953), 290-321; Dunbar Rowland (ed.), *Jefferson Davis, Constitutionalist: His Letters, Papers and Speeches* (Jackson, Miss., 1923), VIII, 213.

How the unspoken assumptions of party politics might or might not govern men's behavior may be illustrated by another pair of cases, this time involving the runners-up for the presidency—the men who did not quite make it. When the supporters of William H. Seward arrived in Chicago for the Republican convention of 1860, they had every reason to be confident that their man, the new party's most prominent national figure, would receive the nomination. The most astute correspondents reported that Seward's candidacy was irresistible, and he was clearly preferred by a majority of the delegates. Seward led on the first two ballots, though he gained little ground on the second, and was overtaken on the third by the forces of Abraham Lincoln. Lincoln's views on the leading issues may in fact have been no less positive than Seward's, but they, like Lincoln himself, had been considerably less exposed to the public in the years just preceding; he thus represented a principle then known, in the idiom of politics, as "availability." He also had an extraordinarily energetic and well-disciplined Republican organization in the state of Illinois. As the result was announced, Thurlow Weed, Seward's manager and friend of over thirty years, sat and wept.[11]

The standards of party, as has been remarked more than once, generate a morality of their own. William H. Seward, with both his virtues and his foibles, and Weed with his, had been in some way governed by that morality ever since they had been young men together in the 1820's. Thurlow Weed could now act (if the thought does not seem ironically strained) as Seward's conscience, in case he needed one. "Whatever your ultimate purpose may be," he wrote to his heartbroken friend, "I cannot doubt that a prompt and cheerful acquiescence . . . is not only wise, but a duty." Seward knew his cue. "I wish that I was sure that your sense of the disappointment is as light as my own," he replied. "It ought to be equally so, for we have been equally thoughtful and zealous, for friends, party, and country. . . ."[12] Weed, during the months that followed, made two trips to Springfield. No bargains were made, but Weed and Lincoln got on remarkably well, each recognizing in the other a man of ability, and each no doubt understanding that, owing to a certain shared fund of experience, communication did not always need to be on an absolutely explicit level. Communication on whatever level was made meaningful—indeed,

11. Glyndon G. Van Deusen, *Thurlow Weed: Wizard of the Lobby* (Boston, 1947), 231-54.

12. Ibid. 255; Seward to Weed, May 18, 1861, in Frederick W. Seward, *Seward at Washington, as Senator and Secretary of State: A Memoir of his Life, with Selections from his Letters, 1846-1861* (New York, 1891), 453.

possible—by what Weed represented, a party organization in New York state that already counted for a great deal in the way of power, influence, and a set of clear loyalties. William H. Seward entered the campaign wholeheartedly, making a number of very strong speeches for Lincoln all around the country. Rumors reached him that Lincoln was planning to invite him to become Secretary of State, and the evidence indicates that there was, for a time, much doubt in Seward's mind as to whether he really wanted it. Yet the offer was duly made, and Seward accepted. Throughout the entire war, whatever may have been his personal quirks, Seward's loyalty to the party, to the national cause, and to the administration were never in doubt.[13]

In the Confederacy, Seward's counterpart was Robert Toombs. One of the ablest Southerners of his time, Toombs had served in Congress since 1844 as a Whig from the state of Georgia, first in the House and later in the Senate. He was genial and gregarious, a man of much practical knowledge, and a great debater and parliamentarian whose performances combined gusto, brilliance, and flourish. As a statesman and defender of Southern rights in the 1850's he had been ardent but certainly not foolish. Having once opposed the Mexican War, supported the Compromise of 1850, and defended the Union, he was carried by the events of that decade to the point where he could with perfect consistency stalk out of the Senate in January 1861, never to return, furiously denouncing Black Republicanism for all time: "Treason; bah!"[14] He was, in short, rather an ideal Southerner and knew it, a man of both éclat and high intelligence, widely popular, and lionized by his friends. It has been said that when the delegates to the Confederate convention arrived in Montgomery in February 1861, the first choice of most of them for the presidency was Robert Toombs. He himself ached to be President, and would no doubt have made a good one, perhaps better than the man actually elected. Of that, too, he seems to have been convinced. The process by which he was passed over in favor of Davis was in certain ways not comparable to that whereby William H. Seward had lost out to Lincoln a few months before. It was not a "political" process, in the sense that it would have been with a party system, nor was there any desire that it should be. There was no trading in the usual sense, and virtually none of the sort of communica-

13. Hendrick, *Lincoln's War Cabinet*, 87-123.
14. Ulrich B. Phillips, *The Life of Robert Toombs* (New York, 1913), *passim.* For Toombs's last speech in the Senate, see *Congressional Globe*, 36th Cong., 2nd sess., 267-71.

tion between delegations that characterizes a real nominating convention, because the group was obsessed with the notion that the choice should appear spontaneous and unanimous. As a result it was sufficiently haphazard that we are still not certain, except in a general way, how it was arrived at. Five of the six delegations present—each state with but one vote—apparently favored Toombs, but someone seems to have carried the untrue rumor that Georgia itself planned to present as its candidate not Toombs but Howell Cobb, the former Speaker of the House, Governor, and Secretary of the Treasury in Buchanan's cabinet. Under this misapprehension (Cobb being somewhat controversial) the other delegations in their separate conferences switched to Davis, a development of which the Georgians only learned through a messenger sent around at the last minute. The crestfallen Georgians thereupon felt they had no choice but to follow suit, not discovering the reason for the change until after the ballot was taken. (Cobb's brother, it appeared, had been at the bottom of this.) So goes, at any rate, one story of Jefferson Davis's "unanimous" election as President of the Confederacy.[15]

Toombs never swallowed his bitterness. He was duly offered the Secretaryship of State, which he accepted grudgingly. But he never tried to make anything of the office or to invest it with any distinction. Indeed, he held it rather in contempt, declaring on one occasion that he "carried the State department in his hat." He resigned after a few months for a brigadier's commission in the army, to the despair of his own brother, who, knowing Toombs had no military talents whatever, vainly implored Alexander Stephens to talk him out of it. As a warrior he was hardly a success. (Once, while charging about on his horse, he was dumped, "purple with

15. This is the version given by Toombs's biographer (see Phillips, *Life*, 222-6), following that of Alexander Stephens, though it is not the only one. For others, see F. M. Gilmer, "Memoir concerning organization of the Confederate Government, election of President Davis, &c, &c," in Rowland (ed.), *Davis*, VIII, 462-3; Ralph Richardson, "The Choice of Jefferson Davis as Confederate President," *Journal of Mississippi History*, XVII (1955), 161-76; and Albert N. Fitts, "The Confederate Convention: The Provisional Constitution," *Alabama Review*, II (1949), 83-101. The very mystery which still hangs over the proceedings illustrates the point of their "nonpolitical," or non-party, character. The Confederates were afraid of the more-or-less open bargaining and maneuvering that a convention would entail, because it might generate doubts as to their unity, and as a result the normal channels of communication through which political leaders learn the specific needs, interests, and ambitions of their supporters (and opponents) were blocked. Thus Davis had no clear sense of the combinations that had put him in power and that, if properly managed, might enable him to govern effectively. The Republican convention, on the other hand, gave Lincoln a very precise measure of the various interests that made up the Republican coalition.

rage," before an aghast party of ladies.) Before quitting the army in disgust at not being promoted to major general, Toombs was elected by his legislature to the Confederate Senate. Since the election was not nearly unanimous, and thus not the mandate he wanted for opposing the administration, he refused to go. His hatred of Davis, whose "incapacity" he called "lamentable" and whom he characterized as "that scoundrel," grew ever hotter with the passing of time. None of the once-great "Georgia Triumvirate"—Stephens, Toombs, and Cobb—ever came close to lending his immense talents and prestige to the success of the Confederate government. And one of Alexander Stephens's closest allies, in his unrelenting warfare upon the administration, was Robert Toombs. Of his President, Toombs declared, "I shall be justified in any extremity to which the public interest would allow me to go in hostility to his illegal and unconstitutional course." In the absence of party platforms and party morality, there could be as many separate versions of "the public interest" as there were contentious men who thought themselves qualified to say what it was. By the same token, there were far fewer checks on purely "personal" politics.[16]

A further contrast between the Federal and Confederate governments, looking now at their formation from still another viewpoint, might consist in the standards whereby the cabinets as a whole were organized. For Davis, the chief concern was that each state had to be represented. For Lincoln also, geography counted as a strong consideration; but for him, both merit and geography as factors in choice had to operate within the limits of another criterion, which gave the problem a certain focus and required a certain precision. His cabinet had to be primarily a party alliance, which was its true functioning character, and its character as a coalition of state interests was thus quite secondary. He wanted every shade of commitment within the party, from border-state conservative to antislavery radical—and the influence they commanded—represented in his cabinet and, as it were, under his eye. A further nicety was that, owing to the comparative newness of the party, considerations of present and future support required that a man's antecedents also be weighed: there

16. Patrick, *Davis and his Cabinet*, 78-90; Ulrich B. Phillips (ed.), *The Correspondence of Robert Toombs, Alexander H. Stephens, and Howell Cobb* (Washington, 1913), 573, 592, 595, 608, 611, 619, 630, 638-9. The story about Toombs and his horse is in Ben Ames Williams (ed.), Mary B. Chesnut, *A Diary from Dixie* (Boston, 1949), 99. The history of political life in eighteenth-century England is an endless chronicle of this "personal politics" aspect of a pre-party or non-party situation.

should be some balance between former Whigs and former Democrats.[17] On the other hand, Davis had no choice but to follow the principle of state representation, and had he not done so he would undoubtedly have suffered even more general dissension and public attacks on his cabinet than he did. But judging both from this and from the cabinet's own instability, the political symbolism of a coalition of states, just in itself, as a focus for loyalty was somehow abstract, lacking in sharpness, and not very compelling. In the Union cabinet such men as Seward, Chase, Gideon Welles, Edward Bates, and Montgomery Blair represented the most powerful elements that made up the party alliance, which was exactly how they were seen both in the party councils and in the country at large. It was understood that the state of the cabinet reflected the state of the party. Thus the chronic tug-of-war which ensued over the relative standing of Seward, Chase, and Blair should be read not primarily as a matter of individuals and their capacities, as such cases would tend to be in the Confederacy. The struggle was over the party influence those individuals represented in the administration, and how, or whether, the balance ought to be altered. Correspondingly, the changes Lincoln made, as well as the ones he refused to make, were on the whole governed not by the official's performance of his duties but by what the result would reflect in the way of party unity. Except in the case of Simon Cameron, which involved both incompetence and corruption, Lincoln's major moves in the management of his cabinet were made for studied party reasons.

The Seward-Chase crisis in the winter of 1862-63 furnishes an outstanding example. During this time Seward became the target of many Republican senators, who had been persuaded by stories that his influence was preventing a sufficiently vigorous war policy and causing dissension within the cabinet. Chase had done much to encourage these rumors. A delegation of senators met with Lincoln to demand that he reorganize the cabinet in order to end the dissension. Sizing this up, Lincoln perceived that what they really wanted was to force Seward's resignation and have the cabinet reconstituted with Chase as a sort of prime minister; he also knew that Seward's resignation would split the party. He thereupon executed what amounted to a virtuoso maneuver to keep the cabinet intact. Seward had already offered his resignation. The President invited the delegation to come back the next evening, and when they arrived the entire cabinet, except for Seward, was waiting for them. In the

17. Hendrick, *Lincoln's War Cabinet*, 3-123.

presence of all, Lincoln blandly asserted that full harmony prevailed and asked Chase whether in his opinion the rumors of dissension were true. Chase was trapped between the choice of supporting the senators' claims and thus showing himself as a talebearer, or of upholding the President —which he shamefacedly did—and losing prestige with the senators. Next day the smarting Chase brought in his resignation—to Lincoln's delight, since that was the way he had planned it—and the President, with both resignations now in his pocket, knew that if the senators still demanded Seward's dismissal they would lose Chase too. He refused to accept either one. "If I had yielded to that storm and dismissed Seward," he later remarked with something of a connoisseur's relish, "the thing would all have slumped over one way, and we would have been left with a scanty handful of supporters. When Chase gave in his resignation I saw that the game was in my hands. . . ."[18] Lincoln's patience with Chase lasted through five resignations, which came to be offered quite regularly. But by 1864 the secretary's activities and ambitions had created a threat to Lincoln's own renomination, which was quite another matter. By keeping him in the cabinet until the nomination was secure, the President inhibited the scope of Chase's mischief and at the same time retained the use of his talents and influence, but as soon as that danger was over he decided that he had had enough. Chase's sixth offer to resign, over a matter of patronage, was happily accepted, much to Chase's own consternation. Chase's usefulness had been calculated with some nicety just to the point of diminishing returns. He was later made Chief Justice of the Supreme Court, but this was not until after the election, and after he had done his duty in the campaign.[19]

And yet Chase's removal created a new kind of party imbalance which would hardly solve itself, since Chase's bitterest enemies, the conservative followers of Postmaster-General Montgomery Blair, took this as a triumphant vindication of themselves. The fact was that Blair's influence in the party at large had been steadily diminishing, and a radical movement for Blair's head thereupon became, in Lincoln's judgment, too dangerous to resist. Though both the personal and official relations between the two had always been characterized by great warmth, Lincoln judiciously decided to cut Blair adrift in September 1864. (Jefferson Davis, as many instances show, would never have played that sort of trick on a

18. John G. Nicolay and John Hay, *Abraham Lincoln: A History* (New York, 1890), VI, 263-71.
19. Harry J. Carman and Reinhard Luthin, *Lincoln and the Patronage* (New York, 1943), 265-7.

loyal subordinate.) Yet this did not prevent Blair from working vigorously for the President's re-election. He was not prepared to sacrifice his claim on the party, which he would have done had he refused to campaign, nor was he willing to risk a Democratic victory.[20]

There were relatively few changes in Lincoln's cabinet, and they were all made under circumstances firmly controlled by Lincoln himself. The historian of Jefferson Davis's cabinet is unable to account satisfactorily for its lack of stability, except to chronicle a long series of resignations, most of them under fire. (There were six secretaries of war, five attorneys-general, and four secretaries of state.) The legislative branch of government has no constitutional right to interfere in the business of the President's cabinet, and in this light Lincoln would have been quite justified in refusing to deal with the senatorial delegation that challenged him on Seward. But constitutional formality was only one of the guidelines. These men confronted him in at least two capacities, as senators and as leaders of the party, and in their latter capacity, as Lincoln well knew, they could not safely be turned away. The resulting adjustment, though exhausting and worrisome, brought rich dividends in the repair of morale. Davis was not required to adjust to any such principle. He too was harassed by informal groups of legislators on similar missions. In February 1865, with the Confederacy rapidly deteriorating, the legislative delegation of Virginia urged him to make certain changes in his cabinet. He thought it proper to declare, as he had on other occasions: "The relations between the President and the Heads of the Executive Departments are . . . of the closest and most intimate character . . . and it is not a Constitutional function of the Legislative Department to interfere with these relations. . . ."[21] Lincoln's cabinet represented an ever-uneasy alliance, which is why it required so much of his attention. But in the very process of managing it he was, in effect, at the same time managing the party and fashioning it into a powerful instrument for waging war. In reference to that cabinet, it is not too much to say that the choice of its members, its stability, its management, and the major changes made in it, are all to be understood largely with reference to a single principle, the exigencies of party politics.

The whole corps of federal officeholders may be understood in much

20. Ibid. 273-7.
21. Patrick, *Davis and his Cabinet*, 60-76 *et passim;* Rowland (ed.), *Davis*, VI, 459. Having to deal with *ad hoc* congressional committees and caucus groups seems to have been a feature of executive routine on both sides. Yet it is probably safe to generalize that most such groups that waited on Lincoln were constituted on a party basis, whereas those Davis faced tended to speak for state interests.

the same light. We have no full study of Jefferson Davis's patronage policies, which is probably symptomatic; there may never be much of a basis
for generalizing about them. But there certainly was one striking, self-
evident difference between Lincoln's and his, which was clarity of standards. Davis wanted merit, zeal, and loyalty. (As one writer puts it, he
"favored civil service reform.") Lincoln also, naturally, wanted merit, zeal,
and loyalty. But he also had some very straightforward criteria for determining in a hurry what those qualities actually meant and how they
were to be found. The appointee had to be a Republican—which was at
least helpful in narrowing a swarming field by roughly half—and the most
dependable general standard for assessing loyalty and zeal was services
to the party. It was within this category that he made his choices on
"merit." The rules of procedure were also quite precise. For example:

> The appointments of postmasters, with salaries less than $1000 per
> annum, will be made upon the recommendations of the [Republican]
> members of Congress in the different districts. Applications addressed
> to them will receive attention earlier than if sent to the Department,
> and save much delay and trouble.

Lincoln was, moreover, very meticulous about "senatorial courtesy."[22]

Though Davis, as might naturally be supposed, accepted the recom-
mendations of others, he does not seem to have felt bound by any given
rule in acting upon them. For example, by insisting on having his own
way over the postmastership of Montgomery, Davis deeply alienated both
the senators from Alabama. Wrote Senator Clement Clay to the equally
outraged Senator Yancey: "He did not recognize the duty to respect the
wishes of the Senators and Representatives, even when the office was in
the town of a Senator and a Representative." And Davis loftily declared:
"I am not aware of the existence of any such usage. . . . I must add that
the Senate is no part of the *nominating* power, and that according, as I
do, the highest respect to the opinions of Senators when they recommend
applicants, I decline to yield to any dictation from them on the subject of
nominations."[23]

Patronage is a care and a worry; it is also a cherished prerogative, with

22. Patrick, *Davis and his Cabinet,* 63; Carman and Luthin, *Lincoln and the
Patronage,* 70-71, 111-12.
23. Harrison A. Trexler, "Jefferson Davis and the Confederate Patronage," *South
Atlantic Quarterly,* XXVIII (1929), 45-58; John W. DuBose, *The Life and Times of
William Lowndes Yancey* (New York, 1892, 1942), II, 743; Rowland (ed.), *Davis,*
V, 234, 529.

gratifications for those who give as well as those who receive. They are all part of the same sensitive network. The responsiveness and *esprit* of such a network thus require that both the giving and the receiving be widely shared, and on some understood basis. We have no way of measuring the energy with which the men who made up these two patronage systems supported their respective administrations and worked to carry out their purposes. But we do know that one administration had an intricate set of standards for appraising energy and rewarding it—in addition always, of course, to standards of patriotism—which was not available to the other.

IV

The field of comparison in which contrasts between the two governments are perhaps most grossly striking is that of state-federal relations. In both cases there was a set of natural fault-lines, inherent in a federal structure, between the state and national governments. In the Confederacy, these cracks opened ever more widely as the war went on. Toward the end, indeed, some states were in a condition of virtual rebellion against the Confederate government. In the North, the very opposite occurred. The states and the federal government came to be bound more and more closely in the course of the four years, such that by the end of that time the profoundest change had been effected in the character of their relations. In the course of things, moreover, the people themselves would come to be more closely bound to their national government. But the mechanisms are by no means self-evident. It cannot be taken for granted that in the nature of things such a process was bound to occur.

For the Confederacy, one very good way to tell this story is in terms of states' rights. The late Frank Owsley made a seminal contribution to historical thought on just these lines when he published his *State Rights in the Confederacy* over forty years ago. With a number of impressive examples, Owsley asserted that it was the mystique of state sovereignty, the inability of the South to overcome the states' rights mentality in order to operate as a nation, that ultimately did in the Confederacy. Most subsequent writers, including the present one, agree that the argument is essentially sound. For comparative purposes, however, something more is required. There was, after all, considerable states' rights sentiment in the North as well. Yet there, states' rights pressure came to be counterbalanced over time by other pressures. What kind? What was the process? How did it work?

There are two areas in which this may be observed most aptly. One is that of control and recruitment of troops; the other, of dealing with disaffection and disloyalty.

For the Confederacy, the great problem in raising and organizing armies was far less a matter of insufficient manpower than it was of divided authority. The various efforts of the Confederate government to get full access to and control over military manpower in the states were successfully obstructed throughout the war by the state governors. The patriotic ardor of the governors for mobilizing troops need not in itself be doubted. The perpetual question was rather how it ought to be managed and how troops were to be used; state resistance to Confederate policy always came down to one of two principles: local defense, or the dangers of a centralized military despotism. Referring to Confederate recruiting in his state, one of the most co-operative of the governors, John Milton of Florida, wrote angrily to Davis in December, 1861: "These troops have been raised by authority of the War Department in disrespect to State authority . . . and I do most solemnly protest, the tendency of the assumption and exercise of such power by the Confederate Government is to sap the very foundation of the rights of the States and . . . to [promote] consolidation."[24]

The organization of the army in the spring and summer of 1861 was held up by shortages not of men but of arms, substantial amounts of which were in possession of the state governments. They were held back partly for what were seen as local needs, and partly in pique at the War Department's receiving of volunteers raised without the intermediary of the governor. Efforts of the states to control the appointment of field officers led them either to hold back regiments until they were fully formed —instead of sending them forward by companies—or else by tendering "skeleton regiments" with a full complement of state-commissioned officers and only a few privates. Their insistence on controlling the clothing and supply of their own state troops in Confederate service led to consequences that were almost disastrous. Resources being not only unequal but at the very best limited, the maximum co-ordination of both purchasing and distribution was imperative. Yet as it was, Confederate purchasing agents had to engage everywhere in the most ruinous competition with

24. *Official Records*, 1 Ser., VI, 342.

agents from the states for sources of supply at home and abroad, while at the same time the output of state-controlled factories was kept consistently out of general reach. Governor Zebulon B. Vance of North Carolina actually boasted that, at the time of Robert E. Lee's surrender (of a tattered and starving army), he himself had huge stores of uniforms, blankets, cloth, leather, overcoats, and bacon in his state warehouses.[25]

Conscription was adopted in the Confederacy in April 1862, a full year before the same step was taken in the North. One of the objects was to reorganize the twelve-months' volunteers whose terms were then running out; the other was to get control of the aggregations of militia which had been built up during the previous year and held in the states for local defense. This latter purpose was never properly achieved. State guards were once again built up, the condition of whose discipline and training made them worthless for almost any purpose so long as they were withheld from general service; and conscription itself, especially after the Act of February 1864, was resisted by the governors in a variety of ways. The chief device was that of exemptions, wherein wide categories of persons were sweepingly redefined as "state officers."[26]

In all such respects, Governor Joseph E. Brown of Georgia stands as an almost incredible Confederate legend. Units of Georgia men who had volunteered directly for the Confederate service (rather than being mustered by the state) were forbidden by Brown in the spring of 1861 to take any arms, whether from state arsenals or even owned by themselves, beyond the borders of Georgia. He organized and fully equipped a brigade —though Confederate law would not allow the Secretary of War to accept such a unit—and then kept it idle during the first Manassas campaign because the War Department wanted him to send it by regiments and would not let him commission a brigadier for it. In order to keep eligible Georgians away from Confederate conscription officers, and his state militia out of Confederate service, he proceeded in 1864 to exempt as "indispensable state officers" a total of about 15,000 men, including everyone remotely connected with the state and county governments as well as factory and railroad employees and some 3000 newly commissioned "officers" of the state militia. When Sherman began his Atlanta campaign, Brown

---

25. Frank L. Owsley, *State Rights in the Confederacy* (Chicago, 1925), 7-24, 86-149; "Address Delivered by Governor Z. B. Vance, of North Carolina, Before the Southern Historical Society, at White Sulphur Springs, West Virginia, August 18, 1875," *Southern Historical Society Papers*, XIV (1886), 506-21.

26. Owsley, *State Rights*, 203-18.

raised 10,000 men for local defense and insisted on their being used as militia. He "loaned" them to General John B. Hood (subject to withdrawal at any time), but when it appeared that the War Department was about to requisition the whole force into general service, he declared that the "emergency" was over and sent them all home on thirty-day furlough to harvest their crops. This was a week after the fall of Atlanta, and at the very time Sherman was preparing for his march to the sea. Brown's endless quarrels with Davis and his attacks on the "tyranny" of the central government were grimly abetted and assisted throughout by the Stephens brothers and Robert Toombs. Indeed, one of the governor's most vicious messages to his legislature was virtually ghost-written by the Confederate Vice-President.[27]

In the North, the story of the recruitment and control of the army was, at least by comparison, relatively straightforward. The raising of troops was at the outset fully in the hands of the state governors, and so in a nominal sense it remained throughout. And yet by a series of steps the actual initiative tended to pass increasingly to the national government. By calling for three-year volunteer enlistments during the first month of hostilities and enlarging the regular army without the authority of law before the assembling of Congress, Lincoln took clear control of the national forces. Through most of the first year the recruiting activities of the governors proceeded with the utmost energy. The first major shift in initiative occurred after the failure of the Peninsular Campaign, when patriotic fervor began wearing thin and volunteers became increasingly harder to find. At this point Secretary Seward persuaded all the governors to unite in memorializing the President to call for 150,000 more volunteers, whereupon Lincoln promptly called for twice that many, together with 300,000 nine-months' militia. Both calls were more than met. Under the threat of a militia draft, the governors threw themselves with renewed zeal into a very aggressive campaign of recruiting. After the Emancipation Proclamation, the administration agreed to the enrolling of Negro troops. Aside from the raising of a few independent regiments, this recruiting was done directly by field commanders, entirely outside the control of any state government, and approximately 186,000 men were thus added to the national army. A further step was the adoption of conscription with the National Enrollment Act of March 1863, which gave the President full

27. Louise B. Hill, *Joseph E. Brown and the Confederacy* (Chapel Hill, 1939), 57-63, 89-96, 183-6.

power to raise and support armies without state assistance. The unpopular Act was not fully exploited, and conscription as such accounted for no more than about 6 per cent of the total Union forces. It was successfully used, however, from 1863 to the end of the war, as a device for filling deficiencies in state volunteer quotas and for encouraging the governors to see that such deficiencies did not occur. In the mobilization of military manpower the state governors on the whole performed their function with exceptional vigor, even while becoming—as one writer somewhat extravagantly puts it—"mere agents" of the national government.[28]

The energy of the Union government may be seen with even greater clarity in its actions against disaffection and disloyalty. Without any special legislation, Lincoln immediately assumed executive authority to suspend the writ of habeas corpus and make summary arrests in areas particularly endangered by disloyal activities; and in handling such cases the government made very little use of the courts. A blanket proclamation of September 24, 1862 (previous ones had designated specific localities), made "all persons discouraging volunteer enlistments, resisting militia drafts, or guilty of any disloyal practice . . . subject to martial law and liable to trial and punishment by Courts Martial or Military Commission," anywhere in the country and at any time "during the existing insurrection." Congress made some effort to define the President's powers in the Habeas Corpus Act of March 3, 1863, but whether the Act intended to grant these powers for the first time or to recognize powers he had exercised all along was not clear, and in any event executive policy and practice proceeded unaltered. For such activities as aiding desertion, circulating disloyal literature, bushwhacking, bridge-burning, forming and promoting disloyal secret societies, and so on, the State and War Departments with their network of provost-marshals and other agents made thousands of arrests throughout the war. The exact number will never be known. The chief voices of opposition to these policies came from the Democratic party; the chief supporters were the Republican governors, especially in the Midwest.[29]

28. William B. Hesseltine, *Lincoln and the War Governors* (New York, 1948), 274. On this subject in general, see Fred A. Shannon, *The Organization and Administration of the Union Army, 1861-1865,* 2 vols. (Cleveland, 1928).

29. Roy P. Basler (ed.), *The Collected Works of Abraham Lincoln* (New Brunswick, N.J., 1953), V, 436-7; James G. Randall, *Constitutional Problems Under Lincoln,* rev. ed. (Urbana, 1964), esp. chaps. 6-8. "The records of the Commissary General of Prisoners were found to contain the names of 13,535 citizens arrested and confined to military prisons from February, 1862 to the end of the war. To this one

No such freedom or directness of action was ever permitted to Jefferson Davis. He could make no summary moves against practices whose effect was to obstruct the war effort until the badly unsettled conditions of early 1862 finally persuaded the Confederate Congress that something needed to be done. The Act passed on February 27 thereupon permitted the executive to suspend habeas corpus and apply martial law to places threatened by invasion. But though Davis used his power in a very restricted way, the resulting hostility to martial law as imposed on Richmond and certain other places was such that Congress in April felt constrained to put further limits on the executive and to amend the law by giving it a fixed date of expiration. A second Act was also limited to a fixed term—it was passed on October 13, 1862, and expired five months later—and did not authorize trials of civilians by military courts. During this time, the writ of habeas corpus was suspended in fewer places than before. But despite Davis's urgings the law was allowed to lapse, and for a year nothing was enacted to take its place. A third Act, in force from the middle of February to the end of July 1864, contained many limits on executive discretion, and after that time the most desperate pleas by the Confederate President could not induce his Congress to pass another. The reason which the Congress gave for its refusal was the opposition of the states.[30] That opposition had, indeed, been so bitter that Confederate law was in many places rendered practically unenforceable. Governor Brown insisted that the people of Georgia had "more to apprehend from military despotism than from subjugation by the enemy," and when Alexander Stephens harangued the Georgia legislature in March 1864 on the government's "despotic" suspension of habeas corpus, Brown had the speech printed and mailed to the company officers of every Georgia regiment and to every county clerk and county sheriff in Confederate territory. The legislature of North Carolina passed an Act making it compulsory for state judges to issue the writ, in effect nullifying Confederate law. A meeting of governors in October 1864 adopted a resolution "virtually condemning" the suspension of habeas corpus.[31]

---

would have to add those arrested under authority of the Navy and State Departments and those confined in State prisons and penitentiaries. Even when these allowances are made, however, the number would be much less than 38,000, which was the exaggerated guess of Alexander Johnston in Laylor's Cyclopedia. . . ." Ibid. 152n.

30. Owsley, *State Rights*, 150-202; Robinson, *Justice in Grey*, 383-419.

31. Robinson, *Justice in Grey*, 191; Phillips (ed.), *Toombs, Stephens, Cobb*, 605, 639-41; *Official Records*, 4 Ser., III, 735.

One result was a serious weakening of the South's military system. State judges in Virginia, Texas, North Carolina, and elsewhere issued writs of habeas corpus indiscriminately to persons accused of desertion or evading military service, and Governor Vance used his militia to enforce them. Robert E. Lee complained to the Secretary of War that the drain on the army thus caused by the use of habeas corpus was "more than it can bear." Moreover, the deterioration of civil government in many areas made a wide field for lawless bands, disloyal secret societies, and trading with the enemy. Persons arrested for such activities were again and again freed by habeas corpus on grounds of insufficient evidence. All this despite Davis's plea that "the suspension of the writ is not simply advisable and expedient, but almost indispensable to the successful conduct of the war."[32]

The chief mechanism that prevented such centrifugal tendencies from developing in the Northern states, as William B. Hesseltine pointed out some years ago, was the Republican party. It was the energy of the Republican party that established the political structure with which the North began the war, and through which the war was prosecuted to the end. More specifically, the governors of every Northern state in 1861 had been put there through the efforts of that party, and these men represented both the state organizations and the national coalition responsible for bringing a Republican administration to Washington. They were politically committed from the very first to positive measures for suppressing disunion. With remarkable unanimity they invited Lincoln at the outset to take steps—indeed, they insisted he take them—which could only draw more and more power into his hands, leaving them with less and less initiative. As with the raising of armies, there was something cumulative about this process; it came to take on a life of its own.[33]

In turn, the various state administrations—especially after the resurgence of the Democratic party with the reverses of 1862—came more and more, despite their traditions of particularism, to realize their growing dependence on the federal government for political support. There are numerous examples of this. One is the famous case of Governor Oliver Morton of Indiana, whom the elections of 1862 had confronted with a

32. *Official Records*, 4 Ser., III, 660, 1134.
33. William B. Hesseltine, *Lincoln and the War Governors*, vi. This work, despite a tone of cynicism which occasionally fails to do justice to its worthy subject, is of seminal importance to an understanding of the change in state-federal relations which occurred during the war.

Democratic legislature. These Democrats, denouncing Morton, Lincoln, conscription, emancipation, and arbitrary arrests, tried to remove the state's military affairs from Morton's control and successfully held up appropriation bills until the session expired, leaving the governor without money to run the state. The distraught Morton, not wanting to call a special session and at the same time convinced that treasonable Copperhead conspiracies were about to engulf the entire Northwest, appealed in his extremity to the President, who was no more anxious than he to have Indiana's Democrats crippling the state's war effort. Funds were found in the War Department, which, together with private subscriptions, enabled Morton to steer through a critical period without state appropriations.[34]

The state elections of 1863—notably those in Connecticut, Ohio, and Pennsylvania, where the full resources of the federal government were exerted for the Republican candidates—show even more clearly this process of growing dependence. In Connecticut, Governor Buckingham was running for re-election against the Democrat Thomas H. Seymour, who flatly opposed the war. Buckingham's 3000-vote victory was assisted by the Secretary of War, who got as many of the state's Republican soldiers furloughed home as the armies could spare; by the President, who wielded the federal patronage where it could best influence the result; and by the Ordnance Department, which let it be understood that Connecticut's arms manufacturers would do well to see that all their workers turned out and voted—for Buckingham. The Democrats of Pennsylvania nominated Judge George W. Woodward, who held that federal conscription was unconstitutional, to run against Governor Andrew G. Curtin; and in Ohio the Republican candidate John Brough was opposed by Clement L. Vallandigham, who had recently been arrested by military authorities for seditious utterances tending to discourage enlistments. Lincoln gave both campaigns his fullest attention. Government clerks from the two states were given free railroad passes, sent home on leave to vote, and assessed one per cent of their salaries for campaign expenses. Secretary Chase, assisted by governors Morton of Indiana and Yates of Illinois, made rousing speeches in Ohio. Workers at the Philadelphia arsenal were marched to the polls on election day "like cattle to the slaughter." Field commanders were again authorized to furlough troops, who thereupon performed the double service of voting themselves and encouraging the

34. William Dudley Foulke, *Life of Oliver P. Morton* (Indianapolis, 1899), I, 213-41, 253-72.

whole citizenry to do the right thing. Curtin defeated Woodward by 15,000 votes in Pennsylvania; Brough, who had barely received the Republican nomination, beat Vallandigham by over 100,000 in Ohio.[35]

In the broadest sense the dependence of the state and national administrations was mutual, and was mutually acknowledged; but in any case the binding agency and energizing force was the Republican party. And this in turn was maintained—indeed, made possible—through the continued existence of the Democrats.

V

There is certainly no need here to discuss the beneficial functions of a "loyal opposition." But something might be said about the functions of an opposition which is under constant suspicion of being only partly loyal. The Northern Democratic party during the Civil War stood in precisely this relation to the Union war effort, and its function in this case was of a double nature. On the one hand, its legitimacy as a quasi-formal institution would remain in the last analysis unchallenged, so long as it kept its antiwar wing within some sort of bounds. But by the same token there was the rough and ready principle that "every Democrat may not be a traitor, but every traitor is a Democrat."

Thus, the very existence of the Democratic party provided the authorities (who badly needed some standard) with a ready-made device for making the first rough approximation in the identification of actual disloyalty. It also provided a kind of built-in guarantee against irrevocable personal damage should the guess turn out to be wrong. When in doubt they could always round up the local Democrats, as many a time they did, and in case of error there was always a formula for saving face all around: it was "just politics." There was, in short, a kind of middle way, an intermediate standard that had its lighter side and alleviated such extremes in security policy as, on the one hand, the paralysis and frustration of doing nothing, and, on the other, the perversions of power that accompany political blood-baths. For example, elections in the doubtful border states were always accompanied by rioting, skulduggery, and various kinds of

35. J. Robert Lane, *A Political History of Connecticut During the Civil War* (Washington, 1941), 202-38; T. Harry Williams, *Lincoln and the Radicals* (Madison, 1941), 281; Stanton L. Davis, *Pennsylvania Politics, 1860-1863* (Cleveland, 1935), 311-16; and George H. Porter, *Ohio Politics During the Civil War Period* (New York, 1911), 178-84.

dirty work; a familiar technique for preventing this was to make whole-sale arrests of Democrats just beforehand. Or, in the case of Clement L. Vallandigham, the man was arrested in 1863 by order of General Ambrose Burnside, convicted by military commission, and lodged in a Cincinnati military prison for expressing sympathy with the enemy and speaking with intent to hinder the war effort. Vallandigham's prominence in the Democratic party of Ohio both created a dilemma and provided for its solution. On the one hand, it would hardly seem safe to have such a man in high public office; on the other hand a shade might be established somewhere between "treason" and "mere politics." Lincoln's solution, without exactly repudiating General Burnside's, was to commute Vallandigham's sentence to deportation through the Confederate lines.[36]

Two state governments, those of New York and New Jersey, actually did fall into Democratic hands for a time during the war. But despite much talk of states' rights and arbitrary central authority, neither of these administrations did anything that materially hindered the war effort. Both, in fact, did much to promote it, and it was not as though either state was lacking in Democrats ready for almost any measure which might tie up the federal government. But a strong stimulus to the Democratic governors, as well as to the state Democratic organizations, for keeping such elements in check was the existence in each state of a formidable Republican organization which was watching their every move.[37]

Meanwhile Jefferson Davis also had opposition, in his Congress as well as in the states, and it grew ever larger. But it was not "an" opposition in any truly organized sense. It was far more toxic, an undifferentiated bickering resistance, an unspecified something that seeped in from everywhere to soften the very will of the Confederacy. Davis could not move against this; he had no real way of getting at it. He had no way, for example, without either an organized opposition party or an organized administration party, of dealing with a man like Joseph E. Brown. Had there been such organizations, and had Brown himself been at the head of either the one or the other of them in the state of Georgia, the administration forces would have had some sort of check on him. As it was, Brown could claim expansively and with the fullest justice that he simply represented the whole people of Georgia; and had Davis directly challenged

36. *Official Records*, 2 Ser., V, 657.
37. Charles M. Knapp, *New Jersey Politics during the Period of the Civil War and Reconstruction* (Geneva, N.Y., 1924), 72-141; Stewart Mitchell, *Horatio Seymour of New York* (Cambridge, Mass., 1938), 300-301.

Brown's loyalty he would have challenged the good faith of an entire state. Not being held to the administration and the other states by party ties, Brown and others like him were without any continuing mode of instruction in the requirements and interests of the Confederacy as a whole. His supreme parochialism and reluctance to co-operate need not be seen as a matter of mere spite. The world's history is full of political elites—such as the Polish nobles of the eighteenth century, unwilling to give up their *liberum veto* to a king to achieve a strong Polish state—that literally did not know their own best interests. Although Brown could not see beyond the borders of Georgia, it ought to be said for him that what he did see he saw very clearly. His whole sense and image of power was tied up in the relation between himself and the population of his state. Thus to him, Davis's efforts to mobilize the total resources of the Confederacy were as great a threat as was the Union army—Brown as much as said so—and they intruded, in any case, an element of uncertainty into his own political world so gross as to be intolerable. Unlike the Northern governors, Brown had no informal national structure with a clear set of organizational interests, and on which his own power depended, to persuade him otherwise.

If Abraham Lincoln could be said to have had any sort of counterpart to Davis's Brown, perhaps the man who came closest to filling that role was Horatio Seymour, the Democratic governor of New York. Seymour was a man of strong intelligence who had been elected in 1862, at a time when the administration's prestige had suffered a number of setbacks. He spoke vigorously for states' rights and individual liberties, attacked conscription, emancipation, arbitrary arrests, suspension of habeas corpus, and the consolidation of national power. His sayings gave much anxiety to the administration, and much heart to its enemies everywhere. And yet the structure of political parties provided every element needed for containing what mischief Seymour might make, in case he ever intended any. Lincoln's technique for handling Seymour was to keep him off balance by receiving all his high pronouncements of principle—though with elaborate politeness—as the utterances of a man who, as a matter of course, wanted to be the next Democratic President. Seymour was treated, in short, as a partisan political schemer. At the same time, there was in Seymour's own state an alert and powerful Republican organization ready to pick up the faintest treasonable echoes that might be coming out of Albany. They would catch at the governor's every word—as with his innocent blunder of addressing an antidraft mob in New York City as "my friends"—in an effort to make the charge stick. The man's leeway was not very wide. He tried without success to have the draft suspended in New York, yet was as energetic as anyone in raising the state's quota of volunteers. He was defeated for re-election in 1864 by Republican Congressman Reuben E. Fenton.[38]

A further note on "opposition" might involve the relations of Lincoln with the "Radical" faction of his own party. This question has produced some strong debate among historians, though the principal issues appear by now to have been largely settled. One side of it was opened by the publication in 1941 of T. Harry Williams's *Lincoln and the Radicals,* which represented the President's greatest political burdens as having been heaped on him not so much by the Democrats as by extremists within the Republican ranks. This determined phalanx of "Radicals," or "Jacobins" as John Hay first called them, hounded Lincoln without mercy. Their Committee on the Conduct of the War, with its investigations into military policy and its eternal pressure for changes of generals, was a serious hindrance to the administration. Their insistence on emancipation, Negro troops, and confiscation of rebel property embarrassed Lincoln in his policy of moderation toward the border states during the early stage of the war. They tried to refashion his cabinet; they tried to force his hand on reconstruction; they even tried to replace him as the Republican candidate in 1864 with someone more forceful. On every issue but the last, the Radicals "conquered" Lincoln. Nor was Williams seeing mirages. It may be, indeed, that he saw things in much the way Lincoln himself must at times have seen them. There *were* Radicals; they did harass him constantly; more than once they drove him virtually to despair. It might even be said that in the end they "won." But whether this should mean that Lincoln "lost" is another question. How fundamental, really, was the "struggle"? Williams was eventually challenged on just this ground by David Donald in 1956, and as a result the entire tone of the matter has since become much altered. Donald pointed out that "presidents are always criticized by members of their own parties," but that this is hardly the same as out-and-out warfare. The Radicals were not in fact a very cohesive or disciplined group; they were far from agreed among themselves on a great many things; and they were certainly not inveterate enemies of the President. He wanted their support, and at the most critical

38. Mitchell, *Horatio Seymour,* 273-7, 324-8, 353, 361, 376.

points he did not fail to get it. Personal relations were always reasonably good; with one of the leaders, Charles Sumner, they were excellent. As Donald says, "to picture Lincoln at swords' points with the Radical leaders of his own party, then, is an error."[39]

The one point which may need further emphasis is that these Radicals, whatever may have been their many differences, represented the most articulate, most energetic, most militant wing of the Republican party. The one thing that did unite such men as Trumbull, Wade, Greeley, Chandler, Fessenden, Julian, and the rest was their implacable insistence that the war be prosecuted with ever more vigor, and that the President use the national power to the utmost in doing it. There is every evidence that in this over-all objective they and the President were at one, inasmuch as the war was, in the end, so prosecuted. Whether Lincoln welcomed his tormentors is doubtful. But whether he or anyone else would have moved as decisively without them is equally doubtful, and what the Union war effort as a whole would have been without the energy they represented is more doubtful still. The tensions and conflicts of the Lincoln administration—such as those having to do with emancipation, the use of Negro troops, and the complexion of the government that was to stand for re-election in 1864—were, as we know, considerable. But without a party apparatus to harness and direct them, they would surely have been unmanageable.

In any event, we might imagine Jefferson Davis as being quite willing to exchange this sort of "opposition" for the one he had. In the Confederate Congress there seem to have been some who pressed for greater vigor than Davis's in fighting the war; a much larger number inclined to measures that would have resulted in less. But perhaps more fundamental was that these men were all mixed in together. There was no recognized way of segregating or defining them, no basis of expectations, no clear principle for predicting what they might do. "There were no political organizations seeking undivided loyalty," as the historian of that Congress puts it, "nor was there consistent pressure from the electorate. Conditions changed, opinions changed, consequently administration sympathies changed." This lack of sharpness seems to have been accompanied by a

39. David Donald, "The Radicals and Lincoln," in Lincoln Reconsidered: Essays on the Civil War Era (New York, 1956), 103-27. See also Hans L. Trefousse, "The Joint Committee on the Conduct of the War: A Reappraisal," Civil War History, X (1964), 5-19; and Grady McWhiney (ed.), Grant, Lee, Lincoln and the Radicals: Essays on Civil War Leadership (New York, 1964).

certain lack of initiative which is quite noticeable when contrasted with the wartime federal Congress, and it is apparent that lack of party responsibility had much to do with it. Davis's Congress for the most part was not violently obstructive, in the sense that groups within it confronted him with formidable alternatives in policy to which he had to adjust. Much of his legislation, indeed, was rather passively enacted, which is to say that at best he could drag his Congress along. At the worst, however, it ended by being a drag on him. Perhaps his snappishness and rigidity were, after all, only appropriate to the circumstances. Professor Yearns mildly concludes:

> He despaired at Congress's amendments, delays, and occasional rejections. Only subservience satisfied him, and, as his influence with Congress was based primarily on an agreement of ideas, not on party discipline, he ultimately lost some of this influence.[40]

Certainly Davis had no counterpart of Lincoln's "Radicals" to spur him on. Could the rabid secessionists of the 1850's, the so-called Southern "fire-eaters," the Robert Barnwell Rhetts, the William Lowndes Yanceys, the Edmund Ruffins, have made such a counterpart? There is little evidence that they could, or would. Such men are quite absent from the roll of the Confederacy's leading statesmen. The most dynamic "fire-eaters" who came into their own in the war years were two obstructionist state governors, already mentioned, Zebulon Vance and Joseph E. Brown.[41]

40. Yearns, *Confederate Congress*, 226, 234. The strongest proponents of a vigorous war policy, in fact, were the representatives from Union-occupied areas, i.e. men who for practical purposes had no constituencies and who were thus politically without responsibility. Ibid. 59.

41. Edmund Ruffin's prominence in the secessionist agitation of the 1850's, one is tempted to think, was a natural extension of his own lifelong habit of resigning from one thing after another (including the Virginia Senate) on the ground of his being insufficiently appreciated. Public service in the ordinary sense was not compatible with his temperament. Indeed, in Ruffin's later years his behavior was that of a man obsessed with the idea of self-destruction. He beheld with fascinated admiration, for example, the demeanor with which John Brown went to his death in 1859. Though nearly seventy, he ran about Charleston in April 1861 dressed up in military costume and attracted much attention, whereupon someone thought to invite the old man to fire the first gun in the bombardment of Fort Sumter. Throughout the war he kept signing up, despite his age, with various military organizations. When it was all over, he shot himself. Robert Barnwell Rhett served in the Confederate Provisional Congress, but his states' rights extremism was too much even for his fellow South Carolinians, and he was twice defeated for a seat in the permanent Confederate Congress. While still in the former body Rhett began attacking Jefferson Davis—according to his one-time friend Robert W. Barnwell, even "before he had time to do wrong." One of his last acts in a public capacity was to oppose a measure for a Confederate-sponsored program of railroad construction because, as he put it, a railroad was "a

VI

It has been asserted throughout this essay that the Republican party, in the presence of an organized party of opposition, performed a variety of functions in mobilizing and managing the energies needed for sustaining the Union war effort. These were carried on both inside and outside the formal structure of government, and by men active in party affairs whether they held office or not. The absence of such a system in the Confederacy seems to have had more than a casual bearing on the process whereby Southern energies, over and beyond the course of military events, became diffused and dissipated. National commitments in the North were given form and direction by an additional set of commitments, those of party. This hardly means that the Republican party is to be given sole credit for the success of the war effort, which was in fact supported by overwhelming numbers of Democrats. But it does mean, among other things, that there were political sanctions against the Democrats' *not* supporting it, sanctions which did not exist in the Confederacy. When Democratic leaders were inclined to behave irresponsibly they could not, like Brown and Vance, play the role of state patriots. A hint of Democratic disloyalty anywhere tightened the Republican organization everywhere.

The emphasis hitherto has been upon leadership, upon how the process of politics affected the workings of government, but a final word should be said about how that process affected the body of citizenry. What may have been the function of a party system as a vehicle of communication? What did it do toward making popular elections a mode whereby the people were in effect called upon to define and reaffirm their own commitment to the national cause? In 1862, 1863, and 1864, through a series of elections which made the heaviest psychological demands on the entire country, the North had annually to come to terms with the war effort. The Republicans, with varying degrees of success, everywhere made attempts to broaden their coalition by bringing as many Union Democrats

---

military convenience, not a military necessity." For the remainder of the war he bitterly attacked the administration in his paper, the Charleston *Mercury*. William L. Yancey was sent by the Davis government on a diplomatic mission to England, where his violent proslavery sayings gave deep offense. He also served in the Confederate Senate, where his anti-administration tirades made him a nuisance. He died in 1863. See Avery Craven, *Edmund Ruffin, Southerner: A Study in Secession* (New York, 1932); Laura A. White, *Robert Barnwell Rhett: Father of Secession* (New York, 1931); and DuBose, *Yancey*, II.

into it as possible, and naturally tried to attract as many Democratic voters to it as they could. The national party even changed its name in 1864, calling itself the "Union" party to dramatize the breadth of its appeal. And yet the result was in no true sense an all-party front or bipartisan coalition; rather it was a highly successful device for detaching Democrats from their regular party loyalties. The distinction is of some importance. The initiative for this effort remained throughout in Republican hands, and the Democrats everywhere maintained their regular organizations.[42] The structure of parties was therefore such that every election became, in a very direct way, a test of loyalty to the national government.

The tests were by no means consistently favorable. In the fall of 1862, the time of the mid-term elections, the Republicans were significantly divided on the President's policy of emancipation, and a heavy majority of Democrats opposed it. This was reflected in the state and congressional election results, which were deeply depressing to the administration. The Democrats elected governors in two states and majorities in the legislatures of several, and substantially increased their numbers in Congress. This had several important consequences. One was that, inasmuch as the Republicans still maintained their control of Congress, the weakened state organizations were brought a step farther in that progress, already described, of growing dependency on the national party and the national administration for leadership and support. Another was that the Republicans were inspired to great exertions in justifying emancipation as an integral feature of the party program and in minimizing the Democrats' claim that the purposes of the war had been altered to make it an abolition crusade. Still a further consequence was that the Democrats were

42. There was some controversy over this point when the essay was first presented at the 1966 Conference on Political Parties, which prompts me to underline the distinction referred to above. For example, it was noted that Lincoln made his appointments in a bipartisan spirit. This is certainly correct, provided one may add what I believe is an important qualification, which is that Lincoln actually made his appointments in two capacities. As head of the state in wartime, he appointed large numbers of Democrats to office, most notably to military commands, which ordinarily he would not have done. But as head of the party, he appointed mostly Republicans to the regular patronage posts—collectorships, surveyorships, postmasterships, and the like. The effect of appointing some Democrats to office and of changing the name of the Republican party was to broaden the party's base, not to remake the party into something else. Lincoln's bipartisan efforts gained him the help of individual Democrats but not of the Democratic party as such, which was just as well both for him and for the Republican party. In the face of an organized opposition the Republicans maintained their discipline, despite much internal dissension, throughout the war.

sufficiently emboldened by their successes that in a number of places they overstepped themselves. The "peace" theme in the Democrats' case against the administration emerged with a clarity that had hitherto been muted, making them much more vulnerable than before to the Republicans' "treason" theme, and drawing clear lines for the state elections of 1863. Ohio in that year was something of a showcase, with the entire country watching. Vallandigham's "martyrdom" at the hands of General Burnside had delivered Ohio's Democratic party over to the "Peace" men, who had made Vallandigham their nominee for governor. The crisis which thus confronted the Republicans called forth their utmost efforts, not only in Ohio but in neighboring states and even in the national capital. Brough, the "Union" candidate, insisted again and again that the people had to choose between treason and disunion on the one hand, and Lincoln, emancipation, and a final crushing of the rebellion on the other. James G. Blaine of Maine, himself an anxious observer, later wrote his own history of the period, and when he noted the importance of this election he did not even mention the name of the winning candidate. He simply said that the people gave "a majority of one hundred and one thousand for the Administration."[43]

Once again in 1864, the Democrats, amid the military discouragements of the summer, assisted in clarifying the choices by writing a peace plank into their national platform and nominating a general, George B. McClellan, who had been dismissed for the failure of the operations of 1862 in the Eastern theater. The re-election of Lincoln was accompanied by the restoration of Republican majorities to every legislature and every congressional delegation, and of Republican governors to every state.[44]

The people of the Confederacy, of course, continued to hold elections. Yet we know surprisingly little—indeed, almost nothing—about these elections. No study has ever been made of them, which is some measure of how comparatively little importance was attached to them at the time. The people were asked in November 1861 to choose Davis and Stephens as heads of the "permanent" government. The election "was marked, however, by general apathy." The first elections to Congress, according to Professor Yearns, "went off quietly." There was virtually no campaigning, and "balloting everywhere was light, as is usual when issues are absent."

43. Wood Gray, *The Hidden Civil War: The Story of the Copperheads* (New York, 1942), 108-10, 140-43, 145-6, 150ff., 158-9; James G. Blaine, *Twenty Years of Congress: From Lincoln to Garfield* (Norwich, Conn., 1884), I, 497.
44. Gray, *Hidden Civil War*, pp. 202ff.

The elections of 1863, from what little glimpse we have of them, seem aggressive only by contrast. The increased activity at that time was principally a product of increased dissatisfaction with Davis's government. Yet even here the opposition was unorganized and unfocused, and candidates "failed to offer any clear substitute for policies they denigrated." "Mixed with rodomontade was the familiar state rights ingredient which gave much criticism a respectable flavor. All of the strong war measures were condemned as evidence of centralized despotism which was abusing the states."[45]

The sluggishness of communication in the Confederacy has often been commented on, and yet here the contrast with the North is one which the disparity in technology does not quite fully account for. There was no counterpart in the South of the resonance which party elections provided for the Northern cause. The historian of Confederate propaganda asserts that official efforts in this direction were very deficient, which is not surprising when it is recalled how preponderantly such efforts in the North were handled through party agencies. We have a description of how such activities were carried on in Washington with the heartiest co-operation of the national government during the fall of 1864:

> The National Republican Committee have taken full possession of all the Capitol buildings, and the committee rooms of the Senate and House of Representatives are filled with clerks, busy in mailing Lincoln documents all over the loyal States. . . .
> The Post Office Department, of course, is attending to the lion's share of this work. Eighty bags of mail matter, all containing Lincoln documents, are daily sent to Sherman's army.[46]

Not long after this time, a measure was timidly offered in the Confederate Congress whereby the government frank might be used for mailing newspapers to soldiers in the field. The Confederate Postmaster-General was distressed. His department was required by law to be self-supporting, and he was very proud of its being the only one to show a surplus, which he had achieved by doing away with all but the bare minimum services. He spoke to the President about this new bill, and the latter solemnly vetoed it as being unconstitutional.[47]

45. Patrick, *Davis and his Cabinet*, 31; Yearns, *Confederate Congress*, 48-50.
46. James W. Silver, "Propaganda in the Confederacy," *Journal of Southern History*, XI (1945), 487-503; Carman and Luthin, *Lincoln and the Patronage*, 287.
47. *Journal of the Congress of the Confederate States of America* (Washington, 1904-1905), G.P.O., IV, 496-497.

Whether Northern wartime elections served to give refinement and precision to the issues is perhaps less important than that they served to simplify and consolidate them. When the people of Indiana were urged in 1863 to vote for Republicans in their local elections, they were really being asked to do more than elect a few county officers. And by the same token the candidate for such an office accepted, along with his nomination, a whole train of extraordinary responsibilities: Governor Morton, President Lincoln, emancipation, arbitrary arrests, and war to the end. There was no separating them; under the circumstances of war, the voter who took the Republican candidate took them all. And the candidate, if successful in his debates with his Democratic opponent, would have enacted something akin to the principle of the self-fulfilling prophecy. He defined his position, he defended the administration, he persuaded his audience, and in the process he repersuaded and recommitted himself.[48] It may be quite proper to say that it was, after all, the Union's military success that made political success possible. The fall of Atlanta in September 1864, for example, certainly rescued Lincoln's chances for re-election. But conceivably it was not that simple, and short-term correlations may be deceiving. How was the Northern will sustained for the three and a half years that were needed before it could reap successes of any kind in late 1864? A continual affirmation and reaffirmation of purpose was built into the very currents of political life in the Northern states. It is altogether probable that the North's political energies and its military will were, all along, parts of the same process.

Every election, moreover, was a step in nationalizing the war. The extension of local and state loyalties into national loyalties during this period was something of a revolution, and it did not occur easily. This profound change cannot be taken for granted, nor is it best understood simply by examining the formal federal structure through which it began. It is revealed rather through the far less formal political process whereby the national government in the Civil War was able to communicate its purposes, to persuade, and to exercise its will directly upon individuals in state, city, town, and local countryside.

48. Even these county elections were watched in Washington, and the results duly noted. See Lincoln to J. W. Grimes, October 15, 1863, in Basler (ed.), *Works*, VI, 515.

VI | SAMUEL P. HAYS

UNIVERSITY OF PITTSBURGH

Political Parties

and the Community-Society Continuum

AMERICAN POLITICAL HISTORIANS are badly in need of conceptual frameworks through which they can formulate problems for research and develop contexts of understanding. Existing conceptual categories are, for the most part, traditional and conventional; as such, moreover, they are sterile. They have not given rise to the imaginative formulation of new problems, nor have they proved capable of responding creatively to new types of evidence or new ideas suggested by those working in other disciplines. It is time that we gave serious attention to this problem, for today it constitutes the major roadblock to advance in the study of the American political past. The repeated conventions of traditional views have become a steel chain of ideas which restrict rather than liberate, which confine rather than release the historical imagination. This is especially true for the period from the Civil War to the Great Depression, the period from about 1865 to about 1929, on which this chapter will focus.

Two general considerations should underlie the formulation of these conceptual frameworks. First, they should be oriented toward *structure* rather than *event*.[1] They should focus on patterns of human relationships in the political system rather than on the succession of outcomes of political decisions. History is concerned with descriptions and analyses of societies as they change over time—that is, with social structure and social process. Political history is concerned with the struggle for dominance among people with varied political goals within that context of structure

1. The concept of political structure is dealt with more fully in Samuel P. Hays, "The Social Analysis of American Political History, 1880-1920," *Political Science Quarterly*, LXXX (1965), 373-94; and in "New Possibilities for American Political History: The Social Analysis of Political Life," Inter-University Consortium for Political Research (Ann Arbor, 1964).

and change. The broad patterns of political relationships cannot be pieced together from a multitude of conceptually separate and distinct events, but must arise from a context which is structural in form.

Second, a satisfactory framework should encompass a wider range of systems of decision-making than the political party itself. Functional and corporate systems co-exist with but differ sharply from parties in urban-industrial America. The geographical representation inherent in the party system, for example, differs markedly from the functional representation inherent in the interplay of interest groups. Moreover, changes in one system of decision-making may well be related to changes in another. Here I shall be concerned especially with the impact of functional and corporate systems upon political parties in the process of industrialization.

There is a special need to develop a framework which will link top-level national policies and grass-roots political behavior. Much of the criticism of past writing focuses on the overemphasis on national events, a perspective which has guided the preservation of records, the development of data, and the formulation of general ideas. Critics have urged, therefore, that attention must be shifted toward the grass roots. The analysis of popular voting behavior has stimulated this trend of thought, but a primary focus on the grass roots would be as one-sided as one on national events. Moreover, historians have erroneously assumed a uniform perspective in local and national political history, emphasizing that national history is either local and state history writ large or that local and state history is national history writ small. But political life at one level is of an entirely different order from that at another. They are linked not by logical similarity but by human interaction. A framework is needed which will account for different levels of political behavior and the interaction between them.

This essay suggests that a community-society dimension provides such a framework.[2] This dimension consists of a continuum of types of human relationships and therefore of identifiable group differences ranging from

2. The most important early statement of this view is Ferdinand Tönnies, *Community and Society*, translated and edited by Charles P. Loomis (East Lansing, 1957). The view has been extended by American sociologists—e.g. Robert K. Merton, "Patterns of Influence: Local and Cosmopolitan Influentials," in Merton, *Social Theory and Social Structure* (Glencoe, 1949), 387-420. I make no pretense of applying these concepts in their original meaning, but only wish to acknowledge them as sources of inspiration. The most immediately relevant statement of the social theory underlying the argument in this paper is in Roland L. Warren, *The Community in America* (Chicago, 1963).

personal, community, face-to-face contacts on the one hand, to impersonal, mass relationships in the wider society on the other. It involves
distinctions in the geographical scope and thereby the quality of human
relationships; hence "community" and "society" as traditional terms. One
conceives of community as human participation in networks of primary,
interpersonal relationships within a limited geographical context. At this
level there is concern with the intimate and the personal, movement
within a limited range of social contacts, and preoccupation with affairs
arising from daily personal life. Knowledge is acquired and action carried out through personal experience and personal relationships. Society,
on the other hand, involves secondary contacts over wide geographical
areas, considerable geographical mobility, and a high degree of ideological
mobility with much variety and choice of what one can do, think, and be.
It also involves the development of human relationships on the basis of
similar functions, the establishment of organizational structures to co-ordinate activities beyond the confines of community, and the development
of techniques to influence public affairs over broad geographical areas.

One can discover a community-society continuum in pre-urban-indus-
trial society, such as William Benton describes for Pennsylvania army
officers whose attitudes toward the federal Constitution of 1789 were
closely related to whether they served inside or outside the state during
the Revolution.[3] Yet the modernizing forces of science and technology
gave rise to cosmopolitan tendencies in the late nineteenth century which
were far more dynamic and extensive than those which existed in earlier
periods of our history. The innovating sector of urban-industrial society
was highly mobile, both ideologically and geographically; it involved
the rapid elaboration of impersonal rather than personal relationships; it
gave rise to modern bureaucratic organizations with their emphasis on
technical knowledge and professional expertise. Innovation constituted
a world apart from local communities; the cultural values of cosmopolitan
life, which grew rapidly in the cities, differed sharply from those in more
traditional sectors of society.

Several elements of this social structure are of special relevance for
political history. One concerns *social institutions*, those ongoing relationships among people of similar circumstance. These can be ranged on a
continuum from the family institutions of residence, school, church, and

3. William Benton, "Pennsylvania Revolutionary Officers and the Federal Constitution," *Pennsylvania History*, XXXI (1964), 419-35.

recreation to those which bring together people of similar skills or economic functions, such as manufacturers, political scientists, or ministers, over broad geographical areas. Different positions on this continuum give rise to different political perspectives, values, and relationships. These differences are reflected in such matters as the relative absence of evidence about ethno-cultural politics in nationally oriented literature and its abundance in locally oriented literature; the relative inability of the cosmopolitan reformer, whether a Bull Mooser Republican or a "reform" Democrat, to communicate with working-class voters; and the conflict between the state highway commission and local county or township road officials.

A second aspect of the continuum concerns distinctions in *social perception*. One of the most important avenues for investigating political life is the distinctive way in which people in different circumstances perceive their political world. What is their conception of the range of political values, of their past, of their current situation and the causes for it, of the kind of society which should be created in the future? A community-society framework provides an excellent setting for the examination of political perception. For the range of human consciousness can be subdivided in terms of its geographical scope and variety, whether limited to a community of one's personal relationships or extended to the larger world of impersonal media, whether tolerating a limited or an extended variety of ideas and possibilities of human thought and action. Although historians cannot recapture attitudes through survey data as students of contemporary events can, they can often reconstruct through documentary data the perceptual worlds of different segments of the political structure.

Still a third feature concerns the *mechanisms of decision-making*. At one end of the continuum local communities have preferred a political system with units consistent with their local community institutions. Urban communities battled for the ward system of city council representation, small-town bankers argued for a Federal Reserve structure which rested on local clearing houses rather than central or regional units, townships fought against state highway and county educational authorities to retain local control. Those involved in institutions organized over large geographical areas sought systems of decision-making the scope of which would be equally broad. Corporations involved in nationwide economic activities sought to shift public regulation from the state to the

national level, professionals and executives of large-scale economic enter-
prises to shift city council representation from the ward to the city at
large, and statewide groups to expand the administrative apparatus of
the state as opposed to the local community. Preference as to the location
of the level of decision-making, therefore, was directly related to the
scope and location of the activities which one wished to influence.

It should be emphasized that I am not speaking about a rural-urban
continuum. In the past many have assumed that the community-society
dimension was consistent with a rural-urban distinction, but it is not.
Within the city, for example, both communities with locally oriented institutions and more cosmopolitan groups with geographically broad and
often impersonal relationships exist face to face. Suburbs contain not only
communities of a wide variety of class levels, but also of different degrees
of involvement in local or cosmopolitan life. Rural areas may often be
populated by cosmopolitans who prefer to live in the suburbs or city
dwellers vacationing in summer homes or recreational havens. In his classic article on local and cosmopolitan influentials Robert Merton emphasized that both groups live within the same urban geographical context
but in different social worlds.[4] The types of human relationships stressed
here, therefore, are independent of their physical location in city or country.

The community-society dimension is a useful framework for sorting out
values, perceptions, and mechanisms in many fields of history. As mentioned above, William Benton has used it to distinguish Federalist and
anti-Federalist attitudes of Revolutionary army officers. It is involved in
the church-sect distinction in religion and in Robert Doherty's distinctions
between those on opposite sides of religious controversies involving Pres-
byterianism and Quakerism in the first half of the nineteenth century.[5] It
has helped to sort out proponents and opponents of municipal reform in
the early twentieth century.[6] It can provide meaningful distinctions between segments of the educational world, whether students or faculty.[7] It

4. Merton, "Patterns of Influence."
5. Robert W. Doherty, "Religion and Society: The Hicksite Separation of 1827,"
American Quarterly, XVII (1965), 63-80; "Religion and Society: The Presbyterian
Schism of 1837-1838," mimeo; "The Growth of Orthodoxy," *Quaker History*, 54
(1965), 24-34.
6. Samuel P. Hays, "The Politics of Reform in Municipal Government in the Progressive Era," *Pacific Northwest Quarterly*, 55 (1964), 157-69.
7. James A. Davis, "Locals and Cosmopolitans in American Graduate Schools,"
International Journal of Comparative Sociology, II (1961), 212-23; Alvin W. Gould-
ner, "Cosmopolitans and Locals: Toward an Analysis of Latent Social Roles," Parts I
and II, *Administrative Science Quarterly*, 2 (1957-1958), 282-306, 444-80.

facilitates investigation into the vertical as well as the horizontal dimension of human organization, in which larger units of institutions, perceptions, and actions are not merely smaller units writ large, but of a different quality. It is an especially useful framework for the investigation of a period of history in which forces of industrialization and urbanization created a more highly systematized and organized society with varying degrees of involvement by different segments of the social order.

II

The community-society structure of American life has been reflected in the structure of the political party. The party relied for victory on voters who formed their political values within the parochial context of community, yet it mobilized those voters for wider action by means of regional and national ideologies. At the same time, elected political leaders, while retaining close community ties, became involved in cosmopolitan political forces relatively divorced from community. Their political situation often thereby became paradoxical, for the party encompassed both local and cosmopolitan levels of thought and action.

Political parties, in contrast with other systems of decision-making, were uniquely capable of expressing community impulses. Since the party's roots lay in geographically organized wards and precincts, in which it had to contend for majority support, it reflected closely the characteristics of community life. The party's leaders were closely akin to the community's leaders. If the community sustained a leadership of its more affluent families, so did the party; if it gathered around such local functionaries as the real estate developer, the saloonkeeper, or the grocer, so did the party. Moreover, the party's position on substantive demands reflected the community's values. If the community supported striking coal miners or opposed Prohibition, so did the party. Often the community's indifference or the diversity of its impulses gave rise to initiative at other levels of political structure, but the party rarely could ignore clear-cut community demands.

Despite all this, however, historians have usually reconstructed political parties from the top down, rather than from the bottom up. While arguing that political leaders invariably manipulated grass-roots political forces, they have failed to examine the data—popular voting and local leadership—which might lead to a different view. They have argued, for example, that the Republican party won in 1896 because it bribed or threatened workingmen to vote against Bryan, and that the urban "machine" controlled unsophisticated and ignorant immigrant voters contrary to their own wishes. Both contentions rest on slim evidence. They fail to take into account the shared patterns of values and the social organization of the local community as a fundamental and persistent force in political life, or the long-term durability of the alignments in question. A major task of American political history is to reconstruct the community roots of political parties.

Analysis of popular voting, for example, reveals the vast importance of community ethno-cultural factors in electoral behavior. Liberal historians, stressing the political battles over the public regulation of private business, have argued that railroad, trust, tariff, and banking controversies shaped party followings in the Populist-Progressive Era. Ethno-cultural issues, such as Sunday observance and Prohibition, they consider to be "red-herrings," emotional rather than "real" issues, often concocted or played up by politicians to divert attention from the "more fundamental" controversies over public regulation of private business.[8] But ethno-cultural issues were far more important to voters than were tariffs, trusts, and railroads. They touched lives directly and moved people deeply. The experience of voters was not related to national and cosmopolitan political perspectives but to day-to-day community life.

Several examples illustrate this rooting of voting patterns in community rather than in society. Party divisions after the Civil War grew out of the impact of evangelical Protestantism on the political world of the late 1840's and the early 1850's.[9] In the form of Prohibition, nativism, and antislavery, that movement produced both a sharp realignment of voting behavior and a cultural unity for the Republican party.[10] The Democratic party, in turn, combined Catholics and German Lutherans and nonevangelical Protestant native-born Americans in a common hostility to evan-

8. See e.g. Harold U. Faulkner, *Politics, Reform and Expansion, 1890-1900* (New York, 1959), 115-16. Hofstadter's "status" theory is based upon the argument that ethno-cultural issues were less real, more derivative, less rational than were economic issues. See his recent concise statement of this argument in his "Fundamentalism and Status Politics on the Right," *Columbia University Forum*, VIII (1965), 18-24.

9. A general survey of ethno-cultural factors in politics is Seymour Martin Lipset, "Religion and Politics in the American Past and Present," in Robert Lee and Martin E. Marty (eds.), *Religion and Social Conflict* (New York, 1964), 69-126.

10. Clifford S. Griffin, *Their Brothers' Keepers* (New Brunswick, N.J., 1960), 219-41.

gelical imperialism and the negative reference groups espousing it. This alignment persisted with little change until the depression of 1893, with variations. In the late 1880's, for example, nativist groups secured laws in Illinois and Wisconsin which prohibited instruction in a foreign language in primary and secondary schools, public or private. Immigrant groups who were normally Republican joined immigrants who were already Democratic to provide the first Democratic victories in those states since the Civil War, most notably bringing victory to John P. Altgeld as governor of Illinois in 1892.

The years from 1893 to 1896 witnessed the first major voting realignment in American politics since the 1850's.[11] This realignment seems to have been a product of the depression of 1893 and of the shifting attractiveness of parties and candidates to ethno-cultural groups. Many voters turned Republican in the elections of 1893 and 1894 and remained so in 1896. At the same time, moreover, William Jennings Bryan, as a political spokesman for evangelical Protestants, drew numbers of Protestant Republican voters into the Democratic party, while William McKinley established strong new roots among many urban-industrial immigrant and labor voters. The Republican party in the early twentieth century was very sensitive to these voters—see, for example, Theodore Roosevelt's appointment of Oscar Straus as Secretary of Commerce, or the Republican party's move in Congress to bottle up a proposal for a literacy test for immigrants. The Northern Democratic party, on the other hand, often served as a vehicle for Prohibition as well as anti-immigration sentiment, a position not unrelated to the party's electoral gains in the state and national contests of 1908, 1910, and 1912.

World War I and its aftermath brought about a massive shift of voters toward the Republican party.[12] The vast number of state legislative races in which the Democrats did not field candidates in 1918 and 1920 indicates the depth of the revolt. The proposed League of Nations was only partially responsible. Beginning as early as 1918, the shift arose from the

11. See Duncan MacRae, Jr., and James Meldrum, "Critical Elections in Illinois, 1888-1958," *American Political Science Review*, LIV (1960), 669-83. Further supporting data for the conclusions in the text were developed for the five East Central states during the summer seminar for historians at the Inter-University Consortium for Political Research, Ann Arbor, Michigan, in 1965, but has not as yet been published.

12. This interpretation is based upon two state studies: one of Iowa, John T. Schou, "The Decline of the Democratic Party in Iowa, 1916-1920," M. A. Thesis, University of Iowa, 1960; and one of Pennsylvania, Joseph Makarewicz, Doctoral Dissertation now in progress.

adverse effect of the war on the personal lives of millions of Americans: resentment against sugar and flour rationing; price ceilings on agricultural products; the policies of the national Railroad Administration, the Fuel Administration, and other wartime agencies; the official and popular treatment of Germans, Scandinavians, and other immigrants; the Eighteenth Amendment; Prohibition, as a Democratic measure; the disappointment of ethnic groups with the peace. In the elections of 1920 these personal resentments, focused on Woodrow Wilson, produced an astounding Republican majority.

An equally impressive shift in voting patterns took place in the late 1920's and early 1930's. Emphasizing ethno-cultural issues, Al Smith of New York forged a Democratic majority in the twelve largest cities in 1928.[13] Even more important, ethno-cultural community voting patterns gave way to socio-economic divisions, as workingmen increasingly voted Democratic—a change V. O. Key, Jr., noticed in New England industrial towns in the first decade of the twentieth century.[14] The votes for Eugene V. Debs in 1912 and Robert M. La Follette in 1924 both seem to be intimately tied in with this development.[15] From the midst of previously dominant ethno-cultural concerns now emerged impulses arising from the technological organization of modern industrial society. Crystallizing these tendencies, the Depression and the early New Deal policies brought them into full force.

These examples relate voting behavior to the underlying patterns of local community attitudes. Those attitudes did not arise from broad cosmopolitan considerations, but from the patterns of value at the local, personal level. Larger national and cosmopolitan forces played a role when they touched directly the lives of voters in their community setting, as they did so dramatically in crises associated with war and depression; and these forces often only crystallized or exacerbated differences in value

13. Samuel J. Eldersveld, "Influence of Metropolitan Party Pluralities on Presidential Elections," *American Political Science Review*, 43 (1949), 1189-1206; Samuel Lubell, *The Future of American Politics* (New York, 1952), 28-57; J. Joseph Huthmacher, *Massachusetts People and Politics* (Cambridge, 1959).

14. V. O. Key, Jr., "Secular Realignment and the Party System," *Journal of Politics*, XX (1959), 198-210.

15. On this point I am indebted to Bruce Stave for the development of relevant data for Pittsburgh. The Franklin D. Roosevelt vote in 1932 was correlated with the Smith vote in 1928 at a level of .72, with the La Follette vote in 1924 at a level of .84 (but with the 1924 Davis vote at —.37), and with the Debs vote of 1912 at a level of .75 (but with the 1912 Theodore Roosevelt vote at —.34). The Democratic strength of 1932, therefore, seems to be positively related to the Debs, La Follette, and Smith votes, but negatively related to the Theodore Roosevelt and Davis vote, in the city of Pittsburgh.

orientation which were already imbedded in social structure. One cannot deal long with election returns without delving more deeply into the dynamics of community life and its social structure out of which political thought and action arose.

Political parties involve far more than local community life. They form hierarchies of organization from the precinct to the national level, and they involve national leadership, national strategies, and national ideologies. There is no more crucial aspect of this for the historian than political ideology, for ideologies are frequently instruments of mass communication which mobilize local impulses for national, cosmopolitan objectives. The party activist, such as the partisan newspaper editor, was not just an organizer of machinery but an organizer of ideas; he had the task of defining a common ground within the party and a ground of distinction from other parties. Through ideology he developed party cohesion by explaining to voters how, though often diverse, they were really alike, and how they were similar in their differences from voters of other parties. To do this he called upon ideas relatively divorced from community concerns and more relevant to the cosmopolitan world. Historians have assumed that national political ideologies represented beliefs which were homogeneous throughout all levels of the political structure. But, in fact, they arose more from cosmopolitan than from local segments of the party structure, reflected leadership strategy more than grass-roots values, and linked together the several levels of party activity. For the decades from 1890 to 1920, for example, highly visible national policies such as tariff and trusts provide an incorrect view of voter preferences. Those preferences rested primarily on ethno-cultural attitudes which rarely appeared in national debate. This may seem to constitute inconsistent evidence about political behavior, but such inconsistency exists only if one assumes that local and national political perspectives *should* be consistent. The point is that they were not: different levels of political life gave rise to different concerns. The party mobilized voters on the community level by stressing ethno-cultural issues which sustained local party loyalties and party differences, and at the same time emphasized altogether different issues, such as tariff and trusts, on the national level of debate. It may well be, in fact, that the stress on national ideology functioned primarily to obscure ethnic and religious differences which, if given free expression, might have hampered effective national party action.

Examination of the tariff as a substantive issue has confused historians.

Tracing ideological tariff differences back into legislative votes and grass-roots impulses, they have failed to find clear, continuous distinctions—there were high-tariff Democrats and low-tariff Republicans—and have concluded that the tariff controversy was an "unreal" issue. Consequently, they de-emphasize the issue and those periods of history, such as the 1880's, in which tariff debates ran high within and between parties. We can make more progress if we examine the tariff as an ideology. To both parties it constituted a process of self-identification and self-explanation. Whether or not congressmen voted consistently with that distinction in committee, and whether or not political economists believe that the distinction was substantive, are not important. Tariff arguments were ideological instruments of voter mobilization and party combat. The question arises, for example, as to whether the tariff or the money question was the major issue in the election of 1896, but the question itself is irrelevant. The important struggle during that campaign was not over two sides of an issue, but over whether or not one issue or the other should be the primary focus of attention. Party leaders contended over alternative explanations for the depression of 1893 and the ensuing economic crisis, and Bryan and McKinley each sought to persuade voters that he had the correct explanation for the cause of the depression as well as the most effective cure. Each tried to mobilize voters around explanatory ideological positions with which those voters could identify. In the end, McKinley's explanation in terms of the tariff made sense to discontented urban-industrial workingmen. His election was a victory not only for a particular group of voters but also for a particular explanation of events.

A recent study of party loyalty in the United States Senate during the period 1909-15 sheds some light on the distinction between grass-roots impulses and ideology.[16] One of the authors' major aims was to measure party cohesion. They discovered that tariff votes brought forth a high degree of party unity for both Democrats and Republicans: but much lower rates obtained for immigration and Prohibition roll calls, which indicated a sharp intra-party division on these issues. I would suggest that the low cohesion on questions of immigration and Prohibition reflected grass-roots voter preferences. Republicans who had inherited urban, immigrant, wet support in the political turnover of the 1890's, and who con-

16. Jerome M. Clubb and Howard W. Allen, "Party Loyalty in the United States Senate in the Taft and Wilson Years," mimeo, Inter-University Consortium for Political Research (Ann Arbor, 1965).

tinued to be sensitive to the anti-Prohibition views of these voters, disagreed sharply with dry Republicans. Democrats, on the other hand, came from both the immigrant wet cities of the North and the dry, native-American South and West. High cohesion on the tariff issue represented not common constituency views, but party ideology. One can readily discover Northern Republican support for lower tariffs, especially in committee, and southern Democratic votes for higher rates. But on final votes, considerable regularity obtained because of the tariff's role in ideological cohesion for the parties.

Political leadership provides a useful means of examining the different levels of party activity within the community-society dimension. National leaders have predominated in party studies; state leaders have been much less examined; local leaders have gone almost unnoticed. We have assumed that local leadership either can be ignored or can be understood from knowledge about national leaders. The result is frustrating for a proper treatment of political structure, for leadership differs markedly at different levels of the hierarchy of political life. We must examine not only the levels separately, but also the interaction between them.

Investigations of "Progressive" leaders during the early years of the twentieth century suggest the possibilities. By investigating one hundred individuals in each of three groups of Iowa Republican leaders—Progressive, Cumminsite, and Old Guard—E. D. Potts established that all three were similar in socio-economic and ethno-cultural backgrounds; they differed only in age and previous political experience.[17] William T. Kerr discovered a similar pattern in the state of Washington.[18] At the state level, therefore, it appears that the "Progressives" differed little from the typical Republican leaders. On the other hand David J. Carey examined one hundred ward and precinct officials and candidates for local office in the Cummins and Old Guard factions in Burlington, Iowa, an especially heated center of Republican intra-party controversy.[19] These leaders differed in cultural and occupational characteristics; but, contrary to the findings of earlier studies by Chandler and Mowry, the

17. E. Daniel Potts, "The Progressive Profile in Iowa," *Mid-America,* 45 (1965), 257-68.
18. William T. Kerr, Jr., "The Progressives of Washington, 1910-12," *Pacific Northwest Quarterly,* 55 (1964), 16-27.
19. David James Carey, "Republican Factionalism in Burlington, Iowa, 1906-1908," M. A. Thesis, University of Iowa, 1960.

Progressives came more from blue-collar occupations and newer immigrant, non-Protestant groups than did the Old Guard. More important, however, Carey found that the sharpest differences involved not personal background characteristics, but institutional affiliations. Old Guard leaders were connected with banking, lumbering and railroad groups, "Progressives" with commercial and mercantile interests.

These studies emphasize the vast importance of examining political leadership at all levels of political life, from the grass-roots to the national, from the local to the cosmopolitan, before any safe generalizations can be drawn about a political movement. We need not expect that party leaders at each level would be of the same personal background or institutional involvement. In fact, it would be surprising if this were the case. It would be more reasonable to expect an interaction of different types of people at different positions in the hierarchy, rather than a similarity at all levels. These are distinctions between different degrees of involvement in community and society.

Local leadership was deeply rooted in the local community. To take one example, urban political leaders—councilmen, school board members, justices of the peace, constables—had characteristics that closely resembled those of the ward communities from which they were elected. Liberal historians have completely missed this feature of urban political life. They have examined urban politics largely in terms of the efforts of enlightened people to throw off the influence of the political "machine." They have reduced the conflict almost to a simple notion of a struggle between honest and dishonest men. They have ignored grass-roots political leadership, for they have felt that party leaders manipulated the vote and that community political impulses were not indigenous but the product of external influences. Yet ward political leaders, even prior to the era of municipal reform, were a direct product of ward community life. They can be understood as community leaders, not in the sense of the kind of leadership the liberal analyst would like to have seen, but of the kind which the community in fact produced. In Pittsburgh, for example, the personal socio-economic position of councilmen varied directly with the socio-economic composition of the wards they represented.[20] Working-class wards most frequently elected workingmen, labor leaders, or men who provided the focal point of community contacts, such as saloonkeepers or grocers. Middle-class wards elected small businessmen such as grocers,

20. Based upon an examination of Pittsburgh City Councilmen from 1860 to 1911.

druggists, undertakers, community real estate dealers, bankers, and contractors. Upper-class wards elected central-city bankers, lawyers, doctors, manufacturers. The leadership of such men, identified with their urban sub-communities, rested on community confidence. They spoke for their communities, rolled logs for them in the city council, and represented their economic and cultural interests.

As councilmen came to represent broader geographical areas, they became divorced from local community life and more involved in cosmopolitan urban impulses which were extra-community in scope. Council candidates who ran in citywide rather than ward elections—this municipal reform was widespread in the Progressive Era—required citywide, rather than local prominence, and such recognition came only with involvement in extra-community activities and institutions. The small storekeeper and clerk gave way as the typical city councilman to the prominent lawyer, the large-scale merchant, or the businessman with wide interests. Such men as these came to dominate the reformed city councils and the city school boards.[21]

Leaders at different levels of the community-society party dimension had correspondingly different perspectives. The scope of consciousness of the ward community leader was parochial and limited. When he thought of schools he thought of the ward school, the employment of teachers from the local community, and the use of the school building for community social activities. When he thought of justice, he thought of ways in which community residents could be helped through petty scrapes with the law. But the leader at the cosmopolitan end of the scale thought in terms of the city as a whole, of the need for smooth citywide traffic flows, of general problems of health and sanitation, of education as a system of training which should conform to professional standards. By the very nature of his position in the social structure, his consciousness, his contacts and his knowledge were far more extensive in geographical scope than the ward community.

III

Changes wrought by science and technology in modern America have had an enormous impact on the political party and its traditional local foundations. These changes fashioned not merely new subject matter for

21. Hays, "The Politics of Reform."

political controversy and new demographic roots for voting, but also new types of human relationships which in turn led to new systems of decision-making. Arising at a level in the community-society continuum far above the grass roots, they shifted initiative upward in the expression of political impulses and were responsible for a decline in community involvement in the party. Preference for these systems of decision-making, moreover, led to hostility toward political parties. Examination of these new systems provides, through comparative study, more insight into the community-society dimension as it pertains to political parties. It also brings into focus important changes in parties themselves as they adjusted to the new competition from rival decision-making institutions.

Urban, industrial society involved a fundamental reordering of human relationships which permeated not only economic and social life but political life as well. This reordering went through two stages. First, the revolution in transportation and in the acquisition and transmission of empirical knowledge destroyed the separateness and parochialism of economic, social, and ideological life in the grass-roots community. It brought about a more mobile society. Second, it gave rise to new forms of social organization at levels above that of the community, involving human relationships over broad geographical areas and often in impersonal rather than face-to-face contacts. Locally-established relationships remained. But superimposed upon them now were larger relationships called forth by the new accessibility of things, of people, and of ideas which the technological revolution and the expansion of empirical inquiry had fashioned.

This greatly expanded scope of human relationships established new contexts of control. It increased manyfold the factors which one had to take into account if he wished to influence the course of events. Now it became increasingly difficult even to understand the situation which one wanted to influence; confining one's knowledge to the personal communication of man to man no longer sufficed. The vast world of complex circumstances intruded into decision-making and required new perceptions of the scope and complexity of the political arena and new devices for gathering information upon which decisions could be based. It also gave rise to new political mechanisms, to new means of control commensurate with the new scope of things to be controlled. It called forth devices for influencing selected types of human relationships over wide geographical areas rather than a majority of the voters in a limited community. It gave rise to functional interest groups and systems of corporate decision-making. The local community remained as the basic element of the political party, but it no longer sufficed as the focal point for organizing new political impulses which arose beyond the local community.

Functionally organized economic groups in business, labor, and agriculture developed rapidly in the late nineteenth and early twentieth centuries to influence the wider price-and-market system. They drew together into separate instruments of action not a majority of those living in a limited geographical area, but those who performed similar economic functions over wide geographical areas. Such groups constituted supra-community organizations with roots in only specialized segments of local communities. People found that as individuals they could not influence the price-and-market system, but that as groups they could—either directly, or indirectly through the instruments of government.

These groups sought to influence the political parties, for example influencing planks in their platforms, and their legislative and administrative decisions as well. Many historians have tended to look upon such groups as influences outside the legitimate political system rather than as a set of forces in their own right. Yet they constituted a system of decision-making which paralleled the political party but which differed in its structural roots. Functional interest groups rejected parties as appropriate instruments of political action. Since the party was geographically based, it rarely could speak with a clear-cut, single-interest voice; only rarely, and then at the smallest level of organization, did it rest on a homogeneous constituency. More often it faced conflicting and contending elements within it which had to be compromised for effective action. If one were concerned with a particular political goal he found himself supporting other political goals in which he was far less interested, simply to secure sufficiently broad support for his own proposal. Since his aims were compromised, diluted, or sidetracked, he rarely felt that his view secured sufficient political expression.

In the latter part of the nineteenth century and the early twentieth century, labor and agriculture became disillusioned with their close connection with parties. Their inability to speak clearly through parties led them to establish other methods of political action based more clearly on function. Trade unions, through the Federation of Organized Trades and Labor Unions and later the American Federation of Labor, as well as through city and state organizations, adopted the policy of supporting and opposing legislators irrespective of party and solely in terms of their commitment to labor legislation. Farm organizations, such as the National Farmers Union, admonished their members to disavow partisan politics but at the same time not to give up political rights—in other words, to change political tactics. Commodity trade groups, frequently based on co-operative economic functions, became the major source of farm political power and political action. These functional groups were nonpartisan political organizations which sought to disentangle themselves from a geographical system of representation they found to be ineffective.

Heavy emphasis upon the relationship of functional groups to legislative and administrative decisions has obscured their characteristics as a political structure independent in origin from the formal institutions of government. The private interplay among functional groups was basic to and more fundamental than their public interplay. The injection of public agencies into the process often came as a result of the failure of groups to enter into or accept privately settled accommodations. Such measures as antitrust laws, or railroad, banking, and agricultural legislation in the years from the 1880's on to the Great Depression of 1929, were not so much attempts by the general public to restrict private business in the "public interest," as devices of some segments of private business to restrict other segments when their objectives could not be reached through private accommodation. The results of such legislation should be interpreted as governmental co-operation with private groups in the development and maintenance of a political structure and a decision-making system. The process can be observed in detail in the movement for railroad regulation.[22] Behind federal regulation lay the gradual organization of shippers and railroads, as well as railroad labor unions, as functional groups to protect their interests as consumers or producers of transportation service. Shippers, engaged in regional economic competition, complained that rate patterns gave cost advantages to other shippers. Bargaining between different groups of shippers went on through the medium of the railroad; mediators and arbitrators were called in. At the turn of the century both shippers and railroads became dissatisfied with this process and sought to shift it to a federal agency; hence Congress strengthened the law in the Hepburn Act of 1906. Federal regulation was only a new technique to resolve an old kind of conflict. It came not out

22. Kathel Austin Kerr, "American Railroad Politics, 1914-1920," Doctoral Dissertation, University of Pittsburgh, 1965.

of the nebulous blue of public demands, but from political bargaining between shipper and shipper which had been developing over the years.

Liberal historians have long been reluctant to take this development seriously. They have considered functional groups to be undesirable intrusions into a more desirable system of decision-making represented by the rational voter choosing between candidates for public office. They have looked upon such groups as limiting, confining, and distorting a more legitimate political process, thereby reducing the opportunity for political expression. But, considered in terms of the social relationships in which they were rooted, functional groups expanded the opportunities for political expression by providing alternatives for the transmission of political impulses which the party could not clearly express. The party's need to appeal to diverse groups within given geographical areas, while giving single-minded expression to none, was a limiting and confining method of political expression to those who wished to give more concentrated support to specialized objectives.

The systematization of human relationships in large-scale, centralized corporate activity, whether private or public, constituted still another process of decision-making which affected political parties adversely. While the party rested upon geography, and the interest group upon function, the corporate system rested upon the integration of different functional groups, often located in different geographical areas, into single systems of activity and under centralized control. Beginning with the latter part of the nineteenth century, this process of decision-making grew steadily in private economic affairs and in education, religion, and government; indeed, hardly a realm of life remained untouched. The corporate form of organization was primarily a political or decision-making system. The specialization of functions which divorced the entrepreneur from the capitalist gave rise to a separate group of decision-makers within the corporate system and to a sharp differentiation between those who exercised control and those who were controlled—in short, between the managers and the managed. The integrative tendencies of the corporate system differed sharply from the system of functional-interest interaction which emphasized the give and take of bargaining among equals, and from the political party which stressed national mobilization of grassroots political values. In the corporate system the initiative came from the top down, not from the bottom up or the middle out; and control flowed only in one direction. The relationships between center and periphery were administrative, and were designed to translate central decisions into peripheral action rather than to translate peripheral impulses into central action.

Systematization was closely related to professionalization, and especially to the growth of the empirical professions. The scope of interest of the professional concerned with such matters as education, health, welfare, and public works was increasingly universal rather than parochial, increasingly cosmopolitan rather than local. He valued ideological mobility rather than confined perspectives. Moreover, since his scope of vision tended to expand, he sought larger units of action, larger corporate systems of operation, through which he could apply his knowledge. The public health expert sought to reach and influence an increasing number of people; the educational leader wished to generalize his standards of education to all. Such professionals were influential in shaping the character of reform movements from the late nineteenth century onward. They found corporate systems of decision-making to their liking, and they approved them not only because of their scope of coverage, but because of their coercive potential. The professional sought to carry standards of life generated by a few to the population at large. His task was to persuade the yet unconvinced, rather than simply to express the values dominant in the general public.

This upward flow in the location of decision-making in private affairs gave rise to a similar upward flow in public affairs. The movement to reform municipal government after 1890, for example, was primarily an effort to centralize the location of decision-making.[23] Prior to municipal reform, representation in city councils had been decentralized in a system of ward representation; council action, therefore, constituted a process of bargaining between locally oriented spokesmen. Mayors, often dominated by the councils, were weak. After 1890, however, reformers demanded more centralized decision-making. They promoted the strong-mayor, then the commission, and finally the city-manager form of executive authority; and they urged that ward representation be abolished in favor of centralized, citywide representation. By 1929 the transition had had a profound effect. It produced a shift in political initiative upward from the urban sub-communities to forces of citywide scope.

The same upward shift in decision-making took place between town-

23. Hays, "The Politics of Reform."

ship and county on the one hand and the state on the other. The focal points of this transition were schools and roads. For several decades after 1890 state functions expanded rapidly, producing growth in appropriations and debts, in programs and administrative personnel.[24] Schools and roads constituted the major items of state expenditures. In each case the upward movement of decision-making involved a shift in control over these affairs from local units of government to higher units. While the local units wanted local control in order to retain farm-to-market roads or local schools insulated from the wider, cosmopolitan world, the state units wanted statewide, hard-surfaced road systems, and more modern standards of school curricula and administration. In each case professionals with cosmopolitan rather than local perspectives were extremely influential in shifting the scope of interest and level of decision-making. The state highway commission supplanted the township trustee in road affairs and the state superintendent of public instruction became an increasingly influential figure.

A similar upward shift in decision-making took place between the state and federal governments. The most dramatic aspect of this process was the change in regulatory legislation. It is often argued that federal regulation of private business developed in an atmosphere of laissez-faire; actually, federal regulation more often merely shifted the location of regulation from state to federal levels in accordance with the expansion of the scope of economic activity itself from state and regional to national dimensions. State regulation of transportation, for example, was traditional in the United States; the perfection of the Interstate Commerce Commission only shifted this regulation upward. Many state pure food and drug laws were in force in the late nineteenth century; the federal law of 1906 nationalized regulation. In each case nationally organized businesses with markets and other interests beyond the confines of a single state actively promoted national regulation. They preferred a system of control consistent in scope with their scope of operations; they preferred to deal with one regulatory agency which had a uniform national policy rather than with many state agencies which had diverse policies. They preferred to narrow and limit the number of political forces with which they had to cope.

24. Morton G. Keller, "The Economic Policy Making of the States Since the Civil War," Paper delivered at the meeting of the Mississippi Valley Historical Association, Omaha, Nebraska, April 1963.

Initiative in these upward shifts in decision-making and initiative in the formation of corporate systems of activity did not come from the grass roots or from the middle layers of political structure which were represented by functional interest groups. It came, instead, from the top. It came from those who had the scope of perspective to define possibilities in large ways, from the professionals, the businessmen, usually from upper-income rather than from lower-income groups, from those whose institutional involvements were already geographically broad.[25] This initiative, moreover, involved a process of influence and domination over centers of initiative of smaller scope: if desirable activity was now to be defined in terms of large areas and large numbers of people considered from a single vantage point, one could not accept more parochial definitions. Cosmopolitan life must overcome local life. The development of citywide representation and the city-manager system coerced and restricted centers of initiative in the urban ward communities. The growth of state highway commissions vastly reduced the influence of township and county officials. Far-flung corporate activities produced policies at variance with those of local communities, such as the use of injunctions in labor disputes instead of jury trials which had usually reflected local rather than corporate views. National regulatory policies inevitably reduced the scope of jurisdiction of state regulatory agencies.

The domestic politics of World War I played a significant role in sharpening the conflict between cosmopolitan and local forces within the context of a system of corporate decision-making. For example, during the war the federal government assumed management of the nation's railroads through the United States Railroad Administration.[26] The USRA developed policies geared to objectives which were national in scope. Its officials thought in terms of a single, most efficient, transportation system; and they sought to persuade everyone involved in the entire process, from corporate executives to divisional traffic managers to local merchants, to dovetail their practices in that over-all system. In fact, they forced them to do so. But each of these groups—local buyers and sellers of coal, for example—saw their problems from their own local point of view. They wished not to conform to a national system but to their own plan to maximize their business. They looked upon the USRA as coercive, authori-

25. Hays, "The Politics of Reform"; Joan S. Miller, "The Politics of Municipal Reform in Chicago During the Progressive Era: The Municipal Voters' League as a Test Case, 1896-1920," M. A. Thesis, Roosevelt University, 1966.
26. Kerr, "American Railroad Politics."

tarian, usurping executive power, and they demanded that the railroads be returned to private management and that the power of the Interstate Commerce Commission, suspended for the war, be restored. This they secured in the Transportation Act of 1920.

The growth of systematized decision-making created a new structure of political relationships quite different from those in other systems. The relationship was clearly hierarchical, with a vast gap between those at the top and those at the grass roots in scope of perspective, in source of initiative, in ability to reach levels of decision-making. A continuum of relationships developed which can be differentiated in terms of geographical scope of movement, perception, and influence. A continuous tension arose between those at different points of the community-society continuum, a tension which was a major element of political conflict. The systematization of modern life, in short, created a structure of relationships in which cosmopolitan elements, corporately organized, looked upon local life—including traditional political party life—as parochial, narrow, and unenlightened. Local communities, on the other hand, considered cosmopolitan influences and their bureaucracies to be imperialistic, dictatorial, and destructive of established values.

IV

The development of systems of decision-making at levels of political organization above the local community had significant repercussions on community political life and on political parties. The growth of functional and corporate systems not only created new processes of decision-making alongside the old, but also inevitably involved the reduction of local political influence in favor of influence at a higher level of organization. The vitality of the roots upon which parties rested diminished drastically. The party itself was subjected to attack; it was forced to adjust to influences from new levels of political initiative. For their part, local community impulses became increasingly traditionalist and conservative. Innovation in the political order in urban-industrial America came from cosmopolitan rather than local sources, through administrative action and empirical inquiry which entered the social order not through community but through society. The local community, on the other hand, feeling threatened by these innovations, adopted a posture of defending and perpetuating those patterns of life and custom familiar to and sustaining it. It became tradition-oriented, seeking to preserve the past; in the midst of rapid social change, it took on a protective stance. The political party, resting uniquely on a geographical base and reflecting geographically organized community forces, was an especially appropriate vehicle of conservatism.

The transformation of evangelical Protestantism from an innovating to a protective political impulse illustrates this process. When evangelical religion swept through American Protestantism in the first half of the nineteenth century it was innovating, hopeful, progressive, positive about scientific inquiry, anxious to be involved in the larger world. It won out over more conservative religious tendencies. This stance provided much of the spirit and drive which the early Republican party possessed. By the early twentieth century, however, this same religious impulse faced a new industrial, urban, and scientific environment, one which was marked by the emergence of Catholics and Jews and the increasing popularity of secular thought. In the face of these changes, evangelical Protestantism became protective. It feared ideological mobility, the unpredictable ventures of the secular mind, the changing religious culture, the growing cities. Rooted in rural areas of the country, it launched a drive to protect its cultural heritage against erosion. From the 1890's on it concentrated on such efforts as Prohibition, Sunday observance, anti-evolution laws, and the preservation of rural political power in state legislatures. The rural political party became the special instrument of this protective stance.

Community impulses in the city equally sought to maintain the past, but their efforts were less successful. For here cosmopolitan impulses were more powerful and better organized. Ward political forces could do little but fight a rearguard action against the innovating forces of cosmopolitanism. The attempt to retain the ward school quickly collapsed before the drive for the citywide school board. The feeble fight against urban city council reapportionment stands in dramatic contrast to the successful rural opposition to state legislative reapportionment of over more than half a century. Cities had the same conditions of unequal representation as did the states. As peripheral sections of the city grew, central sections grew less rapidly and then declined. For a short while the central city was overrepresented and the periphery underrepresented, but this did not last long. Almost every municipal reform movement in the early twentieth century involved the effort to shift representation toward areas of population growth. Where the movement did not reduce the power of older sections of the city through citywide representation, it did so by reapportioning council seats. The change came about so swiftly and often so quietly amid the claims and counterclaims of corruption that historians have not noticed it. It reveals that traditionalist forces were overcome in the city far more readily than in the countryside through the destruction of their crucial base of political action—geographical representation.

Community political impulses not only became more conservative; they also declined. Initiative now moved upward to extra-community forces. As a consequence grass-roots areas felt a loss of involvement in decision-making and became more alienated from the wider political community. Those functions of the local political leader which consisted of conveying impulses from the community to the larger centers declined; and communities, in turn, felt that they had a decreasing influence on those more distant centers. As city-manager plans and citywide systems of representation arose, ward communities felt that decisions which affected them were made elsewhere and that they no longer had personal intermediaries through whom they could reach the centers of decision-making.[27] In rural areas considerable influence was still retained over schools, but even here the township official increasingly lost authority to the county superintendent; moreover, his jurisdiction over roads gave way to the state highway commission. The transformation was driven home dramatically to the rural community when, because of the commission's power of eminent domain, roads were constructed through rather than around farms. Urban communities would experience the same powerlessness in later years when redevelopment authorities used a similar power of eminent domain to replace older patterns of physical community organization with new.

As the local political leader's function as a community representative declined, he was replaced by representatives of larger functional and corporate decision-making systems. These appeared in the community not as spokesmen for the community but as agents of extra-community forces. They served primarily to transmit decisions made elsewhere to the community, to secure information useful for decision-making elsewhere, and to cushion the impact and enhance the acceptability of decisions made elsewhere. Firemen and policemen no longer were stationed in the communities where they lived, nor did they represent community organizations, but were assigned to their stations by citywide commis-

27. For expressions of this view see Harold A. Stone *et al., City Manager Government in Nine Cities* (Chicago, 1940), 20, 225, *et passim.*

sioners and boards. Community welfare councils were established to cushion the impact of the shift from the personal attention given by the ward leader to the more impersonal contact with the public welfare agency. The parent-teacher association replaced the ward school board as the representative of community interests, but it functioned more as an aid to the principal, the agent of the larger school system, than as a dominant and independent influence in the formation of school policy. Many functions formerly carried out by ward leaders who were closely interwoven with the party system were now taken up by others who were more closely connected with functional and corporate systems of decision-making. Some indigenous community influences persisted. In some cities, for example, the ward judicial system, with its local justices of the peace and constables, remained as a community institution. Yet such indigenous leadership in the corporate city was rare. Community autonomy persisted and developed most fully in the suburban political jurisdictions, which vigorously defended their legal separateness precisely to retain a sense of influence and power over affairs which affected them. Within the city precinct and ward leaders remained, but with sharply changed functions. Although in some precincts they retained many of their older functions, in most they were reduced to petty affairs of party organization and to mobilizing votes on election day. The functions of the local party leader declined sharply as the focal point of social and political organization shifted to a higher level.

The emergence of new systems of decision-making gave rise to a widespread attack on the political party itself. From national to local levels the political party was considered to be dominated by the corrupt "machine," which rendered it unreliable as an instrument of public action. Demands for direct election of senators; for primary rather than convention nominations; for initative, referendum, and recall; and for other devices to reduce the influence of the party in the selection of candidates persisted throughout the Progressive Era. In fact, when reformers could not agree on substantive issues, they could agree on procedural political reforms. Political reform was touted as a means whereby political power would be shifted from the "interests" to the "people," and mass involvement in decision-making would be restored. In reality, however, the movement for political reform was an attack on the entire party system as it had developed in the nineteenth century, a rejection of community involvement in decision-making, and a demand that public decisions be made through mechanisms other than the political party. It stemmed from fear of rather than faith in community political impulses.

This attack on the political party came not from the grass roots but from people involved in institutions at higher, extra-community levels of social organization. Very frequently they were themselves involved in newer forms of decision-making. In Pittsburgh, for example, they came from the upper levels of society, from the highest echelons of the corporate world, and from the advanced segments of professional life.[28] In Chicago the Municipal Voters' League was composed of men from the city's dominant social and economic groups.[29] In Seattle and Des Moines the drive was spearheaded by the chambers of commerce. The characteristics of the candidates whom these reform groups backed, as contrasted with those whom they opposed, indicated that they preferred as decision-makers those from their own levels of institutional organization and from occupational groups associated with corporate business and professional life. Those who sought political reform, therefore, were far more involved in a cosmopolitan than a local world, far more receptive to the political processes inherent in the corporate rather than the party system of decision-making.

By the same token, the reform image of an appropriate decision-making system also arose from the cosmopolitan world. The reformer's model was the business corporation, not the political party.[30] The political party was too open to a variety of compromising and debilitating influences. It had to respond to the multitude of impulses arising from the community electorate; it had to compromise in making legislative decisions to secure majority support; it had to reward friends and defeat enemies on a party basis. In the business corporation, on the other hand, decisions could be made on the basis of efficient, systematic analysis, from a single vantage point, in which the overriding objective was the "common good." Increasingly through the years those involved in cosmopolitan life sought to divorce decisions from the electorate, in order to enhance the efficiency and system which they felt would implement their goals.

The attack on the party system and on its community roots frequently came only indirectly. Most emphasis was placed upon the corruption of political leaders and the capacity of the "machine" to command loyalty

28. Hays, "The Politics of Reform."
29. Miller, "The Politics of Municipal Reform."
30. Hays, "The Politics of Reform."

and influence votes. Most reformers, therefore, looked upon their activities as attempts to purify rather than to change drastically the system of decision-making. But, in fact, they sought to make fundamental changes, for to them the shortcoming of the party system was its constant susceptibility to influence from the grass-roots community. Reformers frequently made explicit their objection to the community choice of workingmen, clerks, petty shopkeepers, and saloonkeepers as local political leaders. They often argued, in fact, that ward leaders could not make acceptable political decisions precisely because they were too close to their constituents. The political reform movement in the Progressive Era sought not to extend community involvement in political decision-making, but to restrict it in accord with the requirements of new methods of decision-making.

Faced with the rise of new such systems and the atrophy of the community roots of its impulses, the political party in the twentieth century experienced a series of adjustments. As the location of decision-making in the entire political system shifted upward, so did initiative within the party. No longer did community impulses of the ward and township play such a significant role. Now the party assumed a wider geographical perspective; and, in turn, forces organized on an extra-community level assumed a greater influence within it. This larger context of party activity produced at least two significant changes. First, the party increasingly selected decision-makers who represented not geographical but functional areas of society, such as segments of the economic, ethnic, and religious communities. Second, these decision-makers increasingly came, not from all socio-economic levels, depending upon their community of origins, but from a particular segment of the socio-economic system, the upper-middle class. In both of these changes the party made an adjustment to the new patterns of social organization with which it now was forced to compete. These changes were most dramatic in the cities. No matter what new forms of government emerged there, the geographical base from which decision-makers were chosen through the party expanded sharply, and the number of people and variety of institutions which each decision-maker represented expanded as sharply. Drastically reduced in size, city councils could provide representation to few distinct geographical communities. In this circumstance councilmen were often elected at large; but even when ward representation was retained areas of representation increased sharply in size. Decision-makers now had to appeal to a broad range of the electorate. Party leaders, in selecting nominees for office, recognized this change in the structure of representation. They wished to select candidates who would appeal to the largest number of voters. What would be the criteria? To some extent they retained an area distribution, making sure that candidates came from different sections of the city. More important, however, they sought to grant representation to all the major functional groups of the city.

The process of "balancing the ticket" among economic and ethno-cultural groups could be observed in the earliest departures from the ward system. Often suggestions arose for functional representation along economic lines: for councilmen chosen, for example, from manufacturers, bankers, professionals, labor, and merchants. At times only political defeat gave rise to an effective "balance." In Des Moines, for example, the first slate of candidates for the new city commission was drawn entirely from the business community, though balanced among its various sectors. No one identified with labor was nominated. The result was a disastrous defeat for the "businessmen's slate." Cities in Iowa that followed Des Moines in the drive for the commission form of government—Des Moines was a pioneer in this innovation—profited from its mistakes and "balanced" their tickets with workingmen's representatives. In Pittsburgh the new city council, reorganized in 1911 by replacing ward with citywide representation, included a labor spokesman; the position he held was referred to in the newspapers as "reserved for labor." The choice of the functional groups to be represented remained a major party choice; but the shift from geographical to functional representation was widespread.

The change in the character of working-class representation in city councils was significant. Formerly these representatives had often been unskilled or skilled workingmen, many of whom had no official position in a trade union. Although trade union officials were frequently members of city councils, many working-class councilmen were not union leaders. Moreover, people of other occupations—store clerks, bartenders, and small shopkeepers—often represented working-class wards. Now, however, as the initiative for selecting candidates moved upward to higher levels of social organization, the top-echelon trade union official became the functional representative of working-class people. The labor representative chosen for the Pittsburgh city council in 1911 was the immediate past president of the Amalgamated Association of Iron, Steel and Tin Workers, the largest organized labor group in the city's major industry. In other

180 THE AMERICAN PARTY SYSTEMS

words, spokesmen for labor as an organized functional group replaced working-class community leaders as decision-makers when the party made the adjustment to new systems of social organization.

The occupational characteristics of city councilmen as a whole shifted sharply upward in the community-society continuum. Councilmen now were lawyers and doctors with city contacts far wider than the local community, and bankers and businessmen of far more extensive activities than the community store. There were others, of course, but the center of gravity of the occupational structure of city councilmen clearly shifted from the lower and lower-middle class to the upper-middle class. While few of the council members during the days of ward representation in Pittsburgh, for example, were listed in the *Blue Book* (the city's social directory), an increasing number were so listed after citywide representation replaced ward representation. The change was most striking in school government, where the shift to citywide representation was more rapid and more complete. A study of school bo--ds throughout the nation by George S. Counts in the 1920's indicated that their members came overwhelmingly from the upper occupational and professional groups.[31]

Political parties were equally sensitive to religious and ethnic functional groups. They maintained religious and ethnic balance on city councils, the particular balance depending upon the community's ethno-cultural composition. The gradual involvement of "newer" ethnic groups came about as the party felt it necessary to recognize these segments of the community. But just as candidates who represented labor as a functional group were drawn from the top echelons of working-class organizational and social levels, so were the candidates who represented ethnic groups. The first Negro members of the Pittsburgh city council came from the Negro upper class—professionals and businessmen—a class level which gave rise to an outlook approaching that of the upper-middle-class segment of the white community.

The upward shift in decision-making brought about an upward shift in the characteristics of decision-makers in the community-society dimension, and a related upward shift in their socio-economic class level. One observes a gradual exclusion of local community leaders from the decision-making process which, in turn, involved a gradual exclusion of direct representatives of lower socio-economic groups. Decision-makers, increas-

31. George S. Counts, *The Social Composition of Boards of Education: A Study in the Social Control of Public Education* (Chicago, 1927).

ingly drawn from the upper-middle class, admitted other functional groups to the decision-making process only as they developed spokesmen of a similar community-society and socio-economic position. A functional system of representation in a cosmopolitan upper-middle-class context had replaced a geographical system of representation which had involved leaders from all segments of the community-society and socio-economic structure.

V

Political parties function within given environmental contexts. Both the goals which they seek and their techniques of action are closely related to the social circumstances within which they work. The most pervasive characteristics of that environment, moreover, are structural, those patterns of social organization which interconnect the shared experiences, perceptions, values, and actions of different groups of people. Just as the entire social order is a system of human relationships, so is the political party. Its various facets, whether they be popular voting, social and political perception, ideologies, leadership, or the interaction between levels of political activity, can be understood adequately only if each is located within a precise segment of the social and political structure. Our major current task in historical political research is to describe political structure and the changes therein over a period of time. We must root political parties in that structure.

A community-society dimension is a useful conceptual framework in this task. It brings out more sharply than do other frameworks the changing human relationships within the party in the context of the changing human relationships in the larger social order. It enables one to examine the upper levels of political life, the grass roots, and their interrelationships within a single context. It stimulates examination of a large variety of political phenomena such as voting behavior, ideology, leadership, and the vertical dimension of the political order as closely interrelated facets of political life. It provides an opportunity, within a single system of thought, to examine differences in the geographical scope of human perception, of human relationships, and of systems of decision-making in the political world. It provides a basis for fruitful investigation and examination of modern American political development.

VII | Donald E. Stokes

UNIVERSITY OF MICHIGAN

Parties and the

Nationalization of Electoral Forces[1]

THE FACT that party systems have flourished in the modern world is at least partly due to the ease with which parties are seen as significant political actors by the mass public. Their presence can simplify wonderfully the *dramatis personae* of politics for a remote and very imperfectly informed audience, a fact that helps account for the durability of partisan attitudes once formed.[2] Among the gentle reifications by which the public makes sense of politics, imputing reality to the parties may be the most important of all.[3]

Over the past quarter-century, survey studies of the American voter have detailed the importance of parties as cognitive objects.[4] Parties are

1. I am greatly indebted to Michael J. Kahan, Ronald May, and Arthur C. Wolfe for their aid in preparing this report. The immense task of assembling historical election returns was undertaken by Peter Axelrod, John Francis, Barbara Lazarus, Cathy Miller, Philip Quarterman, Margaret Squires, and Jill Wescott. Finally, I owe large debts to David Butler and Warren Miller, with whom I have explored various aspects of the British and American data discussed here.
2. Graham Wallas wrote years ago that the citizen requires "something simpler and more permanent, something which can be loved and trusted, and which can be recognized at successive elections as being the same thing that was loved and trusted before; and party is such a thing." *Human Nature in Politics* (London, 1910), 83.
3. One suspects that a majority of political scientists specializing in parties could be carried for the proposition that American parties as unitary entities don't exist; but the reasons that would lead them to think so trouble the American voter almost not at all. Perhaps the achievement represented by the reification of parties can be seen more clearly if we consider a rival schema for classifying leaders, such as that of Left and Right. As a means of typing political actors, liberal and conservative identifications probably are more real than party labels to many elite observers, but they have repeatedly been found to be of little meaning to the mass public.
4. The empirical literature treating partisan attitudes in the adult and pre-adult years is by now vast. For a discussion of party identifications in the adult electorate, see Angus Campbell, Philip E. Converse, Warren E. Miller, and Donald E. Stokes, *The American Voter* (New York, 1960), chaps. 6 and 7. For a seminal discussion of the development of partisan orientations in the young, see Fred I. Greenstein, *Children and Politics* (New Haven, 1965), esp. 55-84.

among the first political objects visible to the very young, and the partisan identifications into which the child is "socialized" within the political culture of the family have a remarkable capacity to survive into adulthood. As an adult, the voter relies on his party allegiance to value new leaders and issues and to impose some order on the choices that are presented by a ballot of spectacular length and complexity.

Moreover, the conserving role of party identification by no means exhausts the significance of parties as objects of political attitude. The issues and events which deflect the partisan voter from his established allegiance, temporarily at least, and which can provide the whole grounds of choice for the independent voter of no fixed allegiance, may also be seen in terms of party. To cite an example which has echoed through much of our political history, the cry to throw the rascals out has generally identified the rascals in party terms.

The reality which parties have as objects of mass perception is the more remarkable in view of the actual fragmentation of party structure and the diffusion of authority produced on all levels of government by the doctrine of separated powers. Indeed, the ambiguity of parties as stimulus objects suggests that the focus of partisan attitudes may vary a good deal and that the modern American experience may differ from that of other liberal democracies or earlier periods of our own politics. The very richness of contemporary American survey data poses the danger that conclusions of unwarranted generality will be drawn from the evidence at hand.[5]

This possibility is the backdrop to the empirical argument which I shall give. An analysis of election returns for the United States House of Representatives has made me feel that the past century has witnessed a profound change in the degree to which a local politics has produced the forces moving the electorate in our congressional elections. I shall describe this evolution here, drawing for purposes of contrast on comparable returns from parliamentary elections in Britain. Both the American development and the contrast with Britain seem to me to have important implications for political representation.

---

5. The need for restraint in extrapolating from contemporary survey evidence has been sensed by many writers, including a number of survey analysts. See the cautionary argument advanced by Walter Dean Burnham, "The Changing Shape of the American Political Universe," *American Political Science Review*, LIX (1965), 7-28.

II

This analysis had its origin in a study of legislative representation in
Britain and America, a study which has paid a good deal of attention to
popular influence on the cohesion of the parliamentary and congressional
parties. Many influences affect the solidarity of a legislative party, but the
members' perception of forces on their constituents' voting behavior is
surely among them. Part of what is involved here is exactly the sort of
cognitive question I have touched: what political actors are salient to
the mass electorate? If the member of the legislature believes, on the one
hand, that it is the national party and its leaders which are salient and
that his own electoral prospects depend on the legislative record of the
party as a whole, his bonds to the legislative party will be relatively
strong. This is the situation posited by the model of responsible party
government. But if the legislator believes, on the other hand, that the
public is dominated by constituency influences and that his prospects
depend on his own or his opponent's appeal or on other factors distinctive
to the constituency, his bonds to the legislative party will be relatively
weak. To these two levels of forces the intermingling of American elections adds a third: public response to statewide political leaders, whose
coattails may extend into congressional contests via the long ballot.

To assess the relative importance of forces at these various levels I
have utilized a statistical model which partitions the total variation of
turnout and the party vote over a series of legislative elections into distinct components corresponding to the several levels at which influences
on the electorate may arise. I shall say very little here about the model's
formal properties since they are treated at length elsewhere.[6] The model
detects the relative influence of forces at several levels by exploiting the
nesting of a number of constituencies within a state or region and of a

6. The model represents the proportion Y_{ijk} turning out or voting Republican in
the jth congressional district of the ith state in the kth election year as a sum of three
fixed and three random terms:

$$Y_{ijk} = \alpha + \beta_i + \gamma_{ij} + a_k + b_{ik} + c_{ijk} \tag{1}$$

where α is the fixed effect of national politics; β_i the fixed effect of politics in the ith
state; γ_{ij} the fixed effect of politics in the jth district of the ith state; a_k the effect of
national politics in the kth year; b_{ik} the effect of politics in the ith state in the kth
year, and c_{ijk} the effect of politics in the jth district of the ith state in the kth year.
It follows from this that the variance of Y_{ij} over the five congressional elections of a
decade $(k = 1, \ldots, 5)$ depends only on the variances and covariances of the

number of states or regions within the country as a whole. It can be seen intuitively that if the forces moving the electorate were perfectly idiosyncratic to individual constituencies, variations of turnout or party strength would show no more than a chance similarity across the constituencies of a state or region or across the whole nation. Detecting no more than chance similarity, the model would attribute all forces on electoral change to the constituency level. But if politics at the state or national level did have common effects across a number of constituencies, turnout or party strength would show parallel movements, and the model would attribute an influence to these higher levels of politics according to the degree of observed similarity. In this manner the total average variance of turnout or party strength can be partitioned into components due to forces acting on the electorate at each of several levels.

In the case of recent congressional voting, for example, there can be little doubt of the presence of national forces, especially when a congressional election is joined to a contest for the presidency. Likewise there can be little doubt that congressional voting reflects forces that arise in the individual constituency—the personal stature of the candidates, the hold of local party organizations, the intrusion of purely local issues. And it is part of the lore of American politics that statewide contests for governor or senator may also affect congressional races. The question therefore is not which of these forces are felt at all but rather what is their relative magnitude. It is this question which the model seeks explicitly to answer.

III

When applied to the congressional returns from the 1950's, the most recent full decade yielding the required data, the model gives strikingly

---

three terms which vary over time; that is,

$$\text{Var}\,(Y_{ij}) = \text{Var}\,(a) + \text{Var}\,(b_i) + \text{Var}\,(c_{ij})$$
$$+2[\text{Cov}\,(a, b_i) + \text{Cov}\,(a, c_{ij}) + \text{Cov}\,(b_i, c_{ij})]. \tag{2}$$

A detailed discussion of the model appears in Donald E. Stokes, "A Variance Components Model of Political Effects," in John M. Claunch (ed.), *Mathematical Applications in Political Science* (Dallas: Arnold Foundation, 1965), 61-85. The paper gives the detailed formulas by which each of the terms of equation (2) may be calculated for individual congressional districts and averaged across the nation to reach explicit estimates of the magnitude of national, state, and constituency components of the total variance of turnout and party strength in the five elections of a given decade.

186 THE AMERICAN PARTY SYSTEMS

dissimilar results for turnout and party choice. In the five elections from 1952 to 1960 by far the largest component of the variance of turnout was that measuring national influences. As shown in Table 1a, forces beyond the constituency, especially those attendant on contests for the presidency, played the foremost role in the rise and fall of participation in congressional contests. Indeed, inspection of the components in the table's third column shows that national forces accounted for very nearly seven-eighths of the total variance of congressional turnout in this decade. It is interesting to note that statewide forces were at least as influential on congressional turnout as were forces arising within the constituency.

TABLE 1

Components of Variance of Vote for U.S. House of Representatives over Five Elections, 1952-60

a. TURNOUT

Political Level	Variance Component	Square Root of Variance Component	Normalized Variance Component
National	72.87	8.54	.86
State	7.20	2.68	.08
Constituency	5.22	2.28	.06
			1.00

b. PARTY VOTE

Political Level	Variance Component	Square Root of Variance Component	Normalized Variance Component
National	9.32	3.05	.32
State	5.32	2.31	.19
Constituency	13.98	3.74	.49
			1.00

A very different pattern of variation of the party vote in the 1950's appears in Table 1b. Much the largest component of the variance of party support is that measuring constituency influences; indeed, the third column of Table 1b shows that almost half of the total variance could be attributed to this level. National forces were again substantial, although nothing like as influential as they were in the voter's decision whether or not to go to the polls. Apparently the coattails of presidential candidates are much more likely to pull voters to the polls than to govern what choices for

Congress they make. The partisan influence of statewide contests on congressional races was by no means negligible, but was plainly the least important of the three.

Comparisons across the several political levels of Table 1 suggest a good deal about the dynamics of voting for Congress in the recent past. These figures take on new sharpness, however, when they are compared to values obtained for other periods or other electoral systems. Indeed, no comparison is more instructive than that with Britain, the other great representational system to which I have given attention.

IV

Empirical comparisons across national frontiers are notoriously vulnerable to institutional and cultural dissimilarities extraneous to the problem at hand. Two structural differences between Britain and America have had to be dealt with in the comparison I shall give. The first of these has to do with the party system. The presence of the Liberals deprives British politics of a "pure" two-party character and confronts the investigator with a choice of ways to calculate variations of the electoral strength of the two main parties. Fortunately, for my purposes here it makes almost no difference which of several reasonable alternatives is chosen.[7]

A more serious structural difference arises from the absence in Britain of the intermediate state level of the American federal system. The fact that single-member constituencies are the basis of representation in both the House of Representatives and the House of Commons provides the

---

7. The differences between the several proposed measures of change turn on whether shifts of party strength are to be percentaged in terms of the total vote for one, two, or three parties, or the total registered electorate. I have chosen to use as a percentage base the combined total of the Conservative and Labour vote. For the kth election we may calculate for any parliamentary constituency the quantity

$$M_k = \frac{Con_k - Lab_k}{2}$$

where Con_k is the Conservative per cent of the two-party vote, Lab_k the Labour per cent. M_k can be thought of as the margin by which the Conservative share departed (positively or negatively) from 50 per cent, that is, from being even with Labour's. Then the "swing" (positive or negative) to the Conservatives between a first and second election may be defined as $M_2 - M_1$, and the total variance of M_{ij}, that is, of the Conservative margin of the jth constituency of the ith region over a set of K elections ($k = 1, \ldots, K$), may be partitioned into national, regional, and constituency components by the model described above.

ground for comparing the national and constituency components in the two nations, but there is of course no direct British analogue to the effect of statewide contests on American congressional voting. I have nevertheless retained in the British analysis an intermediate "regional" component to detect common movements of party support in regional groupings of parliamentary constituencies.[8] This component keeps such regional movements from being falsely incorporated into the constituency component, but its interpretation must necessarily differ from that given the American state component.[9]

With these qualifications, the partisan components obtained from parliamentary election returns over the six British general elections of 1950, 1951, 1955, 1959, 1964, and 1966 show a profound divergence from the American congressional components of the past decade. These contrasts are set forth in Table 2, which reproduces in 2a the American

TABLE 2

Components of Variance of Party Vote
over Five National Elections

a. FOR THE U.S. HOUSE OF REPRESENTATIVES, 1952-1960

Political Level	Variance Component	Square Root of Variance Component	Normalized Variance Component
National	9.32	3.05	.32
State	5.32	2.31	.19
Constituency	13.98	3.74	.49
			1.00

b. FOR THE BRITISH PARLIAMENT, 1950-1966

Political Level	Variance Component	Square Root of Variance Component	Normalized Variance Component
National	5.13	2.26	.47
Regional	1.42	1.19	.13
Constituency	4.45	2.11	.40
			1.00

8. The definition of regions is very close to that given in the appendix to David Butler and Anthony King, *The British General Election of 1966* (London; 1966), 300-310.

9. In particular, it is possible that regional effects are actually differential responses of regional clusters of constituencies to *national* forces. To some extent such "downward" deflections of forces are monitored by the model's covariance terms, as explained by Stokes, "A Variance Components Model of Political Effects," 74-5.

partisan components of Table 1 for comparison with the partisan components for Britain, which are given in 2b. A first observation to be made from a comparison of Tables 2a and 2b is that the electoral strength of the parties has been a good deal less variable in Britain than in America. Inspection of corresponding entries in the first two columns of Table 2a and 2b shows the British figures to be uniformly smaller, in most cases markedly so. The more revealing comparison, however, is the relative size of the several partisan components within these two systems. In Britain the national component was the most important element of party change: very nearly half the total variance could be attributed to national forces. The constituency component contributed a somewhat smaller proportion of the total variance than in the United States. And when the contrast of constituency forces is made in terms of absolute magnitudes, rather than of proportions, the difference is remarkable. Indeed, the ratio of constituency components in the first column of Tables 2a and 2b is three to one.

The marked difference of constituency forces in the two countries may be clearer if we take the simpler problem of change between two elections only and compare the dispersion of change across constituencies. For this comparison I have chosen pairs of elections in Britain and America which exhibit fairly equal average change: the mean swing between parties across the parliamentary constituencies of Britain from 1951 to 1955 was 1.8 per cent; the mean swing across congressional districts contested both in 1952 and 1956 also was 1.8 per cent. Variation about these means, however, was very unequal in the two countries, as the distributions superimposed in Figure 1 make clear. To focus attention on constituency influences in the two countries, both these distributions have been adjusted to remove the effect of state or regional, as well as national, forces.[10] The much sharper peak of the British curve makes clear how seldom forces centered in the individual parliamentary constituency yield a result which diverges strongly from a wider pattern of change.

10. The correction for state or regional forces is a straightforward one. Adopting the notation of footnote 7, we may define M_{i1} as the average Conservative margin within the constituencies of the ith region in a first election; M_{i2} as the average Conservative margin in the ith region in a second election; M_{ij1} as the Conservative margin in the jth constituency of the ith region in the first election and M_{ij2} as the Conservative margin in the jth constituency of the ith region in the second election. The adjusted swing between elections in the jth constituency of the ith region is then calculated as

$$S_{ij} = M_{ij2} - M_{ij1} - (M_{i2} - M_{i1}).$$

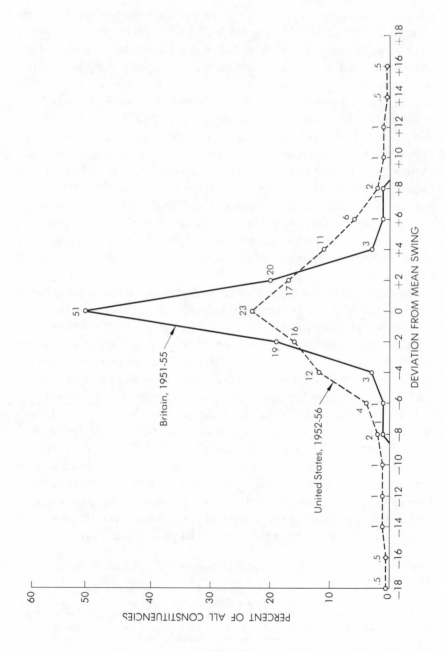

FIGURE 1
United States and Britain: Differentials in Deviations from Mean Partisan Swing,
1952-1956 and 1951-1955

There can be no doubt that Table 2 and Figure 1 describe a difference in electoral behavior which is of immense importance to representative government in Britain and America. The source of changes of voting for Congress lies a good deal within the individual constituency; of voting for Parliament, less so. Of course, these facts will give the legislator a national or constituency orientation only as he perceives the true source of electoral change. Interviews of congressmen and M.P.'s taken as part of the larger research project make clear, however, that the difference of electoral behavior reflected here is vividly apparent to the legislative elites of these two countries.[11]

Britain may well provide an extreme case of the nationalization of political attitude in the Western World; probably it is unique among nations which elect the national legislature from single-member constituencies. What is more, there is reason to believe that this aspect of the party system was strongly evident by the close of the last century, although the fissiparous behavior of nineteenth-century parliamentary elites and the displacement of the Liberals by Labour in this century make it difficult to submit this evolution to orderly analysis. For example, the homogeneity of change across the parliamentary constituencies of Britain between the general elections of 1892 and 1895 was already greater than the homogeneity of change in American congressional districts between successive elections of the 1950's. As shown by Table 3, the standard deviation of swing over the life of the 1892 Parliament was 3.0 per cent on an average swing of 4.0 per cent; between the congressional elections of 1954 and 1958, for example, it was 6.3 per cent on an average swing of 4.6 per cent. The selected additional figures for Britain given in Table 3 suggest that the nationalization of politics increased somewhat from the turn of the century to the present era, although the data would be much less clear for the intervening years of Liberal decline.

Casting the problem in these developmental terms inevitably carries our interest back to the historical antecedents of our American findings. If congressional voting in the middle of this century reveals substantial

11. Data of this kind from American congressmen are reported in Donald E. Stokes and Warren E. Miller, "Party Government and the Saliency of Congress," *Public Opinion Quarterly,* XXVI (1962), 532-46. The data from comparable interviews of Members of Parliament will be reported in a forthcoming analysis of representation in Britain and America. One of my parliamentary respondents, who stood in the Home Counties in 1964, wistfully reported that he had been delighted by the increase of his majority until he realized that his swing was dead on the national average.

Table 3

Some Swing Figures from Britain and the United States

a. BRITAIN

General Elections	No. of Constituencies	Mean	Standard Deviation
1892-1895	307	4.0%	3.0%
1906-(Jan) 1910	419	4.9	4.4
1945-1950	135	4.5	3.7
1950-1951	224	.7	1.4
1951-1955	349	1.8	1.4
1955-1959	455	1.1	2.2
1959-1964	370	3.5	2.4
1964-1966	429	3.2	1.7

Note: The constituencies included in these analyses are those whose boundaries were not subject to marked change between the given pair of elections and whose patterns of candidature (i.e. Conservative vs. Labour, or Conservative vs. Labour vs. Liberal, etc.) were the same at both elections.

b. UNITED STATES

Congressional Elections	No. of Constituencies	Mean	Standard Deviation
1952-1954	318	4.3	5.2
1954-1956	333	2.2	5.1
1956-1958	324	6.9	5.5
1958-1960	327	2.7	5.6
1952-1956	322	1.8	6.4
1954-1958	318	4.6	6.3
1956-1960	333	4.1	6.7

Note: Includes only constituencies contested both years of each pair of elections.

constituency influences on electoral change, what does the more distant past show? What patterns can be drawn from remote congressional returns by the model utilized for the present era?

V

The five congressional elections of a decade provide a natural group for such an analysis of historical returns. The Constitution's requirement that congressional seats be reapportioned among states after each decennial census has supplied an impetus every ten years for redrawing district boundaries. Once in a hundred years—after the 1920 census—Congress failed to discharge its constitutional mandate, and the courts in the 1960's have created special havoc with district lines. But the nine full decades of modern party development, from the 1870's through the 1950's, are accessible to an analysis of the development of congressional voting, and I have applied to the five congressional elections of each decade the statistical model utilized originally for the analysis of the 1950's.

Figure 2 gives the results of this historical analysis first of all for the constituency component of turnout. The results are impressive. Between the mid-nineteenth and mid-twentieth centuries variations of turnout became progressively less distinctive to congressional districts. Almost without a pause, the magnitude of constituency forces on turnout diminished over these nine decades to a level in the recent past which was very low indeed. While in large measure the electorate once went to the polls or stayed away according to the circumstances surrounding individual contests, this sort of influence has become exceedingly weak in recent times.

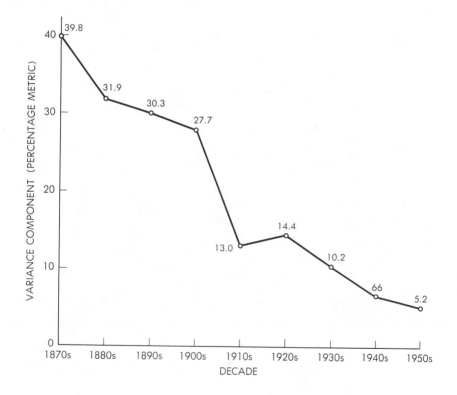

FIGURE 2
United States: Changes in Constituency Influence on Congressional-Election Turnout, by Decade
Note: Only congressional districts with Democratic-Republican contests in all five elections of the decade are included.

During this century there has been a complementary rise of national forces on turnout. The historical series of the national component, superimposed on the constituency series in Figure 3, shows a marked rise over the five decades of this century. This rise followed a decline in the latter

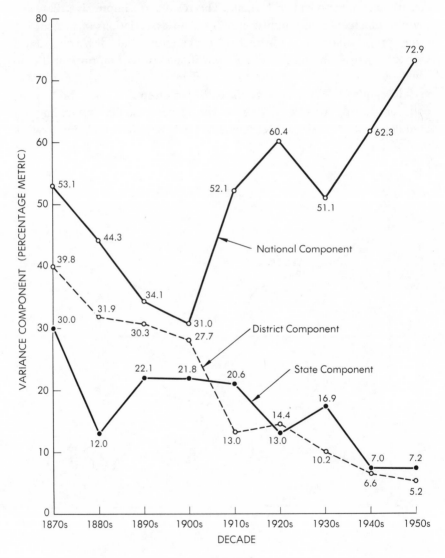

FIGURE 3
United States: Changes in the Relative Influence of Variance Components on Congressional-Election Turnout, by Decade
Note: Only congressional districts with Democratic-Republican contests in all five elections of the decade are included.

decades of the last century; the series indicates substantial national fluctuations of turnout, along with marked constituency variations, in the earliest decades after Reconstruction. In the twentieth century, however, the national and constituency series have diverged strongly, achieving a remarkable difference by the middle of the century. The series for the state component, also shown in Figure 3, suggests that there has been a long-term secular decline of statewide forces on congressional turnout.

The decay of constituency influences on turnout has been paralleled by a decline of constituency forces on the party vote in House races. The historical series for the constituency component of party strength is given by Figure 4, where it is superimposed on the series for turnout. The two patterns are broadly similar. The magnitude of constituency influences

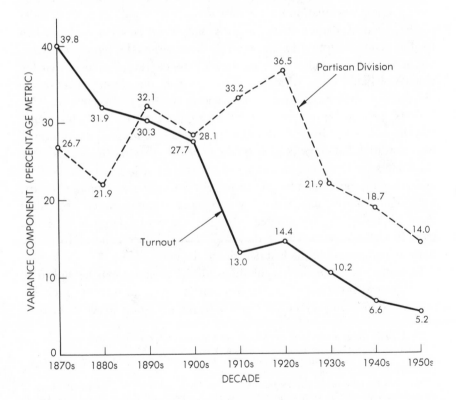

FIGURE 4

United States: Changes in Constituency Influence on Turnout and Partisan Division, by Decade

Note: Only congressional districts with Democratic-Republican contests in all five elections of the decade are included.

on the party division did rise in the middle decades of this period but then fell away to a level in the 1950's which was again, by comparison with the past, very low indeed. The relative position of the two curves in the most recent decades suggests that constituency influences remain stronger in variations of party strength than of turnout, a finding detailed for the 1950's by Table 1. And it is worth recalling that constituency influences on partisan voting for congressional candidates are stronger by a wide margin than constituency influences on partisan voting for British parliamentary candidates. But the primary conclusion to be drawn from the turnout and partisan components in the United States over most of a century is the substantial decline of the constituency as a distinct arena of conflict in congressional elections.[12]

The reasons for this decline must be several, and I shall offer little by way of grand explanation for the nationalization of politics on both sides of the Atlantic. Paradoxically, a fairly simple explanation may account for the major exception to the trend of these series, the temporary peaking of the partisan curve after the turn of the century. I suspect that the change of ballot form, which came in a rush in the closing years of the old century, may have been a main reason for this divergence. In 1888 "tickets" printed by the parties for their supporters were still almost universally in use, but by 1896 all but a few states had adopted some form of the Australian ballot, printed at public expense, carrying the names of all candidates for Congress and other offices contested in a general election, and allowing the citizen to vote in secrecy.[13] Coming at a time when the individual congressional district was a more vigorous arena of conflict than it is today, the encouragement which the consolidated secret ballot gave to variable party voting may well have produced the highs of the partisan component in the first decades of the new century.[14]

In many ways the decline of these historical series can be linked to more general processes of nationalization in American society. Probably one of the most important has to do with the changing structure of mass

12. I shall defer to a later report an examination of the historical series of the national and state components of the partisan vote for Congress.

13. Frederick W. Dallinger, *Nominations for Elective Office in the United States* (New York, 1897), 173ff.

14. This hypothesis ought to be checked in terms of the finer detail of electoral change, particularly by comparing, state by state, variations of the House vote before and after the exact year the ballot was changed. The source and magnitude of this influence would be clearer if a contrast were also drawn between the states adopting "straight-ticket" and "office-group" forms of the consolidated ballot.

communications. In all eras of our politics, those contesting the congressional seat have had to compete for the attention of their electors. The quest for the voter's interest in the congressional district has never been easy, but in a day when the dissemination of news was controlled by local editors, abetted by the face-to-face communication networks of the American small town, it may have been a good deal easier. Certainly the rise of printed and broadcast media disseminating news to huge urban and hinterland audiences, of which any one congressional district is a small part, has worsened the lot of the congressional candidate, although it may in some cases have increased the visibility of state or urban candidates. Our interview studies of constituents in the present era show how much more salient to his voters is the congressman whose district comprises a "natural" community—Dayton, Ohio, let us say—than the congressman whose district is a fraction of a great metropolitan complex. The increasing mismatch of constituency and media audience can therefore have lessened steadily the visibility of congressional contests and, with it, the magnitude of forces distinctive to the constituency.

We can only believe that the centralization of mass communications has deeply influenced the nationalization of British politics. Today eight national morning newspapers achieve a coverage of four-fifths of British households, and very rarely does a single constituency provide the bulk of readers for a provincial daily. The centralization of news is even greater on radio and television, which have never ventured into local broadcasting. The voter learns even less about his constituency from the mass media in Britain than he does in America.

And yet the evolution of mass communications in Britain should caution us against too facile an explanation of the nationalization of politics. It is true that the individual constituency counts for less today than it did prior to the rise of the national morning press in the first years of this century. But the strong parallelism of change across parliamentary constituencies appeared earlier than that; indeed, we have already noted that this tendency was stronger in Britain during the 1890's than it was in America as late as the 1950's. The change that took place in British electoral politics somewhere in the latter half of the nineteenth century probably had more explicitly political origins, especially the great confrontation of Gladstone and Disraeli across the House, the extension of the franchise, and the rise of the national campaign. There may also have been critical political elements in the nationalization of congressional politics in the United States, especially the enormously increased salience of the federal government and the presidency in the period of Franklin D. Roosevelt and the New Deal.

Questions less of cause than of consequence, however, lay behind the analysis reported here. Whatever the factors in the decay of constituency influences over half a century or more, we may enquire into the effects of this development on political representation. A sure account of its effects would require evidence that is beyond reach, but I shall close with several observations on the nationalization of political attitude and representation in Parliament and Congress.

VI

The link between electoral forces and legislative behavior owes much of its elusiveness to the fact that it will depend on perceptions and motives held by the legislator himself. No electoral forces are likely to reach the man who knows his career is about to end by terminal illness, and the true forces acting on a constituency will not matter to the legislator who misperceives them totally. To enlarge what little we know of these perceptions in the current era, my colleagues and I have systematically interviewed Members of Congress and Members of Parliament, as well as samples of their constituents. But the fragmentary nature of such information from an earlier day precludes our measuring in any careful way the changes of perception which have accompanied the broadest changes of electoral forces.

The relationship between electoral patterns and legislative behavior would, however, be complex enough in terms of whatever it is in electoral "reality" that sensitizes the legislator to the forces on his electors. We may begin with the truism that the legislator who cares about his survival at the polls will defer more to electoral pressure, whatever its source, if his survival may depend on it. Hence, a nationalization of electoral forces will have greatest influence among those whose majorities can be swept away. There are of course many reasons—chairmanships, ministerial assignments, party loyalty, and the like—why a legislator can be concerned about the electoral fortunes of his party without his own seat being in danger. But we would expect electoral change to have a special poignancy for those whom it can put out of office.

The threat of defeat may be said to depend on two things, of which the first is the less tangible: for any existing majority, the possibility of defeat grows with the amplitude of change. If no more than 2 or 3 per cent of voters can be expected to shift between elections, a majority of 10 per cent will look impregnable; but if 20 or 30 per cent can be expected to shift, such a lead will look very modest. Politicians rarely raise estimates of this kind to the level of an explicit calculus, but intuitive judgments as to the volatility of the vote constantly enter their assessments of the safeness of legislative seats.

The second, more tangible factor is of course the size of the legislator's majority. For any given amplitude of change, the threat of defeat will be greater where the margin has been narrow. As a means of classifying constituencies this factor is very often explicitly taken into account, and candidates, party managers, and the press all will make judgments as to the safeness of seats on the basis of the narrowness of prior victories.

It follows from this that we should heed the amplitude of change and the competitiveness of seats as we assess the legislative consequences of a change of the focus of electoral forces. These are matters on which Britain and America once again have differed profoundly. We have noted in Table 2 that contemporary change is a good deal less extensive in Britain than in America. From 1950 to 1966—an interval which twice saw a turnover of party control—the average total variance of Labour or Conservative strength in British constituencies was less than half the average total variance of Republican or Democratic strength in America, and the contrast would be even greater if the congressional elections of the early 1960's were included in the comparison. If the two systems differed in this alone, the American congressman would live under the greater threat of defeat.

In fact, however, this difference is largely nullified by a contrast in the competitiveness of seats. The differences of partisan composition between the safest Conservative and safest Labour constituency is vast, but the massing of constituencies within a competitive range is somewhat more pronounced in Britain than America, even when a reasonable adjustment is made for what would have happened had the Republicans contested a greater number of Southern districts. For example, if we compare the congressional election of 1954 and the parliamentary election of 1955, elections in which the Democrats and Conservatives, respectively, won with comparable fractions of the two-party vote, the party winning the seat polled less than three-fifths of the two-party vote in 53 per cent of Britain's constituencies but failed to exceed this margin in only 42 per cent of congressional districts.

What is more, the competitiveness of American congressional districts is less today than it has been in some prior eras, particularly the era of the greatest change across the nation's constituencies, the decade of the 1890's and the first decades of this century. The distribution of Republican strength over the interval from 0 to 100 per cent is shown in Figure 5 for the elections of 1874, 1914, and 1958, elections which were once

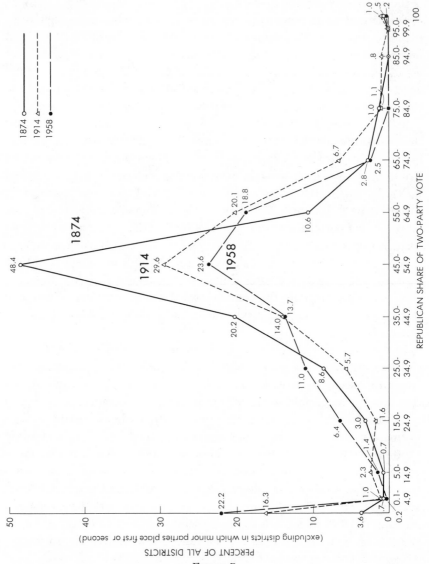

FIGURE 5

United States: Decline in Party Competitiveness in Congressional Elections, 1874-1958

again won by comparable proportions of the whole two-party vote. By the standard of the classical era of Conservative-Liberal competition, the competitiveness of modern British constituencies also is less. The class basis of Conservative and Labour support and the class differences of constituencies have been enough to ensure this. But the concentration of constituencies over a middle range of party strength still is considerably stronger in Britain than it is in modern America. Even with the much greater amplitude of change in American congressional voting, congressmen are no more often than British M.P.'s under a threat of losing their seats in a general election.

This conclusion is borne out by the frequency with which seats change party hands in the two countries. In the parliamentary elections from 1950 to 1966 the average number of seats changing party control was less than 7 per cent. In the congressional elections from 1952 to 1960 the average number of seats changing control was not greatly different. Despite the much greater amplitude of the fluctuations of party strength in the typical congressional district, comparable proportions of seats changed hands in the two countries, as shown by the first column of Table 4. Since the typical parliamentary constituency lay closer to an even division of party strength, it could have the nearly same probability of changing hands on a much smaller average swing.

The pattern of turnover of party control also shows the greater nationalization of political attitude in Britain. Seats changed hands in Britain during this period almost completely in accord with the national trends of party strength. As shown in the second column of Table 4,

TABLE 4

Electoral Turnover in the United States House of Representatives and The British House of Commons

	Mean Proportion of Seats Changing Party Hands	Mean Proportion of Seats Changing Party Hands Which Moved Against Tide
United States, 1952-60	7.7%	22.1%
Britain, 1950-66	6.4%	7.4%

less than 8 per cent of the changes of control within parliamentary constituencies were contrary to national movements of party strength. But in America during this period a very sizable minority of seats changed hands against the national tide. Indeed, if we note that a tide would run at all only as this figure is well below 50 per cent, the actual 22 per cent of changes against the national trend shows how strong were the influences on congressional voting distinctive to the individual district.

It would therefore be wrong to assume that the long-term decay of constituency forces in the United States has led the members of the congressional parties to identify their own fortunes strongly with the public's response to more national leaders and programs. If the competitiveness typical of congressional districts in the years after Reconstruction had survived the party realignment of the 1890's, the decline of the constituency as an arena of conflict might have done more to yield such a result. As it is, the congressman's usual majority and the remaining constituency influences are large enough in American congressional parties to weaken the electoral logic of cohesion so clearly understood in Parliament.

And yet these qualifications in no way diminish the interest of the secular decline of constituency forces apparent in these data. Changes of party strength, and, even more, of turnout, over many decades show that by the middle of this century the public decided whether and how to vote for Congress less than ever before on the basis of influences distinctive to the constituency. If the nationalization of political forces has carried less far in America than in Britain it seems nevertheless an outstanding aspect of our elections for Congress over the life of the modern party system.

VIII | Richard E. Dawson
WASHINGTON UNIVERSITY

Social Development,
Party Competition, and Policy

THIS INQUIRY explores relationships between socio-economic development, inter-party competition, and policy outputs in the American states. It is concerned with the development and functioning of political parties in American society. Its more specific objective is to explore the impact of inter-party competitiveness as an intervening variable between socio-economic conditions and policy outputs. This work is an extension of earlier research on the impact of party competition upon state policies.[1] Unlike the earlier work, however, this inquiry examines these relationships in an explicitly historical and developmental context.

This chapter focuses exclusively on state party systems and their policy-making impact in state politics. My hope, however, is that this form of analysis will help us to learn something about American political party development in general. The method of analysis is comparative. The choice of states as units of analysis and the use of a comparative model rest upon two important assumptions: first, that the American states can be viewed analytically as quasi-autonomous political units, each with its own party system, socio-economic context, and policy outputs; and, second, that comparative analysis, where feasible, is to be preferred to description or historical analysis of a single unit, since comparative analysis is generally a more powerful and useful analytical tool than is a focus upon a single case. If we are correct in viewing the American states as independent political units, we should be able to learn some-

---

1. Richard E. Dawson and James A. Robinson, "Inter-Party Competition, Economic Variables, and Welfare Policies in the American States," *Journal of Politics*, XXV (1963), 265-89.

thing about the development of American parties, and about some of the political and non-political factors associated with party systems, by systematically analyzing similarities and differences in state political systems.

Though in many respects the American states are more properly regarded as sub-units of the more inclusive national political system, they possess enough independent areas of action and perform sufficient political functions to be analyzed as individual political systems. Each of the states has developed its own set of institutions and processes for the formulation and implementation of public policies within its borders. Each state makes for itself a wide range of decisions that determine some important aspects of what David Easton refers to as "the authoritative allocation of values" for its own constituents. Similarly, each state has evolved a system of formal policy-making positions which are sought after in popular elections; and each state system has a complex of groups and individuals that seek to influence the development of state policies, either through gaining control of public offices or by influencing those who hold such offices. In conjunction with the policy-making system and its accompanying electoral system, each American state has a party system, which serves to aggregate group and individual interests and demands within the state, and attempts to translate them into public policy. For these reasons it makes sense to identify and to compare state political systems and state party systems as separate units—noting, of course, that there are significant limitations as to how far the proposition of autonomy can be carried.

The state party systems, though like the states a part of the more inclusive national unit, likewise have at least quasi-independent existences. Commentators on American political parties have often noted the extensive decentralization of party organization and the relative independence of state party systems from the national parties.[2] In a recent discussion of political parties in the American states, Austin Ranney pointed out: ". . . the Democratic and Republican parties in each of the states are in no sense merely local representatives of national firms. Many commentators, indeed, regard the national parties as little more than coalitions of state parties formed intermittently to capture the presidency."[3]

2. See E. E. Schattschneider, *Party Government* (New York, 1942), chap. 6.
3. Austin Ranney, "Parties in State Politics," in Herbert Jacob and Kenneth Vines (eds.), *Politics in the American States* (Boston, 1965), 61.

The American states provide the political and historical analyst with an excellent laboratory for comparative political analysis, one that has only recently begun to be used systematically and effectively.[4] A common national political culture and history, relatively similar formal political structures, and the availability of comparable social, economic, and political data, permit the student of politics to develop comparable measures of state political and non-political characteristics. There are some significant political characteristics which the states share in common. All of the states have written constitutions with formal authority divided between legislative, executive, and judicial branches. Major political officials in each state are elected periodically by popular elections; and in each state there is a political party system which, at least in a formal sense, includes the same two parties. On the other hand, there are many important variations among the states in political processes, in the socio-economic environments within which their politics take place, and in the way values and resources are authoritatively allocated. This combination of inter-state *differences* and *similarities* permits the political analyst to focus on selected variations in some areas while holding other aspects constant; and this condition is, of course, the key to successful comparative analysis. Many of the troublesome conceptual and empirical problems encountered in cross-national and cross-cultural comparative analysis can be avoided in comparing American states, simply because there are sufficient common characteristics, and because there is a much greater reservoir of comparable data than that usually available in cross-cultural analyses.

In studying the American states it is possible to hold important basic political, institutional, and structural factors constant. That is to say, it is possible to assume few fundamental variations between them, and thus to investigate questions such as relationships between wealth and inter-party competition or rate of political participation. It is possible to investigate whether wealthier states are more likely than poorer states to have high rates of political participation, or to analyze the policy consequences of different types of party systems. By adding an historical dimension it is possible also to investigate questions of political and social development through a framework of comparative state analysis. Do relationships between factors such as urbanization and political participation persist

4. See Jacob and Vines, *Politics in the American States,* for a collection of articles which utilizes the American states as components in a comparative analysis.

through different time periods, or are they related only for some particular historical period? How are changes in levels of economic development related to changes in political composition? Or, more specifically,
what impact is increasing industrialization likely to have upon the historical one-party domination in the Southern states? These and many
other issues of development can be investigated best through comparative analysis. Even so, the American states constitute a still little-used
laboratory for the exploration and testing of such hypotheses.

II

The substantive concern of this chapter is with the impact of inter-
party competition as an intervening variable between socio-economic
conditions and state policy outputs. One of the most important issues in
the analysis of American political parties is their role in, and impact
upon, the development and implementation of public policy. Political
analysis is concerned with the investigation of how various formal and
informal institutions and processes, and economic, social, philosophical,
and geographic conditions, influence the adoption and implementation of
public policy. Public policy, in this sense, is a major output of the political
system and a major dependent variable to be explained.[5]

From this perspective, one of the most important functions of political
party systems is that of aggregating or pulling together the varied interests and demands of individuals and groups and of attempting to shape,
integrate, and translate them into some form of public policy. As such,
political parties serve as important links between the socio-economic
makeup or societal structure of a political unit and its policy-making
institutions and policy outputs. They function as a major mechanism
through which societal interests and demands are transmitted into governmental action or inaction, that is, public policies. This being true,
party systems should be closely related, on the one hand, to the socio-
economic makeup or development of any given system; and, on the
other hand, to its complex of policy actions or outputs. More specifically,
the party system should serve to relate or link these two aspects of the
polity.

5. For discussions of the use of policy as a focus for research in political analysis
see David Easton, *The Political System* (New York, 1953), esp. 125-48; and James
A. Robinson, "The Major Problems of Political Science," in L. K. Caldwell (ed.),
Politics and Public Affairs (Bloomington, Ind., 1962), 161-88.

The object here is to focus upon the impact of the level of competition between parties which make up state party systems. The level of inter-party competitiveness has been one of the most widely used criteria for classifying and describing party systems. As Frank Sorauf has pointed out, "basically the single criterion for categorizing party systems has been that of their competitiveness in bidding for voter support."[6] While Sorauf went on to indicate some of the difficulties in defining and measuring competitiveness in party systems, he pointed out that the competitive dimension was a crucial one.

> Despite its weaknesses, the competitive standard for the party system measures the American party system more fairly than it does those of most of the other democracies. For the American parties the electoral function is indeed the cardinal party function. The business of ideology and gov-ernmental power is less important to them than to other parties. The American major parties, by piecing together constantly shifting major-ities of fickle voters, best approximate the kind of inter-party competi-tiveness that the definition of "party system" basically depends on.[7]

Other students, arguing that the level of competitiveness within a state party system has a direct influence on how a state allocates its resources, have pointed more explicitly to policy consequences for this aspect of state party systems. The classical statement of this hypothesis is found in V. O. Key's *Southern Politics*,[8] where he argues that one-party states characterized by multi-factional politics tended to be especially conservative in their public policies. One of the prime causes of this conservatism, Key maintained, was that one-party systems do not pro-vide an adequate institutional mechanism for the expression of the inter-ests and demands of lower socio-economic elements. Policy outputs in these systems thus reflect rather systematically and exclusively the in-terests of better-off and more "conservative" interests.[9] In more competi-tive two-party states, and at least to some extent in one-party states with strong, enduring bifactionalism, the structured and intense competition for control of political institutions provides a mechanism which allows for the expression of lower socio-economic interests—those of the "have-nots." The explanation for this phenomenon, as Key saw it, was that strong competition for offices pushes one or more of the parties to seek the

6. Frank J. Sorauf, *Political Parties in the American System* (Boston, 1964), 15.
7. Ibid. 19.
8. V. O. Key, Jr., *Southern Politics in State and Nation* (New York, 1951), 298-314.
9. Ibid.

votes of the have-nots; parties thus become responsive to and more representative of the lower income and social strata. It was Key's contention that more liberal policies result from more competitive systems, not because of any specific policy orientation or ideological position of the parties, but rather because of the force of competition for office itself. He pointed out that the "great value of the two-party system is not that there are two groups with conflicting policy tendencies from which the voters may choose, but that there are two groups of politicians."[10]

This hypothesis was more explicitly formulated and investigated in Duane Lockard's study of New England state politics. Building explicitly upon Key's work, Lockard sought to test more systematically the impact of party competition upon policy outputs, using the New England states as the analytical unit. On the basis of evidence drawn from these states, Lockard found that the more competitive states were more "liberal" in their public policies.[11] The non-competitive New England states (Maine, New Hampshire, and Vermont) place more of the tax burden on lower income groups and provide less in services for the needy than do the more competitive states (Connecticut, Massachusetts, and Rhode Island). Like Key, Lockard built his explanatory argument around the notion that competition itself pushed the parties to make electoral appeals to, and thus be responsive to, the lower socio-economic groups: "The common assumption is that the political leaders in a two-party system are more responsible to the preferences of the citizenry whether of high or low status in life, not so much out of principle as out of fear of retribution at the polls."[12] Inter-party competition, then, provides a mechanism for participation of the lower socio-economic groups, and for the development of a politics responsive to their interests and needs.

If these notions are correct, the competitiveness of party systems has important consequences for the way party systems carry out their aggregative and policy-making functions. In a similar way a competitive party system may contribute to the level of political integration. Inasmuch as parties in competitive systems seek to win the electoral support of groups that may not be particularly predisposed toward political participation, the parties serve to pull these groups into more active involvement in the polity and thus to integrate them into the political system and its proc-

10. Ibid. 337.
11. Duane Lockard, *New England State Politics* (Princeton, 1959), 326-40.
12. Ibid. 326-7.

esses. This is, for example, what has happened to Negroes who have migrated from the rural South to Northern cities during the past half-century. Political leaders in the more competitive Northern cities and states have sought the votes of the Negro migrants as part of their strategies of political control. As a result the Negro has been more actively integrated into the electoral and political processes in the North than he was in the less competitive South, where his vote was not sought. The politicalization of foreign immigrants by political parties in some of the Northern cities during the early decades of this century is another example of the integrative role of political parties in competitive conditions.

The level of competitiveness of a party system is most likely related, in turn, to various socio-economic conditions within the polity in which it functions. As Paul Goodman has pointed out in Chapter III, a competitive party system probably results from some sort of societal diversity. Thus, Lockard says, "the diversity or lack of diversity of economic interests in a state tends to be reflected in the prevailing party system and the mode of its operation. In the first place, of course, it is the diversity in part that creates the atmosphere for two-party competition, and the absence of diversity facilitates one-partyism."[13] The forms of social diversity which contribute to party competition are many and varied. They include such factors as economic groupings, occupational diversity, urbanization, and racial, ethnic, and religious variations. The patterns of diversity fostering political party conflict and competition in the United States have varied greatly from state to state and from time to time. The high competitiveness of such Middle Western states as Ohio and Indiana during the latter half of the nineteenth century resulted in large measure from the diversity of points of origin of early settlers: those who migrated from New England tended to develop Republican allegiances, and those from the South, Democratic preferences. In the past few decades the competitiveness of party systems in the New England states has stemmed largely from religious and ethnic diversities. Generally speaking, we would expect to find a greater variety of social and economic groupings in the more highly urbanized and industrialized states. Likewise, we would predict that states with a higher proportion of first- and second-generation immigrants would be more likely to have a base for a competitive system than a state with a more ethnically homogeneous population base. More rural and agrarian states, on the other hand, are less apt to have a diversi-

13. Ibid. 337.

fied population, and thus are less likely to develop and sustain a competitive party system.

In short, these notions all suggest that the level of inter-party competition is related both to the socio-economic conditions of a state and to the types of policies adopted by that state system. In this regard the party system serves as an intervening factor, relating socio-economic factors to policy outputs. More specifically, a competitive party system serves as one of the basic mechanisms through which a diversified society makes its demands and resolves its conflicts in the political arena. It is especially a means through which the less socially and economically advantaged population groupings are brought into political participation and given a chance to exert political influence.

These notions about the policy impact of inter-party competition have been developed in a more comprehensive and rigorous way by James A. Robinson and me elsewhere.[14] Constructing indices of inter-party competition, selected socio-economic variables, and welfare policy outputs for forty-six states, we computed correlations between these three sets of variables. In keeping with the propositions advanced by Key and Lockard, we found that the more competitive states tended to be more liberal in the adoption of welfare programs, and also that the more highly industrialized, more urbanized, and especially the wealthier states tended to have more competitive party systems and at the same time tended to be more liberal in welfare policies. All three of the factors were found to be correlated significantly with each other. More liberal policy outputs correlated both with inter-party competition and with levels of socio-economic development as indicated by rates of urbanization, industrialization, and per capita income. In order to examine the relative impact of wealth and of inter-party competition upon welfare policies, correlations between per capita income and policy outputs were computed with inter-party competition controlled, and also between inter-party competition and policies with per capita income controlled. With these controls, the relationships between wealth and welfare policies were found to be substantially higher than those between inter-party competition and welfare outputs. On the basis of this analysis Robinson and I then offered the following conclusion:

> The level of public social welfare programs in the American states seems to be more a function of socio-economic factors, especially per

14. Dawson and Robinson, "Inter-Party Competition," *passim.*

capita income. High levels of inter-party competition do not seem to possess the important intervening influence between socio-economic factors and liberal welfare programs that our original hypothesis and theoretical scheme suggested.[15]

The research and analysis presented here, as pointed out above, are basically an extension of this analysis. The same comparative framework is employed and similar indices are used. I add here an explicit developmental frame of reference and explore the development of these several relationships over time. This should allow us to see more clearly the development and impact of party competitiveness in the American states.

III

The major focus here is upon the relationship between socio-economic development, inter-party competition, and policy outputs, with party competition analyzed as an intervening factor. For reasons which will be made more explicit below, the rate of electoral participation will be treated as a factor that should be related closely to party competitiveness and its policy consequences. In specific terms we will investigate the following two major hypotheses:

1. The higher the level of economic development of a state, the greater the degree of inter-party competition within its party system.
2. The higher the level of inter-party competition, the more "liberal" a state's policy outputs.

The investigation involves a statistical analysis of the relationships between these three sets of variables. The procedure is to construct measurements of each of these sets of variables for the states, and to examine the relationships between them through rank order correlations. Forty-six states are employed in this analysis. Party affiliation of members of state legislatures is used as a part of the index of inter-party competition; thus Nebraska and Minnesota are omitted because they elect members of their legislatures on a non-partisan ticket. Alaska and Hawaii are also excluded because they were not states during most of the time period investigated. The relationships are analyzed within and between three separate consecutive time periods, spanning half a century from 1914 to 1963: (1)

15. Ibid. 289.

1914-29, (2) 1930-45, and (3) 1946-63. These particular time periods are used partly because these years roughly correspond to important periods in American political history, and partly for convenience in methodology and data collection. The first period extends from the end of the Progressive Era and the immediate pre-World War I years through the war and the 1920's. The second period spans the entirety of the Great Depression and World War II, a period of social turbulence and significant political realignment. The third period includes all the years after World War II up to, but not including the 1964 election. The three periods are fairly equal in length and long enough for an adequate measurement of interparty competition within each time span.

1. *Socio-economic development.* One of the central notions of this analysis is that party systems operate within a socio-economic environment, and that the structure and operation of any given party system will be determined, in large part, by the makeup of that societal context. A large number of social and economic factors could conceivably be related to aspects of party systems. Five major indicators of these conditions were selected for this analysis: per capita income and median family income, as indices of wealth and its distribution; percentage of population living in urban areas, as an index of urbanization; percentage of population in the work force not engaged in agriculture, forestry, or fishing, as an indicator of industrialization; and percentage of population either foreign-born or with one or more foreign-born parents, as a measure of ethnic diversity. These five characteristics reflect the socio-economic conditions that are most relevant for the focus on party structures and processes, and allow the identification of significant variations between the states. Within each of the three time periods there are wide differences between the states when measured according to each of these conditions. The ranges for three of these factors are shown in Table 1 for each of the three time spans. One of the striking features of the American states is the wide variance of conditions among them regarding almost every type of socio-economic characteristic, and the persistence of these differences over time. Wealth and urbanization have increased greatly in all of the states during the past half-century, but state rankings according to these characteristics have remained fairly constant. The gaps between the highest and lowest states have decreased, but remain substantial.

The data for these measures are taken from census reports. Census data of 1930 are used for the 1914-29 period, data of 1950 for the 1930-45 period, and data of 1960 for the 1946-63 period. The measure of industrialization is, at best, a crude one. We have taken the census designation of per cent of work force engaged in agriculture, forestry, and fishing, classified them as non-industrialized occupations, and considered that persons not engaged in these occupations were directly engaged in industry or its artifacts. Only three of the indices are employed for the 1914-29 period. Data on median family income and on industrialization, as employed for subsequent years, were not available for that period.

TABLE 1

*Ranges in Socio-Economic Conditions among the States
1930, 1950, and 1960*

Time Period	Per Capita Income		% Urban Population		% Foreign-Born	
1930 Highest	New York	$1,159	Rhode Island	92.4%	Rhode Island	68.8%
Lowest	S. Carolina	$ 270	North Dakota	16.6%	North Carolina	1.2%
1950 Highest	Delaware	$2,146	New Jersey	86.6%	New York	22.8%*
Lowest	Mississippi	$ 733	North Dakota	26.6%	South Carolina	.5%
1960 Highest	Delaware	$3,013	New Jersey	88.6%	Massachusetts	40.0%
Lowest	Mississippi	$1,173	North Dakota	35.2%	Mississippi	1.3%

* The data for the foreign-born are not comparable for the three periods. For 1930 and 1960 the figures refer to the combined percentages of the foreign-born and those with one or more foreign-born parents. The 1950 figure refers only to the percentage of foreign-born. The figures, nonetheless, show the great differences between the states.

For our analysis we consider these several factors as indicators of socio-economic development. Though the concept of levels or stages of economic and social development is not often used in analyzing domestic American politics, this conceptualization seems particularly appropriate for this form of analysis. We want to focus attention on change, and we hypothesize that changes in political and in socio-economic variables are likely to occur in related patterns. At least in the field of socio-economic conditions, excluding ethnicity at the present time, all of the states are moving in a similar direction, but lie at distinctly different points along such paths. The South, for example, may be characterized fruitfully as an economically underdeveloped area *vis-à-vis* other parts of the nation. With very few exceptions, when the states are ranked according to any of the five variables mentioned above, the Southern states cluster at the bottom: they have a series of social and economic, as well as political, conditions which differentiate them from other states. Another series of states—Massachusetts, Rhode Island, Connecticut, New York, New Jersey,

Michigan, Illinois, California—cluster at the top of all of these indicators of socio-economic development. Operationally, when we refer to higher levels of socio-economic development, we mean higher levels of industrialization and urbanization, higher per capita and median income, and a higher percentage of foreign-born or offspring of foreign-born. Except for the ethnicity, or foreign-born, measure, these are all fairly common indicators of economic development. Ethnicity is, however, a more individualized factor, one that has particular relevance for American political development, and particularly for understanding aspects of party development. In addition, the ethnicity of state populations has closely followed the other patterns of social and economic development. For some of the analysis that follows we have combined the ratings of the states according to these five (three in 1930) measures, to give a rough over-all index of socio-economic development.

2. *Inter-party competition and rate of electoral participation.* The most important variable in this analysis, inter-party competition, is also the most difficult one to conceptualize and to measure. A number of students of American politics have struggled with this issue, and a variety of schemes have been developed.[16] We shall not review these efforts here, but will employ a modified version of the measure of inter-party competition developed by Dawson and Robinson.[17] This measure is designed especially to reflect party competition surrounding the major state policy-making bodies. It includes relative party strength in races for governor and for party seats in both houses of the state legislature. Robinson and I identified three separate dimensions of party competitiveness for each of these policy-making units: (1) margin of comparative popular support; (2) the relative percentage of time each party has controlled the offices; and (3) the proportion of time during which control of these three bodies has been divided between the parties.[18] These various dimensions were found to be highly correlated to each other, and a composite index of the

16. Major attempts to measure inter-party competition are in Dawson and Robinson, "Inter-Party Competition"; V. O. Key, Jr., *American State Politics: An Introduction* (New York, 1956), 201; Robert T. Golembiewski, "A Taxonomic Approach to State Political Party Strength," *Western Political Quarterly*, XI (1958), 494-513; Austin Ranney and Willmore Kendall, "The American Party Systems," *American Political Science Review*, XLVIII (1954), 477-85; and Joseph A. Schlesinger, "A Two-Dimensional Scheme for Classifying the States According to Degree of Inter-Party Competition," *American Political Science Review*, XLIX (1955), 1120-1128.

17. Dawson and Robinson, "Inter-Party Competition," 270-78.

18. Ibid. 273-8.

first dimension was found to be the best over-all single measure of a state's party competitiveness.

We follow this course here, adjusting the time spans to fit the time units outlined above. The measure of inter-party competition, then, is based upon a composite rating of (1) the average percentage of total vote the major party candidate for governor has received during the time period under consideration; (2) the average proportion of seats that the major party has held in the lower house of the state legislature during the same time period; and (3) the average proportion of seats the major party has held in the upper house. In each case the major party is the party in the state which won the greatest percentage of seats or votes during that particular time period. A composite index was constructed by averaging each state's ranks on these three different institutional scales. Since the governorship, the house, and the senate each play a crucial role in state policy-making, and since political parties attempt to gain control of each through popular elections, all three should be included in a comprehensive measure of inter-party competition. Following this pattern, a rating of inter-party competitiveness is available for each state in each time period. This index permits the ranking of states from one to forty-six and the making of comparisons both within and between time periods: that is, we can say both that one state is more or less competitive than another, and that a particular state is more or less competitive than it was during a different time period. The ratings and rankings of the states for each of the three time periods are shown in Table 2, and these rankings are used in the correlational analysis which follows.

TABLE 2

Inter-Party Competition
Composite Percentage of Popular Support for Governor, House, and Senate

STATE	1914-29		1930-45		1946-63	
	%	Rank	%	Rank	%	Rank
Alabama	90+*	41	96.2	41	95.7	42
Arizona	70.6	24	87.2	37	71.8	32
Arkansas	89.3	40	96.0	40	92.5	40
California	57.2	9	60.8	17	51.9	2
Colorado	56.9*	8	53.4	4	54.0	6.5
Connecticut	73.9	28	57.9	14	56.9	11
Delaware	55.4	3	57.6	11	54.4	8
Florida	88.3	39	93.8	39	88.5	39
Georgia	100.0	46	99.0	43	98.8	44

TABLE 2
(*Continued*)

STATE	1914-29		1930-45		1946-63	
	%	Rank	%	Rank	%	Rank
Idaho	63.4*	14	59.5	16	55.8	9
Illinois	61.2	12	52.7	3	56.0	10
Indiana	60.7	11	52.6	2	58.0	13
Iowa	77.3	33	66.4	24	70.3	30
Kansas	70.8	25	67.8	26.5	70.0	29
Kentucky	60.4	10	64.1	23	69.2	27
Louisiana	95.0*	43	99.9	44	98.0	43
Maine	74.4	29	78.4	33	71.3	31
Maryland	61.7	13	69.0	29	67.6	25
Massachusetts	69.2	22	57.8	13	52.0	3
Michigan	84.8	37	61.6	18	60.9	20
Mississippi	99.4	44	100.0	45.5	100.0	45.5
Missouri	55.9	4	63.4	22	58.1	14
Montana	64.0	18	55.4	8	50.6	1
Nevada	52.4	2	56.6	10	60.3	18
New Hampshire	63.8	16.5	59.2	15	65.5	24
New Jersey	68.9	21	62.6	20.5	59.5	16
New Mexico	56.7*	6	69.7	30	68.8	26
New York	56.8	7	54.3	7	58.3	15
North Carolina	75.1	31	86.8	36	83.7	38
North Dakota	73.0*	27	76.2	31.5	76.5	34
Ohio	67.4	20	53.5	5.5	62.8	21
Oklahoma	66.8	19	80.8	34	76.7	35
Oregon	76.7	32	66.6	25	60.7	19
Pennsylvania	77.7	35	57.7	12	53.3	5
Rhode Island	56.3	5	55.6	9	57.1	12
South Carolina	99.9	45	100.0	45.5	100.0	45.5
South Dakota	71.0	26	61.9	19	69.5	28
Tennessee	69.5	23	81.3	35	77.9	36
Texas	92.2	42	96.3	42	94.0	41
Utah	50.5	1	68.8	28	52.1	4
Vermont	79.9	36	76.2	31.5	75.0	33
Virginia	86.2*	38	88.1	38	83.5	37
Washington	77.6	34	62.6	20.5	54.0	6.5
West Virginia	63.8*	16.5	67.8	26.5	65.4	23
Wisconsin	75.0	30	50.4	1	64.1	22
Wyoming	63.5	15	53.5	5.5	59.7	17

* These figures are at best only approximate. They have been computed with missing data. In several instances, for example, we were unable to obtain gubernatorial returns for the 1928 elections. In these instances the state averages were computed without the 1928 returns. In other instances all of the data concerning the partisan makeup of the state legislature were not obtainable and the ratings were developed without full data.

The data in Table 2 show an across-the-board increase in the level of inter-party competition from the first period through the second and third periods. This change seems to consist mainly of a movement of moderately competitive states in the earliest period toward more intense party competition during the second and third periods. For example, if a score of 60 per cent or less is designated as highly competitive, the number of highly competitive states increases from nine in the first period to sixteen in the second period to seventeen in the third period. There is less change at the non-competitive end of the continuum. Selecting a score of 75 per cent and above as non-competitive, there is only a slight decrease in the number of non-competitive states, from seventeen in the first period to fourteen in the third period. The trend toward greater competitiveness is also shown by the decrease in scores of the median ranked states for each period. The score of the median ranked state drops from 70.6 per cent (Arizona) in the 1914-29 period to 65.5 per cent (New Hampshire) for the 1946-63 period. In most instances the most dramatic changes took place between the first and second periods. Several of the states—notably Connecticut, Michigan, Massachusetts, Montana, New Jersey, Oregon, Pennsylvania, Washington, and Wisconsin—have become decidedly more competitive through the three time periods. Connecticut, Pennsylvania, and Washington have changed from ranks among the least competitive states to ranks among the most competitive. New Mexico and Oklahoma are the only states that have become decidedly less competitive. The Southern states, on the other hand, are consistently clustered at the bottom of the distributions: on the whole, they appear to have become slightly less competitive since the pre-Depression period. The significant changes in Southern party systems, indicated by some election outcomes in recent years, are too recent and sporadic to be reflected even in the measure of the final period.

The explanatory theory offered by Key and Lockard concerning the relationship between inter-party competition and policy outputs also relates the level of competitiveness to the rate of electoral participation. Higher levels of competitiveness, then, should be related positively to higher rates of electoral participation: party competition, they propose, leads to more liberal policies because more of the "have-nots" are brought into political participation through the force of competition for electoral support. In order to investigate this relationship, we have employed a crude measure of the rate of electoral participation for the states during each of the time periods. As an index of this variable we have taken the percentages of adults voting in the presidential elections falling within each of the three periods and have averaged them into a single rating for each state. This admittedly is not the best measure of participation within the state political system, and it would be more accurate to include turnout for state offices; those data, however, were not readily available. With only a few exceptions, the states show increases in voting turnout from Period I through Period III in presidential elections. The Southern states show substantial increases in turnout, but remain decidedly below the other states in each period. A number of states, including California, Connecticut, Massachusetts, Michigan, Pennsylvania, Rhode Island, and Washington, show increases in turnout of nearly 20 per cent or more. These changes become even more significant when we match this list of states with those given above as having the greatest increases in inter-party competition. Of these seven states all but California and Rhode Island are among the eight states showing significant increases in party competitiveness. The other three states with substantial increases in the level of inter-party competition—Montana, New Jersey, and Oregon—also experienced substantial increases in voting turnout—+14.6 per cent, +13.8 per cent, and +15.1 per cent, respectively. The correspondences between increases in inter-party competition and voting turnout for five of these states are shown in Table 3. The most important changes seem to have taken place

TABLE 3

Development of Competition and Participation in Five Selected States, Periods I–III

	PERIOD I	PERIOD II	PERIOD III
Connecticut			
Competition	73.9%	57.9%	56.9%
Participation	48.7%	64.9%	73.9%
Massachusetts			
Competition	69.2	57.8	52.0
Participation	48.7	65.9	73.9
Michigan			
Competition	84.8	61.6	60.9
Participation	47.4	60.0	65.0
Pennsylvania			
Competition	77.7	57.7	53.3
Participation	43.9	61.4	73.2
Washington			
Competition	77.6	62.6	54.0
Participation	47.4	63.8	65.0

between the first and second periods, with the trend continuing from the second period into the third. These changes, in both inter-party competition and voter turnout, reflect the politicalization of ethnic minority groups in these states during the late 1920's and the 1930's. In these particular states in the past few decades, the second- and third-generation migrants have formed the basis for a competitive party system.

In order to test statistically the relationship between the level of inter-party competition and the rate of political participation in the states, rank order correlations (both Kendall tau beta and gamma) were computed between these two indices.[19] The correlation coefficients for each of the three periods are as follows:

	1914-29	1930-45	1946-63
Tau beta coefficient	.55	.61	.56
Gamma coefficient	.62	.69	.63

These coefficients show a moderately strong statistical relationship between these two factors: that is, states that rank high on inter-party competition tend to rank high also in electoral participation. The relationship, however, falls far short of a perfect correspondence.

3. *State policy outputs.* The American states still perform a wide variety of political or policy-making functions within their own boundaries despite the increase in federal governmental activity. Basic policies in regard to education, highways, and public welfare, as well as a wide range of economic, industrial, and personal regulatory policies, are controlled largely through the states; and through their tax and spending programs, state governments allocate or re-allocate large segments of the wealth of their constituents. The types of programs and policies enacted and enforced by state political systems vary greatly. Even in the field of public welfare, where most state programs operate within the framework of a federally outlined structure and a substantial part of the financing comes from the federal government, there are great differences among the states in actual policy outputs. In 1960, for example, per capita expenditures for public welfare ranged from $55.17 in Oklahoma and $48.52 in Colorado, to $8.57 in Virginia and $11.01 in Maryland. In 1960, 29.27 per cent of the state budget in Oklahoma went for welfare programs, while in Wyoming, only 4.69 per cent of the state budget went for welfare programs.[20]

19. For all of the statistical relations, we show correlation coefficients for both Kendall tau beta and gamma rank order correlation tests. Readers may choose to heed one or the other on the basis of their own preferences. For a discussion of rank order correlation see Herbert M. Blalock, Jr., *Social Statistics* (New York, 1960), 316-25.

20. Data taken from Richard E. Dawson and James A. Robinson, "The Politics of Welfare," in Jacob and Vines, *Politics in the American States,* 386-97.

One of the basic hypotheses of this chapter is that these policy differences are influenced by differences in the level of inter-party competition among the states. More specifically, the more competitive states are more likely to adopt liberal policies or programs, that is, to spend more money and resources for state services and activities. In order to investigate this hypothesis we have developed a series of indices to measure state policies in different substantive policy areas, and we have constructed indicators for each of the three time periods. On the assumption that the effect of inter-party competition is cumulative and takes place over a period of time, policy outputs have been measured at the end of each of the three time periods. Consequently, we have developed policy measurements from programs in the years 1929-30, 1946-48, and 1962-63.[21] Although the development of good comparable indicators of state policy efforts for all of the forty-six states is not an easy task, especially for the earliest time period where data are scarce, we have compiled at least some rough indicators of policy outputs in several important policy areas. The 1929-30 years were the most difficult, because state programs in many areas were sporadic or so varied as to defy good quantitative comparison.

In other situations, data which are comparable from state to state were simply not available. The best policy indicators for these years are in the field of education, where we can use the per capita expenditure for education in the state and the average salary for personnel in public education. Though this is far from adequate as a comprehensive measurement, it is at least a rough index of how much the state and its local subdivisions spent for education at that time. The other major state policy areas present even greater difficulties. We have used welfare and unemployment programs as policy areas in the years 1946-48 and 1962-63, but in 1930 many states were just beginning to enact public welfare and labor relations legislation; thus we were not able to find comparable program and expenditure data in this field. We have, however, found information on the years in which some welfare programs were instituted. On the assumption that the relatively early adoption of a program indicates a more liberal approach to that particular area than a late start does, we have used as state policy indicators the year in which programs of aid for dependent children, aid to the blind, and old age assistance were started. Though several of the states adopted such programs as far back as the

21. These specific years are not always strictly adhered to. For example, education data are for 1947-48 because data for the previous year were not available.

late nineteenth century, most state initiation in these areas took place in the third and fourth decades of this century. We have, thus, five measures of state policy outputs for Period I:

POLICY MEASURES FOR PERIOD I

1. Per capita expenditures for education.
2. Average salary for educational personnel.
3. Year in which program of aid to dependent children was enacted.
4. Year in which program of aid to blind was enacted.
5. Year in which program of old age assistance was enacted.

For the second period, data for the development of quantitative comparative indices in the fields of education, welfare, labor, and income payments were available. For educational policies we have used expenditures per pupil and average salaries for teachers, principals, and supervisors. The same indices were used for the third period, making these the only comparable, or at least vaguely comparable, indices we have for all three periods. By the mid-1940's more comparable data for state welfare and labor programs were available. All of the states by this time were participating in enough similar programs to allow quantitative comparisons. We use the following indicators as measures of state policy outputs:

POLICY MEASURES FOR PERIOD II

1. Per pupil expenditures for pupils in average daily attendance.
2. Average salaries for teachers, principals, and supervisors.
3. Average per recipient payment per family for aid to dependent children.
4. Average per recipient payment for aid to blind.
5. Per capita expenditures for all public assistance programs, excluding funds from the federal government.
6. Average per recipient payment for unemployment insurance.
7. Per capita state expenditure on all income payments.

In developing indicators for policies in the period from 1946 to 1963, we attempted to use indices similar to those of the preceding period so that we could make more accurate inter-period comparisons, while adding a measure of total per capita state expenditure. The policy indicators for this period are as follows:

POLICY MEASURES FOR PERIOD III

1. Per pupil expenditures for pupils in average daily attendance.

2. Average salaries for teachers, principals, and supervisors.
3. Average per recipient payment per family for aid to dependent children.
4. Average per recipient payment for aid to blind.
5. Per capita expenditures for all public assistance programs, including only that portion of funds coming from state sources.
6. An average of the rankings of the states according to per recipient payments on seven welfare programs.
7. Average per recipient payment for unemployment insurance.
8. Total per capita state expenditures.

IV

The first of the major hypotheses to be investigated involves relationships between socio-economic development, inter-party competition, and the rate of political participation. The theoretical basis of these two hypotheses and the indicators used in measuring them was discussed above. Here we report and discuss the statistical testing of these relationships. We have run two different rank order correlation tests between the three variables to learn the strength of relationships between them. The dis-

TABLE 4.

PERIOD I. *Relationships between Socio-economic Development and Inter-party Competition*

INTER-PARTY COMPETITION (1914-29)

Social-economic Development (1929)*	High (50%-59%)		Medium (60%-74%)		Low (75% and over)	
HIGH	(4) Cal. Del.	N.Y. R.I.	(6) Conn. Ill. Mass.	N.H. N.J. Ohio	(4) Mich. Penn.	Wash. Wisc.
MEDIUM	(4) Colo. Mo.	Nev. Utah	(8) Ariz. Idaho Ind. Kans.	Maine Md. Mont. Wyo.	(6) Fla. Iowa La.	Ore. Tex. Vt.
LOW	(1) N.M.		(6) N.D. Okla. S.D.	Tenn. W. Va. Ky.	(7) Ala. Ark. Ga.	Miss. N.C. S.C. Va.

* This measure is a composite of the state's ranking according to per capita income, urbanization, and foreign-born.

RANK ORDER CORRELATION COEFFICIENTS COMPUTED BETWEEN
THREE SOCIO-ECONOMIC MEASURES AND LEVEL OF INTER-PARTY COMPETITION

	Tau Beta	Gamma
Per capita income	.40	.46
Urbanization	.25	.30
Foreign-born	.27	.31

TABLE 5

PERIOD II. *Relationship between Socio-economic
Development and Inter-party Competition*

INTER-PARTY COMPETITION (1930-45)

Socio-economic Development (1945)*	High (50%-59%)		Medium (60%-74%)		Low (75% and over)	
HIGH	(9) Conn. Del. Ill. Mass. Nev.	N.Y. Ohio Penn. R.I.	(5) Cal. Md. Mich.	N.J. Wash.		
MEDIUM	(7) Colo. Idaho Ind. Mont.	N.H. Wisc. Wyo.	(5) Iowa Kans. Mo.	Ore. Utah	(6) Ariz. Fla. Maine	N.M. Okla. Tex.
LOW			(3) Ky. S.D.	W. Va.	(11) Ala. Ark. Ga. La. Miss. N.C.	N.D. S.C. Tenn. Vt. Va.

* This measure consists of per capita income, median income, urbanization, industrialization, and foreign-born.

RANK ORDER CORRELATION COEFFICIENTS COMPUTED BETWEEN
FIVE SOCIO-ECONOMIC MEASURES AND INTER-PARTY COMPETITION

	Tau Beta	Gamma
Per capita income	.60	.70
Median income	.64	.72
Urbanization	.38	.45
Industrialization	.41	.49
Foreign-born	.43	.50

tribution of states and the results of these operations are shown in Tables 4, 5, 6, 7, 8, and 9. Tables 4, 5, and 6 show the relationships in each of the time periods—1914-29, 1930-45, and 1946-63—between inter-party competition and a composite index of socio-economic characteristics. They show the state distributions between two variables, with socio-economic development along the vertical axis and rate of inter-party competition, or rate of electoral participation, across the horizontal axis. The reader can see both the statistical tests of the relationships and the distributions of states that make up the statistical findings.

TABLE 6

Period III. *Relationships between Socio-economic Development and Inter-party Competition*

INTER-PARTY COMPETITION (1946-62)

Socio-economic Development (1962)*	High (50%-59%)		Medium (60%-74%)		Low (75% and over)	
HIGH	(10) Cal. Conn. Del. Ill. Mass.	N.J. N.Y. Penn. R.I. Wash.	(4) Md. Mich.	Nev. Ohio		
MEDIUM	(6) Colo. Ind. Mo.	Mont. Utah Wyo.	(8) N.H. N.M. Ore. Wisc.	Ariz. Iowa Kans. Maine	(4) Fla. Okla.	Tex. Va.
LOW	(1) Idaho		(3) Ky. S.D.	W. Va.	(10) Ala. Ark. Ga. La. Miss.	N.C. N.D. S.C. Tenn. Vt.

* This measure consists of per capita income, median income, urbanization, industrialization, and foreign-born.

RANK ORDER CORRELATION COEFFICIENTS COMPUTED BETWEEN
FIVE SOCIO-ECONOMIC MEASURES AND INTER-PARTY COMPETITION

	Tau Beta	Gamma
Per capita income	.62	.70
Median income	.64	.72
Urbanization	.42	.48
Industrialization	.34	.39
Foreign-born	.46	.52

Looking at the relationships between socio-economic indicators and inter-party competition, we find a moderate statistical relationship in Period I and considerably stronger relationships in Periods II and III.

The strongest relationships are consistently associated with the indicators of wealth (per capita income and median family income). Looking at the state distributions, we can see more vividly some of the phenomena behind these statistical findings. In Period I the fourteen states which ranked high in socio-economic development are distributed almost equally along the index of inter-party competition: four ranked high, six medium, and four low. By Period II none of the states ranking high in socio-economic development rates low on inter-party competition. Instead, nine of these states rank high and five rank medium. By Period III the relationship is slightly stronger. No highly developed state ranks low, and ten of the fourteen states rank high. California, Delaware, New York, and Rhode Island remain fairly competitive throughout the three periods. Michigan, Pennsylvania, Washington, and Wisconsin, which were low in party competition during the earliest period, move into the medium or high category. New Jersey, Illinois, and Massachusetts move from medium to high ratings of inter-party competition. At the other end of the socio-economic continuum, a movement toward less competition seems to have taken place. Most states falling in the least developed category have moved to the least competitive category. Idaho is the only state in Period III which has a relatively low socio-economic rating and a highly competitive party system.

These findings support the hypothesis that party competitiveness is related to socio-economic conditions, at least during the two recent time periods. The relationships during the first period, however, are fairly weak. The weakness of these relationships suggests that party competitiveness during that period was not influenced by the particular socio-economic factors analyzed here. Party identification and voting patterns prior to the 1930's were more strongly influenced by regional factors, early settlement patterns, and other conditions which are not accounted for by these indices of socio-economic development. The movement toward greater congruence between these measures of socio-economic characteristics and party competition after 1930 is quite pronounced. By the period 1946-63, all of the highly developed states have either highly or moderately competitive party systems, with more than two-thirds falling in the highly competitive category. Likewise, better than two-thirds of the least highly developed third have low competitive systems, and only one supports a highly competitive party system. From a developmental standpoint these findings indicate that a fundamental shift has taken place in the social bases of party support since the early 1930's.[22] Some of the traditional sectional and early settlement patterns of party support have become less relevant, while socio-economic factors such as wealth and urbanization have become more significant.

These changes are most apparent in lower New England and in the Northern and Eastern industrial states. They rank at the top along the socio-economic indices throughout the three periods, but only in the latter periods do they show uniformly competitive party systems. A similar but more recent change has been taking place in northern New England and in the middle prairie states, a transition not reflected in our composite index of party competition. This index shows that these states remain fairly constant with low levels of inter-party competition. There is a different picture, however, when competition for the office of governor in the past few years is considered alone. In all of these states—North Dakota, South Dakota, Nebraska, Iowa, Kansas, Maine, New Hampshire, and Vermont—recent elections for governor have become distinctly more competitive, and 1954 seems to have been an important breakthrough year for the Democratic party in these states. Prior to that year, Democratic candidates rarely came close to winning as much as 40 per cent of the two-party vote for governor. Since 1954, however, Democratic candidates have not received less than 40 per cent; moreover, in each of these states a Democrat has won the governorship at least once. These states are also going through important changes in socio-economic conditions. Urbanization and industrialization are creating the social and economic foundations for a competitive party system, and the relative significance of more traditional foundations of party support is decreasing.

A similar, but less pronounced, pattern of relationships has existed between socio-economic development and electoral participation. The state distributions and statistical results for these relationships are shown in Tables 7, 8, and 9. These statistical relations are consistently weaker than those between socio-economic development and inter-party competition, but the same over-all trend pattern is apparent. Again, the relationships are weak during the first period when states with high rates of voter turnout represented all levels of socio-economic development. By Period II the relationships are slightly stronger. All of the highly developed states have moved out of the low participation category, though only two are in

22. This notion has been discussed by V. O. Key, Jr., *Politics, Parties, and Pressure Groups* (New York, 1958), 576-9; and Samuel Lubell, *The Future of American Politics* (New York, 1952), chap. 7.

TABLE 7

PERIOD I. *Relationships between Socio-economic Development and Presidential Voting Participation*

PRESIDENTIAL VOTING PARTICIPATION

Socio-economic Development[*]	*High*		*Medium*		*Low*	
HIGH	(2) Del. N.H.		(10) Conn. Ill. Mass. Mich. N.J.	N.Y. Ohio R.I. Wash. Wisc.	(2) Cal. Penn.	
MEDIUM	(6) Idaho Ind. Iowa	Kans. Mo. Utah.	(8) Colo. Maine Md. Mont.	Nev. Ore. Vt. Wyo.	(4) Ariz. Fla.	La. Tex.
LOW	(3) Ky. N.D. W. Va.		(3) N.M. Okla. S.D.		(8) Ala. Ark. Ga. Miss.	N.C. S.C. Tenn. Va.

[*] This measure is a composite of the state's ranking according to per capita income, urbanization, and foreign-born.

RANK ORDER CORRELATION COEFFICIENTS COMPUTED BETWEEN
THREE SOCIO-ECONOMIC MEASURES AND LEVEL OF
PRESIDENTIAL VOTING PARTICIPATION

	Tau Beta	*Gamma*
Per capita income	.18	.20
Urbanization	.09	.10
Foreign-born	.19	.22

the high participation grouping. There are still a number of states in the category of low socio-economic development which also have high rates of voting participation. These relationships become slightly stronger during Period III, with the distributions of states beginning to approach the hypothesized pattern. Several of the more highly developed states—Connecticut, Massachusetts, and Rhode Island—have moved into the high participation grouping, and more of the medium states have moved toward the middle of the participation distribution. It is the Southern states, ranking low in both socio-economic development and political participation, that most consistently follow the hypothesized pattern and contribute much to the strength of the statistical relationships.

The data analyzed thus far offer considerable support for the hypothesis which relates the impact of socio-economic factors and inter-party com-

TABLE 8

PERIOD II. *Relationship between Socio-economic Development*
and Presidential Voting Participation

PRESIDENTIAL VOTING PARTICIPATION

Socio-economic Development*	High		Medium		Low	
HIGH	(2) Del. Ill.		(12) Cal. Conn. Md. Mass. Mich. Nev.	N.J. N.Y. Ohio Penn. R.I. Wash.		
MEDIUM	(9) Colo. Idaho Ind. Iowa Kans.	Mo. N.H. Utah Wyo.	(6) Maine Mont. N.M.	Okla. Ore. Wisc.	(3) Ariz. Fla. Tex.	
LOW	(3) N.D. S.D. W. Va.		(2) Ky. Vt.		(9) Ala. Ark. Ga. La. Miss.	N.C. S.C. Tenn. Va.

* This measure is a composite of the state's ranking according to per capita income, median income, urbanization, industrialization, and foreign-born.

RANK ORDER CORRELATION COEFFICIENTS COMPUTED BETWEEN
FIVE SOCIO-ECONOMIC MEASURES AND LEVEL OF
PRESIDENTIAL VOTING PARTICIPATION

	Tau Beta	*Gamma*
Per capita income	.34	.38
Median income	.37	.42
Urbanization	.16	.18
Industrialization	.19	.22
Foreign-born	.26	.30

petition. What is more significant from a developmental standpoint, however, is the marked trend over time toward greater correspondence between these two factors. This trend can be seen in the political party transitions of the past few decades and in the developments which are currently taking place in the prairie states of the Midwest, in upper New England, and in the South. These trends point toward increasing party competition within states which currently show low or moderate levels of competitiveness. For the Midwest and New England states this movement follows the national trend of the past few decades toward greater Democratic electoral support, as traditional voting patterns wane and

TABLE 9

PERIOD III. *Relationship between Socio-economic Development and Presidential Voting Participation*

PRESIDENTIAL VOTING PARTICIPATION

Socio-economic Development[*]	High		Medium		Low	
HIGH	(5) Conn. Del. Ill.	Mass. R.I.	(9) Cal. Md. Mich. Nev. N.J.	N.Y. Ohio Penn. Wash.		
MEDIUM	(5) Ind. Iowa Mont.	N.H. Utah	(10) Ariz. Colo. Kans. Maine Mo.	N.M. Okla. Ore. Wisc. Wyo.	(3) Fla. Tex. Va.	
LOW	(4) Idaho N.D.	S.D. W. Va.	(2) Ky. Vt.		(8) Ala. Ark. Ga. La.	Miss. N.C. S.C. Tenn.

[*] This measure is a composite of the state's ranking according to per capita income, urbanization, industrialization, and foreign-born.

RANK ORDER CORRELATION COEFFICIENTS COMPUTED BETWEEN
FIVE SOCIO-ECONOMIC MEASURES AND LEVEL OF
PRESIDENTIAL VOTING PARTICIPATION

	Tau Beta	Gamma
Per capita income	.35	.39
Median income	.39	.45
Urbanization	.39	.45
Industrialization	.17	.19
Foreign-born	.43	.50

occupational and residential patterns shift. For the South, on the other hand, an increase in competition involves the development of more Republican support. Although developments in the South are complicated by the race issue and federal civil rights legislation, there is some evidence from recent elections that this is the developmental pattern in the South.

V

The second major hypothesis of this inquiry links higher levels of inter-party competition and electoral participation with more liberal policy

outputs. As in the preceding section, we have computed rank order correlations between the states, ranked in this instance along the two political dimensions and according to a series of state policy outputs. The
correlation coefficients computed between these two sets of variables are
shown in Table 10. With few exceptions these coefficients show moderate
to fairly strong statistical relationships between inter-party competition
and policy measures. The relationships increase in strength from Periods

TABLE 10

Relationships between Inter-party Competition,
Political Participation, and State Policy Outputs

POLICY OUTPUTS	INTER-PARTY COMPETITION		ELECTORAL POLITICAL PARTICIPATION	
	Correlation Coefficients		*Correlation Coefficients*	
	Tau Beta	Gamma	Tau Beta	Gamma
	PERIOD I			
Per capita expend. for education	.42	.48	.37	.41
Aver. salary for educational personnel	.39	.45	.10	.11
Year aid to blind enacted	.16	.20	.20	.24
Year aid to dependent children enacted	.28	.34	.31	.38
Year old age assistance enacted	.44	.52	.36	.42
	PERIOD II			
Per pupil expend. for education	.42	.49	.29	.34
Aver. salary for educational personnel	.42	.49	.18	.20
Aver. payment for aid to dependent children	.47	.55	.34	.39
Aver. payment for aid to blind	.32	.38	.23	.27
Per capita expend. for public assistance programs	.33	.38	.30	.35
Aver. payment for unemployment insurance	.41	.47	.28	.33
Per capita expend. on all income payments	.59	.69	.44	.50
	PERIOD III			
Per pupil expend. for education	.62	.70	.37	.43
Aver. salary for educational personnel	.52	.58	.23	.27
Aver. payment for aid to dependent children	.57	.65	.57	.66
Aver. payment for aid to blind	.42	.47	.37	.42
Per capital expend. for public assistance programs	.44	.50	.27	.31
Aver. payment for unemployment insurance	.59	.68	.40	.47
Aver. rankings of states on seven welfare programs	.53	.60	.44	.51
Total per capita state expenditures	.41	.47	.31	.35

I through III. By the third period nearly all of the coefficients are higher than any of those for Period I and almost any in Period II. This developmental trend is similar to that discussed in the previous section.

The relationships between the two indices of competitiveness and educational policy are among the strongest in all three time periods. The gamma correlation coefficients between inter-party competition and expenditures on education range from .43 in 1929-30 to .49 in 1947-48 and .70 in 1962-63. This trend toward a stronger relationship is similar to the one Robinson and I found in tracing developments from 1941 to 1960 in state welfare policy and inter-party competition.[23] The indices used here for educational expenditures are not entirely comparable. The 1929 measure is of per capita expenditure for education, while the measure for the two latter periods is for per *pupil* expenditures. Nonetheless, these measures can serve as rough indicators of state efforts in education.

The distribution of states and correlation coefficients between these two variables are shown in Tables 11, 12, and 13. The data in these tables al-

TABLE 11

PERIOD I. *Relationship between Inter-party Competition
and Per Capita Expenditure for Education*

PER CAPITA EXPENDITURE FOR EDUCATION

Inter-party Competition (1914-1929)	High		Medium		Low	
HIGH	(5) Cal.	N.Y.	(4) Mo.	N.M.		
	Colo.	Utah	Del.	R.I.		
	Nev.					
MEDIUM	(9) Ariz.	N.J.	(6) Ill.	Mass.	(5) Ky.	Okla.
	Conn.	N.D.	Ind.	Ohio	Maine	Tenn.
	Idaho	S.D.	Md.	W. Va.	N.H.	
	Kans.	Wyo.				
	Mont.					
LOW	(1) Mich.		(6) Iowa	Vt.	(10) Ala.	Miss.
			Ore.	Wash.	Ark.	N.C.
			Penn.	Wisc.	Fla.	S.C.
					Ga.	Tex.
					La.	Va.

Both Tau Beta and Gamma rank order correlations were computed between these two variables. The correlation coefficients are as follows:

Tau Beta coefficient   .42
Gamma coefficient   .48

23. Dawson and Robinson, "The Politics of Welfare," 404-9.

TABLE 12

PERIOD II. *Relationship between Inter-party Competition
and Per Pupil Expenditure for Education*

PER PUPIL EXPENDITURE

Inter-party Competition (1930-45)	*High*		*Medium*		*Low*	
HIGH	(8) Conn. Del. Mass. Mont.	Nev. N.Y. R.I. Wyo.	(6) Colo. Ill. Ind.	Ohio Wisc. N.H.	(2) Idaho Penn.	
MEDIUM	(5) Wash. Cal. Mich.	Ore. N.J.	(7) Iowa Kans. Ky. Md.	N.M. S.D. Utah	(2) Mo. W. Va.	
LOW	(1) Ariz.		(3) Fla. La. N.D.		(12) Ala. Ark. Ga. Maine Miss. N.C.	N.D. Okla. S.C. Tenn. Tex. Va.

Both Tau Beta and Gamma rank order correlations were computed between these two variables. The correlation coefficients are as follows:

Tau Beta coefficient	.42
Gamma coefficient	.49

low us to see more clearly the developing pattern of relationships between inter-party competition and expenditures for education. In Period I less than a third of those states which ranked high in per capita educational expenditures were highly competitive states; indeed, three-fifths of them are in the category of medium competition. The states which ranked high on inter-party competition are distributed almost evenly between the high and medium expenditure categories. The hypothesized relationship is indicated, but it is not very strong. During Period II more of the high spending states are located in the highly competitive category and more of the low spending states in the low competitive grouping, making the relationship slightly stronger, although only 50 per cent of the highly competitive states rank high in per pupil expenditures for education. By Period III the states approach the hypothesized relationship much more closely. Twelve of the fourteen high expenditure states are in the high inter-party competition category, and twelve of the eighteen highly competitive states rank high in educational expenditures. At the other end of the continuum of educational expenditure, ten out of the fourteen states

TABLE 13

PERIOD III. *Relationship between Inter-party Competition
and Per Pupil Expenditure for Education*

PER PUPIL EXPENDITURE

Inter-party Competition (1946-63)	High		Medium		Low	
HIGH	(12) Cal. Conn. Del. Ill. Mass. Mont.	N.J. N.Y. Penn. R.I. Wash. Wyo.	(4) Colo. Ind.	Mo. Wisc.	(2) Idaho Utah	
MEDIUM	(2) Md. Ore.		(6) Mich. Nev. N.H.	N.M. Ohio S.D.	(2) Ky. W. Va.	
LOW			(8) Ariz. Fla. Iowa Kans.	La. N.D. Tex. Vt.	(10) Ala. Ark. Ga. Maine Miss.	N.C. Okla. S.C. Tenn. Va.

Both Tau Beta and Gamma rank order correlations were computed between these two variables. The correlation coefficients are as follows:

Tau Beta coefficient	.62
Gamma coefficient	.70

categorized as low in per pupil expenditures rank low in inter-party competition. Only two of the highly competitive states rank low in education, and none of the non-competitive states ranks high in educational effort.

The correlation coefficients computed between electoral participation and various policy measures, as given in Table 10, show that most of these relationships are somewhat lower than those between inter-party competition and policy outputs. Like the relationships between competitiveness and policies, they grow stronger from Periods I to II to III. Very few of the statistical relations here, however, could be classified as strong. The rate of electoral participation appears to be less significant for understanding public policy outputs than is inter-party competition.

VI

The data presented thus far appear to offer at least limited support for the major hypotheses concerning the social base and policy consequences of inter-party competition. The competition of party systems, at least since the early 1930's, has been closely associated with higher levels of socio-economic development. Party competition, in turn, seems to be related to the liberality of state policy outputs; this relationship is particularly strong during the period since World War II. The rate of electoral participation is related positively, but only weakly, to both socio-economic conditions and policy outputs.

From a developmental perspective, two significant patterns are discernible. First, there is a general increase in the ratings of states in most of the measures of socio-economic variables (ethnicity is an exception), in inter-party competition, and in electoral participation. It is more difficult to portray state policy outputs in a similar quantitative pattern, but states have increased their expenditures and their involvement in most policy fields. The increases, and even the decreases, in inter-party competition registered over the three time periods coincide with an almost universal increase in support for the Democratic party. While an increase in competition has generally involved an increase in the proportion of votes and legislative seats won by Democrats, the few states that have become less competitive have also done so through increasing Democratic voting and legislative strength.

Equally significantly, there has been a general increase in the strength of association between the several sets of variables over the fifty-year time span. The most significant increase is shown in the strength of relationships between socio-economic conditions and party competition, with the most marked shift occurring between Period I and Period II. A similar, though less pronounced, increase is indicated in the relationship between party competition and policy outputs. For this relationship the greatest differences are between Period III and the two earlier time spans. These data suggest that the socio-economic conditions isolated for consideration here were not particularly relevant for the development and sustenance of inter-party competition in the period preceding the 1930's, but that they have become increasingly significant since that time. These particular findings raise two questions for further investigation into the patterns of American party development. Does this lack of relationship between these common socio-economic factors and party competition extend back before the first time period employed here? What kinds of social and economic factors, if any, were related to party competition prior to the 1930's?

The meaning of these findings for an understanding of the impact of

TABLE 14

Relationships between Socio-economic Development and State Policy Outputs

POLICY OUTPUTS	PER CAPITA INCOME		MEDIAN INCOME		URBANIZA-TION		INDUSTRIAL-IZATION		FOREIGN-BORN	
				Correlation Coefficients						
			(*Tau Beta—Left Gamma—Right*)							
PERIOD I. (1914-1929)										
1. Per capita expend. for education	.53	.60	No Data		.35	.40	No Data		.58	.65
2. Aver. salary for educational personnel	.75	.84			.66	.76			.59	.67
3. Year aid to blind enacted	.33	.40			.36	.44			.32	.39
4. Year aid to dependent children enacted	.46	.56			.41	.50			.50	.60
5. Year old age assistance enacted	.45	.51			.30	.36			.39	.46
PERIOD II. (1930-1945)										
1. Per pupil expend. for education	.66	.76	.65	.74	.50	.57	.48	.55	.63	.71
2. Aver. salary for educational personnel	.64	.75	.64	.73	.68	.79	.69	.79	.55	.63
3. Aver. payment for aid to dependent children	.50	.59	.56	.65	.44	.52	.43	.50	.58	.67
4. Aver. payment for aid to blind	.55	.65	.56	.64	.44	.52	.38	.45	.58	.68
5. Per capita expend. for public assist. programs	.44	.51	.39	.45	.42	.49	.26	.30	.48	.55
6. Aver. payment for unemployment insurance	.61	.71	.64	.74	.53	.62	.54	.63	.56	.66
7. Per capita expend. on all income payments	.79	.88	.79	.89	.52	.60	.49	.57	.66	.74
PERIOD III. (1946-1963)										
1. Per pupil expend. for education	.83	.92	.76	.85	.56	.63	.39	.46	.55	.63
2. Aver. salary for educational personnel	.80	.90	.83	.93	.72	.82	.60	.69	.48	.56
3. Aver. payment for aid to dependent children	.60	.68	.67	.76	.41	.48	.37	.43	.67	.77
4. Aver. payment for aid to blind	.62	.70	.62	.71	.42	.48	.35	.40	.57	.66
5. Per capita expend. for public assist. programs	.51	.58	.47	.54	.39	.45	.26	.30	.47	.54
6. Aver. payment for unemployment insurance	.64	.73	.67	.77	.49	.57	.29	.34	.43	.51
7. Aver. rankings of states on seven welfare programs	.65	.73	.72	.81	.50	.57	.37	.43	.58	.67
8. Total per capita state expenditures	.49	.55	.50	.56	.24	.28	.11	.13	.50	.58

party competition upon policy outputs is more difficult to pull together. As a final step in this analysis we have computed correlations between the several indicators of public policies and the socio-economic variables. If the original hypothesis that inter-party competition serves as a factor intervening between socio-economic conditions and policy outputs is correct, policy outputs should be strongly correlated to socio-economic conditions as well as to inter-party competition. The data presented in Table 14 show that the socio-economic factors are indeed highly correlated with policy outputs throughout all three time periods. In most cases the statistical correspondence between socio-economic factors and policies is

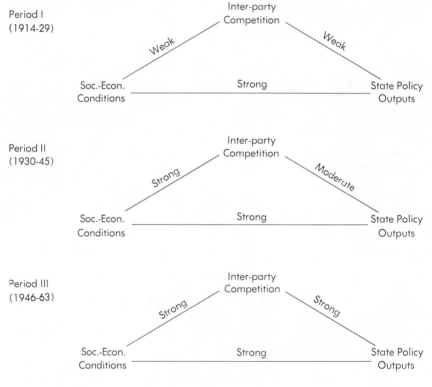

FIGURE 1
*Relationships between three sets of variables over three
time periods**

* These diagrams are designed as rough summaries of the statistical relationships found between these various sets of variables for each time period. The solid lines identify particular relationships, and the words "strong," "moderate," and "weak" are summary descriptions of the strength of relationships found between specified relationships. The correlation coefficients upon which the summary designations are based are found in their appropriate places in the text.

stronger than that which relates party competition to policy outputs. This is particularly true for the third period, and for the relationships with measures of state wealth. There is little indication of any time trend toward stronger or weaker relationships. Socio-economic factors are more highly and more consistently related to policies than is party competition with either socio-economic conditions or policy outputs.

These findings have particular import for our understanding of the policy consequences of party competition. The findings for all three sets of relationships in each of the three time periods are summarized by diagrams in Figure 1. These diagrams show that socio-economic factors have been related to policy outputs over time regardless of the level of inter-party competition. More highly developed states become more competitive politically, and party competition has become more closely associated with policy outputs in a similar way. The developmental findings do not allow us to affirm that inter-party competition has played any role in the development of more liberal policies. What they do suggest is that wealthy, urbanized, and ethnically diversified states tend to be more liberal in their public policies, regardless of the level of party competition. These trend findings, along with the multivariate analysis findings of Dawson and Robinson,[24] lead us to conclude that the level of inter-party competition is not the crucial factor, intervening between socio-economic factors and policy outputs, that our original hypotheses and theory suggested. A fairly strong association between party competition and policy outputs exists during the final period analyzed here, but the indications are that the relationship is probably spurious. High levels of party competition and liberal state policies both seem to be related independently to highly developed socio-economic conditions.

24. Dawson and Robinson, "Inter-Party Competition," 286-9.

IX | THEODORE J. LOWI

CORNELL UNIVERSITY

Party, Policy,

and Constitution in America

RECENT ADVANCES in the study of comparative politics and political development call for a fresh appraisal of the United States and other developed democracies. Reappraisal will yield valuable insights for the students of new nations, and will also be valuable for further study and understanding of the developed countries themselves. Until the past decade, students of American politics in particular were weak on the translation of empirical work into broader theoretical constructs. Separation of facts from values, made in the name of science, became for many a means of semi-retirement into the riches of American research operations and the easy infinitude of four-cell tables. The developmental approach has helped restore a preoccupation with theory and a sense that every political analyst may carry a bit of Aristotle in his knapsack.

Plagued with a superabundance of political facts and narrow-gauge hypotheses and findings, the political scientist who specializes in American politics will have the weightiest tasks as theorist in the new, post-behavioral world of political development. He must simplify a universe made complex by the heights of its development, and still more so by the superb researches of over two generations of modern historians and one generation of excellent political analysts. Yet, in order to join in the efforts of modern political theory, the student of American politics will also have to match the student of undeveloped countries in the simplicity, comprehensiveness, and intuitive validity of his theses. This volume is a sign that some foolhardy souls are willing to take the risk. Some of the chapters have concerned themselves with theses about the development of the political party, taking party as the dependent variable. This essay is an effort to formulate and employ a single thesis regarding the role of party in the development of the larger political system. Other ways to say the same thing would be the "functions of party," or "party as an independent variable."

The best place to begin an analysis of the functions of party in American political development is with a proposition about party in democracies that is general, abstract, and sufficiently non-controversial as to be almost a definition of party. The statement is this—*party in a democracy institutionalizes, channels, and socializes conflict over control of the regime.* In such a characterization the basis or substance of the conflict is less important than the conflict itself. In some systems parties may be regularly associated with clear policy alternatives and, in governing circles, may indeed function as policy-shapers and policy-makers. But policy-making is not the *sine qua non* of party in democracies. Parties that provide the essential level of competition and succession are, in short, not necessarily "responsible parties," in the policy sense.

To put the same proposition still more concretely and positively, party performs a *constituent* or *constitutional* function in the polity. "Constituent" is not used here merely to mean the person or unit being represented in an assembly. That is part of a broader, formal definition. The term "constituent" may reasonably be defined as "necessary in the formation of the whole; forming; composing; making as an essential part." Constituent means that which constitutes. A country holds a constituent assembly to draw up a constitution. Constitution is the setting up, the way in which a political regime is organized and the laws which govern its organization. A party whose functions are constituent or constitutional must have something regular and essential to do—whether intended or not —with the structure, the composition, and the operation of the regime or system. That is to say, the significance of democratic party systems is to be found first in the *regime* and in the *type* of regime rather than directly and specifically in the substantive outputs of the regime. The consequences of party and party development ought to be sought in govern*ment* rather than in govern*ing*.

This paradigm of party and its functions, therefore, rests upon the distinction between constituent processes and functions on the one hand, and policy processes and outputs on the other. Political parties may perform both constituent and policy functions; such parties we can call "responsible parties." On the other hand, political parties may only perform constituent functions. Parties in the European democracies tend to be bi-functional, or "responsible"; parties in the United States tend to be unifunctional, or "constituent." The key to understanding American political development and modern American party politics lies in this distinction; it is decisive to distinguishing between European and American party experience. A satisfactory placement of American experience into a general comparative theory rests upon this distinction and upon translating American politics in these terms. Such, at least, is the governing proposition of this chapter.

There are many reasons why American political experience differs so much from that of other developed democracies. These same factors are the basis for the expectation that American parties and not European parties have been unifunctional, or constituent. (1) There is the problem of the feudal past and the fact that every European state entered modernity faced with class structures, class consciousness, class politics, and the immediate need for centralized and coercive public policies. (2) The fairly early presence of socialist commitments in Europe arose out of the feudal problem but deserves special appreciation because socialist parties were the first really programmatic parties; in turn, they forced "programme" upon the older, middle-class parties which might otherwise have remained recruiting-agencies and boodle-boards like the American parties. As Maurice Duverger observes, there was a "contagion from the Left." (3) Latter-day democratic parties were almost all extra-parliamentary in origin. Unlike the American and British grand old parties, most modern parties all over Europe, including Britain, arose out of the masses. Extra-parliamentary parties were most likely to arise out of social movements tied together by ideology. Parliamentary parties were most likely to arise out of the mutual needs of existing oligarchs for self-defense and re-election. (4) There was also the undoubtedly related fact that most policy-oriented parties outside the United States were performing their functions in a multiple-party system. Except for Great Britain, it can be said that one of the constitutional consequences of programmatic, policy-oriented parties has been to prevent the rise of a two-party system or to destroy it where it existed. Parties have simply been unable to incorporate well-defined purposes with a majoritarian position. Even Britain did not possess a pure two-party system for most of the period between 1870 and 1931, during which time there were often four strong parties in Parliament. Britain returned to a two-party system after World War II, but since that time the policy differences between the two parties have also become considerably weakened and muddied. Even at the height of its power in 1945-51, the Labour party was criticized not for what it failed to do but for what it "failed to *want* to do." (5) There is yet another factor often offered to explain the difference between American and European political development. This is the constitutional factor, which refers in this context primarily to the structure of government and the electoral system—the American presidential system (or separation of powers) versus the European parliamentary system (or fusion of powers), and elections in single-member districts by plurality as contrasted with multi-member districts and proportional representation. Undoubtedly these are important factors in party development, but, at least in the United States, the stronger influence has been the other way around.

All of these factors except the last make very plausible, at least at the beginning, the central thesis here: that American parties are constituent parties and have almost never been "responsible," policy-making parties; that any attempt to understand them as bi-functional would not be supported by the available data; and that any serious attempt to reform the parties toward policy responsibility would do violence to history and to modern political institutions. In this chapter the constituent thesis will first be formulated as the most plausible and consistent interpretation of the facts of American political development from 1789 until about 1850. It will then, as a theory, be applied in several forms to the data of contemporary political behavior and institutions. The inquiry thus boils down to two questions: (1) What were the general political consequences of party development in the United States in the past? (2) What are the continuing consequences of developed parties in the political development of the United States today?

II

The consensus necessary for drafting and ratifying the new Constitution and getting the new federal government going was lost in new issues. The assumption and funding of over $75 millions of debt, the creation of a national bank, the future of relations with England, and the location of the tax burden—students of the period generally agree on the influence of these issues upon the political institutions that eventually emerged. Indeed, George Washington was hardly in harness before he must have found the reins held by his ministers, particularly Alexander Hamilton, whose every act of manipulation brought about polarization and organization in Congress. By the end of the Second Congress (March 1793) over 80 per cent of the members of the House of Representatives were regularly affiliated with either the emerging Federalist or Republican leadership.[1] By the end of the 1790's, even as the membership of the House increased from 65 to 105, the proportion of affiliated Federalists and anti-Federalists rose to and stuck at around 90 per cent. As conflicts within the national elite persisted, so organization around the issues intensified. It is no paradox that the very men who were "above party," the very men who were on principle opposed to party, were the men who created political parties and led them, first in Congress, then around the presidency, and then in the states and localities.[2] Probably the most useful and widely used index to the emergence of party is the startling show of party regularity that led to the Jefferson-Burr tie in the electoral vote and the constitutional crisis of 1800.

The period of fundamental national political party development in the United States began with the establishment of the national government in 1789 and came to an end during the 1840's, when most of the patterns and practices we identify with our parties today were established. In earlier chapters in this volume, Paul Goodman and Richard McCormick are able to identify two fairly distinct phases in this development, which they entitle the first and second party systems. However, while the basis of the party system of the late 1820's and afterward was different from that of 1800, the system of party politics was never absent after its initial establishment by 1800. The period between 1824 and 1828 was an interlude during which new parties supplanted the old. The new system was sufficiently different to warrant the special treatment that McCormick gives it, but developmentally the system can also be viewed as one continuous process. It was, moreover, a process that profoundly affected the course of American political development as a whole. Some important consequences of the course of party development are set forth here.

1. William N. Chambers, *Political Parties in a New Nation* (New York, 1963), 90-91, and citations there.

2. For a dramatic if not always careful account, see E. E. Schattschneider, *Party Government* (New York, 1942, 1959). See also Joseph Charles, *The Origins of the American Party System* (New York, 1956); and Noble E. Cunningham, Jr., *The Jeffersonian Republicans: The Formation of Party Organization, 1789-1801* (Chapel Hill, 1957).

1. *Decentralization and dispersion of national power.* Many factors contributed to decentralization and dispersion of power in the United States, but no factors are more direct and palpable than those of party development. Most of the real indices of decentralization are, in fact, part of normal party activity and manifest party goals. As measured by the backgrounds of top personnel, crude as the measures necessarily are, it appears that party competition, without intending to, broke up the original friendship and kinship aristocracy of deference in one peaceful generation. There has been much recent revisionism among historians concerning the revolutionary or not so revolutionary character of the "Jacksonian revolution," but nonetheless Andrew Jackson's presidency does coincide with the beginning of a new political generation. His own election is significant as the election of the first interloper, the first "rank outsider," to the office of President.[3] His nomination and election in the face of original opposition from the Republican oligarchy that controlled the congressional caucus is the more significant in light of the type of coalition that was built for him by the first state and local bosses. The ambiguity or even the absence of class influence may reduce the significance of Jackson's election in 1828, but that is far less important here than the clarity of the nominating, organizing, and campaigning leadership— the cadre of professional politicians around Martin Van Buren who spanned, *without benefit of common program*, New York, Virginia and the South, and the new West.[4] Thenceforth parties were not "built *out* from the center of government," like the earlier formations, but "built *up* as a Federal structure of existing national factions and state components."[5]

The results in the national inner circle were astonishing. Of twenty-four individuals most clearly identified as leaders within the Jacksonian inner circle,[6] *fourteen* came from states other than those in which they were born and reared; of these fourteen only one was foreign-born, and

3. Cf. Schattschneider, *Party Government,* 152.

4. Cf., for example, Chambers, *Political Parties in a New Nation,* 206.

5. William N. Chambers, *The Democrats, 1789-1964* (New York, 1964), 28, emphasis in original.

6. The Jacksonian inner circle was defined as the top administration (Jackson and his cabinet) plus the several non-cabinet leaders singled out most consistently by political historians of the period (most particularly Schlesinger, aided by Agar and Binkley). These were: Van Buren, Livingston, McLane, Forsyth, Ingham, Duane, Taney, Woodbury, Eaton, Cass, Butler, Branch, Dickerson, Barry, Kendall, Berrien, Polk, Cambreleng, Overton, Lewis, Grundy, and Blair.

he of a native-born father, a journalist and traveler. In other words, 60 per cent of the key Jackson men were both outsiders to Washington circles *and* outsiders to the societies in which their initial recognition was marked.[7] Most of these men were also self-immigrants to the new Western states,[8] but this is only an additional mark of the dispersion of national power and of how quickly national political competition had brought the new states and territories into central roles. Of those who were neither alienated from the communities of their birth nor representatives of the new states, at least four had been noted state political organizers and leaders and were more important for that than for House or Senate service.[9]

Evidence of decentralization is not limited to the presidential circle or to the period 1828-32. While not all trends shown in Table 1 are dramatic,

TABLE 1

Recruitment to the United States House of Representatives
Offices and Statuses of Congressmen Prior to Election

Congress (Year)	Holders of Federal Office	"Local Nota-bles"	College Edu-cated	State Elective Office	County and Local Office	Freshmen
1st (1789-91) N=66	54% or 14%*	76%	56%	79%	24%	45%†
12th (1811-13) N=150	3%	59%	43%	72%	29%	39%
22nd (1831-33) N=222	8%	54%	50%	68%	36%	42%
32nd (1851-53) N=239	9%	50%	49%	60%	36%	53%

* Two different equivalents were used for "federal office" prior to 1789. If Continental Congress is used, 54% had served at the national level. If delegate to Constitutional convention is used, the 14% figure is obtained. Data were not available on other possible equivalents.
† Relative to service in the Second Continental Congress.
Source: Richard Humphrey, Unpublished Doctoral Dissertation, University of Chicago, in progress.

all consistently point to decentralization in the recruitment of members of the House of Representatives in the years from 1789 to 1853. "Local

7. We might legitimately add Martin Van Buren to this enumeration of the "alienated," because he was self-made from poverty through modern machine politics, even though he was a New Yorker from beginning to end.
8. Twelve of the twenty-four can be identified as coming from one of the new states.
9. It seems safe to include Van Buren, Taney, Woodbury, and Butler. Of course, many of those from the new states were also primarily state politicians. Cf. Chambers, *The Democrats,* 28; ". . . it was from the outset a 'party of politicians'. . . ."

notables," defined as individuals whose biographies cited civic or business leadership but no identifiable public office, had dropped by more than 20 percentage points between 1791 and 1833 and more than 25 percentage points by mid-century. The number of those who had backgrounds of college education dropped by a noticeable degree in the earlier periods and, more significantly, did not increase during the sixty years, despite the increasing availability of colleges and universities throughout the country. Matching the relative decline of local notables and the college-educated among congressmen was the decline of the use of state elective office—governors, legislators, and so on—as a channel of recruitment. Consistent with this, though not proportionate, was the expansion of local office in the backgrounds of the congressmen of the period. This is as far as available data allow us to go, beyond the educated impressions of party historians; however, these patterns are strengthened by the consistency of other data reported below.[10]

2. *Democratization of the presidency.* Although it is simply another aspect of decentralization, the democratization of the presidency is worthy of separate treatment. The efforts to settle the original, divisive issues that led to organizing Congress into parties also led to heightened efforts to control the presidency, and *those efforts did something to the office itself.* The first great organized effort to carry an opposition candidate, Thomas Jefferson, into office in the campaign of 1800 was also the first giant step toward the plebiscitary presidency—namely, *the pledging of electors.* By such means the *election* of the President was decentralized and popularized by the parties.[11] The designation of electors by state legislatures was all but abolished by 1828, another important step toward popularization. Further decentralization came with the replacement of the old system of presidential nominations by the congressional caucus with the new national delegate convention, an extreme and dramatic step in decentralization and democratization. Thereafter *nomination* as well as election was to be by mass and relatively popular processes.

3. *Restoration of the separation of powers.* One of the most profound

10. Cf. also Gabriel Almond, "Plutocracy and Politics in New York City," Unpublished Doctoral Dissertation, University of Chicago, 1939, for another view of the departure of the "local notables" from public office, especially in the most highly organized party city.

11. In 1804, only one of the slates of electors in the fifteen states split for more than one candidate. After that no more than two states split until 1824, when five of the twenty-four states split. After 1832, all states chose their electors on a winner-take-all basis.

and permanent contributions of party development was to the revival of the separation of powers. In contrast to the tendency in most modern states toward concentration and consolidation of governmental power, the United States seems to have held more closely to a pre-modern distribution. All the evidence points toward the emergence of a "fusion of powers" in the United States during the first decades of political development, despite the letter and spirit of the Constitution. At the very first the relation between the two major branches of government was one of executive dominance under Hamilton and Jefferson; and later it became one of clear congressional dominance. But in either situation the separation had become unclear; the lack of separation was virtually institutionalized. The Ways and Means committee in the House, a feeble early attempt to fight fusion, quickly became a center of ministerial government; and as President, Jefferson, who probably contributed most to the fusion of powers, established many regular channels to Congress through the committee. He had John Randolph deposed as chairman; his Secretary of the Treasury participated regularly in Ways and Means meetings; he replaced Randolph with George Washington Campbell, who later became a Secretary of the Treasury under James Madison. He also named his own Speaker and floor leaders as well. The House floor leader (also Republican caucus leader) was William Branch Giles of Virginia, who had only just returned to Congress in 1801, after nearly four years of retirement. By his contemporaries he was called "first lord of the treasury," "chancellor of the exchequer," and so on,[12] and he went on to the Senate and to even larger influence.

Following Jefferson and with the beginning of the period of Republican one-party dominance, the lodging of government in Congress became more pronounced. The "Senate cabal" included Vice-President George Clinton;[13] the cabinet came increasingly to be viewed as a collection of administrators almost independent of the President and responsible to Congress;[14] and Robert Smith, Madison's first Secretary of State, was apparently forced upon him by the Senate leadership. All the cabinets of this period were strongly stamped with direct congressional consensus and coalition building. They were long on holdovers from one adminis-

12. Wilfred E. Binkley, *President and Congress* (New York, 1962), 65: "The expressions were not applied, as in Washington's day, to executive heads but to chairmen of the Committee on Ways and Means."
13. Herbert Agar, *The Price of Union* (Boston, 1950), 198.
14. Cf. Binkley, *President and Congress*, 79.

tration to another, long on adversaries for nomination or election to the presidency, and very short on personal loyalty to the man who appointed them. This institutionalizing fusion of powers is strongly suggested in Wilfred E. Binkley's observation that "the later conception of the department heads as the personal representatives and advisers of the President . . . is not at all apparent."[15] "Indeed . . . unless the trend were checked . . . the presidency bade fair to represent, in time, not much more than a chairmanship of permanent secretaries of the executive departments to which Congress at times paid more attention than to the President."[16] Further institutionalizing is strongly suggested in the establishment of a pattern of presidential succession through the Secretary of State.[17]

Party development directly checked or reversed these forces which tended toward the fusion of powers, mainly through the influence that party exerted upon recruitment and succession. In the absence of constitutional provisions for presidential succession in the fullest sense, Congress had at first provided a solution in its nominating caucus. It was a solution, however, that fed into all of the policy issues in which the branches were involved. Furthermore, through this initial pattern of succession Congress had become the President's constituency. Inevitably there was going to be a fusion, either in a cabinet system in everything but name, or a return to congressional government. The Framers had rejected congressional election of the President as part of their espousal of the Separation of Powers, but this system was "establishing itself by accident."[18] Despite earlier Republican condemnations of the caucus system, Jefferson secured his formal nomination by use of the caucus. Later, of course, he had to return to Congress to secure his own election. From that time until Jackson's election in 1828, all presidential successions were affected, one way or another, by Congress. The caucus granted Jefferson's renomination in 1804 as a matter of course and Madison's nomination in 1808 as a matter of duty, although the latter's renomination in 1812 was secured only on rather severe conditions laid down by a caucus of growing identity and strength. The incumbent Secretary of State, James Mon-

15. Ibid. 79.
16. Ibid. 78-9. See also Agar, *The Price of Union*, 227 and 241, on the "congressional plan" of government under Adams.
17. After Jefferson the succession was direct up to Henry Clay who, until 1825 at least, was considered heir presumptive. This is one of several patterns broken forever by the emergence of the party system.
18. Agar, *The Price of Union*, 213 and 199; Binkley, *President and Congress*, 67 *et passim*.

roe, had his nomination ratified in 1816 by the caucus without even any need of laying down explicitly the condition that he be a servant of the caucus. Finally the caucus lost control of the succession in 1824 by foolishly nominating the ailing William H. Crawford in a rump session. Even so, the three favorite-son candidates—Jackson, John Quincy Adams, and Henry Clay—forced the electoral decision right back into the House of Representatives when none of the candidates won a majority of the electoral vote.

It was Jackson's failure to win preference as an insider in 1824 that turned him to Van Buren and the sorts of strategies that men like Van Buren would inevitably use to elect him President. Without any particular intention this process would, by 1832, destroy the established system of succession and thereby begin the restoration of the separation of powers. Organizing the presidency literally from the bottom up tended further to democratize national power. Even more important for the general course of political development, *Jackson's strategy resulted in giving him and succeeding Presidents a base of power independent of Congress;*[19] *moreover, insofar as parties perpetuated the system of succession Jackson employed for himself, to that extent parties would perpetuate the independence of the presidency.* The system of nomination by convention, coupled with the earlier removal of the choice of electors from the state assemblies and the even earlier devolution of the electoral college, totally split Congress off from the presidential succession and established, for the first time, an institutionalized, *real* separation of powers.[20] This was to remain in existence thereafter, despite variations of caliber and energy in the presidential incumbents.

4. *Democratization of the electorate.* This development is easiest to document by the sheer expansion of political activity at local levels. In the urban areas of the Eastern seaboard, recognizable political organizations and neighborhood clubs were beginning to form in the period of the second party system. One of the most significant steps along these lines

19. According to Agar (*The Price of Union*, 221 ff.), Jackson had at least a few clubs in every state by the end of Adams's term. He also had a party press.

20. Congressmen remained major combatants for President and for access to the presidency, but *Congress* was no longer the channel of presidential recruitment, election, succession. Except for the vain effort at usurpation in Andrew Johnson's term in 1868 and the unfortunate involvement in the Hayes-Tilden dispute of 1876-77, Congress had been maker of Presidents for the last time. With that also passed Congress's opportunity to be the seat of government, young Woodrow Wilson's views to the contrary notwithstanding.

was establishment of a Naturalization Bureau by Tammany Hall in 1840.[21] As a result of such expansions of organized political activity individual involvement also spread greatly, and mass participation in nominations and elections became highly visible at all levels of public office. In only two of the then twenty-five states—New Hampshire and Maine— did the dominant party carry more than 90 per cent of all counties in the presidential election of 1836. Eliminate Missouri, with 84 per cent of its counties Democratic, and one finds that in twenty-two of the states the second party carried at least 20 per cent of the counties.

The spread of political activity and involvement that accompanied party formation also expanded the size of the electorate significantly. Inspection of available data between 1808 and 1828 tends, as McCormick states, to confirm a positive relationship between party and turnout;[22] and if we convert McCormick's figures into a time series and extend them to 1844, as we have in Figure 1, a very dramatic relationship appears. The expansion of the electorate was no mere reflection of Jackson's personal popularity: the turnout was still higher with the far less charismatic Martin Van Buren and William Henry Harrison in 1840, and the more regularly contested gubernatorial elections during earlier periods brought higher turnouts than did the presidential elections.[23] Confirming data are available in Robert A. Dahl's study of New Haven, where between 1810 and 1832 the turnout was sporadic, only once rising above 40 per cent: voting "had oscillated . . . with the intensity of campaigning and organization." Around 1832, however, "modern party organizations" developed, and with them regular party competition. Thereafter the turnout swings upward from a low of 8 per cent in 1832 to 15 per cent in 1834, to nearly 60 per cent in 1836, and above 70 per cent in 1840.[24]

21. See Gustavus Myers, *The History of Tammany Hall* (New York, 1917). Despite its prejudice against allowing the foreign-born into the inner councils (299), the Tammany leadership was led to its husbanding role through competition for control of New York City: "After the election of April, 1840 . . . the Committee of Whig Young Men issued a long address . . . charging that prisoners had been marched from their cells in the City Prison by their jailers to the polls to vote the Tammany ticket . . . [and that] naturalization papers had been granted at the Marine Court on tickets from Tammany Hall, under circumstances of great abuse" (129). See also Theodore J. Lowi, *At The Pleasure of the Mayor* (New York, 1964), 34-53 and chap. 8.

22. Richard P. McCormick, "New Perspectives on Jacksonian Politics," *American Historical Review*, LXV (1960), 294. Turnout is defined as per cent of adult white population voting.

23. Ibid. 295.

24. Robert A. Dahl, *Who Governs?* (New Haven, 1961), 20ff.

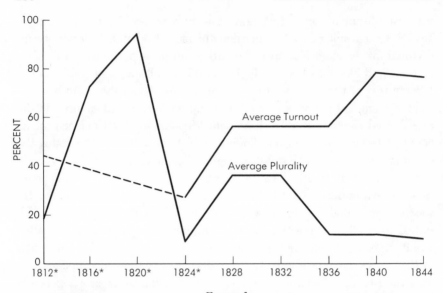

FIGURE 1
*The relationship between turnout and party competition in presidential
elections: state averages, 1812-44.*

Pluralities for 1812 and 1824 are based on electoral votes. Multiple candidacies in 1824 confuse the
picture; using House election by states, Adams won by 8%. A fair turnout estimate exists for 1812 but
not for 1816 and 1820; thus a broken line is used to connect 1812 to 1824.
Sources: Richard P. McCormick, "New Perspectives on Jacksonian Politics," *American Historical
Review*, LXV (1960), Tables I, II, III; and *Historical Statistics of the U.S.*, Washington, 1960.

III

At some point in the 1840's the national party system seemed to pause
in its development. It had made a place for itself in the political system;
although not consciously intended as such by party leaders, the consequences observed so far were probably necessary adjustments to the new
institution of party politics. All serious candidates for President would
henceforth be chosen by the major parties, and there were going to be
only two such parties from 1832 onward, with the exception of the con-
fusions of the mid-1850's and 1860. Parties would henceforth monopolize
all important elections; and party machinery would dominate, if not
monopolize, all nominations. Parties would also monopolize the procedures and administration of Congress as well as virtually all of the state
assemblies. Not excepting even the Civil War period when, as Eric
McKitrick has shown, party was a crucial factor in the Union war effort,
the relation of parties to the national government was pronounced, and
it was not to change appreciably for at least three-quarters of a century.

The scheme of party organization and procedure was also to remain about the same for decades to come.

It is not surprising to find that the consequences of political parties for the political system have not been the same since the end of the great period of development. What is surprising is the nature of the change in function. The historical patterns seem to support the following proposition: the end of important steps in party development was accompanied by *a change in the direction of party function from liberal to conservative, from innovation to consolidation, or from change to a resistance to change.*

1. *Developed parties and the electorate.* A more intensive analysis of the electoral data at the end of the time series in Figure 1 turns up a pattern that is not at all consistent with the conclusion warranted by its over-all character. Comparing "degree of competition," 1836-40, against the turnout for 1840 yields a correlation coefficient of −.28 (Figure 2). That is to say, competition, as measured by the size of the winning plurality over two elections, accounts for barely a tenth of the turnout.

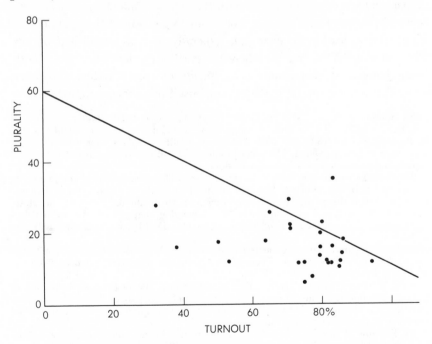

FIGURE 2
*The relationship between party competition and voting turnout, 1836-40,
state by state.*

Mere inspection of Figure 2 shows how relatively haphazard was the relationship between competition and turnout in the 28 states of the period.[25] The function of party in the electorate has simply not been as complete and as regular as many friends of party government have believed.[26] The most plausible proposition here is that *party formation and dissolution are functional and dysfunctional for electorates, but established systems of competing parties are only negligibly so.*[27] In many instances closely balanced parties have actively resisted further democratization of politics. For example, the only notable recent expansions of electorates have appeared in certain Southern states, and this is mostly attributable to the fact that the first competitive system since the 1880's is only now developing there. Other electoral phenomena confirm the essential conservatism of developed parties in the United States. For example, party development (see Table 1) was associated with very low measures of tenure in Congress. In the Twelfth Congress 39 per cent of the numbers were freshmen, and by the time of the Thirty-second Congress, 53 per cent were freshmen. Contrast this with 1911, when just over 30 per cent were freshmen, and with the typical contemporary Congress, in which freshmen comprise no more than 15 per cent of the membership. Resistance to leadership change is generally true of established parties. Elite composition in systems where the parties are developed has usually been changed by social movement outside the party system altogether, or by the minority party "redeveloping" itself after severe defeat.[28]

25. Source of data: Walter Dean Burnham, *Presidential Ballots, 1836-1892* (Baltimore, 1955). For "degree of competition" we took size of plurality ($D\% - R\% = P$) averaged for 1836 and 1840 ($1836P + 1840P \div 2$) for each state. Turnout was taken as earlier defined. The great problem with all this is the error of population reports and whether error is biased or random.

26. Cf. Schattschneider, *Party Government*, 48: "The enlargement of the practicing electorate has been one of the principal labors of the parties, a truly notable achievement for which the parties have never been properly credited." Contrast this statement with Figure 2 and with Burnham, "The Changing Shape of the American Political Universe," *American Political Science Review*, LIX (1965), 7-28, and with the sources cited there, 13.

27. It also supports the argument I made in an earlier paper about the conditions for innovation in party systems, "Toward Functionalism in Political Science: The Case of Innovation in Party Systems," *American Political Science Review*, LVII (1963), 570-83. If "party formation" is not taken as analogous to the single event in the life of an organism but as a state to which all seriously defeated parties return, if only temporarily, the distinction between developed and developing becomes a functional tendency of considerable importance.

28. See my "Toward Functionalism in Political Science," and my analysis of the "reform cycle" in *At The Pleasure of the Mayor*, 178-210. Dahl and Almond document many of the types of nineteenth-century elite changes associated with party

2. *Party and the maintenance of federalism.* During the formative period of party development nothing was more important than the federal structure of the regime, and much has been made of the impact of federalism on party.[29] However, once the parties had formed around this constitutional structure, the constitutional force of party itself weighed strongly in favor of federalism despite the extremely strong nationalizing pulls of economics and of the efforts of many national political leaders to cope with economic problems. Whatever viability and utility is left to the states, for better or worse, is a result for which the forces of developed parties can take a great deal of credit.[30] The mechanisms involved in this influence of party are simple. The influence is epitomized in the phrase, "the Tiger shall not cross the bridge," the Brooklyn rallying cry against Tammany efforts to bring all of Greater New York within a single Democratic organization.[31] Party leaders developed a fundamental stake in the integrity of the state boundary because it was the largest unit for electoral office: everything beyond that was imponderable, unpredictable. And besides, what was beyond the state level? Only the other states, for even control of the presidency is not a national political process but a series of fifty separate state processes. Efforts to establish parties on even the regional level have never succeeded, largely because state leadership has enjoyed internal resources too valuable to risk losing to an expansive neighbor.[32]

---

development. However, see *At the Pleasure of the Mayor,* 110ff, for further examples of types of opposition established parties have erected to further alteration, except under the special conditions proposed, 178ff.

29. See e.g. Schattschneider, *Party Government,* 124ff and chap. VI; and David B. Truman, "Federalism and the Party System," in Polsby, Dentler, and Smith (eds.), *Politics and Social Life* (Boston, 1963), 513-27.

30. Cf. Morton Grodzins, in one of the few efforts to focus on this neglected aspect of the dependence of federalism upon party: "The parties become a chief avenue for the achievement of decentralized government. But governmental (here formal constitutional) factors are partially responsible for the manner in which parties are structured. So government 'causes' the form of party; party 'causes' the form of government." Morton Grodzins, "American Political Parties and the American System," *Western Political Quarterly,* XIII (1960), 994.

31. Schattschneider, *Party Government,* 145.

32. Tammany never succeeded in crossing the river; in fact, New York City government under the modern (1898) charter reflects the separatism in its Borough structure. And the states have remained fairly separate from one another. They support each other in their separateness, particularly when a strong national leader poses a threat. Following Franklin D. Roosevelt's vain "purge of 1938," Congress passed the Hatch Act, forbidding political activities by federal employees, in order to guard against any chance that a President might try to build a party independent of the states. Cf. Truman, "Federalism and the Party System," 526; and Schattschneider,

As a result the state became a vital political unit. It might have become more a political unit than a governmental one, but for the fact that the commitment of the parties in Congress to the states strongly influenced the substance of much important national legislation, often carving out a totally unwarranted role for the state governments. In his unique study of the influence of party on the system, Morton Grodzins analyzed the state bias of many important federal programs and the role of party in bringing this about, even when "there existed compelling reasons for establishing [the] programs without state participation."[33] The two programs he had most particularly in mind were the Social Security Act of 1935 and the National Airport Act of 1946, but he also identified several other major areas of policy in which the spirit of party determined a structure of "state sharing" in the programs.[34] One gets the impression from the various accounts of the Social Security Act of 1935 that congressmen were more concerned over the role of the states than they were over the fact that this Act created the welfare state.[35] The role of parties in providing work for the state governments can be seen as especially systematic in land-use and resources programs, but it also marks a goodly part of recent welfare legislation.[36] Thus, even as the national government and the Constitution expanded to meet the problems of a nationally integrated country, the parties participated in a silent conspiracy to prevent that expansion from departing too far from eighteenth-century constitutional structure.

Despite significant differences of impact as between developing and developed parties, there is one thing all of these consequences have in common. This is that none of them has anything to do directly with the promulgation or enactment of public policy. In the chronicles of party development, policies or issues seem to have contributed to the formation of parties; but parties seem to have played only a negligible role in the direct formation of policies. Assuming that the Jacksonian period had

---

Party Government, 166-7. See McCormick's chapter in this volume for an excellent treatment of how the highly sectional responses of voters to the presidential candidates of the 1830's helped produce non-sectional parties.

33. Grodzins, "American Political Parties," 980ff.

34. Ibid. 980ff.

35. See sources cited in Grodzins, "American Political Parties"; and also Edwin Withe, The Development of the Social Security Act (Madison, 1962).

36. See e.g. my "How the Farmers Get What They Want," Reporter, May 21, 1964. The best recent example in the welfare field is the governors' formal participation in the Appalachia program and their veto power over Appalachia projects.

been one of class and issue politics, Herbert Agar observed that William Henry Harrison's demagogic, no-commitment campaign of 1840 "re-established the normal pattern of American politics . . . the usual method of seeking votes by regional bribes and balances, and of bolstering the union by regional compromise."[37] "Responsible" parties, "policy-making" parties, "mandate" parties are only occasional phenomena in American political history. And if policy-making is only an occasional activity of political parties in America, even if an important one when it occurs, then it ought not to be brought into the center of a functional definition of party.[38]

The positive proposition which arises out of this review of the consequences of developing and developed parties is that they all have to do with *constituent* or *constitutional* processes. They all had something to do with the structure or composition or regimes, the recruitment of leaders, the size and composition of electorates, the structures of decision-making. Developments of this sort occurred without any particular association with public policies or specific issues. Policy issues at the beginning contributed mightily to the creation of the first party system. Policy issues at the end of the first constitutional epoch, the 1850's, contributed to the destruction of party. But for the functioning of party itself, the important fact has been the existence of competition, not so much what the competition was about. Party in America arose out of the interstices and flaws of the formal constitutional structure, was shaped by that constitutional structure, and developed its particular functions primarily out of the flaws in that structure. Party continues into the twentieth-century world of mass democracy as the same kind of institution, with an amazingly similar structure and astonishingly similar functions. Popular ideology about democracy and party has continually demanded that the parties be reformed toward some concept of "responsibility," some function of mandate or policy-making. Parties and party leaders have successfully resisted these demands, however, perhaps more because of the unappreciated success of party as a constituent institution than because of the conservatism or the wisdom of party leaders.

Thus the several consequences of party formation and activity in the

37. Agar, *The Price of Union*, 291. Agar approves; Lord Bryce agrees with the facts, but disapproves, in *The American Commonwealth*, as quoted in Agar, 688.
38. Function is defined simply as a regular and abiding relation between a given institution or practice and other institutions and practices within the system of which they are defined to be a part. See my "Toward Functionalism in Political Science," and the citations there.

early period of the development of the first and second American party systems can be put within the confines of a single thesis about party and party function. This thesis, in turn, can be taken as the single functional hypothesis governing the analysis of party development in the contemporary period. If party is a basic part of the constitutional process, then it is, like the constitution (small "c"), not likely to change much in either structure or function. If this thesis gets close to the reality of party, we must predict that modern phenomena, especially political phenomena that could be recorded only since the development of modern polling and quantifying techniques, will support this thesis with a clarity of distribution superior to any alternative theses.

IV

How contemporary and continuous this particular constituent function of party has been is shown by Grodzins's analysis of party and its contribution to the maintenance of federalism. But the relation of the party system to the maintenance of the separation of powers may go unappreciated precisely because it is so regular and so successful. Appreciation can be renewed simply by speculating upon the consequences of a successful Dixiecrat party in 1948 and after, or the success of Governor George Wallace's movement in 1964. A three-party system would regularly deprive presidential candidates of majorities. Very quickly and directly, the entire pattern of recruitment and succession would change. The separation of powers would begin to recede until the presidency and both houses of Congress had become a single institution. The functions of the cabinet and the very purpose of cabinet officers would change. These patterns would develop whether the basis of the new system was civil rights, foreign affairs, or labor relations. The parties would inevitably be more policy-oriented. Ironically, this more decentralized, three-party system would result in a shift toward a more centralized Constitution.

To what extent can the constituent function also be seen in the behavior of the electorate and of modern leaders? To what extent can the clearest patterns of party influence be explained by an argument extended from the single thesis of the unifunctional (and conservative) constituent party?

Two dimensions of modern political life will be analyzed here, the electorate and the legislature. These do not exhaust the possibilities, but they will be sufficient. Analysis of party and the electorate, with which we will begin, is in turn divided into (1) the sociological impact, and (2) the impact of party on political opinion and choice.

1. *Maintenance of existing social cleavages.* The voting studies produced by Berelson and his associates provide one of the few opportunities in the literature to assess the "social effects of the campaign."[39] Their data are unusual because they are drawn from interviews of the same respondents before and after the campaign, and because the items isolate and allow for analysis of leaners and switchers. What they found was simply this: Between the 1944 and 1948 campaigns, trends among voters were relatively independent of the modal pattern of affiliation for each of the major social groupings. There was, in brief, a general drift of Catholics and Protestants and of union and white-collar labor toward the Republican party. Between May and November of 1948, however, the pattern altered dramatically. Catholic and union labor patterns of switching differed drastically from that of Protestants and white-collar workers. For example, in May of 1948, 55 per cent of the 1944 Protestant Democrats and 43 per cent of the 1944 Catholic Democrats had decided that they had defected to the Republican party. Between May and November of 1948, however, there was virtually no more defection of Catholics to the Republican party, while 37 per cent of all Catholics identified as Republicans in June had "re-defected" to the Democrats.

These figures are interesting not merely because they show predicted patterns in the ultimate voting decision. They are significant as an index to party functions in the electorate. During the period of most pronounced party activity—indeed a period short enough to allow us to attribute observed changes to party influence—respondents displayed their strongest identification with their status and class groupings. Parties compose electoral slates to maximize voter identification; candidates frame strategies and appeals around audience identification—down to the finer points of Protestant candidates eating indigestible blintzes. In appealing to whatever characteristics are perceived as even remotely salient to voters, campaigns tend to restore and reaffirm the identifications of voters with these very characteristics.[40] This is a pronouncedly conservative influence, and it suggests that party works in opposition to the "melting

39. Bernard R. Berelson *et al.*, *Voting: A Study of Opinion Formation in a Presidential Campaign* (Chicago, 1954), 140-41.
40. Cf. Lowi, *At the Pleasure of the Mayor*, 44ff.

pot" tendencies of many institutions in American society. Unlike economic endeavor, many kinds of which are a good deal more permeable
by new social elements than the political parties are,[41] the parties make
a special effort to symbolize to their advantage all of the characteristics
a candidate or an appointee might possess.[42] Even if a party gains no
votes, its effort is likely to produce the effect indexed by the Berelson
data.[43] This conservative influence of party on the electorate suggests, second and more to the point, that the clearest of party influences is constituent. Regardless of any influence party may or may not have on voter information or the structuring of voters around issues, and so on, *party tends to
have this regular influence on the composition of the electorate: party
activity, without any necessary intention on the part of the campaigners,
tends to determine the degree to which social characteristics will be salient
in any political situation.*[44] Party functions tend strongly toward the maintenance of many political response patterns and social identifications long
after the original and most self-conscious bases for these patterns have
broken down.[45]

41. Ibid. 110ff.
42. Ibid. 46. "Success in economic fields is highly individualized; . . . there is
relatively little group symbolization of success. . . . Economic mobility is more truly
assimilative because economic success homogenizes values and tends to erase social
differences. If the melting pot is insisted upon as the proper metaphor for the American social process, then it should be added that the political process reduces the
flame."
43. Assessment of the full extent of ethnic, religious, and class reawakening during
campaigns would require data bearing directly on these identifications rather than the
data here, which are made to perform as an index to this reaffirmation. This index,
clear as it is, is bound to mask some of the impact of party on social identifications
because it only measures that part which is expressed in party affiliation. For example, many Catholics or Irish might insist on remaining Republican but still find themselves feeling more Catholic or Irish as a result of the campaign appeals. For another
example, new appeals to Negroes in the South by both major parties will probably
produce more Negro solidarity rather than less. Cutright and Rossi, "Grass Roots
Politicians and the Vote," in Polsby *et al.* (eds.), *Politics and Social Life*, 778, offer
some further evidence on this point. They show how strong reaffirmation of identification can be even when the group is split in voting patterns. In their predominantly
Catholic community they found that actual vote was up noticeably over "expected
vote" for either party whenever the precinct captain was a Catholic. Protestant Democratic captains reduced "expected vote" by as much as 70 per cent; Catholic Republican captains increased expected Republican vote by 39 per cent.
44. Some have accepted the melting pot idea and project a decline in relevance of
established social cleavages, especially ethnicity, in politics. Cf. Dahl, *Who Governs?*,
42ff. However, one of Dahl's associates in the New Haven series, Raymond Wolfinger,
disagrees and supports his disagreement with some extremely strong data in "The
Development and Persistence of Ethnic Voting," *American Political Science Review*,
LIX (1965), esp. 902, Table II.
45. Cf. Wolfinger, "Development and Persistence of Ethnic Voting," 907-8; see
also V. O. Key, Jr., and Frank Munger, "Social Determinism and Electoral Decision:

2. *Party and the organization of disagreement.* Nothing finds students of voting behavior in closer agreement than the issue of the relation of party to public policy issues, and nothing is so disturbing to existing theories of party. American parties are not "responsible parties." Campbell and his associates, in *The American Voter*, devote the entire concluding section of their careful analysis of "public policy and political preference" to an explanation of why there is so little difference between the two parties.[46] They propose, as they must, that "where there is a babel of perceptions about party positions on a prominent issue, the significance of the public mandate becomes inscrutable"; and they offer some reasonable explanations for the babel.[47] Schattschneider provides a veritable inventory of such conclusions for the twentieth century,[48] and Agar and Bryce offer corresponding conclusions for the nineteenth century.[49] A typical picture of the relation of American parties to the electorate on a single, major issue appears in Figure 3. Rather than a "responsible" position of two-party bimodality ("differences between the parties"), there is a strong tendency toward *bimodality within each party*—although the Republicans are more internally bimodal than the Democrats, the same pattern is still clear for the latter. This same tendency of ambiguity between and bimodality within the parties can be observed—see Figure 4—even among the more active party members, and even in as organized an area as Wayne County (Detroit) has come to be.[50]

The constituent party thesis rests comfortably with such findings. How-

---

The Case of Indiana," in E. Burdick and A. J. Brodbeck (eds.), *American Voting Behavior* (New York, 1959), 281-99; and Edgar Litt, *The Political Cultures of Massachusetts* (Cambridge, Mass., 1965), 64-7, esp. Table 3.3.

46. Angus Campbell *et al.*, *The American Voter* (New York, 1960), 8, and 183ff.

47. Ibid. 183.

48. Schattschneider, *Party Government*, 131-2.

49. Agar, *The Price of Union*. See 291 for Agar's propositions on the "normal pattern of American politics." See 688ff for his views and for a concise statement of Bryce's views.

50. Samuel J. Eldersveld, *Political Parties: A Behavioral Analysis* (Chicago, 1964), 186. The same pattern can be found in the 1964 Survey Research Center's data, but the presentation cannot be made comparable to Figures 3 and 4 because the responses to the attitude questions were only threefold rather than fivefold. Turning the figures around, however, and using the fivefold party identification against simple Agree-Disagree, we find:

	Strong D	D	Ind. D.	Ind. R.	R.	Strong R	N
Agree	38%	27%	11%	3%	10%	5%	563
Disagree	11	20	7	10	18	25	352

(These figures based upon all respondents [915] who could be scaled on six issue questions, as discussed below.)

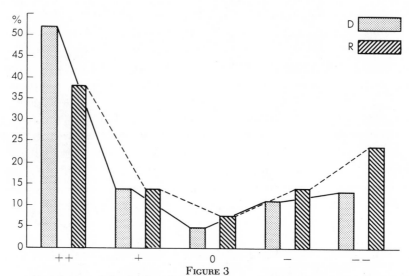

FIGURE 3

Distribution of clearly identified Democrats and Republicans according to response to, "The government in Washington ought to see to it that everybody who wants to work can find a job."

Source: Survey Research Center, 1956.

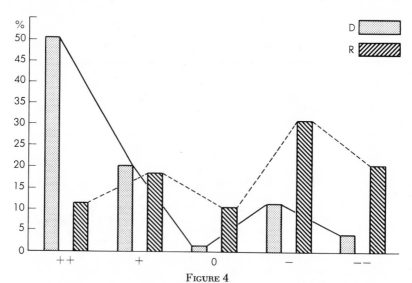

FIGURE 4

Distribution of Democratic and Republican precinct leaders according to response to, "The government ought to help people get doctors and medical care at low cost."

Source: Samuel J. Eldersveld, *Political Parties: A Behavioral Analysis* (Chicago, 1964), 186, Table 8.2.

ever, they are the beginning point of the analysis, not the conclusion of it. To approach real parties it is wrong to isolate an issue; one must take several issues simultaneously in a composite analysis rather than one issue at a time. An election is not a series of individual referenda offered on the same day. All identifiable Democrats and Republicans are distributed in Figure 5 according to their scores on a simple scale consist-

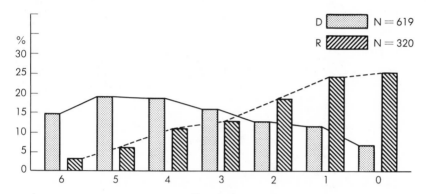

FIGURE 5
All Democrats and Republicans, according to their scores on six domestic issues, 1964.

Source: Survey Research Center, 1964.

ing of their responses to six domestic policy questions.[51] Here for the first time we begin to get clear two-party bimodality, a bimodality far clearer than any array of the two parties according to social class or other demographic characteristics.[52] The picture in Figure 6 is the same, except that it involves only the *clear* party identifiers, by eliminating the categories

51. Six domestic issue questions were identified in the Survey Research Center's 1964 election study. All respondents were arranged in seven categories, as follows:

SCORE:	6.	5.	4.	3.
RESPONSES:	6Y, or	5Y, 1N, or	4Y, 2N, or	3Y, 3N, or
(Y=Yes;	5Y, 1NA	4Y, 1N, 1NA	3Y, 2N, 1NA	2Y, 2N, 2NA
N=No;	108	147	160	151
NA=No Answer)				

	2.	1.	0.
	2Y, 4N or	5N, 1Y, or	6N, or
	2Y, 3N, 1NA	4N, 1Y, 1NA	5N, 1NA
	158	164	136

The scores were then gang-punched and cross-tabulated against party identification. Because there were too many NA responses, 545 respondents from the original sample could not be scored.

52. See e.g. the figures in my "Toward Functionalism in Political Science," 574, based on data drawn from 1951 and 1959 Roper surveys. See also Angus Campbell and Homer C. Cooper, *Group Differences in Attitudes and Votes* (Ann Arbor, 1956), esp. 56, and Table IV-18.

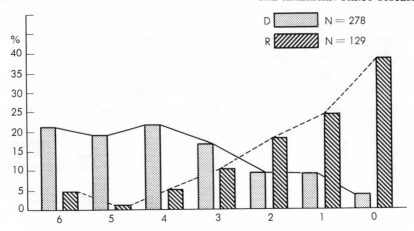

FIGURE 6
*Clearly identified Democrats and Republicans, according to their scores
on six domestic issues, 1964.*

Source: Survey Research Center, 1964.

of "Independent, closer to Democrats" and "Independent, closer to Republicans." If all respondents were always in the same position on all issues, then the composite profile would look like the individual issue profiles. Since this is not the case, the combining of issues as in Figures 5 and 6 *tends above all to reduce the strength of deviancy and the statistical influence of the deviants in each party*. The Left tail of the Republican and the Right tail of the Democratic distributions are spread out thinner and thinner from the mode, and the farthest part of each is reduced toward numerical insignificance. Expansion of the scale to include ten issues and more, and foreign as well as domestic issues, *would virtually eliminate the deviating tail of both parties*.[53]

This inconsistency between the single issue and the composite of the single issues is, of course, a statistical mirage. But, more than that, it is also an accurate view of a real phenomenon—how the parties work. Parties combine and compose without doing much influencing along the way: "to speak of party politics as if it were a case principally of the creation and manipulation of opinion is to miss the point entirely," said Schattschneider, in his magnificently suggestive book. "*Persuasion is unnecessary or secondary*. Politicians take people as they find them. The politician has a technical specialty based on a profitable discovery about

53. This does not mean it eliminates members. Combination reduces the number of members who consistently disagree with the modal position of the party.

the behavior of numbers."[54] In this sense we can say that the contrasts shown above between single issues and composites of issues are both statistical *and* real phenomena, and that together they represent the party in the most realistic way. The contrasts constitute a single finding, a single datum whose support for the constituent thesis is direct and clear. Parties present few issues to electorates as referenda or quasi-referenda and therefore represent few real majorities before, during, or after elections. In mixing up the deviants among a congeries of issues, the party represents "artificial majorities";[55] and those, of course, are not majorities in any sense but a numerical one. This occurs on a base-line of ideology, or at least of traditional tendencies, supported by perceptible differences in the leadership.[56] This means that, electorally, American parties represent outcomes *in general;* parties seldom shape or represent outcomes *in particular.* Representing *in general* is not the same as responsible policy-making by party, or even the shaping of policy along lines of electoral influence or electoral choice.

Party is a means by which electorates structure themselves in some manner which is institutionally related to government. This institutionalized and even partially ordered relation of mass to elite is a constitutional fact about stable democracies which, however, students of African politics are more likely to appreciate than are students of stable democracies. The political process can be conceived as beginning with irritants and interests too amorphous and many-sided to be the basis of much formal discourse. A major function of leadership in society is the organization of these interests into public issues. Party leaders have always been instrumental in picking among interests and issues those which will constitute the agenda of formal public discourse, a process C. J. Friedrich calls agreeing on what to disagree about.[57] This organizing of disagreement actually amounts to the creation of a working agenda. It is a mat-

54. Schattschneider, *Party Government,* 41-2, emphasis in original. Schattschneider was talking about caucus and coalition politics in groupings considerably smaller than electorates, but his point seems to be no less applicable here.

55. Cf. William H. Riker, *Democracy in the United States* (New York, 1953), 108-9. Riker does not see the same implications in this as I do. He goes on, 109-11, to demand that somehow parties must make these majorities meaningful and be responsible policy-making parties in spite of the artificiality of the majorities they help create. But his concept is a potent one.

56. Eldersveld, *Political Parties,* 186. See also Herbert McClosky, "Issue Conflict and Consensus Among Party Leaders and Followers," *American Political Science Review,* LIV (1960), 406-27.

57. Carl J. Friedrich, *The New Belief in the Common Man* (Boston, 1942), 171.

ter of high statecraft; but, while an agenda does influence what becomes policy, the specific policy outcome is clearly an indirect part of this process.[58] On an agenda, broadly defined, interests have reached a relatively late stage of development where they are likely to be perceived as having two sides ("issues"); party leaders, however, find themselves in the uncomfortable position of leading a party comprised of *both* sides of each issue. The leaders inevitably become brokers with the agenda items as they were with items not yet well enough organized to be on an agenda. The pronounced internal bimodality of American parties helps explain why more clear debates on the issues, and more mass decisions on candidates that are clearly associated with specific policies alternatives, have been made *within* parties between candidates for nomination rather than between two candidates for election.[59]

It is in this sense that party can be termed basically a container, composer, and cumulator, a statistical rather than a rational or conscious order. As such it may be a more or less passive channel for regular expression without influencing or being influenced much along the route. In this it is as much a part of the constitutional process as any institution could be. In other words, party in America continues to make possible a popularly based policy-making process without very much directing the policy outcomes themselves.

V

Facts to the contrary notwithstanding, scholars and reformers have insisted most strongly on the presence and on the desirability of responsible parties in Congress.[60] Studies of the presidency and the executive already tend toward a constituent interpretation of party functions, even to the

58. An aspect of this worth pursuing, though we cannot do so here, is the possible influence of party in keeping some things regularly *off* the public's agenda. I am not referring to any conspiracies between candidates to avoid some issue, but to the less conscious but possibly quite real deadening effect of consensus between the two parties. Among others, Key, Eldersveld, and Campbell *et al.* report how nearly unanimous are all the party indentifiers on foreign policy attitudes. Data in *The American Voter*, 198, show that breaks in the internationalism scale scores are almost identical for Republicans and Democrats and for every level of identification. This is bound, for better or worse, to have a structural impact on any such issue or issue area.

59. Compare e.g. Willkie-Taft to Willkie-Roosevelt as an illustration of this point.

60. See the debate between the American Political Science Association Committee on Political Parties and Julius Turner, wherein the resolution was that parties ought to be responsible and are not, and the rebuttal was that parties ought to be responsible and chi-squares say they already are. Reprinted in Theodore J. Lowi (ed.), *Legislative Politics U.S.A.* (Boston, 1962).

extent of treating party processes and functions as relatively constant since the 1830's.[61] For these reasons the data on party-in-government presented here will be taken exclusively from congressional experience.

1. *Legislative party behavior.* The same principle of analysis used for electoral behavior can be brought to the legislative arena, and for the same purpose: to show and to evaluate the contrast between party influence as measured by voting on issues taken one at a time, and party influence as measured by voting on a composite of issues. The presentation will look different because legislators have obliged us with no fivefold shadings of opinion, but only a yea or nay vote. Evidence of party influence on a series of single roll calls taken one at a time is drawn in Table 2 from six roll call votes as tabulated by the Americans for Democratic Action in 1961 in order to calculate their "liberalism score." Voting behavior for each roll call in House and Senate is summarized by a simple index widely employed in testing the relative influence of party and other forces—the index of likeness.[62] Parties in the House, as is well known, display greater differences than in the Senate, but in both chambers and in both parties there are regularly considerable numbers of defecting party members. Only in marginal instances do party leaders even try to exert pressure to get determined dissenters to change their votes. Thus, with dissenters in both directions, the parties typically lack distinction. Even on the most prominent and controversial issues of a session, such as those listed in Table 2, only a chi-square test could say without

TABLE 2

Party Influence as Measured By Index of Likeness on Six Roll Calls in House and Senate, Compared to Contrived Index of Likeness for the ADA Scores, 1961

	I.L. HOUSE	I.L. SENATE
"ADA COMPOSITE I.L."	23	36
Extend Minimum Wage	42	63
Housing Bill	30	54
Foreign Aid Authorization	78	87
Education Bill	37	50
Enlarge Rules Committee	38	—
Cloture Rule	—	90
Average I.L. for Five	45.0	68.5

61. See e.g. V. O. Key, Jr., *Politics, Parties, and Pressure Groups* (New York, 1958), 434 and 474. See also my "Ritual and Power: Senator Kennedy and the First Ballot," *The New Republic*, April 11, 1960.

62. Julius Turner, *Party and Constituency: Pressures on Congress* (Baltimore, 1951), 26 and 36.

embarrassment that the parties were "significantly different." The average index of likeness for the six roll calls was 45.0 in the House and 68.5 in the Senate. The index of likeness for a "party vote" (where 90 per cent of the members of one party vote in opposition to 90 per cent of the members of the other party) is 20.

Two comparisons can be made with this weak and ambiguous record of party influence and discipline, the first of which can be seen in Figures 7 and 8.[63] The ADA liberalism score is a composite of a dozen key roll calls. Ranging the senators and representatives according to their scale scores presents a picture of extreme two-party bimodality, just as we found it was with composite opinions of party affiliates in the electorate. As expected, this bimodality appears greater in the House, but this accurate impression is exaggerated somewhat by the larger size of the House and the fact that the arrays of Figures 7 and 8 are based on numbers rather than on percentages of seats. Based on this composite,

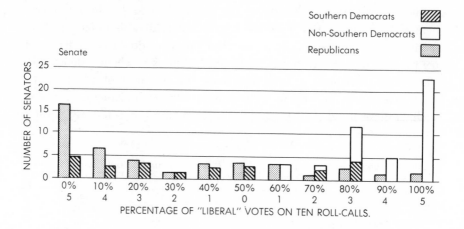

FIGURE 7
Liberalism scores of Democratic and Republican senators, 1961.

Source: Fred I. Greenstein, *The American Party System and the American People* (Englewood Cliffs, 1963), 79.

63. Figures published in Fred I. Greenstein, *The American Party System and the American People* (Englewood Cliffs, 1963), 79. Each senator and representative is assigned a score according to the proportion of the key votes on which he voted "right" in the eyes of the ADA; this is essentially the same as our earlier scoring of survey respondents according to the number of Y or N answers to the issue questions. Greenstein names six of the roll calls employed in the score, but he fails to state how many there were in all. Usually ADA, AFL-CIO, *New Republic*, and Committee for Constitutional Government scores are based on 10-15 key votes.

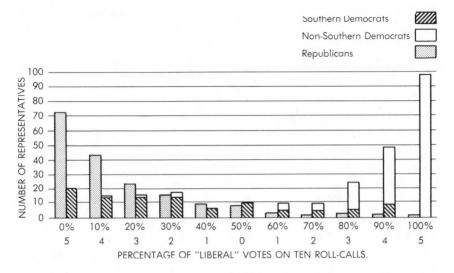

Southern Democrats
Non-Southern Democrats
Republicans

PERCENTAGE OF "LIBERAL" VOTES ON TEN ROLL-CALLS.

FIGURE 8
Liberalism scores of Democratic and Republican representatives, 1961.

Source: Fred I. Greenstein, *The American Party System and the American People* (Englewood Cliffs, 1963), 79.

two-party bimodality makes Congress appear almost as a parliamentary body if we disregard the Southern Democrats, and still with a quite disciplined and responsible two-party system even with the Southern Democrats included. Using *New Republic* and AFL-CIO scores, V. O. Key, Jr., presents almost exactly the same pattern of clear two-party bimodality in selected sessions between 1949 and 1960.[64]

By inspection alone, the contrast between the index of likeness for single roll calls and the arrays of scale scores in Figures 7 and 8 in Congress is altogether consistent with the contrast observed earlier in the electorate. But a more direct comparison of behavior on single issues versus composites of issues can be made. In Table 2 we can compare each individual index of likeness, or the average index of likeness, with the "ADA Composite Index of Likeness" at the top. This ADA composite is simply a means of converting Figures 7 and 8 into summary numbers by weighting the distance away from a perfect party position.[65] The re-

64. Key, *Politics, Parties, and Pressure Groups* (4th Ed.) 732-5, especially the pattern for the House, 1955-56, and the Senate, 1949-50.
65. The index of likeness (I.L.) is a summary of the relative support given on an issue by one party in relation to another party. It is computed: 100 − (%Y Dem. − %Y Rep.): the higher the score the more the parties are alike, the lower the score the

sults are dramatic. This composite index, which is simply a direct, numerical translation of the Figures 7 and 8, almost gives us party government in the House (comparing the composite I.L. of 23 to the index of likeness of 20 for a "party vote"), and is closer than senators would like to believe it to be in the Senate. But this is not classic party government where party leaders and whips line up their members on every vote. This is simply a measure of the party as composer and container—again, more a statistical than a conscious and disciplined order. These data only make sense in a constituent interpretation where the impact of party is least of all on public policy formulation.

2. *The party institution in Congress.* A look at the actual party institutions in the two houses will support the constituent thesis and will provide an ample and intuitively satisfactory basis for explaining why party influence in Congress can be so clear in general (or in composite), and yet so ambiguous in particular. In sum, *congressional parties are built manifestly to perform constituent functions and not to perform— indeed, perhaps to avoid performing—policy functions.*

Since the caucus or conference no longer exercises sanctions in Congress, party structure begins and ends with a much smaller and more oligarchic organization. The majority party in the House is comprised of the Speaker, the Majority Leader–whip system, and the committee on committees. Other features are essentially auxiliary and need not concern us here. The minority party in the House consists of a Minority Leader, the whip system, and the committee on committees, and the same holds true for both parties in the Senate, except the majority party of course has a Majority Leader. Party leaders have resources that may appear outwardly impressive but in reality are hardly dependable resources at all. For example, assignment and reassignment of committee posts is a valuable activity over which the Speaker or Minority Leader and his associates have unquestionable influence.[66] However, the number of highly

---

more unlike. The ADA Composite Score was computed the same way except for the addition of the following preliminary step. The points on Figures 7 and 8 were assigned weights from 5 to zero to 5. These were used as multiples for the numbers of seats represented by each bar. The derived Yeas and Nays became the basis for a derived index of likeness. Actually, the weights assigned as multiples *reduce* the difference represented by the resulting I.L. Weights of 10 to zero to 10 could have been justified, because 10 or more roll calls are involved.

66. There is no need to mention such potential but nearly useless resources as withholding the party label in elections, or binding members to conference decisions, or removal from committee assignments.

preferred positions open at any one time is small, and can only be granted —but not readily taken away. These resources are further removed from the discretion of the Leaders by the fact that so large a proportion of the assignments and reassignments is determined almost automatically through seniority and by zone apportionment. The "Johnson rule," whereby no senator may serve on a second major committee until all senators serve on one such committee, introduced an element of discretion, and it may help explain Lyndon Johnson's success during and after his Senate leadership. Discretion is still heavily constrained in both houses, however, and even if the process were more flexible the Leaders would probably avoid using it as an influence mechanism except in the most extreme circumstances.

This leaves relatively little by way of systematic influence. We can talk about the importance of different types of personalities in leadership—a popular contrast would be between Lyndon Johnson and his successor Mike Mansfield—but while that sort of appeal or influence is doubtless important it is not institutional and is therefore not basic to party itself. The only source of regular, systematic influence seems to be the whip systems in the respective chambers. Increasingly in the past generation or more, the whip organizations have become the core of party in House and Senate, and Randall Ripley's analysis of the whip organizations in the House provides important clues to the nature and extent of party activity.[67] He lists the four main tasks of both party whip organizations in the House in the following order: attendance, information, polling, and the guiding of pressure.[68] He does say later that the fourth task is "in some ways, the most important";[69] but it is that, really, because it ought to be, and at later points his own data and documents show that exerting pressures is a very special undertaking. The Democratic whip in the House does not even keep systematic voting records, and neither party attempts to check after the fact on voice votes. Instead, the most systematic pressure is exerted after the whip polls are taken and the waverers and unreliables have been identified, and *it is this group of waverers and unreliables on which regular pressures are exerted.*[70] Otherwise the

67. Randall B. Ripley, "Party in Congress: Whip Organizations in the United States House of Representatives," in Lowi (ed.), *Legislative Politics U.S.A.*, 2nd Ed. (Boston, 1965), 93. Longer version first published in *American Political Science Review*, LVIII (1964).
68. Ibid. 98.
69. Ibid. 105.
70. See Ripley, "Party in Congress," 104. "Probably the most important use for the poll results is in helping the leadership determine where to apply pressure." However,

whip polls on attendance and on voting intention are used to help the leadership set up the agenda of weekly congressional business, including keeping some still badly organized items off the agenda altogether; to keep members informed of what is on that agenda; and to maximize attendance.[71] Finally, the whip system helps facilitate the recording and enforcing of contingencies between two or more members of the party, including deals made with the leadership and deals made between two members in a log-roll.[72]

The most extraordinary data on the nature of whip-organization influence can be found in Table 3. For the House sessions of 1961-63, Froman and Ripley have placed categories of roll calls in descending order according to the degree to which *substantive* rather than procedural issues were involved. The top three categories are the farthest removed from substance, although there are substantive implications to everything; and the bottom four are the farthest removed from procedural questions. With some interesting variations, which Froman and Ripley pursue,[73] the pattern is clear, especially in the last column which shows the average cohesion for the three years. The more procedural the issue, the clearer the party influence. For many earlier sessions, Julius Turner devised similar controls with similar results. Comparing the average index of likeness for all roll calls in a given policy category to all substantive roll calls in the same category, he found almost invariably an increase to a higher index of likeness. Table 4 gives a few examples, to which should

---

in the whip system, "Loyalty is less important than accuracy and thoroughness" (98). And, with Froman, Ripley stresses more strongly that the focus of whip "pressure is on the waverers" and that "the Speaker seriously endeavored to change the votes of about twenty Democrats on each of the roll calls. He received varying answers from them, ranging from flat refusals to all-out promises of support." L. A. Froman, Jr., and Randall B. Ripley, "Conditions for Party Leadership: The Case of the House Democrats," *American Political Science Review,* LIX (1965), 55-6.

71. This includes occasionally misinforming members whose intention to oppose a forthcoming bill is known.

72. Examples of deals with the leadership include "pocket votes," offers by members who intend to vote against but will vote with the leadership if the vote is needed. See Ripley, "Party in Congress," 107 and 109.

73. Ibid. Most interesting is the difference on recommittal motions and on rules. As the minority, the Republicans would tend to be more cohesive, because the minority almost invariably offers recommittal. On rules, invariably sponsored by the majority, the Republicans are a good deal less cohesive. Cf. also Key, *Politics, Parties, and Pressure Groups,* 730-31. In 1953-54, Key found that the average index of likeness on 73 roll calls at early legislative stages was 51; on 72 roll calls at late to final stages, the average index of likeness was 81.

TABLE 3

Party Cohesion On All Contested House Roll Calls, By Category, 1961-63*

Category	1961	Rank	1962	Rank	1963	Rank	Average	Rank
	(%)		(%)		(%)		(%)	
DEMOCRATS								
Election of Speaker	100.0	1	100.0	1	100.0	1	100.0	1
Rules	83.7	4	90.2	2	94.0	2	90.6	2
Misc. procedure	81.2	5	83.3	5	89.2	3	84.5	4
Final passage	84.3	3	85.9	3	85.6	5	85.2	3
Recommittal Motions	86.9	2	85.6	4	80.9	6	84.1	5
Conference Reports	77.2	7	82.2	6	89.2	4	82.6	6
Amendments	77.4	6	73.6	7	79.8	7	76.6	7
REPUBLICANS								
Election of Speaker	100.0	1	100.0	1	100.0	1	100.0	1
Rules	80.0	4	75.7	7	79.0	6	77.9	6
Misc. procedure	91.8	2	87.2	2	97.6	2	91.9	2
Final passage	77.9	5	77.1	4	78.8	7	78.0	5
Recommittal Motions	87.7	3	85.4	3	89.9	3	87.8	3
Conference Reports	76.1	6	77.0	5	81.8	5	78.1	4
Amendments	72.5	7	75.9	6	89.0	4	77.7	7

* "Contested roll calls" are those with more than ten dissenting votes. The figures in this table represent the percentage of Democrats and the percentage of Republicans voting alike on the roll calls analyzed.
   Source: L. A. Froman, Jr., and Randall B. Ripley, "Conditions for Party Leadership: The Case of the House Democrats," *American Political Science Review*, LIX (1965), Table V.

TABLE 4

Average Index of Likeness on All Roll Calls Compared to Substantive
Roll Calls Only, A Selection

Issue	ALL ROLL CALLS		SUBSTANTIVE ROLL CALLS	
	Number	Average Index	Number	Average Index
Tariff	11	13.7	5	21.4
Public works, general	5	74.8	3	59.0
Public works, specific	8	38.9	7	39.4
Social and labor	18	40.8	13	43.7
Farm	27	42.7	20	44.6
Government regulation	30	58.3	16	64.1
Executive and Congress	32	39.4	21	51.0
Foreign affairs	17	51.0	9	68.4
Civil Service	7	85.3	7	85.3

Source: Julius Turner, *Party and Constituency: Pressures on Congress* (Baltimore, 1951), 38.

be added the reminder that the contrast is reduced by Turner's inclusion of substantive roll calls with his averages in the first column.[74]

74. The average index of likeness is superior to Froman and Ripley's measure of cohesion, because it expresses the prevailing relationship between the two parties,

What all this amounts to is another case of the party managing to agree on what to disagree about. From the workings of the whip system to the high-level agreements between a Mike Mansfield and an Everett Dirksen that keep the Senate running most of the time, the regular, *institutionalized* activities of party support the notion of the constituent party. On the other hand, no amount of data on congressional behavior or on the whip organization has been sufficient to disprove the contention that "no consistently great influence in policy directing or in establishing party accountability for legislative program" exists.[75] If party influence is clearest and strongest wherever party has an institutionalized, *functional* position, then the analysis of the electorate and Congress ought to leave no doubts as to what party is in its institutionalized, functional reality. So clearly is this the case in Congress that "manifest" and "latent" functions are almost identical. Party in Congress is virtually built around its constitutional role; its resources, sanctions, traditions, and informal relations to its members are as impressive for this role as they are unimpressive for policy-making.

Many party historians have been impressed by the degree of party discipline in Congress during the nineteenth century. Party discipline seems to have begun a decline at the very beginning of the twentieth century from which it seems never to have recovered. There were indeed many spectacular examples of party discipline in Congress between 1845 and 1912, but the extent, scope, and regularity of that discipline can be overestimated. Although A. Lawrence Lowell's review of several sessions of Congresses in the nineteenth century shows that the discipline of parties in Congress was to some extent greater than it is today, it was not appreciably greater, except for a relatively brief period between roughly 1895 and 1905. The number of roll calls that reached the cohesion of party votes (I.L. = 20 or less) came to 50 per cent during William McKinley's administrations, but only to 11 per cent under James K. Polk and to 30 per cent during 1863-65 under Abraham Lincoln. Selected sessions under Franklin D. Roosevelt show an incidence of party votes of 22, 12, and 10 per cent by sessions.[76] Furthermore, there was good reason for the slightly higher degree of party discipline in earlier eras in

---

something that can only be inferred from their measure. Also, their measure leaves us unable to compare directly their findings with the earlier ones of Key and Turner.

75. Hugh A. Bone, quoted in Ripley, "Party in Congress," 110.

76. See Turner, *Party and Constituency*, 28.

the fact that national government was not the same before 1890 as after: national policies and programs began to change and, as suggested above, policy in the United States has had more impact on party than party has had on policy. Even with the so-called decline of party discipline since World War I, one finds parties more disciplined on nineteenth-century policy issues than on twentieth-century ones. Thus in Table 5, for example, where seventy of Turner's roll call analyses from the House sessions

TABLE 5

Party Influence in Two Types of Public Policy

Type of Policy	Number of Party Votes*	Roll Calls with I.L. below 30	Roll Calls with I.L. over 70	Total Roll Calls
Distributive	15	24	1	40
Regulative	1	6	11	30

* I.L. below 20

of 1921, 1930-31, 1937, and 1944 are classified according to a simple twofold substantive scheme,[77] party influence emerges as a significant factor in votes on "distributive" policies, where on fifteen of forty roll calls the parties emerged as very nearly parliamentary institutions. Votes on regulative policy processes find the party situation much more ambiguous.

The emergence of party influence primarily on distributive issues almost proves the rule that parties are constituent. Distributive policies include all the "pork-barrel" and related policies that are still important, but were almost the sum total of federal action until the twentieth century. Decisions on these hardly amount to policy decisions at all; rather, they tend to be congeries of small, piecemeal decisions that can be called a policy only after the fact. These decisions have been the bread and butter of party. They have been part of party life itself, and such "policy"-making has really been a latent function of keeping the organization together.[78] The strength of party control in the distributive type of policy indicates mainly that log-rolling, although widespread in Congress, is not indiscrim-

77. For more on the typology and its rationale, see Theodore J. Lowi, "American Business, Public Policy, Case Studies and Political Theory," *World Politics*, XVI (1964). Here only two of the three categories of policy could be clearly identified in Turner's roll calls, *Party and Constituency*, chap. III. "Distributive" policies include public works, tariffs, natural resources, military procurement, and so on. "Regulative" is used conventionally.

78. Cf. Schattschneider, *Politics, Pressures, and the Tariff* (New York, 1935); see also Lowi, "American Business."

inate. It tends to take place primarily within the party and is enforced by the party through the whip system. Party is still primarily a conduit and cumulator. Party shows up suddenly as "responsible" in this type of policy mainly because log-rolling is the fundamental decision-making process in distributive policy and much more marginally involved in other types of policy; and log-rolling is most frequent and most efficient along party lines.[79] The strength of party in this one kind of policy also indicates that, from the time of its completed development, party in America has changed very little in structure or function, and that, as the responsibilities of government change, the most fundamental features of party have become even more clear.

VI

Analysis of data from many generations and many institutions seems to support several propositions about American political parties and their relation to the broad question of American political development. First, the function of party in development is constituent as the term has been defined here. Second, the function of party throughout the entire history of party in America has been constituent. Together these propositions imply, third, that parties themselves did not develop after a certain point in time, if development requires the functions of an institution to alter appreciably. Those few notable aspects of development in structure, process, and leadership composition—which other chapters in this volume deal with—do not seem to have changed the place of party in the system. Fourth, the impact of this constituent function of party in America has been conservative, or anti-innovative, ever since the full development of party ended around 1840.[80]

79. Cf. Lowi, "American Business."
80. On rare occasions, American parties have been programmatic and innovative, along European lines. At such times—most clearly in 1856-60, 1912-14, and 1933-35 —clearer "differences between the two parties" on issues taken one at a time appear, and parties seem to have been innovative rather than consolidative. However, these periods reinforce rather than weaken the constituent thesis. First, each period was ushered in by the "redevelopment" of a party after an earlier disaster: as proposed earlier, parties are more innovative during periods of development than at other times. Second, during that time, and only then, are party oligarchies particularly susceptible to direction by interest group leaders with strong policy commitments. Third, the constituent impact during these periods remains more striking than the policy impact. Leaders are temporarily more susceptible to real mass opinion; the separation of powers is temporarily ineffective (for example, Woodrow Wilson's use of the confer-

This combination of influences is evidently one of the main sources of the uniqueness of American political development as a whole. *In the exercise of primarily constituent functions, the party system became almost inherently conservative.* To put the matter on too conscious a level, it is as though parties, having no institutional involvement with public policy, were under no pressure to alter the system in ways which each new public problem might require. In fact, the existing system can be presumed to be a vested interest of party leaders. The new economic system of the twentieth century obviously required some nationally integrated solution, but Grodzins's studies suggest how parties kept such national integration from taking place. The extraordinary ethnic and regional heterogeneity of American society has also required an integrative solution. Various data show that the party solution was rather one of "agglutination," however, in which some minimum of common political culture was brought about while the heterogeneity was not weakened, at least not by party, but in most cases was strengthened. Many other cases reveal the mechanisms whereby normal and unintended party activity has preserved the basic formal structures of the regime. Thus Samuel P. Huntington captures the arrested development of the American Constitution by seeing in it the perpetuation of a "Tudor polity," copied from a Great Britain that was in the process of casting it off at the very time of its imitation in America. Separations among formal powers, divisions of sovereignty among regions (states), maintenance of the separation of public and private spheres, resistance to a centralized bureaucratic executive, and so on, have had vastly important and direct political consequences. They are also indicative of the old-fashioned notion of higher authority that limits sovereignty and checks in very important ways the centralization and rationalization of governmental power. They are all indicative of an almost retrograde political system in the midst of the most continually developing of all modern societies.[81]

In sum, what sort of intuitively satisfying party system does the con-

---

ence in Congress not merely to depose a leader but to enact a program); and control becomes executive-centered. Cf. my "Toward Functionalism in Political Science." For an excellent supportive essay, see also Edward C. Banfield, "In Defense of the American Party System," in Robert A. Godwin (ed.), *Political Parties U.S.A.* (Chicago, 1961), 22-33.

81. Samuel P. Huntington, "Political Modernization: America vs. Europe," Paper presented at the Annual Meeting of the American Political Science Association, September 8-11, 1965, Washington, D.C.

stituent thesis leave us with? It leaves us with a party system that is part of the regime itself but not an instrwment of any particular interests of the regime. It is a party system that shapes the regime by monopolizing succession and decentralizing leader-mass relations without implying any commitments of leaders or mass. It is a party system that, as in other democracies, made numbers an effective power basis. But, unlike the case in some other democracies, the American party system did not produce "mass democracy" because it preserved and reinforced many identifications and groupings within the mass; that is, as a result of party, we have not one electorate but many hundreds of electorates. In terms of the present notions of political development, all of these tendencies are retrograde. Yet they have supported an extraordinary stability relative to the extreme stress and strain of our heterogeneous and dynamic society—which might serve as a warning to theorists, consultants, and leaders of new nations today that "political development" *can* be dysfunctional for the society.

Finally the constituent thesis, for all the reasons stated above, leaves us with a party system that splits regime off from policy. It leaves us with parties that virtually exist to keep leadership, succession, and the constitutional structure separate from the actual settlement of issues. Just as responsible, programmatic parties, like Europe's, tend to centralize authority, so programmatic parties tend to democratize regimes by keeping legitimacy and policy in close association. Although Great Britain has been a stable polity despite this (probably because of its small size and social homogeneity), most other large, modern, democracies have not developed into stable polities and have undergone a major constitutional crisis with every major failure of public policy. One of the secrets of political stability in democratic development is the indirectness of the relation between the mass and the authoritative policies by which they are governed. Plebiscitary democracies are either unstable or totalitarian; and in this sense Great Britain, not the United States, is the exception. The United States possesses as many of the conditions of instability or of mobilization as France and Germany do, but with the major difference that our irresponsible parties have managed to keep legitimacy and policy separated. This is a peculiar but important type of differentiation. Given the contemporary world tendency for legitimacy to become intertwined with policies and for constitutions to fall over issues, it is remarkable that American parties manage to maintain this particular kind of differentiation at all.

The salient fact is that they do.

X | Walter Dean Burnham

MASSACHUSETTS INSTITUTE OF TECHNOLOGY

Party Systems

and the Political Process

THE MORE DEEPLY one reflects on the characteristic properties of political parties in the American party system of today, the more exceptional these parties seem to become by comparative standards. American mass-mobilization parties are the oldest such phenomena in the modern world. After an impressive trial run which extended from the 1790's to about 1820, they emerged as full-grown, recognizably modern structures by 1840—at least thirty years before the development of the first stable mass parties in Britain. During the enormously creative period extending roughly from the establishment of state nominating conventions in the 1820's to the creation of the Democratic National Committee in 1848, the party system took on a recognizably modern shape. But once that era had passed, very few major changes in organization occurred until the replacement of the convention by the direct primary during the years 1900-1915, and very few have taken place since.

No "branch" or "indirect caucus" types of party organization—still less "cell" or "militia" types—have been able, for example, to establish themselves in the American context.[1] Recruitment of elective elites remains closely associated, especially for the more important offices and in the larger states, with the candidates' wealth or access to large campaign contributions.[2] To this day the financing of the parties themselves remains to a substantial degree in the hands of those relatively few individuals and

1. For a useful typology of modern party organizations, see Maurice Duverger, *Political Parties* (New York, 1954), 1-60. A discussion in terms of the American party system of the present is found in Frank J. Sorauf, *Political Parties in the American System* (Boston, 1964), esp. 38-58, 153-69.
2. This is especially the case at the crucial nominating stage. See Alexander Heard, *The Costs of Democracy* (Chapel Hill, 1960), 34-5, 318-43.

277

groups who make large donations; it does not rest on any stable mass base. This is, of course, but one reflection of the failure of European concepts or practices of party membership or organization to develop with democratization in the United tates. Typically the American party is composed of an inner circle of office-holding and office-seeking cadres together with their personal supporters and a limited number of professional party workers. This structure has been decentralized but probably not significantly broadened under the direct primary system. Outside this circle lies the mass of party identifiers, only a tiny fraction of whom are involved in any more extensive partisan activity than voting every two or four years. Still further outside is the extraordinarily large part of the potential electorate which is not politically involved at all.[3]

All of the available evidence suggests that the American party systems, viewed comparatively, have exhibited an arrested development which stands in particularly striking contrast to the extraordinary dynamism of the nation's socio-economic system.[4] This arrested development is visible both organizationally and functionally. There are at least four broad functions which are performed by fully developed democratic parties. The first of these is a nation-building, integrative, or in Lowi's term, "constituent" function. This involves the regularized amalgamation and priority ordering of conflicting regional, ethno-cultural, group, or class interests through the mechanisms of the political party. In modern politics, broad acceptance of the legitimacy of the political regime as a whole depends in large measure on the successful performance of this function. Second, political parties carry out an office-filling function; orderly and democratic procedures are prescribed for elite recruitment to a limited number of elective and appointive positions. Third, parties perform a function of political education or political socialization for their mass clienteles. In its most developed form, this function is carried out through a network of party-controlled structures of eduction and media, with the intent of producing a more or less coherent frame of political reference among those clienteles. Fourth, major parties may perform a policy-making function. This involves not only the capture of office, but the capture of the policy-making machinery of government for programmatic purposes.

3. Walter Dean Burnham, "The Changing Shape of the American Political Universe," *American Political Science Review*, LIX (1965), 7-28.

4. This peculiarly nondevelopmental aspect of American party development has also been noted by Robert A. Dahl (ed.), *Political Oppositions in Western Democracies* (New Haven, 1966), 34-69.

While the American parties have historically engaged in political education to some extent, and have occasionally been genuine policy-making
vehicles, their involvement with such functions has been limited. Particularly in our own century, American political parties have been largely
restricted in functional scope to the realm of the constituent and to the
tasks of filling political offices. So far as the function of political education
is concerned, indeed, there is evidence that during the nineteenth century
the parties were engaged in propaganda and political-socialization activities on a scale which knows no parallel today. This intense activity seems
to have been closely related to the quasi-monopoly which election campaigns and the partisan press of that period had on entertainment prior to
the development of other mass media, and also to the relatively extreme
frequency of elections and variability in election dates which existed prior
to about 1880.[5] But as the party press faded out of the picture toward the
end of the nineteenth century, as elections became concentrated in November and terms of office were lengthened, and as non-political mass
media undermined the salience of the political campaign as a species of
entertainment, the educative functions performed earlier by the parties
tended to atrophy. American parties during the twentieth century have
not been organized to provide political education or indoctrination for
their clienteles on a month-in-month-out basis. Such an effort would require, in all probability, stable dues-paying memberships and the development of permanent ancillary party agencies for reaching a mass clientele
whether or not an election was pending.

Similarly, the norm in American politics has been that the major parties
lack the internal cohesion and organizational capacity to perform policy-
making functions systematically or over a long term. In Great Britain,
down through Lord Palmerston's time, majorities in the House of Commons—like those of the House of Representatives today—tended to be
complex mixes of party and coalitional elements. Only after the sequential
development of mass party organization following the Reform Bill of 1867
did the party whips in Britain become more than intelligence agents and
persuaders for the leadership. In the United States, on the other hand, the
development of mass parties in the 1830's destroyed the basis for consolidated party leadership which had existed during the time of the first

5. An illuminating discussion of the exacerbating effects of perpetual electioneering
on antebellum politics is found in Roy F. Nichols, *The Disruption of American
Democracy* (New York, 1948), 5-7.

party system, permanently activated the cleavage between executive and legislature, and gave an enormous impetus to the decentralizing influence of federalism.[6] Since then, American parties have performed the policy-making function only very infrequently—as a rule, only in situations marked by unusual social and political tension. Indeed, Dawson's study for this volume strongly implies that the link between party and policy outputs at the state level has been so ambiguous during this century as to generate doubt as to the weight of party influence upon those outputs.

The history of American party development, taken as a whole, suggests that every major upsurge of democratization has led to a dispersion rather than a concentration of political power in the policy-making arena. In this the United States has been quite exceptional. Students of comparative party organizations and their development have often argued that mass-based parties develop in an industrial era in order to array on a broad scale the power of numbers against the power of wealth, interest, and social position enjoyed by existing elites. Concentration of organization and decision-making authority is essential to this end. Were this argument to be accepted as a binding generalization about party development in advanced societies, we should be confronted with an intriguing paradox suggested by the late Morton Grodzins: that American parties may actually be anti-parties.[7]

II

But this is not the end of analysis; it is merely a beginning. To make such an assumption is not only to take sides immediately in a substantive dispute with strong normative overtones, it is to plunge into a sea of analytical difficulties. It presupposes that there is, or more precisely ought to be, a clear-cut European confrontation between Left and Right in this country. It presupposes, moreover, that the cultural differences between the middle and working classes must necessarily dominate our domestic politics, and thus receive concrete expression in terms of party organization and evolution. But why should these differences receive such expression if they have not been dominant in the political culture? Nothing, indeed, is clearer than that the two major American parties are and always

6. Wilfred E. Binkley, *President and Congress* (New York, 1962), 83-104. See also Theodore J. Lowi's contribution to this volume.

7. Morton Grodzins, "American Political Parties and the American System," *Western Political Quarterly*, XIII (1960), 974-98.

have been overwhelmingly middle-class in organization, values, and goals. From a European point of view, they can hardly fail to appear as exquisitely old-fashioned, as nineteenth-century anachronisms. Yet they have not only survived, they have totally dominated the American electoral scene—and at no time more completely than during the past generation. If parties seeking to organize the lower strata of American society along collectivist lines have been so evanescent, if the two major components of the system have so feebly performed the educative and policy-making functions, the reason for this must lie not only in our dispersive political institutions but more fundamentally within the American political culture itself.

Of all theses regarding that culture, the one which has the greatest explanatory power is the theory of the liberal tradition in America which has been developed by Louis Hartz.[8] According to this analysis, the United States is a fragment of Europe, which was detached at a bourgeois point in history and subsequently developed a nearly monolithic, absolutist commitment to the values of individualist liberalism. These values, for most Americans at most times, have been so pervasive and have been so feebly challenged from within that they have tended to assume some of the properties of natural law in the American mind. Absolutist individualism has, of course, been buttressed both by the frontier experience and by the enormous relative affluence which most of the population has enjoyed throughout the country's history.[9] But the quite differing political experiences of other societies which have been relatively prosperous, or which have passed through a frontier stage, suggest the importance of the liberal cultural monolith in shaping the course of American political development.

Economic and social development consequently took place under very different political conditions than in Europe, other fragment cultures, or the modernizing states of the third world. During an initial period in which there was inadequate capital which was both private and internally generated, governments at all levels played a major promotional role, especially but by no means exclusively in the fields of transportation and finance. This period was comparatively short, however, and was supplanted by an era in which an adequate supply of domestic take-off

8. Louis Hartz, *The Liberal Tradition in America* (New York, 1955); and Hartz, *The Founding of New Societies* (New York, 1964), 1-122.
9. David M. Potter, *People of Plenty: Economic Abundance and the American Character* (Chicago, 1954).

capital in private hands and a widely accepted economic theory of laissez-faire combined to restrict governmental intervention in the private sector. This arrangement, in its turn, survived with little effective challenge until the corporate world of private enterprise had clearly lost its capacity to regulate the development of the American economy without incurring ruinous social costs. But from beginning to end—from the age of neo-mercantilism down to the modern welfare-warfare state—the overwhelming value consensus in this field has been in favor of maximum private enterprise and minimum intervention by public authority. Neither the New Deal nor the post-New Deal periods can be adequately understood unless it is appreciated that this has remained official doctrine. Controversies over public involvement in the American economy have essentially tended to be differences, based on interest and ideology, over what "minimum intervention" ought to be at any given time.[10] Under such conditions there is hardly room for political parties to undertake sustained policy-making or government-control functions even if their leaders were for some reason inclined to make the attempt. Nor would such an attempt be likely to take place, since such control functions have not been considered necessary by any significant part of the population.

But this hardly means that there have been no political conflicts—or even that there have been no significant elements of class conflicts—in our history. Still less does it mean that the party system itself has played an insignificant role in that history. To be sure, it may be argued that its role has been peripheral and institutionally supportive of the American consensus concerning the primacy of the private sector in economic affairs. But there are other, and extremely important, dimensions of conflict which must be considered. Lee Benson is clearly right in his argument that the very consensus on economic and other fundamentals in the United States has produced not a lack of political cleavages, but a striking variety of them.[11] If the political culture and the party system have given only limited expression to vertical divisions within American society, they have accommodated an enormous variety of horizontal cleavages. Of these, three have been of paramount importance in our political history and, as the 1960 and 1964 elections have demonstrated, remain vital factors in American party politics to the present day.

1. *The clash of sectional subcultures.* The literature which emphasizes

10. Andrew Shonfield, *Modern Capitalism* (New York, 1965), 298-329.
11. Lee Benson, *The Concept of Jacksonian Democracy* (Princeton, 1961), 272-7.

and documents the vital historical importance of cultural and economic divergences along sectional lines is enormous. It may be enough here to mark the role of mass party politics in contributing to the full articulation of these cleavages. A student of the Missouri Compromise has pointed out that if the intense struggle in Congress over its terms had resulted in civil war, the war would have been fought out in the halls of Congress itself, with the rest of the country looking on in some amazement.[12] If a vastly different public reaction to its repeal was manifested a generation later, one can hardly doubt that the development of a mass-based party system, and the mobilization of mass opinion which accompanied it, bore much of the responsibility for the difference. In particular, the more Americans of the New England and Southern subcultures came to learn about each others' social values and political goals, the more pronounced their hostility toward each other grew. A strong argument can be made for the proposition that the Civil War was far more directly the product of the expansion of public political consciousness which is inherent in the dynamics of democratic development than of any economic causes.

The twofold decision of the period from 1861 to 1877—first to keep the South in the Union by force, and then to permit it to reassert substantially complete autonomy in its political affairs—enormously increased the need for the components of the party system to place major emphasis on integrative activities and functions. It is enough to recall that the influence of sectional cleavages was overwhelmingly dominant in American political history from 1854 to 1932, or to note the evidences of the age-old antipathy between the New England and white Southern subcultures which emerged in the massive voter shifts of the 1964 election. The South over the past century has influenced American politics in ways not dissimilar to the influence of Quebec in Canada or of Ireland in the United Kingdom in the years from 1870 to 1922. The massive influence of that deviant subculture upon national party politics and policy outputs has scarcely run its course a century after Appomattox.

2. *The clash between "community" and "society."* This cleavage, like the sectionalism with which it has some relationship on the national level, can in a sense be traced back to the controversies between the Hamiltonians and the Virginia agrarian school in the infancy of the republic. But it becomes particularly significant in the industrializing and post-industrializ-

12. Glover Moore, *The Missouri Controversy, 1819-21* (Lexington, Ky., 1953), 175.

ing eras of our history. As Hays points out in his illuminating study in this volume, between 1880 and 1920 a substantial portion of our industrializing elites and their supporters were pitted against the parties themselves. Whatever may have been the parties' contributions to centralized policy-formation prior to the industrial takeover, after the end of Reconstruction the parties became bulwarks of localist resistance to the forced-draft change initiated by cosmopolitan elites. Thus was born a tradition of hostility to the political party as such, with an associated theme which emphasized that political centralization at any level in the system required the displacement rather than the further development of the political party as an instrument of popular government. This anti-partisan tradition of the Progressive Era, and the power shifts which developed from it at the local level, were both in profound harmony with the dominant function of the alignment system of 1896 to 1932: the insulation of industrial elites from the threat of effective, popularly based "counterrevolution." The persistence of this tradition and its consequences has undoubtedly made a significant contribution to the truncating of American party development during this century.

Viewed somewhat more broadly, this local-cosmopolitan cleavage may also be related to a larger regional phenomenon in post-Civil War America. This is the ongoing conflict between the Northeastern metropole on one hand and the Southern and Western regions, which stood in a quasi-colonial relationship to the metropole, on the other.[13] William Jennings Bryan, as H. L. Mencken sarcastically noted, was the political evangelist of white Anglo-Saxon provincial "locals" who were in revolt against "their betters"—by which Mencken meant metropole cosmopolitans like himself.[14] After the shattering blow which fell upon the Democratic party in the Northeast during the 1890's, the Democratic party became to a substantial extent the party of the "locals" or the community-oriented, while the G.O.P.—especially in its Bull Moose wing—tended to become the dominant partisan vehicle of the "cosmopolitans" or the society-oriented.[15] This helped, no doubt, to reinforce the persistent Republican charge, which was reiterated down through the 1930's, that the Democratic party was incompetent to govern in an industrial society. Many of the urban "locals"

13. An excellent statement of the case from a self-consciously colonial point of view is Walter Prescott Webb, *Divided We Stand* (New York, 1937).
14. H. L. Mencken, "In Memoriam: W. J. B.," in Alistair Cooke (ed.), *The Vintage Mencken* (New York, 1959), 161-7.
15. The *locus classicus* here, on the level of the Progressive intellectual, is surely Herbert Croly, *The Promise of American Life* (New York, 1909).

—the working-class elements who were deliberately bypassed by Progressive-era reform in local government—supported this Republican position, at least at the presidential level, by their votes. That they did so probably reflects their memory of the "Democratic depression" of 1893-97, as well as their ethno-cultural hostility to the Bryan crusade and its clienteles. It is possible that this support may also have been a manifestation of "working-class imperialism" akin to the support which Disraeli and his Conservative party successors enjoyed in England during the last third of the nineteenth century. By the beginning decades of the twentieth century the differential in economic development between the Northeast and the rest of the country had become enormous; to a greater or lesser extent most politically active groups in the metropole shared in its relative affluence.

Nor has intersectional antagonism disappeared as a force in contemporary American politics since, even though regional differentials in economic development have been severely eroded since World War II. While the terms of the political discourse involved have shifted beyond recognition, at the bottom of this antagonism may well be an ongoing "community" resistance—which still tends to be geographically concentrated —to massive, centrally directed social change. It seems reasonable to suppose that both the growth of a doctrinaire Right and the contemporary conflicts between the executive and Congress can be at least partially explained in terms of this community-society continuum.

3. *The clash of ethno-cultural groups.* It is by now axiomatic that the diversity of ethnic origins in the American melting pot has been basic to American political alignments since the creation of the first party system in the 1790's. There appears to be a curiously circular relationship between ethnic diversity and the limited role which class alignments have played in the history of American politics. On one hand, as Benson argues, the American liberal value consensus on such fundamentals as economic and church-state relationships helped make possible a full articulation of ethno-cultural antagonisms in party politics at a remarkably early date.[16] On the other hand, however, the very existence of ethnic fragmentation—especially after the "new immigration" of 1882-1914 added novel elements to the American melting pot—severely inhibited the formation even of mass trade unions, and was instrumental in preventing the emergence of socialism as a major political force.

In the Northeast, for example, lines of class and ethnic division tended

16. Benson, *The Concept of Jacksonian Democracy,* 165-207.

to coincide during and after the era of industrialization. Most of the middle classes in such centers as New York, Boston, and Philadelphia were of old-stock Protestant background, while many of the working-class elements were relatively recent arrivals with wholly different cultural traditions. But if class and ethnic lines tended to coincide in the conurbations, the lower classes were also enormously internally fragmented along ethnic lines. Some groups, such as the Jews of Manhattan and the Germans of Milwaukee, had cultural traditions which favored the growth of socialist movements among them.[17] Groups such as these, coupled with certain radical native-stock farm elements in the colonial regions of the country, gave the American Socialist party most of such vitality as it possessed at its apogee around 1912. But most of the "new immigrant" groups came from a European stratum, the peasantry, which had no counterpart in the social experience of most other Americans. Such groups required the most extensive acculturation simply to come to terms with urban-industrial existence as such, much less to enter the party system as relatively independent actors.

It is hardly surprising, consequently, that the typical American form of urban political organization during and after the industrializing era was the non-programmatic, patronage-fueled urban machine rather than the disciplined, programmatic Leftist party of the type which was emerging in European conurbations during the same historical period. As Robert K. Merton's pioneering analysis has made clear, the urban machine developed as an unofficial means of concentrating political power in an official context of power dispersion.[18] Its functions, at least on the latent level, were overwhelmingly integrative. For the lower strata, in return for their votes, it provided a considerable measure of primitive welfare functions, personalized help for individuals caught up in the toils of the law, and political socialization. For business elements it provided a helpful structure of centralized decision-making in areas of vital concern to them. Of the classical urban political machine it may be said, first, that it provided services for which there was a persistent social demand and which no other institution was capable of providing; and second, that the extraordinary

17. See e.g. Lawrence Fuchs, *The Political Behavior of American Jews* (Glencoe, 1956). To this day Jewish voters are very atypically Democratic (or "Leftist") at levels of socio-economic status where substantial Republican strength is normally encountered in other population groups. Angus Campbell *et al., The American Voter* (New York, 1960), 302, 306.

18. Robert K. Merton, *Social Theory and Social Structure* (Glencoe, 1957), 72-82.

fragmentation and lack of acculturation among its mass clientele ensured its preoccupation with ethnic-coalition politics to the virtual exclusion of class politics.

Here, as elsewhere in the study of American political cleavages and organizational structures, there appears to be an inverse relationship between the integrative or "constituent" functions of parties and their policy-making or government-control functions. If the social context in which a two-party system operates is extensively fragmented along regional, ethnic, and other lines, its major components will tend to be overwhelmingly concerned with coalition-building and internal conflict management. The need to unite for electoral purposes presupposes a corresponding need to generate consensus at whatever level such consensus can be found. Surely, at the primordial level, the American liberal consensus in its various nuances provides a framework for party action. Yet this essentially middle-class frame of reference and the feebleness of social solidarities above the level of the primordial have worked together throughout our history to exclude programmatic politics—or programmatic parties—from the mainstream of American political development. More than a decade ago Samuel Lubell argued that the major task of American politics was that of building a nation out of a congeries of regions and peoples.[19] So long as that task remains unfinished, there is little reason to suppose that our major parties will break out of the mold in which they were cast during the generative years of the second party system.

III

A study of the history of American voting alignments, paradoxically enough, reveals that, notwithstanding the substantial exclusion of the parties from the policy-making and educative functions, the voting public has made vitally important contributions to American political development approximately once in a generation. Studies of American elections, especially in the past decade, have uncovered a remarkably stable pattern involving two broad types of elections which differ from one another not in degree but in kind. Most American elections, most of the time, are relatively low-pressure events. In such elections the voting decision seems to be a mix of traditional party identifications and short-term, "surge" fac-

19. Samuel Lubell, *The Future of American Politics* (New York, 1952), 245-61; and Lubell, *White and Black* (New York, 1964), 153-74.

tors associated with specific candidate or issue appeals.[20] Taken in the aggregate, such elections—whether "maintaining," "deviating," or "reinstating"—are part of a broad pattern of system maintenance.[21] They constitute reaffirmation of a "standing decision," even though the parties themselves may alternate in power as they did in the 1880's or the 1950's.[22]

Approximately once every thirty years, however, an entirely different cycle of elections emerges—a realignment cycle which precipitates massive grass-roots changes in voting behavior and results in a new coalitional pattern for each of the parties. Each of these critical realignments has been associated with a major turning-point in the development of the American political system as a whole. There appears to be a typical pattern in the alignment cycle, although not all of its stages have clearly been followed in each historical realignment. After a more or less extended period of stability, broadly-based discontent with the existing political order begins to emerge and then to crystallize. At a certain point the intrusion of a proximate tension-producing event, in a context of growing discontent, triggers either the creation of new major-party organizations or the capture of one of the older parties by insurgents against the political status quo. This proximate event may be economic, as were the depressions of 1893 and 1929, or political, as were the events leading from the Kansas-Nebraska Act of 1854 to the election of Lincoln; usually it has been a mixture of both elements. In the campaign or campaigns which follow this breakthrough, the insurgents' political style is exceptionally ideological by American standards; this in turn produces a sense of grave threat among defenders of the established order, who in turn develop opposing ideological positions. The elections which follow produce massive realignments of voters, and usually result in a stable majority for one of the parties which endures until the beginning of the next realignment phase a generation later.[23]

This cyclical pattern—long-term continuity abruptly displaced by an

20. Angus Campbell, "Surge and Decline: A Study of Electoral Change," *Public Opinion Quarterly*, XXIV (1960), 397-418.

21. Angus Campbell *et al.*, *Elections and the Political Order* (New York, 1966), 63-77.

22. For a useful discussion of the "standing decision," see V. O. Key, Jr., and Frank Munger, "Social Determinism and Electoral Decision: The Case of Indiana," in Eugene Burdick and Arthur J. Brodbeck (eds.), *American Voting Behavior* (Glencoe, 1959), 281-99.

23. V. O. Key, Jr., "A Theory of Critical Elections," *Journal of Politics*, XVIII (1955), 3-18.

explosive but short period of change—seems not only to reflect the constituent function of the party systems and the electoral system in the United States, but to be a prime manifestation of the dominance of that function in our politics. The critical realignment, to be sure, drastically reshuffles the coalitional bases of the two parties, but it does far more than this. It constitutes a political decision of the first magnitude and a turning point in the mainstream of national policy formation. Characteristically, the relationships among policy-making institutions, their relative power and decision-making capacity, and the policy outputs they produce are profoundly affected by critical realignments. It was far from coincidence, for example, that the Supreme Court reached its height as an economic policy-maker in a period—1890-1937—which almost precisely covers the period of the partisan alignment of 1894-1932, or that this role became untenable after the next realignment. With characteristic properties such as these, the critical realignment may well be regarded as America's surrogate for revolution. One of these experiences led directly to the outbreak of civil war, and every one of the others has been marked by acute political tension.[24]

The existence and significance of the critical realignment in American political history provides an excellent point of departure for analyzing our political development in terms of the constituent decisions and institutional modifications which have been associated with it. Examination of American party politics over time reveals the existence of not less than five national party systems. Each of these, to be sure, has constituted a link in a chain of development within the same polity, and thus has numerous properties which it shares in common with the others. But to a marked degree each is also a discrete entity, with characteristic patterns of voting behavior, of elite and institutional relationships, and of broad system-dominant decisions. While a full exploration of these patterns in all their subtlety is the proper subject of a much larger and more detailed study than this, their broad contours can be briefly outlined here.

1. *The experimental system, 1789-1820.* In a real sense, the first American party system was a bridge between a pre-party phase in American political development and the recognizably modern parties found in the second and succeeding party systems. All of American political life was

24. See a preliminary discussion of these characteristics in Walter Dean Burnham, "The Alabama Senatorial Election of 1962: Return of Interparty Competition," *Journal of Politics,* XXVI (1964), 798-829, esp. 822-9.

experimental and to a degree tentative during this period of nation-building, and the Federalist and Republican parties, as they developed, shared this experimental quality. In a developing society which was overwhelmingly agrarian and spread out along two thousand miles of coastline, a number of fundamental problems had to be faced almost immediately after the establishment of government under the Constitution. Full national independence from Europe—economic and psychological as well as political—remained to be realized. Both living and institutional symbols of a common American nationality had to be forged. In pursuit of the goals of nationality and full independence, it was essential to provide a political framework for "take-off" into sustained economic growth under internally generated capitalist auspices. Finally, certain political issues required authoritative disposition. To what extent, if at all, should public deference to elite rule, characteristic of eighteenth-century British and colonial politics, be continued as a mainstay of republican institutions? To what extent, if at all, was partisan conflict, both over office and over policy goals, legitimate in itself?

The party system which developed in the 1790's exhibited peculiarities which were intimately associated with the attempt to find solutions to these problems. Both because of the narrow base of the active public in the initial phases of development and because of the primitive communication and transportation facilities of the time, both of the opposing coalitions were organized from the center outward toward the periphery.[25] While the importance of state politics and the significance of regional bastions of support for the Federalist and Republican parties should not be overlooked, these parties apparently were loose amalgamations of state organizations to a smaller extent than were their successors. Second, because of the heavy involvement of coastal America with Europe during the era of the French Revolution, foreign-policy controversy played an enormously salient role in the structuring of party conflict. Third, the deferential tradition was paralleled by a nearly complete identification by each rival group of the national good with their own partisan views; and this significantly affected the behavior of both parties during this period. While this identification with deference and the universal validity of their own policy views affected the Federalists especially adversely by rendering

25. William N. Chambers, *Political Parties in a New Nation* (New York, 1963), 103-12. See also Noble E. Cunningham, Jr., *The Jeffersonian Republicans in Power, 1801-1809* (Chapel Hill, 1963), esp. 299-305, and Richard P. McCormick, *The Second American Party System* (Chapel Hill, 1966), 19-31.

them inflexible and resistant to change, many Jeffersonians also tended to regard their opponents as a "disloyal opposition," and their leadership was hardly free of elitist bias.[26]

It would be a distortion to argue that domestic partisan conflict in this period was confined to the problem of defining how broad the ruling elite should be or what regional and economic interests should be included in it. But in practice it can hardly be argued that the election of 1800 produced any revolutionary change in the foundations of national economic policy-making, however important its political effects were. To some degree after 1800, the Jeffersonians were impelled toward active intervention in the economy by the exigencies of foreign affairs, as in the Embargo of 1808. But the rechartering of the Bank of the United States in 1816, as well as the harmony which developed over time between John Marshall's Supreme Court and the other branches of the federal government, are sufficient indications that neo-mercantilism remained on the policy agenda after as well as before 1800. As the democratization of politics in the Jacksonian era was to reveal, such policy could be sustained in an overwhelmingly rural society only so long as systematic partisan mobilization of the vast majority had not yet occurred, and only so long as deference politics continued to display some vitality. In all probability the contribution of greatest lasting significance which the realignment of 1800 made to American political development was the precedent of a peaceful turnover of political power by a Federalist coalition which professed to regard its rival as subversive of the republic. Similarly, the greatest contribution of the parties themselves was to establish the tradition of partisan competition itself, as well as to supply practical working knowledge of such competition to a whole generation of Americans.

After 1800 as well as before, the first party system displayed certain properties which were unique to it and were not clearly transmitted to its successors. First, while contests for the presidency were of major importance in crystallizing party competition nationally, neither the office nor the modes of election involving it were as yet wholly democratized. Legislative choice of presidential electors, like such choice of governors in some states, survived in many states throughout this period. This, coupled with the "inner circle" characteristics of the Republican congressional caucus,

26. Cunningham, *The Jeffersonian Republicans in Power, 1801-1809*, 8-9, 303-4. For an interesting discussion of the ambiguous attitude of many Republican leaders concerning expansion of the suffrage, see Chilton Williamson, *American Suffrage from Property to Democracy, 1760-1860* (Princeton, 1960), 138-64.

permitted a semi-fusion of powers at the federal level which has known no counterpart since the election of Andrew Jackson.[27] Moreover, this system was very incompletely developed. Partisan competition did not spread throughout the country; particularly in the Southern and frontier regions, what weak foothold the Federalists had had down to 1800 virtually evaporated thereafter.[28] The forces which have operated over the past century to restore party competition were clearly inoperative after 1800. In the period from 1802 to 1822 (excluding the unopposed presidential election of 1820), Jeffersonian Republicans won three-quarters of all contests for presidential electors and congressmen, and four-fifths of all senatorial contests.[29] Finally, of course, the system evaporated in a decade-long, nonpartisan "Era of Good Feelings," for which there is no subsequent parallel in American history.

While all party systems can in a sense be regarded as artificial, the extreme imbalance between the components of this first system after 1800 suggests rather strongly that party competition under the first system had accomplished its dominant and relatively narrow purposes by that date. Were it not for disruptive internal pressures generated by repeated collisions with the major powers involved in a European "world war" which lasted until 1815, it seems probable that a non-partisan interregnum would have emerged at least a decade before it did. Once the struggle between uncompromising and moderate elitism had been clearly settled in favor of the latter, there were evidently not enough points of internal conflict at the national level to sustain truly competitive party politics. In this sense, as in others, the first party system left no successors.

2. *The democratizing system, 1828-1854/60.* Of all of the five American party systems, the second was incomparably the most creative from an organizational point of view. The development of national two-party competition centering on a democratized presidency, and growing out of a host of local political alignments, was so massive an undertaking that it

27. Binkley, *President and Congress,* 60-82. See also Leonard D. White, *The Jeffersonians* (New York, 1951), 29-59. White also duly notes that very little break in basic administrative patterns occurred after 1800. For a eulogy of Alexander Hamilton delivered by a Republican Secretary of the Treasury, see pp. 14-15 of White's work.

28. McCormick, *The Second American Party System,* 27-8.

29. For a statistical confirmation of the existence of forces tending to restore two-party competition, extending back to 1866, see Donald E. Stokes and G. R. Iversen, "On the Existence of Forces Restoring Party Competition," in Angus Campbell *et al., Elections and the Political Order,* 180-93.

required more than a decade to complete after the critical election of 1828. There appear to have been three major stages through which the second party system passed before its dissolution. The first was the period of intense partisan organization between the election of John Quincy Adams in 1825 and his defeat at the polls in 1828. In this phase an extremely heterogeneous opposition to "insider" politics was mobilized around Andrew Jackson; this "outsider" was virtually compelled to raise the standard of popular revolt in order to unseat the incumbent political elite.[30] The second phase of development, by which time about half of the potential electorate had been mobilized, was the Jacksonian phase proper. This phase was characterized by the emergence of the convention system as a device for presidential nominations independent of Congress or the state legislatures, by an extreme sectionalism in voting patterns, and by the new separation-of-powers conflicts between President and Congress. This phase was also marked by a heavy majority for Jackson's supporters at the polls and a new issue-oriented politics which resulted in a resounding confirmation in 1832 of the "decision of 1828." The third, or mature, phase was inaugurated in 1834 by the founding of the Whig party, and was completed around 1840. The origins of the Whigs involved not only the definitive collapse of Jackson's "Solid South," but by the recognition by Jackson's opponents that effective opposition depended on acceptance of both the policy and organizational implications of democratization. Thereafter, as McCormick observes, the second party system was notable for the extreme closeness of the party balance throughout the country and for exceptionally high rates of voter turnout.[31]

The "decision of 1828" generated a number of fundamental changes in institutional relationships and policy outputs. Broadly, it was a decision to democratize political opportunity and—at least rhetorically—to eliminate the last vestiges of elitism and deference politics from the American scene. Democratization in the context of the middle period came to involve a dismantling of neo-mercantilism on the federal level and a general recession of the federal government to an extremely low level of positive activity. During the first half of the lifetime of the second party system, this was to a substantial degree the expression of the agrarian yeoman's political style and political goals, just as Hamilton had feared half a century

30. For a lucid discussion of the organizational effort involved, and Martin Van Buren's key role in it, see Robert V. Remini, *The Election of Andrew Jackson* (Philadelphia, 1963), 51-120.

31. McCormick, *The Second American Party System*, 329-56.

earlier. Thereafter, the emergence of sectional conflict reinforced the weakness of the federal government—as has been true in some contemporary societies with problems of regional integration—since systematic federal pursuit of any positive domestic policies gravely threatened the increasingly tenuous union between North and South.[32] In this context the presidential nominating convention produced candidates whose chief virtue was their "availability," and whose tenure was exceptionally short. The Senate's role during this period was that of a congress of ambassadors concerned with working out the terms of intersectional compromise. As for the parties themselves, the democratized political atmosphere, the increase in the number and variety of elective offices, and the perpetual mobilization campaigns necessitated the emergence of the plebeian electoral machine staffed by professionals who had to be paid for their services.[33]

The dramatic collapse of the second party system in the period from the mid-1850's to 1860 disclosed its essential fragility. Each party had been put together piecemeal from a bewildering variety of local cleavages and ethno-cultural hostilities. On the national level, each was an electoral machine which sought to make voting capital out of these local antagonisms and the national symbolic rhetoric of the democratic "revolution." But precisely because the two parties were both so nationwide in their coalitional base, they found it increasingly difficult to accommodate sectionally divergent interests among their elites and mass followings.

The weakest link in the system was clearly the Whig party. In retrospect, it seems quite strange that a general sentiment arose in the aftermath of the 1852 presidential election that the party was already moribund, for even in defeat it had received 46.4 per cent of the two-party vote.[34] Yet two major disruptive forces were at work. In the first place, the Whig party below the presidential level was a good deal weaker than it

32. Studies of elections in certain developing nations can provide interesting comparative insights into the interrelationships between the integrative and policy-making functions under acute conditions of regional heterogeneity. Se K. W. J. Post, *The Nigerian Federal Election of 1959* (Oxford, England, 1963), esp. 437-43; and also Leon D. Epstein, "A Comparative Study of Canadian Parties," *American Political Science Review*, LVIII (1964), 46-59.

33. Still extremely useful for a study of American party development with these particulars in mind is M. Ostrogorski, *Democracy and the Organization of Political Parties* (New York, 1902), vol. II, 207-440.

34. Arthur C. Cole, *The Whig Party in the South* (Washington, 1913), 274-6. It is particularly suggestive that Whig leadership opinion that the party was dead after the 1852 election was concentrated in the North, and that this conclusion tended to be resisted by Southern Whig leaders with the exception of the group around Alexander H. Stephens.

seemed, and this weakness tended to accelerate in every election after 1848. This weakness, and particularly its tendency to increase, probably helped certain Whig elites—especially in the North—to turn their attention to other political combinations which would be more profitable to themselves and the interests which they supported. Second, the structure of opinion on the slavery question and related issues was clearly sharply different among the mass bases of each party. In at least a number of Northern states, the Whigs were the party of the positive liberal state, and this in substantial measure reflected the presence of a large New England subcultural component in their mass base.[35] In the Deep South, on the other hand, there was a significant correlation in many areas between wealth—including slaveholding wealth—and Whig strength in given county units.[36]

TABLE 1

Partisan Strength in the Second Party System,
1834-53, by Categories of Offices

OFFICE	% DEM.	% WHIG	% OTHER
Presidential electors	53.9	46.1	—
U. S. representatives	54.9	42.6	2.5
U. S. senators	54.8	42.5	2.7
Governors	58.7	39.7	1.6

It is unlikely that this tendency toward a bimodal opinion structure among the Whigs was duplicated in anything like the same degree in the Democratic party. A *posteriori*, indeed, it can be noted that the swift and near-total collapse of the Whig party's mass support in the North after the Kansas-Nebraska Act had no counterpart among the Democratic following. Moreover, as elections after 1860 were to demonstrate, the critical split which did come to the Democrats that year was significant as an organizational rupture, but it did not result in permanent mass defections from the Democratic banner.

3. *The Civil War system, 1860-93.* The major "decision" associated with the realignment which culminated in the 1860 election was, of course, the

35. One notes this, for instance, in Benson's estimates of the demographic composition of the major parties in New York around 1844. Benson, *The Concept of Jacksonian Democracy,* 185. The most predominantly Whig area in New York State was also know as the "Burned-over District," because of the plethora of social-reform and millenarian movements which flourished there during the middle period. See Whitney R. Cross, *The Burned-Over District* (Ithaca, N. Y., 1950).

36. Seymour Martin Lipset, *Political Man* (Garden City, N. Y., 1960), 344-54.

reorganization of the party system and of institutional relationships and policy outputs along explicitly sectional lines. This was the only possible restructuring which could lead to the definitive containment and eventual extinction of slavery and the economic-cultural regime built upon it. Since this intersectional issue was neither "negotiable" nor one which the losing elite groups could permit to be resolved through the electoral process, the inevitable result of organizing the party system in this way was civil war. Put another way around, the only possible way to avert a breakup of the antebellum Union and the violence which followed was— precisely as the conservative compromisers of 1850 had always argued— to declare the entire question of slavery off-limits and thus to prolong the life of the second party system indefinitely. But such an attempt to halt further political development in a broader system undergoing the most dynamic change seems to have been foredoomed to failure. It reckoned without the implications of accelerating cultural, demographic, and economic divergences along regional lines. In fact a classic pre-revolutionary situation had developed by the 1850's. The system as a whole tended to be dominated by political elites who represented a declining sector of the national socio-economic system. Elites who represented the values and interests of dynamically evolving sectors at first resented, and later rose in rebellion against, that traditional dominance.

It may be argued with great plausibility that the American Civil War and its aftermath constituted the only genuine revolution in the history of the country.[37] Certainly during the first half of the Civil War the party system was replete with characteristic deviations from normal patterns, deviations which could be expected in an era of violent transition. With the exclusion of an entire region from access to—much less control over— national policy-making institutions, a radical shift in policy outputs occurred. Not only was slavery given a violent *coup de grace*, but an integrated program of positive federal involvement in the fields of banking and currency, transportation, the tariff, and land grants to smallholders was inaugurated. While on some issues the majority coalition was fragmented, the central policy issues of the 1860's were closely integrated. During this era the dominant Republican party was genuinely, if unusually, a policy-making party. On the mass level, the partisan loyalties

37. A most provocative recent discussion, which raises the largest issues of development, is found in Barrington Moore, Jr., *Social Origins of Dictatorship and Democracy* (Boston, 1966), 111-55.

which were forged during this revolutionary era survived almost unchanged until the 1890's, and in some areas left traces which are still visible today.

It is usual to define the end of Reconstruction as occurring at the time of the famous bargain of 1877 between Northern Republicans and Southern Democrats. In reality, however, the revolutionary phase of this party system had largely run its course by 1870.[38] The administration of Ulysses S. Grant can probably best be regarded as a bridge between the era of convulsive revolution which preceded it and the era of industrializing-elite dominance which followed. Into the 1870's, Republican leaders were preoccupied with the danger that a Southern re-entry into the political system might produce an overthrow of their coalition at the polls and a restoration of the Jacksonian coalition to its former dominance. Nor was this a chimera: the success of the Republican revolution in national policy-making had been predicated upon enormous artificial majorities that were produced in a Congress in which the Southern states were not represented. Indeed, the Republican fears were partially realized after 1872. Southern "Redemption" and the persistence of traditional Northern support for the Democrats resulted in a unique period of partisan deadlock which lasted from 1874 until Republican capture of all branches of the federal government in 1896.

The accelerating influence of industrial capitalism produced results,

TABLE 2

Partisan Strength in the Third Party System,
1854-92, by Categories of Offices

A. 1854-73

OFFICE	% DEM.	% REP.	% OTHER
Presidential electors	29.4	70.0	0.6
U. S. representatives	34.4	58.4	7.2
U. S. senators	32.7	60.7	6.6
Governors	25.6	69.2	5.2

B. 1874-92

OFFICE	% DEM.	% REP.	% OTHER
Presidential electors	50.6	48.3	1.1
U. S. representatives	55.9	41.7	2.4
U. S. senators	47.5	51.0	1.5
Governors	48.9	49.5	1.6

38. Kenneth J. Stampp, *The Era of Reconstruction, 1865-1877* (New York, 1965), 186-215.

however, which differed sharply in many respects from those which had been feared by Republican leaders in the Reconstruction era. Both political parties fell substantially under the control of elites who favored industrial development and private enterprise. The Southern Redeemers were not Jacksonians *redivivi;* most of them were upper-class gentlemen who adapted their goals and styles quite well to the new industrial dispensation.[39] Paradoxically, the freezing of alignments along Civil War lines at the mass level gave maximum political latitude to the industrial elites and their partisan assistants to develop the economy on their own terms. As for the Negro, his interests were abandoned by the Republican leadership, in substance if not in rhetoric, as an essential part of the sectional bargain on which the stable deadlock rested. As the nature of the Southern Democratic leadership changed somewhat around 1890 by becoming rather more plebian, it drew the logical consequences implicit in this bargain and, against ineffective Republican resistance on the national level, formally expelled the Negro from the Southern polity. During the 1880's and the 1890's this solution came tacitly to be accepted by the Republicans, by the Supreme Court, and by white public opinion.[40] The modern Solid South thus came into being, and, as a political necessity in a one-party regime, so did the direct primary.

4. *The industrialist system, 1894-1932.* The deadlock of 1874-92, however, was as unstable as the national bipartisan balance which had existed in the 1840's. In both cases a party system whose components were locked in an obsolescent pattern of alignments and partisan ideologies tended increasingly to underrepresent significant disadvantaged elements in the electorate. The processes of industrialization after the Civil War had produced two major strata of the disadvantaged: the farmers, especially in the cash-crop colonial areas of the country, and the growing, ethnically fragmented urban proletariat. As the history of the period from 1877 to 1896 so strikingly reveals, both groups became progressively more alienated from the established order as the Civil War system drew to its close. Suffering from the effects of a long-term crisis in agriculture, the cash-crop farmers in the plains states and the South were already in active rebellion by 1890. Almost immediately thereafter, the second worst in-

39. See, for instance, C. Vann Woodward, *Reunion and Reaction: The Compromise of 1877 and the End of Reconstruction* (Boston, 1951), 23-53.

40. C. Vann Woodward, *The Burden of Southern History* (Baton Rouge, La., 1960), 69-87. See also *Civil Rights Cases,* 109 U. S. 3 (1883); and *Plessy v. Ferguson,* 163 U. S. 537 (1896).

dustrial depression in American history struck the urban centers. The almost instantaneous result, with a conservative Democratic administration in power, was the collapse of the Democratic party throughout the urban metropole in 1894. As many members of the Northeastern elite feared, the stage was thus set for a political coalition of both disadvantaged elements with the objective of overthrowing industrial-elite rule. The fact that full democratization of politics had uniquely occurred in the United States before the onset of industrialization—and thus that such a mass assault against industrial elites could be conducted with constitutional legitimacy—undoubtedly increased the latters' anxiety. While the Supreme Court did what it could in its classic decisions of 1894-95 to undermine that legitimacy, only a critical realignment could dispose of the issues raised with any finality.[41]

In the event, the insurrection under William Jennings Bryan's leadership proved abortive. Among the factors leading to his defeat, several appear decisive. First, the urban working class was too immature and fragmented internally to work effectively with the agrarian rebels. But more than this, there appears every evidence that the combination of the "Democratic depression" of 1893 and severe ethno-cultural hostilities between new-immigrant workers and old-stock agrarians created an urban revulsion against the Democrats which lasted into the late 1920's.[42] Moreover, the issues which appealed to the dominantly colonial-agrarian clientele of the Bryanites—especially currency inflation—meant nothing, and perhaps less than nothing, to workers whose wages were all too obviously at the mercy of employers and economic conditions. Finally, the essentially nostalgic and colonial character of the insurgents' appeal pro-

41. Among the best studies of this interaction are Arnold M. Paul, *Conservative Crisis and the Rule of Law* (Ithaca, N. Y., 1960), esp. 131-235, and Alan F. Westin, "The Supreme Court, the Populist Movement and the Campaign of 1896," *Journal of Politics*, XV (1953), 3-42.

42. One of the many myths—or, more appropriately, half-truths—which are propagated among liberal historians is the notion that employer coercion or intimidation of urban workers was a dominant factor in the 1896 outcome. See e.g. Ray Ginger, *Altgeld's America* (New York, 1958), 172-9. Quantitative analysis of urban election data—especially over time—indicates how dubious this explanation is. It fails to take into account, first, that the realignment of 1896 endured in the cities with very little change until 1908, and remained substantially dominant until the "Al Smith revolution" of 1928; and second, the existence even in 1896 of very considerable ethnic differentials in the impact of the campaigns and realignments of this era on the urban vote. For a study which remains a seminal contribution by an historian, see Lee Benson, "Research Problems in American Political Historiography," in Mirra Komarovsky (ed.), *Common Frontiers of the Social Sciences* (Glencoe, 1957), 113-83.

duced a violently sectional reaction throughout the metropole; the Democratic party in that region sank into an impotence which, save for a limited upswing between 1910 and 1916, lasted for a generation.

The alignment system which was set up during the 1890's marks the point at which American party development began clearly to diverge from developmental patterns in other industrial societies. This system was unique among the five under discussion: it was structured not around competition between the parties, but around the elimination of such competition both on the national level and in a large majority of the states. The alignment pattern was broadly composed of three subsystems: a solidly Democratic South, an almost equally solid Republican bastion in the greater Northeast, and a quasi-colonial West from which protesting political movements were repeatedly launched against the dominant components of the system.[43] The extreme sectionalism of this system can be measured by virtually any yardstick. For example, excluding the special case of 1912, 84.5 per cent of the total electoral vote for Democratic presidential candidates between 1896 and 1928 was cast in the Southern and Border states. Gubernatorial contests during the 1894-1930 period, while showing somewhat greater dispersion of partisan strength, also demonstrate this sectional pattern.

TABLE 3

Sectionalism and Gubernatorial Elections, 1894-1931

REGION	PERCENTAGE OF GOVERNORSHIPS WON BY:		
	DEM.	REP.	OTHER
South[a]	96.8	2.6	0.6
Border[b]	61.1	38.9	—
Midwest and West[c]	31.0	67.2	1.8
Northeast[d]	16.9	83.1	—
Total U.S.	43.0	56.0	1.0

a Eleven ex-Confederate states.
b Kentucky, Maryland, Missouri, Oklahoma, West Virginia.
c East North Central, West North Central (except for Missouri), Mountain and Pacific census regions.
d New England and Middle Atlantic census regions plus Delaware.

A number of major consequences followed from this pattern of politics. With general elections reduced to formalities in most jurisdictions, the

43. This discussion partly follows E. E. Schattschneider, *The Semi-Sovereign People* (New York, 1960), 78-96. See also his "United States: The Functional Approach to Party Government," in Sigmund Neumann (ed.), *Modern Political Parties* (Chicago, 1956), 194-215.

direct primary was developed as an imperfect and ambiguous alternative to party competition. Election turnout dropped precipitately from levels comparable with those of present-day Europe: by the 1920's, national turnout ranged from less than one-third in off years to little more than two-fifths in presidential elections. Viewed in terms of the broader political decision-making system as a whole, the substantial disappearance of party competition, the discrediting of party itself as an instrument of government, the progressive fragmentation of Congress during this period, and the large but negative policy role played by the Supreme Court all fitted admirably into the chief function of the fourth party system. That function was the substantially complete insulation of elites from attacks by the victims of the industrializing process, and a corresponding reinforcement of political conditions favoring an exclusively private exploitation of the industrial economy. One is indeed inclined to suspect that the large hole in voter participation which developed after 1900 roughly corresponds to the area in the electorate where a viable socialist movement "ought" to have developed but, for reasons discussed earlier, did not succeed in doing so.[44]

It can nevertheless be argued that the sectionalism of the 1896-1932 alignment significantly advanced the nationalization of American politics. First, the realignment of the 1890's destroyed or submerged a tangled network of diverse patterns of party allegiance which went back to the Civil War or earlier. It thus created both a severe loosening of the grip of traditional voting patterns and tended to establish broadly regional alignments in their place. Second, the apparently decisive rout of the Democratic party in the industrial-urban centers bore within it the seeds of the party's eventual regeneration. A power vacuum had been created in its state organizations in the Northeast by the desertion of the old, respectable Gold Democratic leadership. This vacuum was in time to be filled by representatives of the newer immigrants.[45] The stage was thus gradually set, via the Democratic convention of 1924 and the "Al Smith revolution" of 1928, for a transition from the old rural-colonial party of Bryan to the winning coalition of rural and urban underprivileged which the party was to become under Franklin Roosevelt.

44. For a more detailed discussion, see Walter Dean Burnham, "The Changing Shape of the American Political Universe."
45. An excellent state case study of this process is J. Joseph Huthmacher, *Massachusetts People and Politics, 1919-1933* (Cambridge, Mass., 1959).

5. *The New Deal System, 1932-?*. The election of 1928, bringing as it did a huge bloc of new immigrant votes into the political system for the first time, has rightly been called the beginning of critical realignment in the Northeast. Even so, it is doubtful that the extremely stable sectionalism of the fourth party system could have been destroyed by any force less profound than the Great Depression. The extended realignment of 1928-36, associated with that great shock and with the coming of age of the new immigrants, has rightly been called an event "very like the overthrow of a ruling class."[46] Permanent federal involvement in the mixed economy which arose from the ruins was substituted for a business rule which could no longer stay the course. The inevitable institutional modifications emerged; the presidency and its ancillary executive establishment moved into ascendancy as a center of policy planning and initiation, and the Supreme Court's veto over interventionist economic legislation was eliminated. The federal government also promoted the development of countervailing institutions of power in the larger society, especially in the labor field. As the Democratic party became the normal majority party, a substantial class cleavage was added to the traditional mix of voting alignments for the first time. Sectionalism was replaced piecemeal by the emergence of two-party competition where it had not existed for decades. The party system became nationalized, although the organizational structures and functions of the major parties themselves remained largely unchanged.

It is important to emphasize, however, that the nationalization of party organization and voting alignments which was inaugurated in the 1930's has been a gradual process which is still far from finished. On the state level, years had to pass before the conservative, old-line Democrats who were suddenly propelled to victory during the 1930's were replaced by leaders more in tune with the programs of the national party. Realignment of party organizations and followings along national lines did not spread into a number of states in the far North until the late 1940's and early 1950's.[47] Similar realignment in the South, at least below the presidential level, has begun to have statewide ramifications only since 1960.

46. Schattschneider, *The Semi-Sovereign People*, 86.
47. In New England and elsewhere, as Richard E. Dawson points out in this volume, 1954 appears to have been a breakthrough year. Duane Lockard, *New England State Politics* (Princeton, 1959), 30, 45. In the upper Midwest, the breakthrough came around 1948. John H. Fenton, *Midwest Politics* (New York, 1966), 18-20, 44-64, 87-100.

TABLE 4

Gubernatorial Elections in the Fifth Party System, 1932-66

REGION	PERCENTAGE OF GOVERNORSHIPS WON BY:		
	DEM.	REP.	OTHER
South	98.4	1.6	—
Border	80.0	20.0	—
Midwest and West	44.4	53.7	1.9
Northeast	43.4	56.7	—
Total U.S.	57.4	41.6	1.0

Here, as elsewhere in the past, American party development has largely been derivative from major changes in the structure of the socio-economic system. Urbanization and the development of autonomous sources of capital in the former "colonial" areas, along with the enormous shift of middle-class populations southward and westward since the end of World War I, have resulted in a severe erosion of the formerly central distinction between economically developed and underdeveloped regions in the United States. Such postwar changes have helped to provide the social diversification essential to two-party competition. Moreover, the federal government during the past decade has conspicuously reversed the "decision" of the 1890's regarding the exclusion of the Negro from the Southern political system. This reversal is as characteristic of the fifth party system as the former decision was characteristic of the fourth. The original national acceptance of exclusion gave the cue for the organization and maintenance of the restrictive one-partyism which was essential to the classic Southern subsystem. The contemporary national insistence upon the inclusion of the Negro has destroyed most of the rationale for the preservation of that one-partyism.

There is much reason for subdividing the fifth party system into two parts at about the year 1950. The first period was that of the New Deal era proper. Broadly speaking, this was a period in which the major concerns of American politics centered on the domestic issues of prosperity and the full integration of the newer immigrants into American social and political life. As the sustained growth in the American economy after 1941 was still in its infancy, the dominant political themes at this time still turned on scarcity and the attendant problems of class relationships in American society. Despite the intrusion of World War II, foreign-policy issues remained on the whole distinctly peripheral to these concerns. The

"American responsibility," about which so much has been heard of late, was barely in gestation among elite circles down until about 1950, and was virtually invisible to the country at large until the outbreak of the Korean War. The election of 1948 may well be remembered in retrospect as the last of the older-style elections: the last before the full emergence of television, the last to turn on explicit class appeals, the last in which the "farm vote" was considered a major factor in the outcome, the last in which foreign-policy issues were conspicuous by their absence from the major-party campaigns.

The period since 1950 may legitimately be described as one of great confusion in American party politics, a period in which the classic New Deal alignment seems to have evaporated without being replaced by an equally structured ordering of politics. The rapid development of public-relations techniques and the projection of candidate "images" have been accompanied at the mass level by a sharp decline in the salience of older-style class cleavages, and an equally significant erosion of party as a dominant factor in electoral decisions. The underlying partisan preferences of the electorate, as survey research has repeatedly demonstrated, have not significantly changed since at least the 1940's.[48] But the electorate since 1950 has displayed a willingness to engage in ticket-splitting on an unprecedentedly massive scale. Probably as a consequence of image voting, the partial replacement of patronage politics by ideologically flavored politics, and the penetration of the mass media, short-term influences on voting have grown tremendously in recent years at the expense of long-term continuities.

For this reason, it remains impossible to say with any certainty whether or not the 1964 election was in fact a critical election, even though some of its behavioral properties would otherwise support this view. It is enough to point out that, as in 1964 the Republicans lost scores of counties in the Northeast which had been steadfast in their support since the Civil War, so in 1965 and 1966 Democratic candidates for major offices lost such once-impregnable party bastions as Boston, Manhattan, and Philadelphia to their Republican challengers. If a realignment is actually going on under these conditions, it is incomparably more subtle and diffuse than any of its predecessors.

48. Philip E. Converse, "The Concept of a Normal Vote," in Angus Campbell *et al., Elections and the Political Order*, 9-39, and esp. 13.

IV

Underlying these developments, as Sorauf suggests, there may well be a party system which is undergoing extensive atrophy because so many of its functions are being performed by other agencies. At the bottom of such a development are certain rather obvious but momentous changes in American life. In the first place, a continually increasing majority of the active American electorate has moved above the poverty line. Most of this electorate is no longer bound to party through the time-honored links of patronage and the machine. Indeed, for a large number of people, politics appears to have the character of an item of luxury consumption in competition with other such items, an indoor sport involving a host of discrete players rather than the teams of old. Connected with this tendency toward depoliticization is clearly a second factor: the extraordinarily complex and technical character of many key political issues as these become translated into concrete proposals for action and policy decisions. In such an intricate political environment, partisan cues to the public are perhaps less relevant than in an age of fewer and broader political issues. In a sense, this may be considered to involve an extension of the principles of civil service to the substance of policy: as there is said to be no Democratic or Republican way to run an agency, so it often appears—whether accurately or not—that there is no Democratic or Republican way to solve highly complex policy problems.

The third and most significant of all these changes has been the international emergence of the United States as an *imperium* in fact, if not in rhetoric or intent. This development has many profound implications for the subordinate role of the political party in the broader decision-making system. Two of these raise particularly serious questions of relevance. In the first place, as is well known, in the United States the making of foreign-policy and military decisions is the province of a bipartisan elite drawn from the executive establishment and from private industry. It is not the province of the political parties, and it is not normally capable of being structured into a cluster of issues on which the parties are opposed and between which the voters can choose. Since these decisions involve the expenditure of between three-fifths and three-quarters of the current federal administrative budget, depending upon which items are included, it is not inaccurate to say that most of the present-day activities of the federal government lie quite outside of areas in which parties can make any positive contributions to the political system. Second, the compartmentalization between foreign defense policies and domestic affairs which used to exist has increasingly dissolved since World War II. The nonpartisan military-foreign affairs sector has come more and more to infiltrate the world of domestic politics and nominally domestic or private activities. Since this growing sector involves areas far removed indeed in complexity and remoteness from the lives of the voters, and consequently tends to escape even the forms of democratic control, its infiltration of the domestic scene suggests a growing restriction of the scope of effective party activity even there.

At the outset it was argued that this country has had a common middle-class, liberal political culture. Even though the absolutism of its assumptions has been brought into serious question in recent decades, the social center of gravity of the active electorate and the structure and financing of our parties have produced elective and appointive elites who have tended not to question the postulates of our traditional liberal absolutism. As the American cultural fragment has rejoined the world, it has been confronted by the most serious challenges to both the relevance and validity of the economic and political values which had so often been assumed to be "givens" in this country. What are the implications of this for the future of American party politics?

On the whole, the outlook is not reassuring. The socialist phase of historical development, and thus of party organization and development, is clearly a thing of the past all over the Western world. Whether for good or for ill, it was a phase through which American party organization never passed. Largely as a consequence of the failure of collectively based vehicles of mass political mobilization to develop here, American major parties have never performed most of the ranges of educative or policy-making functions in any sustained or systematic way. They are most unlikely to begin doing so now. Moreover, as we have indicated, there are large and rapidly growing areas of contemporary public policy from which they—and hence the public at large—have been effectively excluded.

It would clearly be a radical oversimplification, of course, to assert that the parties have been reduced solely to the office-filling function. There is, for example, no hard evidence that the parties have lost their constituent function; indeed, a study of Lowi's discussion might suggest a contrary view. Nor—as any examination of congressional roll calls in recent years makes clear—can it be said that policy differences between Republicans and Democrats are unimportant, much less that such differences do not exist. In the aftermath of the election of 1964, it would be particularly misleading to discount overmuch the very great salience which the political party continues to display in American political life. All that is suggested here is that the relative weight of nonpartisan factors at the top decision-making levels of the American political system has increased substantially over the past generation, and that, granted the massive scope of American involvement in the rest of the world alone, these factors will probably continue to grow in importance. Partisan politics, in such a case, will tend to be confined to a narrowing—though not necessarily unimportant—range of activity.

In politics, as in architecture, form follows function. In an affluent, corporate, technologically complex America, an America whose national policy processes seem likely to be increasingly dominated by its external commitments, it may be asked what functions will be left for political parties to perform? The answer to this question is not at all clear. What does seem clear is that—in the future as in the recent past—the functions which the parties perform and the forms which they assume will be determined by the emergent needs of the broader social and political system, and not by the parties themselves.

XI | WALTER DEAN BURNHAM

MASSACHUSETTS INSTITUTE OF TECHNOLOGY

American Politics in
the 1970's: Beyond Party?

I

THE ARGUMENT of this essay may be summarized very simply. The American electorate is now deep into the most sweeping transformation it has experienced since the Civil War. It is undergoing a critical realignment of radically different kind from any in American electoral history. This critical realignment, instead of being channeled through political parties as in the past, is cutting across older partisan linkages between rulers and ruled. The consequence is an astonishingly rapid dissolution of the political party as an effective intervenor between the voter and the objects of his vote at the polls. As a result, critical realignment and party dissolution have become, uniquely in our time, inseparably linked aspects of the same disruption of the course of our political history. Since it is, in my view, a change of revolutionary scope and implications, we shall first attempt to describe its empirical boundaries, and then make some effort to identify the leading forces that have produced it. Finally, we shall examine some of its probable implications.

II

We start with the premise that the United States is now living through a critical realignment to end all critical realignments in the traditional meaning of the term. This is a realignment whose essence is the end of two-party politics in the traditional understanding; in short, it is a caesura in American political evolution, a point in time at which we close a very old volume of history and open a brand-new one.

Obviously, putting the proposition so baldly invites the rejoinder that it isn't so: tomorrow will look like today, and today's political coalitions and voting behavior have more than a little connection with yesterday's. Agreed: but let us see just how far the argument can be pushed, in the face of the data now available. In doing this, we should look at the meaning of the first operational term, "critical realignment"; then at the second, "party decomposition" (or dissolution); and finally, at the relation between the two in our time.

Critical realignments. A considerable amount of work has been done since 1967 by historians and political scientists on both the conceptualization of the term "critical realignment" and upon specific historic periods and geographic places in which critical realignments have occurred.[1] This is hardly surprising, since, empirically, these events are highly dramatic and easy to measure. Conceptually, the periodic recurrence of critical-realignment sequences in voting behavior clearly provides an admirable point of entry for ordering, classifying, and interpreting the American political experience in new and fruitful ways. Out of this literature a number of propositions have emerged which set apart critical realignments from other types of elections, e.g., those of a "deviating" character such as 1904 or 1956. Critical realignments . . .

—are in the nature of relatively short, sharp, and dramatic movements of many voters away from support of one party to support of another;

—arise as a consequence of severe, cumulative, but uneven stress in the social system (the stress may be of economic, cultural, or other origin);

—are proximately caused by some triggering or "detonating" event or events (*e.g.*, the Kansas-Nebraska Act or economic disruption);

—are very frequently, if not always, associated (normally in pre-realignment or early-realignment stages) with nation-wide third-party up-

1. See Walter Dean Burnham, *Critical Elections and the Mainsprings of American Politics* (New York, 1970); James L. Sundquist, *Dynamics of the Party System* (Washington, 1973); Michael F. Holt, *Forging a Majority* (New Haven, 1969); Paul Kleppner, *The Cross of Culture* (New York, 1970); Michael P. Rogin and John L. Shover, *Political Change in California* (Westport, Conn., 1970); Richard Jensen, *The Winning of the Midwest* (Chicago, 1971).

risings of a "movement" type, with the third party frequently a bridge
for voters in motion from one major-party commitment to another;

—historically have been periodically recurring phenomena, with peaks
spaced approximately 36-38 years apart;

—have involved major and intense struggles over the definition and re-
definition of the most important national policy agendas of their time;

—have resulted in a new "stable phase" in the electoral cycle, grounded
upon durable majorities and minorities in the electorate;

—have been followed by significant alterations in national public policies and by changes in the relative effective political power of our
separate national policy institutions.

On its face, this catalogue of "symptoms" appears very closely to fit
many salient electoral developments of the past decade. Major crises have
erupted in the social system since 1964; we have had, and conspicuously,
such normally "anomalous" phenomena as the emergence of the George
Wallace (American Independent) movement, as well as striking abnor-
malities and polarizations within the Republican convention of 1964 and
the Democratic conventions of 1968 and 1972, and two extraordinary
landslides (1964 and 1972) in the past three presidential elections. Nor
can it be seriously doubted that Richard Nixon's election in 1968 was followed by significant domestic policy changes—including, as by no means
unimportant or accidental, a reconstitution not only of the personnel but
also of the policies of the Supreme Court.[2] Those interested in the peri-
odicity phenomenon, may consider $1928 + 36 = 1964$, or, alternatively,
$1932 + 36 = 1968$.[3] Certainly, too, no one can deny that something very
much out of the ordinary electoral routine was going on in both these latter years.

More to the point, major shifts have taken place very recently in the
structure of attitudes in the electorate, and these require some extended
discussion. The nature of critical realignments and their relation to "nor-

2. See David Adamany, "Legitimacy, Realigning Elections and the Supreme Court,"
1973 *Wisconsin Law Review*, pp. 790-846.
3. For a remarkable application of content-analytic technique to party platforms—
which produces "peaks" of value change precisely synchronous to the mid-point peaks
in voting behavior during national critical-realignment sequences—see J. Zvi Namen-
wirth, "Wheels of Time and the Interdependence of Value Change in America," *Journal of Interdisciplinary History*, III. 4 (Spring 1973), 649-83.

mal" or "usual" politics reflect issue polarizations that are extremely intense by American standards—not only among elites, as in the recent party conventions mentioned above, but also among decisively large parts of the mass electorate. The exceptional nature of the voting shifts that occur in critical realignments—their abrupt departure from hitherto normal standards, their great magnitude in certain parts of the electorate, and the durability of the post-realignment party balance—seems inexplicable unless issue consciousness and issue voting create massively higher levels of voting than could be expected from reading the collected 1954-66 works of the Michigan Survey Research Center group.[4]

Unfortunately, we can only "prove" the existence of such exceptional issue intensity among parts of the mass public in historical realignments by citing largely qualitative reports by contemporaries and later historians. Modern survey research dates back only to 1935, and survey instruments designed to get to basic attitudinal questions associated with critical realignments were really not available until the early 1950's. This was a time falling in the midst of a "stable phase," halfway between the class polarizations of the 1936-40 period and the post-1963 upheaval in the shape of American politics; and the studies produced from these surveys are limited accordingly.[5]

But as attitudinal structures change, so do research findings on the American electorate. Several important studies in the early 1970's have revealed most drastic changes in the kind and quality of the attention the American electorate is paying to politics. Let us recall first what the Michigan group told us about the American electorate in more stable times.

—First, the most important single determinant of voting behavior, consistently, has been the individual's party identification.[6]

—Second, most voters have extremely weak cognitive maps of the political world: in the overwhelming bulk of cases, they do not respond

4. See Philip E. Converse, "Information Flow and the Stability of Partisan Attitudes," chap. 8 of Angus Campbell et al., Elections and the Political Order (New York, 1966); and, by the same author, "The Nature of Belief Systems in Mass Publics," chap. 6 of David E. Apter (ed.), Ideology and Discontent (New York, 1964).

5. Cf. my "Theory and Voting Research: Some Reflections on Converse's 'Change in the American Electorate,' " American Political Science Review, LXVIII (September 1974), pp. 1002-1023 and accompanying discussion by Professors Converse and Jerrold G. Rusk and this writer, ibid., pp. 1024-57.

6. Angus Campbell et al., The American Voter (New York, 1960), especially pp. 528-31.

in a way that reveals what Philip Converse has called "internally constrained belief systems" about politics.[7] Two corollaries to this proposition are:

—Third, the level of political cognition is very strongly associated with level of formal education among individuals, and that the top 10 per cent or so of the electorate in both categories are in some sense the "keepers of the flame" of democratic values.[8]

—Fourth, the large bulk of the electorate responds in a heterogeneous way to a number of durable issue clusters in politics, with particularly little relation or constraint between positions on any issues of domestic policy on the one hand and foreign policy on the other.[9]

—Fifth, presidential elections tend to be decided by the least adequately socialized or "competent" parts of the electorate, who come "surging" in under the pressure of short-term stimuli, as in 1952, and then "decline" out in subsequent off-year elections, as in 1954.[10]

It follows from all these and other portraits of the American electorate that it is at once highly subject to manipulative campaign techniques and functionally incapable of providing the necessary mass base for a "more responsible two-party system," as Gerald Pomper has quite correctly pointed out.[11] It was the popularization of just such findings—more than the findings themselves—which so perturbed the late V. O. Key, Jr., toward the end of his life, and prompted him to dedicate his last book to the proposition that "voters are not fools."[12]

Such is, very briefly, the portrait of the American electorate sketched out for us by academic research on voting prior to the early 1970s. It corresponds precisely to what could be expected of the public midway in the larger electoral cycle, when the "old politics" dominates, consensus is

7. A point stressed in Converse, "The Nature of Belief Systems in Mass Publics."

8. The phrase is also Professor Converse's. Cf. his "Of Time and Partisan Stability," *Comparative Political Studies,* II (1969), 141.

9. This lack of relationship between domestic- and foreign-policy attitudes has been a common theme of attitudinal research ever since Gabriel Almond's *The American People and Foreign Policy* (New York, 1950). Cf. also Campbell *et al., The American Voter,* pp. 187-88.

10. Angus Campbell, "Surge and Decline: A Study of Electoral Change," chap. 3 of Campbell *et al., Elections and the Political Order.*

11. Gerald M. Pomper, "Toward a More Responsible Two-Party System? What, Again?" *Journal of Politics,* XXXIII (1971), 916-40.

12. In *The Responsible Electorate* (Cambridge, 1966), p. 7.

high, and issue polarizations are very modest. As we turn to more recent studies, it is at times difficult to believe that they describe the same country or population of voters that was so intensively analyzed just a few years earlier. Let us summarize the leading findings of this new survey-based work.

In a number of recent articles and commentaries, Gerald Pomper has stressed that a steep upward change has developed in the electorate's perceptions of issue distances between the parties since the age of *The American Voter*.[13] This change did not occur gradually, but was a jump shift associated quite precisely with the 1964 presidential campaign and election. From then on, in a much more sharply defined way than ever before in the history of survey analysis, voters perceived the Democrats to be "liberal" and the Republicans, "conservative." Pomper argues two substantive "implications" from this radical change toward "constraint" in the mass electorate: first, the 1964 election was a critical election; second, the existence of a much more clearly issue-polarized competition between the parties, *and public awareness of this issue polarization,* may have created for the first time in this century the essential attitudinal preconditions for the establishment of a "more responsible two-party system" in the United States.

Unfortunately, Pomper does not reflect upon one very clear implication of his data: that this increasing clarity is associated with increasing conservatism in public attitudes toward the issues and the parties. This shift in opinion has very much to do, it goes without saying, with the shattering of the old post-Roosevelt Democratic presidential coalition, with the rise of George Wallace and George McGovern and the remarkable post-1964 electoral successes of Richard Nixon.

Norman H. Nie continues the empirical attack upon the Eisenhower-era model of the American electorate in an important article, "Mass Belief Systems Revisited."[14] His findings are very similar to, though richer than, Pomper's. There has been a very steep increase in ideological con-

13. Gerald M. Pomper, "From Confusion to Clarity: Issues and American Voters, 1956-1968," *American Political Science Review*, LXVI (1972), 415-28. This issue is devoted partly to a symposium on issue voting, and Professor Pomper's paper forms a part of it. See also Richard W. Boyd, "Popular Control of Public Policy: A Normal Vote Analysis of the 1968 Election," ibid., pp. 429-49; Richard A. Brody and Benjamin I. Page, "Comment: The Assessment of Policy Voting," ibid., pp. 450-58; and John H. Kessel, "Comment: The Issues in Issue Voting," ibid., pp. 459-65.

14. Norman H. Nie (with Kristi Andersen), "Mass Belief Systems Revisited: Political Change and Attitude Structure," *Journal of Politics*, 36.3 (August 1974), 540-91. Page references are to a late draft of the typescript.

sistency in public attitudes. This occurs in breakthrough fashion in the 1964 election, producing a jump-shift in both attitudes and voting behavior in that presidential election and the two that have followed.

This increase in attitudinal constraint has been an across-the-board phenomenon; in particular, it is found at all levels of formal education in the electorate, which means that the phenomenon cannot be adequately explained in terms of the rapid 1952-72 growth in aggregate levels of formal education in the adult population. Nor, of course, can it be explained in terms of the strong static relation between education level and the level of attitudinal consistency and political awareness posited by Philip Converse and others.[15] Perhaps crucial to our subsequent argument here is that, in Nie's words, "in the last three presidential elections [i.e., 1964-72] political attitudes have come to be an increasingly significant force in determining the direction of the presidential vote, while the impact of partisan identification, once predominant, has become much less significant."[16] He goes on, cautiously: "Perhaps voter rationality, like attitude consistency, is also more a function of the political context than a consequence of innate limitations of the mass public"—a point that clearly will have to be kept in the center of scholarly work on voting from now on.[17]

Not surprisingly, Nie concludes that this fundamental and sudden change in 1964, coupled with survival of the change thereafter, may very well be associated with an era of major-party realignment. We shall return later to some speculation on what party politics might look like in an era marked by high position-issue intensities among the voters and a corresponding decline in "free-floating" party identification as a determinant of voting behavior.

The third major piece of research to have been completed in the early 1970s is a study of the 1972 presidential election by a group of Survey Research Center investigators and based upon the SRC sample.[18] Here, as elsewhere, we must remain content with a brief summary of its leading findings, coupled with a recommendation to the reader to study the origi-

15. The key to this, of course, is to control for educational levels. When this is done, as the Nie paper points out, the 1956-72 upward shift in attitude consistency is revealed to be an across-the-board phenomenon, although differentials continue to exist in the predicted direction between better-educated and less-educated groups. See Nie, ibid., MS pp. 17-19, and Figures 5 and 6.

16. Ibid., MS p. 28.

17. Ibid.

18. Arthur H. Miller, Warren E. Miller, Alden S. Raine, and Thad A. Brown, "A Majority Party in Disarray: Policy Polarization in the 1972 Election." Paper presented at the 1973 American Political Science Association convention.

nal work. The authors also find that ideological polarizations were vastly more important in 1972 than in earlier decades, with partisan identification playing a much less salient role as shaper of voter decisions. Suggestively, however, they find that this ideological polarization in 1972 was markedly concentrated among Democrats and Independents, extending much less sharply to Republicans. This reflects a prime reality of contemporary American electoral politics, the disruptive stress that the issues of the post-1964 period have placed upon the Democratic presidential coalition:

> Perhaps the most important revelation of the analysis was that the traditional inertial force of party identification proved less potent than the polarizing effects of the specific issues relevant to the election. Indeed, when the relative weights of the three general factors explaining the vote, namely, the candidates, parties and issues, are compared to previous elections, it becomes clear that not only was this an issue election but that it may more appropriately be labeled an ideological election. Above all else, the outcome of the election was the result of the ideological polarization within the Democratic ranks that pitted the left wing Democrats against those on the right.[19]

The SRC scholars point directly to a fundamental characteristic of politics in a critical-realignment era: the emergence of profound issue cleavages (involving race, the Vietnam War, and antagonistic cultural symbolisms) which cut orthogonally across traditional partisan commitments in decisively large minorities of the electorate. But they go on to make two points that are of profoundly disturbing significance. First, these issue cleavages as they have emerged in 1964, 1968, and again in 1972 have contributed to the political discontent of large segments of the electorate. These new issue polarizations severely disturb pre-existing partisan commitments by many voters without as yet being able to supersede them. Second, there has been no evidence whatever of any significant conversions within the electorate toward identification with the Republican party, despite the results of the elections of 1968 and 1972. If this is a critical realignment, one is driven to ask, In what sense can it be called a *partisan* realignment?

The authors of "A Majority Party in Disarray" end upon an appropriately cautionary note. For them, a crucial part of the over-all context is the steep increase in measurable political disaffection in the electorate

19. Ibid., p. 74 (revised typescript).

over the past decade. As Everett Ladd also points out,[20] the unresolved crisis within the Democratic party has contributed to a situation in which, election after election, significant minorities of the electorate—it may be added, different minorities each time—have been left without an adequate perceived choice at a time when they very much want to make one.

> There is a broader question here, namely, the legitimate representation of the American people. In the absence of realignment or a viable third-party alternative, it appears that until the polarization within the Democratic ranks is diminished, a major segment of the population will go unrepresented at the presidential level; whether their policy orientation is one of social change or social control, their policy expectations and preferences will go unsatisfied. Such a condition of a perceived nonresponsive government can only lead to further political dissatisfaction, discontent and disaffection.[21]

So we may say that many of the most important general preconditions and behavior patterns associated with critical realignments in the past have been manifesting themselves in the current period. Yet something is clearly wrong with this picture as it stands. A quite considerable part of the professional and journalistic literature of the past few years anticipated an old-style partisan critical realignment in our time, or has proclaimed that one is occurring. But—for reasons we shall examine in some detail below—a good deal of this writing is probably an exercise in waiting for Godot. A work like Kevin Phillips's *The Emerging Republican Majority*[22] might have been as well titled *What to Do Until the Critical Realignment Comes*. But supposing it doesn't come? What if the waiters wait in vain? Supposing that the more probable development, one outlined by me in 1970, is best described in the title of David Broder's recent book, *The Party's Over?*[23]

We may find it very useful under these circumstances to think in other categories, categories that deal with the emerging decomposition of party-in-the-electorate as of the essence of the current critical realignment sequence. Stripped of all subsidiary or divisible "accidents" of the phenomenon, what is a critical realignment? It is a major change rooted in the behavior of critically large minorities of American voters which durably

20. Everett C. Ladd, Jr., "The Dynamic of Contemporary American Electoral Politics" (typescript).
21. Miller *et al.*, "A Majority Party in Disarray," p. 90 (revised typescript).
22. New Rochelle, 1969.
23. New York, 1972.

alters electoral coalitions, the shape of election outcomes, and the flow of public policy. It happens when politically decisive minorities of the electorate stop doing what they have been used to doing, start doing something else, and keep on doing it for a long time afterward. All preceding critical realignments in American electoral history have been channeled through parties. But if and to the extent that this one is not so channeled— or even more, cuts across and dissolves party—this precisely forms the core of comparative analysis, an analysis through which alone we can comprehend our present political condition.

Party decomposition. A good deal of work has been done on the phenomenon of decaying partisanship in the American electorate, much of it summarized and elaborated upon in my *Critical Elections and the Mainsprings of American Politics.*[24] This decay in the stability of support for candidates of a given party means several things at once. First, presumably, it entails a decline in the strength and extent of party identification as well as in the degree to which it is autonomously determinative of voting behavior. Second, it is manifested in an increasing longitudinal velocity in aggregate outcomes of presidential elections: the amplitude of partisan swing tends to increase, and presidential landslides become common. Third, decay in partisan-related components in voting decisions is reflected in a systematic tendency toward split-ticket voting at all levels of the electoral system.[25] As I have attempted to show elsewhere, the trend toward party decomposition goes back a long way in American electoral history. It was first visible in the 1904-10 period, reached an intermediate peak in the 1920's, and was reversed to a considerable extent in the two decades following the 1932 realignment. Thus, a clear secular trend away from nineteenth-century levels of partisanship in American electoral politics has existed across most of this century. What is distinctive about the period from 1960 onward is that this decomposition has accelerated at a breakaway pace, reaching all-time highs—so far, at any rate—in the 1972 election.

We have already discussed the recent SRC discovery that autonomous partisan identification in 1972 was much less significant as a determinant of presidential voting decisions than formerly, and "ideology" much more. This implies a basic qualitative change in the meaning of such party iden-

24. New York, 1970.
25. Cf. V. Lance Tarrance and Walter de Vries, *The Split-Ticket Voter* (Grand Rapids, 1972).

tification as remains. On the quantitative side, one of the best-known developments of the past decade has been the volatilization of party identification itself: first, the 1964-65 surge toward the Democrats, and since then a decline among both Democrats and Republicans and a major increase among Independent identifiers. The Gallup data tell this familiar story.[26]

TABLE 1

The Rise of the Independent: Gross Party Identification in the American Electorate, 1940-74

YEAR	% DEM.	% IND.	% REP.
21 and over			
1940	42	20	38
1950	45	22	33
1960	47	23	30
1964	53	22	25
1970	45	26	29
18 and over			
1971	44	30	26
1972	43	29	28
1973	43	33	24
1973/74	42	34	24

This upward shift in Independent identification suggests a corollary to the point made by the 1972 SRC study: If there is any evidence at all of partisan realignment in the contemporary period at this important level of self-identification, the "party" benefitted by it is clearly the Independents. Moreover, there is every reason to conclude two things about this Independent voter pool: first, it is particularly concentrated among the young; second, it contains an increasingly large proportion of "new" Independents, i.e., those who are more or less actively oriented to the political world but are alienated from both major parties.[27] The first suggests a rather dramatic failure of traditional sources of political socialization of the young; the second suggests what Gallup, the SRC group, and others have identified—a growth in "active" modes of political alienation.

The bulk of the discussion of party decomposition to follow focuses upon leading aggregate changes in American voting behavior—changes

26. *Gallup Opinion Index*, No. 105 (March 1974), pp. 21-22.
27. See my discussion of this in Burnham, *Critical Elections* . . . , pp. 127-31. Much the same point is now being made from more extensive analysis of survey data in the most recent period, particularly by Nie and Miller *et al*.

associated with the contemporary jump-shift in split-ticket voting. It is here that we are confronted with apparently durable behavioral changes of the utmost significance to the future development of American political institutions. The general extent of this post-1960 change can be surmised from examining the data from Milwaukee County, Wisconsin—perhaps the only jurisdiction in the nation to report the number of straight party ballots cast in general elections.[28]

TABLE 2

Split-Ticket Voting in the Milwaukee Area, 1960-70*

AREA	PERCENTAGE OF STRAIGHT BALLOTS CAST						
	1960	1962	1964	1966	1968	1970	% Dem. for Governor, 1968
Milwaukee City	68.3	52.8	61.6	50.6	36.8	31.7	59.3
Ward 3	68.4	55.3	58.1	50.7	34.5	25.3	42.8
Ward 6 (Black)	68.9	59.0	71.1	51.8	51.3	43.7	83.8
Ward 1 (White)	66.6	53.1	66.6	56.5	44.1	35.1	73.7
Greenfield	63.0	x	55.1	34.1	31.9	26.4	51.3
Oak Creek	68.1	50.7	63.0	x	28.7	18.1	45.0
Hales Corners	57.1	40.4	53.2	45.8	39.6	31.9	31.3

* As examples, the most predominantly Republican and two most predominantly Democratic wards of the city in 1968 (one white-ethnic, the other overwhelmingly black) have been presented here.

An inspection of the array suggests what a more complete analysis reveals: the decay of straight-ticket voting from 1960 through 1970 is a universal phenomenon, presumably caused by general and powerful processes at work in the political system as a whole.[29]

28. The data are taken from relevant volumes of the *Biennial Report* of the City of Milwaukee's Board of Election Commissioners. Unfortunately, in 1970 Wisconsin joined the lengthening parade of states shifting their state elective offices to four-year terms, elective in non-presidential years; hence, there is no such data for the 1972 election.

29. The "test" here is simple, though N is small. First, one computes the time regression line for each ward, 1964-70 (ward boundaries were changed in 1963). Then one divides b by a in each regression equation to yield standardized rates of decline in straight-ticket voting; then correlates these rates with the mean percentage Democratic of straight tickets cast in the 1964-70 period. Here as elsewhere there are significant differences between black-populated and white-populated areas in their aggregate voting patterns. Excluding the two wards with heavy black concentrations yields an N of 17. The question of the relation between partisan percentages and the rate of decline in partisan voting in white areas is "answered" by $r = -.330$. This indicates that only 10.9 per cent of the decline can be "explained" in terms of an argument that greater Republicanism is associated with greater propensities across time for aggregate levels of split-ticket voting to increase.

We now turn our attention to a phenomenon of very great system-level importance. David Mayhew, the first to identify it clearly, refers to it as the strange case of the disappearing marginal seat in congressional elections.[30] The argument is breathtakingly simple. At one time (down until the later 1950's), partisan outcomes of contested congressional elections with incumbents running distributed themselves in a rough approximation to a normal curve, with the single mode of the curve falling close to the zone of maximum party competition. Similar unimodal and semi-normal distributions could be established for congressional outcomes in seats where no incumbents were running for re-election, and for presidential election results compiled by congressional district. Since that time, the nonincumbent group and presidential elections at the congressional-district level have retained this unimodality—this latter of course by no means always with the mode at the area of maximum party competition.

The crucial change has come to the incumbent group of congressional seats—always a large majority of all congressional races in the modern period. Here the unimodal "competitive" pattern has been decisively replaced by a bimodality, with each mode quite far removed from the normal competitive range of outcomes. The meaning of this is clear. Presidential "coattails" have all but vanished where incumbent congressmen are concerned. The partisan turnover in House elections has been very much reduced, and the number of incumbents actually suffering defeat has fallen from fifty in 1920 to eight in the equivalent presidential-landslide year of 1972. Congressional incumbents, benefiting by large-scale ticket-splitting among the voters, have become very largely immune to the tides of politics outside of congressional elections, and—except in the rare landslide in congressional voting—very largely immune to defeat.

We may begin our discussion of this important phenomenon by extending an earlier discussion of split-partisan outcomes as between presidential and congressional elections held at the same time and at the same level of analysis.[31] The data from 1940 through 1972 in this regard are reported in Table 3.

While an upward tendency in split outcomes can be detected through 1964, the 1972 election showed a tremendous increase. President Nixon carried 377 congressional districts, while George McGovern won 58—in itself an all-time "outcome landslide" for any presidential election at this

30. David Mayhew, "Congressional Elections: The Case of the Disappearing Marginals." Paper delivered at the 1973 New England Political Science Association meeting.
31. See Burnham, *Critical Elections* . . . , pp. 100-111.

TABLE 3

Proportion of Split Results:
Congress and President, 1940-68 [32]

YEAR	NUMBER OF DISTRICTS ANALYZED	% OF SPLIT RESULTS	% OF SPLITS INVOLVING MINOR PARTY
1940	362	14.6	9.4
1944	367	11.2	2.4
1948	422	22.5	33.7
1952	435	19.3	1.2
1956	435	29.9	1.5
1960	437	26.1	2.6
1964	435	33.3	0
1968	435	31.7	34.8
1972	435	44.1	0

level. Of these 377 Nixon districts, 188 elected Republican congressmen and 189 elected Democrats. With 192 districts with split outcomes (44.1 per cent of the total), we begin to approach some kind of maximum empirical limit. Assuming a roughly two-party outcome in terms of House seats won, a *complete* rupture of majority coalitions as between presidential and congressional elections—i.e., with the losing party's candidate losing *all* congressional districts, but with his party winning about half the seats—this limit would be approximately 50 per cent of split outcomes to all district outcomes. As it was, in 1972 Nixon carried over three-quarters (77.4 per cent) of all districts that elected Democrats to the 93rd Congress. One may make the point even more simply: Had the electoral conditions of the 1920 Harding landslide prevailed in the 1972 Nixon landslide, the Republican would have elected about 350 congressmen. Instead, they won only 191, far short of a party majority.

Not only did Republican congressional candidates not "make it" in 1972 despite the Nixon landslide, the President and his advisors adapted their 1972 strategy with this in mind. As Gordon Strachan pointed out in his testimony before the Senate Watergate Committee, more than a hundred Republican candidates in seats held by Southern and labor-backed Democrats were simply written off by White House strategists.[33] This

32. For a continuation of this table back to 1900, see Burnham, *op. cit.*, p. 109. Source for the 1940-64 data above is Milton Cummings, *Congressmen and the Electorate* (New York, 1967), tables 2.1 (p. 32) and 5.1 (p. 139).

33. U.S. Senate, 93rd Cong., 1st Sess., Select Committee on Presidential Campaign Activities, *Presidential Campaign Activities* (Hearings), Phase 1: Watergate Investigation, pp. 2483-85 (testimony of July 23, 1973).

strategy was followed in pursuit of the basic goal of these operatives: the winning of the largest possible majority for the President. Labor, which tacitly supported his re-election, and the Southerners, who openly did so, were not to be antagonized. Thus it is that political elites, in a mutually reinforcing process, adapt to what they see to be the dominant behavioral patterns of electoral politics and, in doing so, reinforce those patterns.

Returning to the "vanishing marginals," a comparison of 1952 and 1972 outcomes reveals this process as it has moved to current levels of coalitional dissociation.

As Table 4 and Charts 1-8 make clear, a major generic change has taken place in the structure of congressional-election outcomes involving incumbents. In 1952—excluding the uncontested Southern Democratic "tail" of the distribution—all three categories of elections had a unimodal distribution, though the modes did not coincide for congressional districts with and those without incumbents. In particular, there was relatively little

TABLE 4

Separation of Voting Coalitions: Outcomes for President,
Non-Incumbent, and Incumbent Congressmen, 1952-72

% DEMOCRATIC BY DISTRICT	% OF DISTRICTS, 1952			% OF DISTRICTS, 1972		
	Pres.	*Non-Inc.*	*Inc.*	*Pres.*	*Non-Inc.*	*Inc.*
0.0-4.9	0	0	3.0	0	0	1.6
5.0-9.9	0	0	0	0	0	0
10.0-14.9	0	0	0	0.2	0	0
15.0-19.9	0	0	0	1.6	0	0.5
20.0-24.9	0.2	2.7	0.8	8.3	0	2.1
25.0-29.9	4.6	4.1	3.0	14.9	1.7	10.1
30.0-34.9	9.9	5.5	10.5	23.2	3.4	7.2
35.0-39.9	19.8	9.6	13.8	21.4	12.1	10.3
40.0-44.9	19.3	13.7	12.4	11.7	20.7	5.6
45.0-49.9	14.0	21.9	6.7	6.4	25.9	4.0
50.0-54.9	8.7	16.4	8.8	4.8	10.3	5.3
55.0-59.9	7.6	5.5	5.2	2.5	5.2	7.2
60.0-64.9	7.8	2.7	5.5	1.2	6.9	11.4
65.0-69.9	3.4	1.4	3.9	1.2	1.7	9.0
70.0-74.9	3.0	0	2.5	0.9	6.9	5.3
75.0-79.9	0.9	1.4	2.2	0.5	0	3.7
80.0-84.9	0.7	0	1.1	0.9	3.4	3.2
85.0-89.9	0	0	0.6	0.2	0	1.6
90.0-94.9	0	1.4	0.8	0	0	1.9
95.0-100.0	0	13.7	19.1	0	1.7	10.1
N =	435	73	362	435	58	377

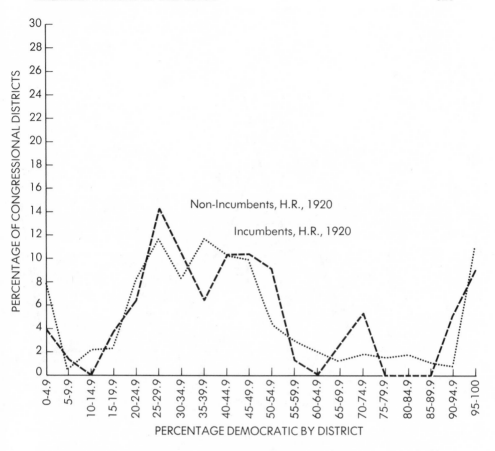

FIGURE 1

Development of "Institutional" Party Systems: Outcomes in House Elections, 1920

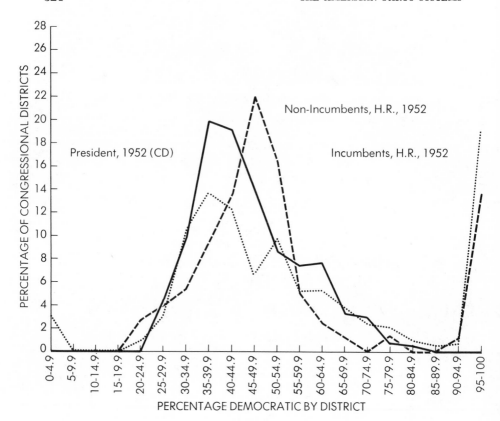

FIGURE 2

*Development of "Institutional" Party Systems: Outcomes for President
and Congressional Incumbents and Nonincumbents, 1952*

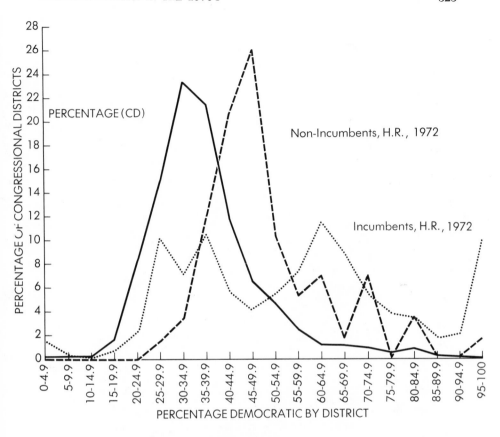

FIGURE 3

*Development of "Institutional" Party Systems: Outcomes for President
and Congressional Incumbents and Nonincumbents, 1952*

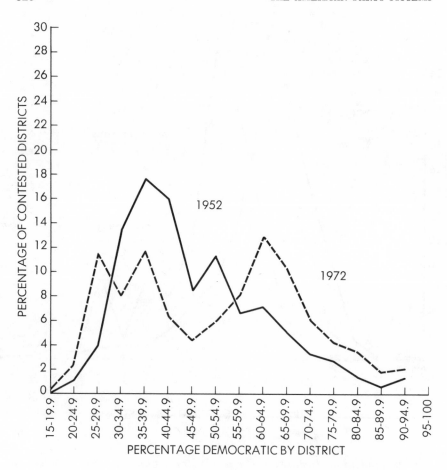

FIGURE 4

From Unimodal to Bimodal: Results of Contested Congressional Elections,
1952 and 1972 (Incumbents Only)

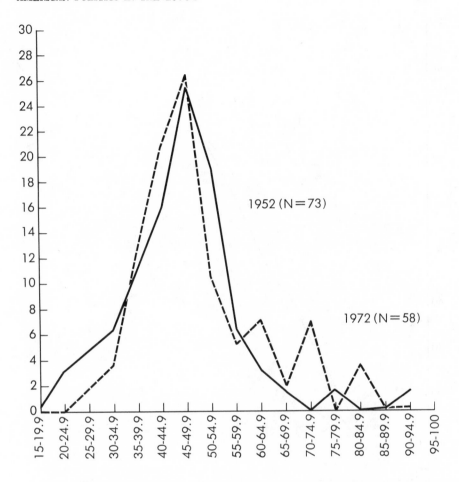

FIGURE 5

Enduring Unimodality of Outcomes: Results of Contested Congressional Elections, 1952 and 1972 (Non-Incumbents Only)

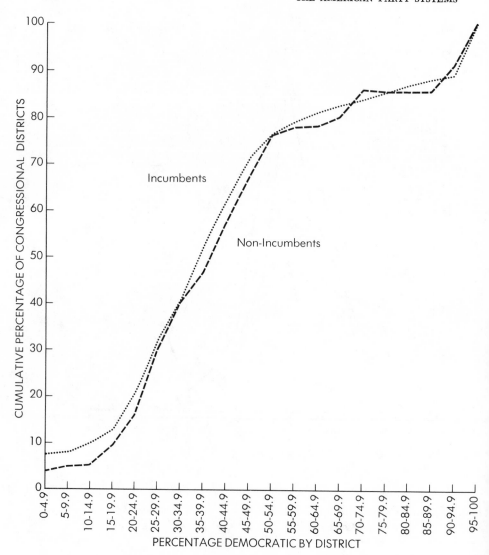

FIGURE 6
Cumulative Frequency Distribution, 1920 (Congressional Districts)

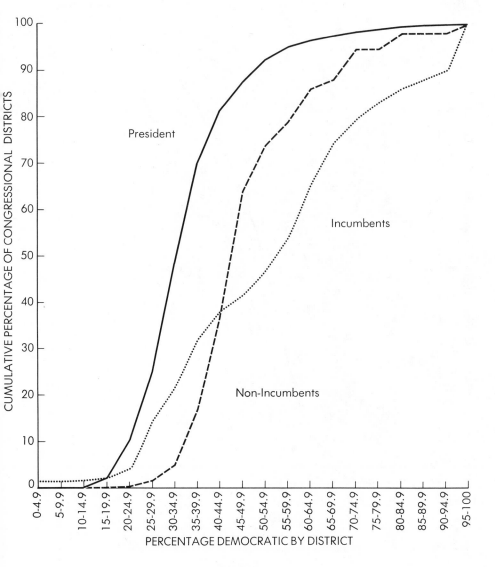

FIGURE 7
Cumulative Frequency Distribution, 1952 (Congressional Districts)

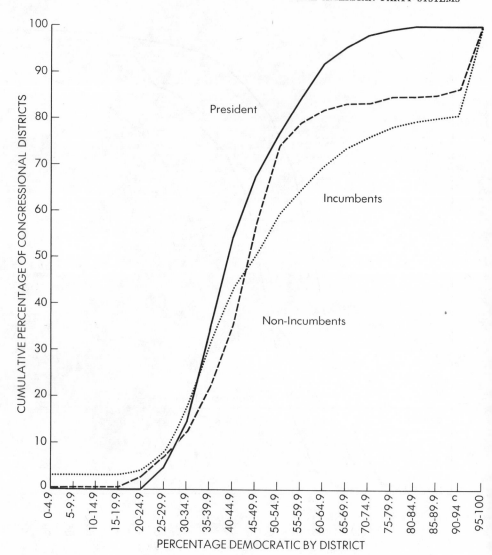

FIGURE 8

Cumulative Frequency Distribution, 1972 (Congressional Districts)

difference in distributional shape between the Presidential and Incumbent categories. Fifty-six Incumbent and 28 Non-Incumbent congressional districts were in the closely competitive 45.0-54.9 per cent range, for a total of 84 in all. Because the distribution had remained what it was in 1952, presidential "coattails" still existed and—for the last time in our history thus far—the Republicans won 221 seats to 213 for the Democrats, and organized the House.

By 1972 this picture had radically changed. The Presidential and Non-Incumbent distributions were still unimodal, though with an enormously increased gap between the first mode (30.0-34.9) and the second (45.0-49.9). The Incumbent congressional elections, however, had developed a very strong bimodality, centering upon 35.0-39.9 and 60.0-64.9. Correspondingly, the number of districts falling into the closely competitive 45.0-54.9 per cent range fell to 35 Incumbent and 21 Non-Incumbent, or 56 in all. This represents a decline in the proportion of competitive congressional seats from nearly one-fifth in 1952 to one-eighth in 1972.[34] Clearly, the prime 1972 beneficiaries were incumbent Democratic congressmen, who in most cases have established themselves in their districts quite irrespective of what happens in presidential or any other elections. But the distancing of incumbents from the competitive range essentially favors those of both parties in the long run. What this means, as Mayhew has pointed out, is that even very large national vote swings in these circumstances will have remarkably little effect so far as turnover is concerned. The 1972 results simply reinforce Mayhew's argument as to developments from the late 1950's to 1970.

That this distancing does appear to work to the benefit of incumbents of both parties can be seen by analyzing paired presidential-congressional outcomes by district in one large state, Pennsylvania.

This table reveals, clearly enough, the crucial point: the mean percentage for Democratic incumbents increased despite the Nixon landslide of 1972. Moreover, the closing up of the standard deviation reveals a growing homogeneity of such non-competitive outcomes. Finally, one may note the great increase in the distance between Republican and Democratic incumbents, an increase from 17.9 per cent in 1952 to 29.5 per cent in 1972.

34. This, it should be noted, occurred despite a very sharp decline in the number of uncontested (mostly Southern-Democratic) seats between these two elections. If one computes the proportion of closely competitive seats (45.0-54.9 per cent Democratic) to all *contested* seats, they constituted 24.3 per cent of this total in 1952, and only 14.4 per cent in 1972.

TABLE 5

Insulation of Congressional Incumbents:
The Case of Pennsylvania

YEAR	PRES.	CONG.	PRES.	CONG.	DIFFERENTIAL (MEAN)	
	Dem. Inc.	Dem. Inc.	Rep. Inc.	Rep. Inc.	Dem. Inc.	Rep. Inc.
1952–N	12	12	18	18		
Mean % D	57.2	58.5	40.0	40.4	+1.3	+0.4
S.D.	7.37	6.24	5.58	5.28	2.98	2.77
1972–N	13	13	11	11		
Mean % D	45.7	62.9	32.4	33.4	+17.1	+0.9
S.D.	10.42	4.41	4.00	5.97	9.71	6.84
1952-72 Shift						
Mean % D	−11.5	+4.4	−7.6	−7.0	+15.8	+0.5
S.D.	+3.05	−1.83	−1.58	+0.69	+6.73	+4.07

Two objections to all this may be voiced. The first, stressed both by Mayhew and by Edward Tufte,[35] is that these profound changes are largely the result of structural factors—for instance, collusive reapportionment by state legislatures to protect incumbents. Consequently, they are not—at least not primarily—the result of recent changes in behavior by the voters. The second objection is that 1972 is a peculiarly inappropriate benchmark when comparing presidential and congressional outcomes. We may deal in a very preliminary way with this second point by observing that—however unpopular Senator McGovern's unique candidacy may have been among Democrats and Independents—the 4.4 per cent increase in the mean percentage for Democratic incumbents from 1952 to 1972, associated with the fact that the variance among these districts was cut almost exactly in two, makes very clear that processes of coalitional dissociation along office-specific lines are going on which quite transcend such considerations.

The first or structural argument requires a little discussion here, if only because research on this dissociation is at such an early stage of development and has, in my view, considerably overstated the importance of

35. Edward R. Tufte, "The Relationship between Seats and Votes in Two-Party Systems," American Political Science Review, LXVII (1973), 540-54.

structural variables in shaping the vast changes we see. No one can doubt that legislatures in recent decades, for example, have typically reapportioned congressional seats in order to protect incumbents of both parties.[36] But we may ask when such practices began, and in response to what changed perceptions of voting behavior in congressional elections on the part of these legislatures.[37] If this is left aside, it is notable that the same processes of coalitional dissociation and insulation of incumbents can be found in states like New Hampshire and West Virginia, where a single party has controlled the reapportionment process for at least the past forty years.[38]

It is also possible to identify districts without any boundary changes at all for the past several decades. One such district, the 24th Pennsylvania, is presented here, in part because it permits us to identify the time at which basic changes in aggregate voting behavior began to occur. This is a three-county district centered on Erie, and it achieved its present shape in 1941. It was first captured by a Democrat (the current incumbent, Joseph Vigorito) in 1964. As Table 6 reveals, that year marked in more

36. Though by no means always. In each of the New York congressional reapportionments of 1951, 1961, and 1971, Republicans dominated both branches of the Legislature and the governorship. They did what they could to draw lines favoring Republicans and undermining Democrats—conspicuously (and successfully) in the case of the 12th district in Brooklyn (1951), and (in 1961) quite unsuccessfully in the the case of the upstate 35th district, represented by Samuel S. Stratton (D). Remarkable examples of political geography can be found in each of these three New York reapportionments, particularly in New York City.

37. Such is the state of our ignorance about practically all systematic, longitudinal patterns surrounding congressional elections that we are quite without information on this vital point, as on others. It does seem reasonably certain that protection of incumbents of both parties through reapportionments on the whole goes back at least to World War II and probably earlier.

38. Thus—taking 1956 rather than 1952 in these two states as benchmark for comparison, because of a number of turnovers in personal (not party) incumbency in 1952 —we find the following pattern.

YEAR	WEST VIRGINIA			NEW HAMPSHIRE		
	% Dem. Pres.	% Dem. Pres.	Difference	% Dem. Cong.	% Dem. Cong.	Difference
1956	51.1	54.2	+3.1	33.8	38.4	+4.6
1972	36.1	66.0	+29.9	35.0	29.8	−5.2
Shift	−15.0	+11.2		+1.2	−8.6	

The number of incumbents in West Virginia, 1956, was five (Democrats), and in 1972 was four (Democrats). In New Hampshire two (Republican) incumbents ran for re-election in both 1956 and 1972.

ways than one the beginning of a new era in the district's electoral politics.[39]

TABLE 6

The Triumph of Incumbency:
The Case of the 24th Pennsylvania District

YEAR	INCUMBENT'S PARTY	% FOR INCUMBENT	MEAN % FOR PARTY, STATE-WIDE OFFICES	DIFFERENTIAL
1942	R	60.5	60.8	−0.3
1944	R	54.6	54.5	+0.1
1946*	(R)	(63.9)	(64.0)	(−0.1)
1948	R	54.5	55.3	−0.8
1950	R	57.0	54.7	+2.3
1952	R	57.1	57.4	−0.3
1954	R	52.0	49.0	+3.0
1956	R	57.8	57.6	+0.2
1958	R	53.8	52.1	+1.7
1960	R	51.0	52.5	−1.5
1962*	(R)	(51.4)	(52.2)	(−0.8)
1964	R	49.2	42.6	+6.6
1966	D	55.3	49.4	+5.9
1968	D	61.1	50.1	+11.0
1970	D	66.8	53.0	+13.8
1972	D	68.8	51.1	+17.0

* Years with no incumbent running. Party shown is that of the preceding incumbent and the winner in the year indicated. Mean per cent includes President, U.S. Senator, and at-large state offices.

Obviously, the 1964 election in this district marked the beginning of a breakaway divergence between congressional voting coalitions and those of other offices. This process has now resulted in the emergence of a safe seat for its Democratic incumbent, while the district as a whole remains closely competitive at other levels of election. Moreover, this process of coalitional dissociation was very far advanced by 1970, and was in no way an artifact of Senator McGovern's candidacy in 1972. Virtually by definition, these very recent changes in this district must be attributed wholly to changes in aggregate voting behavior; for there have been no changes in the structural context of voting here.

The explanation for such profound and rapid transformations in voting pattern may be a relatively simple one. More than a decade ago, Warren

39. The point should be explicitly made here that there have been no significant changes in ballot form or electoral law in Pennsylvania during this period. It is true that, beginning in 1966, the number of state-wide offices separately elective was reduced by constitutional change.

E. Miller and Donald E. Stokes of the Michigan SRC group pointed out that voters knew very little about candidates in congressional elections compared with others in more salient contests, conspicuously the Presidency.[40] What little they knew involved the incumbent, and—except in the unusual case—this tended to give incumbents a considerable electoral advantage. Voters seek cues wherever they can, and conspicuously, as a host of writers have pointed out, through the party affiliation of candidates running for offices. The American ballot is everywhere vastly more complex than ballots in any parliamentary democracy: both separation of powers and federalism vastly proliferate the number of voting choices that voters have to make at any one time.

It would follow that if, for whatever reasons, decisive minorities of voters do not find party (or their own party identification, if any) a useful frame of reference of voting decisions, they will seek other kinds of cues for those decisions. At the highest level of salience—say, in voting for President, U.S. Senator, or Governor—they will respond to a mixture of candidate appeal, major campaign issues, and, third and last, party in ways similar to those described for the 1972 presidential election by Miller et al. At lower levels of salience, and especially when this "nonpartisan" minority turns to voting for congressmen, the incumbency effect suggested by Miller and Stokes will have overwhelming importance.

Such an effect will, of course, be further reinforced by two other considerations. First, the saturation of the electoral process by electronic media results in severe inequalities of media coverage and increases, very probably, the salience gap as between, say, campaigns for President and for Congressman. Second, there is excellent reason to suppose that incumbents have responded to their electoral context by making themselves as visible as possible to their constituents, chiefly as officials whose basic task is servicing the constituency rather than formulating public policies. And so one would expect to find, and does in fact find, an extremely rapid rise in the volume of mail sent out under the congressional frank from the mid-1950s through 1970.[41]

40. See Donald E. Stokes and Warren E. Miller, "Party Government and the Saliency of Congress," chap. 11 of Angus Campbell et al., Elections and the Political Order.

41. It should go without saying that incumbents in the House—much more than in the higher-visibility Senate—have every incentive to perpetuate the existing state of affairs. This is particularly the case so far as proposals to finance from federal funds their largely invisible challengers are concerned. The implications of this for campaign-reform legislation before the Congress in 1974 should be obvious.

The institutional and policy implications of this evolution of bimodal congressional-election outcomes could not be more profound. First, as the proportion of incumbents running for re-election increases from five-sixths of the contests in 1952 to seven-eighths in 1972, and the "trough" in the competitive ranges deepens, turnover of personnel in the House begins to approach the minimum possible. This growing stabilization of outcomes—a further move toward "institutionalizing" the House[42]—stands in the sharpest contrast to increasing volatility across time in other election campaigns. Second, until the Watergate affair destroyed the Nixon Administration in 1973-74, all trends pointed toward a decline in the significance of the Congress as a whole, and the House in particular, in the national policy process.[43]

Obviously, the march in executive hegemony has been abruptly halted for the time being; but it may well be wondered whether this setback will prove to be more than temporary. If not, one may anticipate that the House will become ever more clearly a body whose members maintain job security through being *ombudsmen* and constituency advocates before the immense bureaucracy at the other end of Pennsylvania Avenue. But if the collapse of the Nixonian bid for domination of American national politics should presage a permanent shift of influence over policy toward Capitol Hill, another problem is implied by the bimodal distribution. If turnover rates in the House continue to converge as closely to zero as actuarial realities permit, the absence of fresh blood—occurring as it does in a period of the most rapid changes in society and economy—implies a constantly growing gap between a self-insulated House and the needs of the country at large.

In either event, one point stands out with crystalline clarity: at some time between 1960 and 1964, the voting coalitions in presidential and congressional elections became dissociated from one another to a degree unprecedented in the history of American electoral politics since the creation of the party system nearly a century and a half ago. Some years ago James M. Burns elaborated a theory of a four-party system, composed of

42. See Nelson W. Polsby, "The Institutionalization of the House of Representatives," *American Political Science Review*, LXII (1968), 144-68; and Nelson W. Polsby *et al.*, "The Growth of the Seniority System in the House of Representatives," ibid., LXIII (1969), 787-807. These two articles constitute the first significant effort at the kind of extensive longitudinal and quantitative history of the Congress which is so urgently needed.

43. See, e.g., Samuel P. Huntington, "Congressional Responses to the Twentieth Century," chap. 1 of David Truman (ed.), *The Congress and America's Future*, 2nd ed. (Englewood Cliffs, 1973).

presidential Republicans and Democrats and congressional Republicans and Democrats.[44] But the phenomena he described were analyzed at the level of elites. Today we have such a "four-party system" (if such it can be called) at the grass roots. Not only is this situation likely to add a new dimension to the "deadlock of democracy" that Burns described. It is also likely to add a most potent behavioral reinforcement of the American Constitution's separation of powers, with consequences we can barely foresee.

Considerations of space do not permit us as exhaustive an analysis of contemporary party decomposition elsewhere in the electoral universe as we might wish. Further discussion here will be confined to one state, West Virginia, with a strong tradition of high turnout, straight-ticket partisan voting, and—except for the realignment era of 1930-34—a generally stable pattern of both aggregate party affiliation and electoral outcome across time.[45] In 1938, for example, party registration in this state stood 57.4 per cent Democratic, 41.5 per cent Republican, and 1.1 per cent other or no response—a figure virtually identical to the partisan outcome of the 1940 election for President and other offices. By 1972 the balance had glacially shifted to 64.6 per cent Democratic, 33.8 per cent Republican, and 1.6 per cent other and no response: a pro-Democratic shift averaging 0.2 per cent per year.

Clearly George McGovern was exceptionally unpopular in West Virginia: the 1968-72 partisan swing to Nixon was 18 per cent here, compared with 11.3 per cent nation-wide; and McGovern's 36.4 per cent of the vote was the lowest for any Democratic candidate since the abnormal election of 1864. At the same time, Senator Jennings Randolph won re-election with 66.5 per cent of the vote,[46] and the four congressional incumbents won a statewide total of 66.2 per cent—the latter being the highest Democratic congressional percentage in the entire history of West Virginia congressional elections.

44. In *The Deadlock of Democracy: Four-Party Politics in America* (Englewood Cliffs, 1963).

45. For a general discussion of West Virginia politics down through 1952, see John H. Fenton, *Politics in the Border States* (New Orleans, 1957), pp. 82-125.

46. One major nation-wide aspect of the developments we have been describing is the recent emergence—in *some* cases—of extraordinary majorities for senatorial incumbents running for re-election. Senator Randolph's 1972 percentage was exceeded in the history of West Virginia senatorial elections only by Sen. Robert Byrd's 67.7 per cent in 1964 (but with Lyndon Johnson also winning 67.9 per cent) and 77.6 per cent in 1970. Other prominent examples of this trend, both very recent, include Senator Proxmire's 70.8 per cent in the Wisconsin 1970 general election and Senator Jackson's 82.4 per cent in the Washington 1970 election.

A comparative survey of county-level correlations for 1940 and 1972 suggests something of the extent of the deterioration in West Virginia, and indicates that the 1972 presidential outcome alone cannot account very completely for it.

TABLE 7

West Virginia: Partisan Intercorrelations among
Four Major Statewide Offices, 1940 and 1972[*]

	1940 Office				1972 Office			
OFFICE	PRES.	U.S. SEN.	CONG.	GOV.	PRES.	U.S. SEN.	CONG.	GOV.
		$r =$				$r =$		
President	1.000	+.988	+.980	+.991	1.000	+.734	+.536	+.910
U.S. Senator		1.000	+.992	+.994		1.000	+.680	+.718
Congress			1.000	+.988			1.000	+.513
Governor				1.000				1.000
		$r^2 \times 100 =$				$r^2 \times 100 =$		
President	100.0	97.7	96.1	98.2	100.0	53.9	28.7	82.8
U.S. Senator		100.0	98.4	98.7		100.0	46.3	51.5
Congress			100.0	97.6			100.0	25.3
Governor				100.0				100.0

[*] N in both cases = 55. Based on percentage voting Democratic of total- (and two-party) vote.

The decay in the explanatory power of partisanship in this period is profound, and not merely as between presidential and other electoral coalitions. As Table 7 reveals, there was a single coalition in 1940—one virtually identical with the distribution of aggregate partisanship as revealed in registration data. By 1972 we can see at least three voting coalitions in outline: (1) a presidential-gubernatorial coalition, with one explaining 82.8 per cent of the aggregate county-level variance in the other; (2) a senatorial coalition; and (3) despite the near-identity of gross statewide totals as between senatorial and congressional outcomes, a quite discrete congressional coalition.[47]

We may summarize these developments—and analogous ones elsewhere —by a glance at the basic syndrome of politics described by the late V. O. Key, Jr., in the "pure non-party" systems of the Deep South a generation ago.[48] His description of Democratic-primary politics in states like Ala-

47. Of course, the standard error of estimate around the regression equations shows an enormous increase between 1940 and 1972. In 1940 the maximum was 2.14 (President-Congress), as compared with a maximum of 7.44 in 1972 (also President-Congress). This represents a *twelvefold increase* in the variance of the partisan vote.
48. V. O. Key, Jr., *Southern Politics in State and Nation* (New York, 1949).

bama or Arkansas in that era suggests that there existed simultaneously completely ad hoc electoral coalitions from office to office at the same election, and for the same office from one election to the next; very strong evidence of "friends-and-neighbors" effects, i.e., abnormal support for a candidate in his home county; as a rule, protection of congressional incumbents; and, of course, low turnout and local-oligarchic control of public policy.

For Key, the whole point of competitive party politics was to abolish such dissipation of the potential implicit in electoral democracy—involving among other things party as a "solvent of federalism" and separation of powers as well.[49] Something like this was surely his hope for the South. What has happened instead is that these elements of a nonpartisan syndrome have spread outside the South—in many cases, such as in West Virginia, for the first time in our political history. For what we find in a state like West Virginia in the years since 1960 are these things: increasingly discrete (ad hoc?) electoral coalitions from office to office at the same election, and for the same office from one election to the next; emergence of clear "friends-and-neighbors" patterns in voting; protection of congressional incumbents (the last incumbent defeated in a general election was retired in 1958); and a rapidly declining turnout.

As to the latter, the turnout of 40.3 per cent of the potential electorate in 1970 and 64.9 per cent in 1972 constitute the lowest rate of participation for these respective years since ex-Confederates were readmitted to the West Virginia franchise in 1870. As for "friends-and-neighbors" effects, these have not only been associated with the home counties of congressional incumbents since the early 1960s, but came clearly to the fore in 1972—for the first time on record—in voting for such obscure offices as state auditor.[50] All this suggests a rapid and increasing deterioration of partisan constraints on voting behavior, a deterioration that may au fond be far more a cause than an effect of the 1972 presidential campaign. Such examples could be extended almost indefinitely, but these will suffice as mere fragments of a general pattern. The point must be stressed: If and to the extent that they represent a change in the behavior of po-

49. V. O. Key, Jr., *American State Politics: An Introduction* (New York, 1956), especially chap. 2.
50. It may also be noted in passing that for the first time in the history of West Virginia since the end of the Civil War, a state-wide partisan political office (Commissioner of Agriculture) was won by an incumbent in 1972 *without opposition.*

litically decisive minorities, a change that is largely irreversible, then we have a "critical realignment" of voting behavior. But we have also a critical realignment that works not through but athwart the traditional major parties, and cumulatively dissolves them as channels of collective electoral action.

This dissociation, it would seem, is the most significant of all the electoral developments that have occurred during the past decade. It follows, quite rigorously, from the basic changes in the electorate's perception of political objects which Pomper, Nie, and Miller *et al.* have identified. Bluntly put, to the extent that issues achieve salience and shape voting behavior in the United States of today, the resultant cleavages become both too intense and too numerous to be contained any longer within the traditional two-party electoral matrix. One may speculate that, if electoral law and political tradition in the United States allowed, we would have seen the emergence some time ago of an explicit multi-party system. As it is, we find party decomposition instead. This discussion must now terminate with a brief review of the causes of this decisive change in our electoral politics and a more extended discussion of its implications.

III

The newer electoral literature seems agreed that American voters are polarizing more and enjoying politics less. It also tends to emphasize a related theme: through a combination of contextual stress (including egregious "imperial" decisions by political elites, such as those that took us into Vietnam) and social change, the electorate is now polarized across at least two orthogonal dimensions. As a result, nothing approximating a majority, however factitious, now exists in the American political system as a whole. One may express this set of orthogonal dimensions schematically.

	Wallace following; Johnson/Humphrey/Labor	Hard-core Republicans
RACIAL, WAR, "SOCIAL-ISSUES" AXIS	CLASS-ETHNIC ("NEW DEAL") AXIS	
"Right"	"Left"	"Right"
"Left"	McGovern following; "new" academics, professionals	(A scattering of "Libertarians")

As I have suggested earlier, it seems also possible to think about the emergence of these orthogonalities as eruptions of political response to the kind of post-industrial change in social status and functions suggested by David Apter, a response speeded up by the civil-rights revolution and by the Vietnam experience.[51]

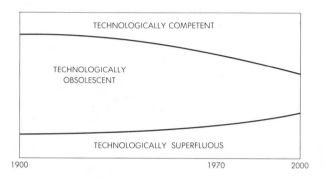

It is obvious that such a classification nicely elides over many many crucial problems of scarcity and political domination in American society. As a "broad brush," however, it is not without some value.

Implicit in Apter's argument is that this emergent technostructural stratification of power and influence cuts athwart, without necessarily superseding, the older industrial upper-middle-working-lower class stratification pattern. The "technologically competent" strata of post-industrial society would include, in addition to many members of the more cosmopolitan and older upper classes, many of the "newer class" of academics—particularly in the natural and social sciences—as well as many of their students; it would include also journalists and people in the electronic media, particularly those in the "center" as compared with the "periphery" of American society. The "technologically superfluous" strata would include those without visible or probable future functional roles in a post-industrial society, by reason of their lack of necessary competence or acquired skills that are marketable in this emerging form of domination. This population would obviously be quite disproportionately composed of unskilled blacks and members of other racially (and otherwise) handicapped groups in the social structure. The "technologically obsolescent" strata would include a very substantial part of what is called "middle

51. In "Ideology and Discontent," chap. 1 of David E. Apter (ed.), *Ideology and Discontent*.

America"—both working class and white-collar strata and older, largely local or "periphery"-concentrated elite groups.

The logic of justification for the old pre-1929 industrial pattern of domination was the dogma of laissez faire, Horatio Alger individualist and capitalist liberalism. Its transitional successor, the "welfare state" born in depression, had group pluralism and governmental benevolence for its ethics of rule. Its technologically oriented successor, pretty clearly, would be grounded in a bureaucratic, "nonpolitical," expertise-oriented ethic, *ceteris paribus;* and we might count ourselves lucky if it were not to contain a significant element of sophisticated imperialism as well. But perhaps the most significant part of the whole picture is that older logics of justification for social activities and socioeconomic rewards have increasingly—but very unevenly—broken down, while those appropriate to a "technetronic society" have not been in any way solidified.

A major consequence of this impaction is, precisely, what Theodore J. Lowi has described as "the end of liberalism" and the proliferation of social conflicts among a host of groups.[52] In such conflicts, members of the opposed groups typically regard themselves as victims of fraternal relative deprivation: "they" (their antagonists and others) get undeserved social rewards; but "we," the virtuous—for example, "we" who still believe in the older values of self-denial, hard work, patriotism, and the sanctity of the nuclear family—are being deprived of these values by "them," in collusion with the Government, and without legitimate right.

Racial antagonisms—arising from the unplanned consequences of such changes as the mechanization of cotton agriculture since World War II—add fuel to the fire. Ex-peasant populations arriving in American cities have always started off at the very bottom of the urban social and economic structure. As is well known, however, the experience of blacks in the United States has been fundamentally different even from that of the Irish immigrants of the mid-nineteenth century; and, what is worse, fundamental, technologically conditioned changes in economic production have heavily reduced the social need for the kind of hod-carrying, pick-and-shovel jobs that sustained the Irish for many decades after their arrival. A pool of "technologically superfluous" people at the bottom of the social structure thus collects, grows, and perpetuates itself. To a large extent, its members of all racial and ethnic backgrounds inevitably become

52. In *The End of Liberalism* (New York, 1969).

a *Lumpenproletariat* of the sort described by Marx and Engels in 1848. The cultural dissonance that the "lowest classes" present to their white working-class (and white-collar) neighbors is paralleled by the latters' sense of physical and economic threat to their own and their children's hard-won place in the social order.

Moreover, it can hardly be said that as yet those strata most likely to benefit positively from a technetronic social universe—academics, students from the older middle class, technicians, and bureaucrats—have established a logic of justification for domination that is coherent or legitimate, even in their own eyes. To the contrary: for many reasons too complex to discuss here, a substantial part of this new cosmopolitan elite has rejected the implications of their own dominant position and has come actively to patronize at least those of the "technetronic" underclass who are members of discrete racial minorities. As it happens, many of these liberal elites—judges, administrators, legislators, academics, and others—occupy a sufficiently exalted position in the social structure to ensure that the direct social costs of combined racial-and-class integration in the metropolitan area will be borne by those elements of the white population that are both economically and culturally least able to bear them. Except in the very rare case, these costs are not borne by these elites themselves or their families. Those who do bear them—or feel acute anxiety that they will be made to bear them in the near future—know this. The result, visible in case after case, has been the repudiation of these elites by the rank and file who gave them support from the age of Franklin D. Roosevelt to that of John F. Kennedy.

To all these pressures must be added the direct costs of the Vietnam War's speed-up of cultural conflict in the white population over issues involving definitions of patriotism, life styles, work and leisure, and other primordial values. Out of this transitional farrago of conflict without overarching *policy* legitimacy have come, in direct succession, Barry Goldwater, George Wallace, Richard Nixon and Spiro Agnew, and the McGovern campaign of 1972. Out of it also has come, by the same token, the destruction of the old presidential Democratic coalition. The 1972 Democratic primaries produced national totals divided almost exactly one-third for Wallace, one-third for McGovern, and one-third for the "vital-center" ABM coalition around Hubert Humphrey, Henry Jackson, and the forces of organized labor. This result quite accurately reflects the impaction of one set of issues on another, with no clear way visible now or in the near future to resolve the conflicts involved.

The dissociation of American electoral coalitions has thus come to take on a very marked institutional division-of-labor character. The bulk of recent analytical work on presidential elections has made crystal clear that this office—more in the ascendancy than ever before (at least until 1974)—has become the vortex of all the combined passions, intensities, and multiple cleavages over values, relative social status, and relative deprivation that are now at work in the electorate. It is a uniquely concentrated symbolic office; and when symbolisms fall apart, when conflicts escalate as policy legitimacy decays, the symbolisms projected come to dominate outcomes in a highly issue-polarized, near-ideological electoral setting. But the shape of the aggregate data alone also makes it obvious that this pattern cannot readily be extended to other levels of election as a matter of course. On the contrary: the emerging shape of congressional elections, with its growing support for incumbents of both parties, bespeaks quite directly the lack of any ideological polarization at all similar to those operating at the presidential level.

As for other levels with some visibility of their own—senatorial elections, gubernatorial elections, and mayoral elections—the pattern is heterogeneous in the extreme: sometimes there are polarizations that parallel those operating at the presidential level, and sometimes there are not. Compare, for example, the two mayoral elections in New York City won by John Lindsay (1965, 1969) with the election won by Abraham Beame in 1973. But there is little doubt that a growing common theme in these contests has been that described by Murray Levin in his analysis of the 1959 Boston election: increasingly, the road to victory lies in a candidate's successfully denying that he ever had anything to do with politics before. And, as Levin correctly observes, this repudiation of politics and politicians is associated with the "alienated voter"—the man in the street who finds tremendous cognitive dissonance between what he learns in public-school civics about how the system *should* work, and what he learns in adult everyday life about how it actually *does* work.

Every indicator suggests that there are many more voters with these attitudes in the mid-1970's than there were in 1959. We can present only a few highlights from the most recent survey study emphasizing this—the study done for the U.S. Senate's Committee on Government Operations at the end of 1973 by Louis Harris Associates.[53] Among the most significant findings of this study are these:

1. The American people's loss of confidence in their government has now reached majority proportions—though, overwhelmingly, the belief is widespread that the system can be made to work well.

2. A remarkably sharp divergence has emerged between the public at large and political elites, who were separately surveyed. The public is much more negative about such matters as the evils of secrecy in government, respect for people who run government at all levels, and supposed improvements in the quality of life in the United States, than are its leaders. The leaders are relatively contented, if not almost complacent; the public, rather intensely, is not.

3. The discontent is pervasive: of twenty-two major institutions and the people in charge of them, a majority of the respondents expressed a "great deal of confidence" in only two of them—medicine and local trash collection. By contrast, only 33 per cent expressed this confidence in the Supreme Court, 30 per cent in the Senate, 29 per cent in the House of Representatives, and 18 per cent in the White House.[54]

4. This discontent has grown rapidly since 1966: the proportion of the sample expressing "a great deal of confidence" in the Supreme Court has declined from 51 per cent to 33 per cent in the 1966-73 period; in the U.S. Senate, from 42 per cent to 30 per cent; in the U.S. House of Representatives, from 42 per cent to 29 per cent; and, far the most dramatic of all, in the Executive branch of the federal government, the decline has been from 41 per cent to 19 per cent.[55]

The over-all 1966-73 decline in the proportion of respondents expressing "a great deal of confidence" in the four federal political institutions was from 44 per cent to 28 per cent, while the decline in confidence for eight non-governmental institutions in this period was from 46 per cent to 37

---

53. "Confidence and Concern: Citizens View American Government": U.S. Senate Committee on Government Operations, 93rd Cong., 1st Sess. (Dec. 3, 1973). This, incidentally, is the first sample survey ever to be commissioned by the Congress of the United States.
54. Ibid., pp. 37-38.
55. Ibid., p. 33.

per cent—suggesting pretty clearly that the decline in confidence is both general and specifically concentrated on political institutions.

Table 8 reveals the same deterioration in confidence and growth in political and social alienation. A set of projective questions, designed to tap such feelings, has been asked by Harris since 1966. The results are set out below, and they speak for themselves.[56]

TABLE 8

Growth of the Alienated Voter:
The Harris Survey, 1966-73

% AGREEING WITH STATEMENT	1966	1968	1971	1972	1973	CHANGE, 1966-73
The rich get richer, the poor get poorer.	45	54	62	68	76	+31
What you think doesn't count much any more.	37	42	44	53	61	+24
People running the country don't really care what happens to you.	26	36	41	50	55	+29
I feel left out of things going on around me.	9	12	20	25	29	+20
Average feeling alienated and powerless	29	36	42	49	55	+26

It can hardly be doubted that this across-the-board increase in public discontent is closely linked to the bankruptcy of the existing top-level leadership cadres of both political parties. This bankruptcy, if not total, has been comprehensive: failures of vision, of empathy with the needs and concerns of non-elite Americans of both races, failures in specific policies, failures, indeed, in common honesty and elemental political morality.

It is something of a truism of critical-realignment sequences—though one not as yet sufficiently integrated into scholarly analyses of them—that established "old politics" leadership in any given period responds to growing political crisis by a rigidity and a rejection of emergent demand which contributes in no small way to the magnitude of the subsequent explosion, and the completeness of their own repudiation. Thus it was with James Buchanan, Grover Cleveland, and Herbert Hoover. So it has been with the Vietnam warriors of the Johnson Administration and virtually

56. Ibid., p. 30.

the whole personnel of the Nixon Administration. Leaving aside peculiarities of personality, this remarkably recurrent pattern of rigidification,
explosion, and repudiation of previously dominant leadership makes sense
when one thinks of critical realignments as moments of convulsive transition—moments when older dominant value sets are being replaced and
challenged by newer ones, but where the replacement is still in a very
early stage of development. "Bankruptcy" thus tends to take on, as it
should, somewhat less of a moralistic cast in analysis, and more of a
probably systemic consequence of the same political lags, the same gaps
between political inertia and social change, which mark these processes.

What is different about the contemporary period in this respect is that
leadership has failed the public for so long a time, and that the failed (or
repudiated) leadership has included in turn the top elites of both major
political parties. By 1976, for example, about 27 per cent of the electorate
will be under 30. This very large segment of the voting population has
lived its entire adult life in this cumulative crisis of leadership: the oldest
among these younger 1976 voters will not have been more than 16 when
John F. Kennedy was assassinated. Moreover, one crucial dimension of
this failure has been the emergence of a manifest elitist illusion among
top American leadership of both parties. It has been very characteristic
of both the Johnson top leadership (especially those involved with the
Vietnam disaster) and of former President Nixon and his aides to blame
the public at large for failing to support their disastrous blunders and, in
the case of Nixon personally, to regard adult American citizens as "children." Quite appropriately, and in a very Greek way, this *hubris* has produced its *nemesis* and has led to *atē:* Pride meets its appointed Fate, and
Destruction follows. For the realities are quite otherwise.

If Key in his generation was correct in arguing that "voters are not
fools"—and he was—still less are they fools today. In the conclusion to his
most recent book, Louis Harris strikes a most appropriate note:

> The facts in this book have pointed up perhaps more clearly than any-
> thing else just how badly the leadership of the country has read the
> temper, mood and serious intent of the American people. Taken to-
> gether, the record is a serious indictment of the political, social and eco-
> nomic leadership of this country over the past decade. There is little
> doubt in this writer's mind that the public, although far from correct in
> many areas, nonetheless is far more sophisticated, far more concerned,

and far more advanced than the leadership believed. It can be said with certainty that the people by and large have been well ahead of their leaders.[57]

Just so; and it may be added that, since this top leadership is ultimately produced by the political parties, we should perhaps not be surprised that the repudiation of this leadership and the dissolution of the older parties should move hand in hand together.

When one is in the eye of a political hurricane, it is particularly difficult to gauge the future with any sense of confidence. Still, the attempt must be made to assess the way ahead. Clearly, the shift toward higher levels of education in the population and radical improvement in the ease of acquiring political information through electronic media and otherwise can be expected to continue. So also will growth in the tertiary sectors of the social structure: across time, professional and technical people will constitute a growing part of the labor force, and organized labor will constitute less. There is no particular reason to assume, on the other hand, that tensions between different racial and cultural groups living in close physical proximity will soon decrease, or that the high level of violent crime now prevailing will show any tendency toward decline. Just beyond the horizon of current issue problems involving culture, race, and economics lie far larger ones having to do with runaway inflation and a contraction of the available natural-resource base to sustain a social structure grounded upon high mass consumption in its tastes, values, and motivations.

If we assume with Anthony Downs that political parties and their ideologies used to be short cuts to voting decisions under conditions of imperfect information and widespread economic scarcity,[58] we may view most or all of these prospective developments as unfavorable to the survival of the traditional parties as effective intermediaries between voters and the electoral decisions they make. The massive growth in ticket-splitting and independent party identification in recent years may well be considered proximate effects of transitional sociocultural stress on one hand and inadequate political leadership on the other. But it also would make sense to suggest that, to the extent that the costs of political information to voters have been drastically reduced by the new communica-

57. *The Anguish of Change* (New York, 1973), p. 286.
58. In *An Economic Theory of Democracy* (New York, 1957), especially chaps. 11-13.

tions technology, many of the older mobilization and concentration functions once performed by the major parties have lost their utility in recent years.

Voters can and do make intelligent decisions on the merits, as they see them, of individual candidates and the specific issue-clusters surrounding their campaigns. Obviously, to the extent that the American electorate in the 1970's and 1980's becomes more affluent, better educated, and with more leisure time on its hands and a number of alternative life styles to choose from, does the kind of social structure emerge which alone could undergird the models of the independent, responsible citizen developed by John Stuart Mill and Moisei Ostrogorski. Except as gatekeepers (reducing the number of electable alternatives on the ballot through an enduring monopoly over effective nominations), the parties could then largely disappear—and our political democracy would be improved by the disappearance.

A surprisingly large part of political-science literature written by Americans over the past two decades has persistently sought to formulate teleological theories of political development and post-industrial "technetronic" society. At the end of such "development"—very much like the "end of days" posited by Marx a century ago—lies the end of ideology and apolitical bliss. One suspects that such utopias have their function in the practical political sociology of rulership. As predictions, however, they will prove as inadequate as most of their predecessors. The old-style American major party-in-the-electorate may very well be on its way out as a channel through which the collective power of the many can at least occasionally control the behavior of the elites who run this political system. And if the foregoing analysis of current electoral developments has been correct, this remarkable development would indeed be a "critical realignment to end all critical realignments." But the ultimate results may be very different from those predicted and hoped for by technocrats and democratic elitists from the age of the Progressives to the present. Let us recapitulate—if by perhaps excessive emphasis—what these developments mean in coalitional and institutional terms.

1. *The Presidential coalition.* The most dramatic developments at this level have involved the nationalization of electoral coalitions and the rupture of the older presidential Democratic coalition into three almost equal parts: the supporters of Wallace, the "vital center" groups around

organized labor, and the McGovernite "left."[59] These things have happened, as we have attempted to point out, because of the growth of multiple polarizations over race, culture, American foreign and military policy, and economic conflicts. The Presidency has increasingly emerged as an imperial office, at home as well as abroad. Dominating the American political system, it has become the vortex for national conflicts over symbolisms and both symbolic and material allocation choices.

As a direct result of these conflicts, and the multiple pressures of change playing upon the American electorate, no stable presidential majority coalition can now be said to exist. The results of both the 1968 and 1972 elections would appear to suggest that a predominantly conservative—though hardly Republican—majority may have emerged. Yet such a view reckons without the enduring importance of economic issues. With a combined double-digit inflation rate and recession as of 1974, and with the added short-term impact of Watergate, it would be a hardy spirit indeed who would predict the outcome of the 1976 presidential election.[60]

2. *The Senatorial coalitions.* It is very hard to establish anything like a uniform set of generalizations at this highly visible level of election. In

59. Of the 15,993,965 votes cast in the 1972 Democratic presidential preference primaries, the distribution from "left" to "right" was as follows:

Candidate	Percentage
McGovern	25.3
Chisholm	2.7
McCarthy	3.5
Lindsay	1.2
(Total "left")	(32.7)
Muskie	11.5
Humphrey	25.8
Jackson	3.2
(Total "center")	(40.5)
Yorty	0.5
Wallace	23.5
(Total "right")	(24.0)
Others	2.8

60. We note, for example, that Eisenhower had a 15.4 per cent margin over Stevenson in 1956, yet Kennedy won in 1960; or again, Johnson had a 22.6 per cent margin over Goldwater in 1964, and yet Nixon won in 1968. Even without Watergate and the economy to concern us, a Nixon margin of 23.2 per cent over McGovern in 1972 would by no means be enough to give any assurance of a certain Republican presidential victory in 1976.

1972, for instance, the Nixon landslide did nothing to prevent four Republican incumbents from losing their seats to Democratic challengers.[61] It is obvious that Democratic senatorial candidates ran far ahead of their presidential nominee as a rule in 1972. Yet six of the sixteen Republican incumbents running for re-election actually ran ahead of Nixon in their states.[62]

If one were to concentrate on the extreme ends of the Republican incumbent continuum, one could perhaps conclude that in 1972 those who lost their seats were older and tended toward the Conservative wing of the party, while the incumbents who ran ahead of Nixon tended to be younger and more liberal. But a review of the names in each category reveals so many exceptions for so few cases that any generalization seems suspect; and that, perhaps, is the point. Some incumbents were popular in their own right, and some were clearly less so; an analysis of the why's and wherefore's would thus require a particularized study of the politics of each state involved and an assessment of the relative effectiveness of the candidates as campaigners.

3. *The House coalition.* Over-all, as we have indicated, from about 1956-58 through 1972 this has increasingly taken a bipartisan incumbent-protection form. In 1972 this development was simply accelerated marginally: the proportion of incumbents running for re-election who were defeated in the general election was 3.4 per cent of all incumbents and 3.0 per cent of the whole House. Over-all, the Democratic share of the total congressional vote in 1972 was 52.1 per cent, compared with McGovern's 37.5 per cent; Republican congressional candidates won 46.5 per cent of the national congressional vote, compared with Nixon's 60.7 per cent—a *net* split-ticket proportion of 14.4 per cent, as compared with a net split-ticket proportion of 5.1 per cent in 1952.

One is inclined almost to the view that critically large minorities of the American electorate have come to behave in a way functionally related to the emerging realities of political power at the center. The imperial Presidency, the vortex of all nation-wide political conflicts in the United States,

61. Allott (Colo.); Boggs (Del.); Miller (Iowa); Smith (Me.), trailing Nixon in their states by a mean of 13.2 per cent. One Democrat from the South also lost his seat (Spong, Va.), but ran 16.0 per cent ahead of McGovern. While only 3.4 per cent of House incumbents running for re-election lost their seats (including a number who were reapportioned out of them), 5 out of 25 Senate incumbents (20.0 per cent) and 2 out of 9 incumbent governors (22.2 per cent) were also defeated for re-election.
62. Brooke (Mass.); Case (N.J.); Hansen (Wyo.); Pearson (Kans.); Percy (Ill.); and Stevens (Alaska).

is electorally dominated by a network of shifting minority coalitions. The Senate is the more "statesmanlike" of the two branches of the Congress: the visibility that produces a greater attrition of incumbents than in the House is the same visibility that produces majorities such as the 82.4 per cent won in 1970 by Henry Jackson (D) of Washington, or the 77.3 per cent won in 1972 by Ted Stevens (R) of Alaska, and has made the post-war Senate a breeding-ground for presidential candidates. The House has increasingly turned toward constituency service and *ombudsman* functions; and its incumbents become both more numerous and insulated from any but the most massive shifts of opinion. What emerges from all this is an immensely significant behavioral reinforcement of the separation of powers.

The reader may well ask at this point, So what? Let us try to answer this from the point of view of, first, the policy analyst and, second, the democratic theorist. The most obvious policy implications of this functional decomposition of voting behavior are, first, a concomitant destabilization of domestic policy initiatives and follow-through; and second, a future for policymaking which rests uneasily between the alternatives of reinforced institutional deadlock and of executive imposition of policy on the rest of the system.

It is clear that a growing velocity of movement from one presidential election to the next has already meant drastic reversals in a number of crucial domestic policy arenas, particularly but by no means exclusively those dealing with the cities, poverty, and race relations. This is so because, however decomposed the electoral coalitions may be, there is a very substantial and probably growing divergence between Democratic and Republican elites over basic contemporary political issues. To the extent that the Presidency changes partisan hands with increasing frequency, to that extent a longitudinal continuity of policy formulation and implementation becomes problematic in the extreme.

Yet it is increasingly obvious that the rest of this decade, and the decades to follow, will be marked by constantly growing pressures for public-sector controls over what used to be regarded as private life. Nowhere more is this the case than with the economy, where multiplying costs of scarce resources are likely simultaneously to intersect with rapid inflation and recession. Eventually, wage and price policies will probably have to be implemented permanently in most advanced industrial societies, including this one. Yet the problem for the policymaker is always how to obtain consent for any such ambitious program as this, and how to insulate it from becoming the plaything of organized sectoral interests.

Now the United States has always been a country whose policymaking processes have been wide open at all stages to the penetration of such interests. One would suppose that any further *institutional* reinforcement of this American pattern could only make such difficulties worse; and yet the current drift toward discrete office-specific electoral coalitions seems to point precisely in that direction. In this context lies a recipe for speeding up the dialectical tension between "drift" (policy deadlock among separated institutions permeated by pressure groups) and "mastery" (executive dictatorship in an atmosphere of acute policy crisis). While "party government" is hardly a panacea, as the current British case amply demonstrates, it is very hard to see how, without it, any prospect for eliminating or softening this excruciating dilemma within the rubrics of democracy can be found.

The energy crisis of 1973-74 is, or should be considered, very much like Jefferson's description of the Missouri struggle of 1820 as a "firebell in the night." For the problems it implies, and the demands its successors will place upon political institutions and leaders in the United States, are at least as profound, and directly involve democratic values at their most basic level. *If* some such massive public controls as those suggested here must be developed and sustained from sheer necessity, they cannot be maintained without consent in a democracy. That consent in turn must be rooted on an ethic of justification. A vital element in any such ethic— assuming that the government must do things that used to be considered possible and legitimate only during a world war, but must now do in peace—must be equality of sacrifice. If democratic consent is to be won for the very hard public choices lying just over the horizon, a bona-fide, sustained, and more than rhetorical effort to approximate equality of sacrifice will have to be made by policy elites. Unfortunately, nothing of the sort seems possible without a revolutionary change in behavior norms among rank-and-file and elites alike, and the capacity of our institutions for sustained, integrated, and coherent public policy.

How revolutionary this revolution would have to be would depend very largely upon how much time this country has left before really hard allocation choices are imposed on it by brute necessity. But the horns of one further dilemma are already coming into our view. In such an age, policy will either have to be much more social-democratic than it has ever been in the United States, or it will have to be established and imposed by an authoritarian oligarchy—an oligarchy whose first forebears were clearly visible in President Nixon's White House Office before Watergate blew it to pieces.

American radicals have long argued that the Democratic party must be destroyed before any truly democratic structures could be built in the United States. They may now be getting their wish, though not in quite the form they had hoped for. If one assumes that the party decomposition we have been describing is the end of the tale, what follows for the voter? First, he is very likely to become increasingly confused by his enormously complex political system: party is a vitally important vehicle for simplifying and concentrating public choice. Second, he is likely to become increasingly aware that the old party organizations—which control nominations—are in some sense in collusion against his welfare: the lessons that Ralph Nader and Common Cause have taught him are not likely to be forgotten, for subsequent experience will most probably reinforce them. Third, he is likely to find himself being forced to make choices— especially in presidential elections—which do not permit him to do more than vote for the lesser of evils. Fourth, he is very likely indeed to conclude that voting makes no great difference anyway: pressures on him arising from race (from *either* side of that gap), war or peace, and inflation continue to weigh on him despite the promises of candidates and parties. Fifth, as to equality of sacrifice—well, really! No one who prides himself on realism about politics in the United States would think *that* a likely outgrowth of this final victory of electoral individualism.

It is hard to escape the conclusion that if such a process continues to unfold, a true crisis of the regime will emerge—perhaps sooner than later. If "partisan decomposition" continues under these conditions of pervasive public discontent, democracy will be progressively emptied of any operational meaning as executive-bureaucratic imperatives come to dominate the political system. In this case, it may be possible to make a relatively peaceful transition to *Imperium* without much disturbance in *formal* institutional structure. It is worth recalling, prehaps, that the Roman Senate survived not only the accession of Augustus but even the fall of the Empire in the West.

Alternatively, this decomposition may be reversed by a renewed "critical realignment" that restores the traditional two-party system and produces a durable policy majority for one of its components. Despite the arguments sometimes made to this effect (e.g., by James Sundquist[63]) we cannot accept the likelihood of this happening unless we can identify the emergence of forces in society and polity strong enough to overcome those that have produced the evolving patterns of electoral dissociation described here. We may doubt that economic stress alone will suffice to restore the party system of the 1930's.

Finally, we may suppose the possibility that a new constellation of parties emerges from the present ruins, broadly arrayed on a "left-right" continuum and not necessarily confined to two major components. *Prima facie*, the emergence of such a new order of things might seem the least likely of all possible alternatives. More likely, one might have thought, would be a situation in which a man on horseback emerges at a point when economic and social crisis are in a much more advanced stage than now, and win the Presidency on either party ticket or as an independent. Nevertheless: *if* we assume that the electorate as a whole has become more sophisticated from recent painful experience, and as educational levels have risen: *if* we assume that there continue to be effective cultural and institutional resistances to authoritarianism; and *if* we assume that outstanding political leadership can be found, can emerge, and can be kept alive, it might happen that political democracy will actually survive. These may appear to be heroic assumptions. But assumptions no less heroic were made *and validated* in past crises, notably the crisis of 1860-61. Quite possibly, the current dissolution of party-in-the-electorate will turn out after all *not* to be a "critical realignment to end all critical realignments," but the prologue to a revitalization of *democracy through party*.

At the very end, our argument in these pages becomes a truism: each generation must win anew, for itself, its own battle for as much liberty as it can wrest from necessity, or to lose what liberty it could have retained both for itself and for its posterity. Now it is our turn to work out this destiny.

A POSTSCRIPT ON THE 1974 ELECTIONS

Neither this book nor this chapter is directly concerned with "current events." At the same time it may be profitable to add a word about the outcome of the 1974 elections, the first since the unraveling of Watergate

63. Sundquist, *Dynamics of the Party System,* chap. 17.

finally resulted in Richard Nixon's ejection from the presidency. In many respects the 1974 election appears to represent a continuation of the recent trends with which this chapter has been concerned. The circumstances were the most unusual on record, and the results tend to fall in line with that context.

In the House of Representatives elections, the Democrats won the largest two-party percentage of the vote ever recorded, just under 59 per cent. But the Republican victims of this landslide were by no means a random sample of marginal or near-marginal incumbents. To the contrary: as in 1964, they were concentrated on the far-right wing of the party, almost as though in certain cases a decisive minority of voters swung against conservative incumbents on policy grounds. On the other hand, the incumbent-insulating effects described in the article were still clearly operative: with 59 per cent of the vote and no biases in the conversion of votes into seats, the Democrats might have won 326 seats, very similar to their performance in the 1930's; and one might be on safe ground in assuming that about 35 Republican incumbents survived because the system is not unbiased. The losses suffered by the GOP were as extensive as they were because so many of the seats they lost were not marginal at all: thus we find two ultra-conservative Republicans—Camp of Oklahoma and Blackburn of Georgia—losing in 1974 despite their having received far more than 70 per cent of the vote in 1972, while a Republican liberal like Joel Pritchard of Washington was re-elected despite having received only 51 per cent of the vote in his first election two years earlier.

In the races for Senate and state offices, the heterogeneity of movement which has been discussed here also manifested itself, although the over-all movement was in a heavily pro-Democratic direction. Where personal popularity prevailed, as with John Glenn in his Ohio Senate race, the candidate could win more than two-thirds of the vote as a Democrat in a typically Republican state. Yet this landslide was not enough to save Governor John Gilligan, also a Democrat, from losing to his Republican challenger John Rhodes. On the other hand, for the first time since New Deal days Governor-elect Rhodes will have to deal with Democratic majorities in both houses of the state legislature. And so the pattern of heterogeneity goes: Vermont, which produced the first Democratic senatorial victory in the history of the state; Maine, where an anti-party independent won the governorship over both major-party candidates; New York and Pennsylvania, where Democratic governors were chosen but

Republican senatorial incumbents (both liberals, it may be noted) were re-elected.

The overwhelming mood of this election appears to have been one of disgust, indeed almost of despair among a very large number of citizens. This expressed itself in each set of elections, in different ways in each. But despite the Democratic victory, there is little in the over-all result to suggest other than that the march toward decomposition of the party-in-the-electorate is continuing. Moreover, one of the most important "events" of 1974 was the tremendous drop in the turnout rate. Nationwide, participation in the House elections fell to just under 40 per cent, thus plumbing depths seen only in the 1920s and in the wartime 1942 election. In a great many states the 1974 turnout rate represents the lowest participation since the creation of the party system in the 1830's. In 1974, far more than in any earlier year since at least the advent of the New Deal, it would be a rash soul indeed who would argue that such mass abstention connoted a "politics of happiness." Confronted as the country has been with malfeasance in the White House, with a rapidly deteriorating economy—but with the doctors of the economics profession in disagreement as to the remedy—and with a new President who has yet to show that he has mastered his office, voters could perhaps be pardoned for deciding that the marginal cost to them of taking the trouble to vote was more than any benefit they might receive from the exercise. Confusion, uncertainty, deadlock, and drift all appear to be on the cards at least through January 1977; and if the Republicans have been rejected, it cannot be said that the Democrats inspire enthusiasm.

What we have described here is a kind of hollowing-out process, the creation of a real vacuum at the center of American political life. Yet nature, in politics as elsewhere, abhors a vacuum, and the need to generate popular support for government remains acute—indeed, is more acute than it has been at any time since the presidency of James Buchanan. This translates, as it must, into a need for effective, creative leadership. Who is to provide it? Will it emerge from within what is left of our two parties, or will it be offered by an entrepreneur who emerges from outside, and against, these parties? In one variant or another, these questions will be at the root of our politics for the rest of this decade; and they will be answered in one way or another because they have to be answered.

Index